# International Marketing Research

## Third edition

# International Marketing Research
## Third edition

**C. SAMUEL CRAIG and SUSAN P. DOUGLAS**

**Leonard N. Stern School of Business, New York University**

John Wiley & Sons, Ltd

Copyright © 2005    John Wiley & Sons Ltd, The Atrium, Southern Gate, Chichester,
West Sussex PO19 8SQ, England

Telephone: (+44) 1243 779777

Email (for orders and customer service enquiries): cs-books@wiley.co.uk
Visit our Home Page on www.wileyeurope.com or www.wiley.com

This publication is designed to provide accurate and authoritative information in regard to the subject
matter covered. It is sold on the understanding that the Publisher is not engaged in rendering professional
services. If professional advice or other expert assistance is required, the services of a competent
professional should be sought.

*Other Wiley Editorial Offices*

John Wiley & Sons Inc., 111 River Street, Hoboken, NJ 07030, USA

Jossey-Bass, 989 Market Street, San Francisco, CA 94103-1741, USA

Wiley-VCH Verlag GmbH, Boschstr. 12, D-69469 Weinheim, Germany

John Wiley & Sons Australia Ltd, 33 Park Road, Milton, Queensland 4064, Australia

John Wiley & Sons (Asia) Pte Ltd, 2 Clementi Loop #02-01, Jin Xing Distripark, Singapore 129809

John Wiley & Sons Canada Ltd, 22 Worcester Road, Etobicoke, Ontario, Canada M9W 1L1

Wiley also publishes its books in a variety of electronic formats. Some content that appears
in print may not be available in electronic books.

*Library of Congress Cataloging-in-Publication Data*

Craig, C. Samuel.
   International marketing research / C. Samuel Craig and Susan P.
Douglas.— 3rd ed.
      p. cm.
   Includes index.
   ISBN 0-470-01095-9
   1. Export marketing—Research.  I. Douglas, Susan P.  II. Title.

   HF1416.C73 2005
   658.8′4—dc21

                                        2005001265

*British Library Cataloguing in Publication Data*

A catalogue record for this book is available from the British Library

ISBN 0-470-01095-9 (PB)

Typeset in 10/15pt Sabon by Graphicraft Ltd, Quarry Bay, Hong Kong.
Printed and bound in Great Britain by Biddles, Kings Lynn.
This book is printed on acid-free paper responsibly manufactured from sustainable forestry
in which at least two trees are planted for each one used for paper production.

To Liz, Mary Catherine, and Caroline
(C.S.C.)

To Nicholas and Stephanie
(S.P.D.)

# CONTENTS

# ABOUT THE AUTHORS

**C. SAMUEL CRAIG** is the Catherine and Peter Kellner Professor, Professor of Marketing and International Business and Director of the Entertainment, Media and Technology Program at New York University's Stern School of Business. He received his PhD from the Ohio State University. Prior to joining New York University, Professor Craig taught at Cornell University. He has taught marketing for executive programs in the United States as well as France, the UK, Thailand, Singapore, Greece and the former Yugoslavia.

Professor Craig has co-authored *Consumer Behavior: An Information Processing Perspective* (Prentice Hall) and *Global Marketing Strategy* (McGraw-Hill). His research has appeared in the *Journal of Marketing Research, Journal of Marketing, Journal of Consumer Research, Journal of International Business Studies, Columbia Journal of World Business, International Journal of Research in Marketing, Journal of International Marketing* and other publications. Over the past 25 years, he and Professor Douglas have collaborated on a wide variety of international marketing projects including this book, numerous scholarly articles, and contributions to handbooks and encyclopedias.

**SUSAN P. DOUGLAS** is the Paganelli-Bull Professor of Marketing and International Business at New York University's Stern School of Business. She received her PhD from the University of Pennsylvania. Prior to joining New York University, Professor Douglas taught at Centre-HEC, Jouy-en-Josas, France, and was a faculty member of the European Institute for Advanced Studies in Management in Brussels. She has also taught international marketing in executive programs in France, Belgium, Italy, Greece, Taiwan, Singapore, India, South Africa and the former Yugoslavia. A past president of the European Marketing Academy, and former vice-president of the Academy of International Business, Professor Douglas was elected as a fellow of the Academy of International Business in 1991 and was Dean of the Fellows from 1999–2002. She was made a fellow of the European Marketing Academy in 2002 and chaired the Fellows from 2002–2005.

Professor Douglas co-authored *Global Marketing Strategy* (McGraw-Hill) with Professor Craig. Her research has appeared in the *Journal of Marketing, Journal of Consumer Research, Journal of Marketing Research, Journal of International Business Studies, Columbia Journal of World Business, International Journal of Research in Marketing, Journal of International Marketing* and other publications.

# PREFACE

In the relatively short time since the second edition of *International Marketing Research* appeared, there have been rapid and dramatic changes in the field. As firms increasingly expand operations in countries outside their home market, they require marketing research to guide decision making. Industry consolidation of research firms has accelerated as they strive to better serve global clients. The Internet has burst on to the scene as an alternative way to gather information and conduct surveys rapidly. Increasingly research is being conducted in developing countries as firms expand operations into markets such as India and China. The third edition of the book is completely updated to reflect changes in both the structure and practice of international marketing research.

Generally speaking, the volume of commercial research on international markets has expanded more rapidly than academic research. This is particularly true within the EU and nearby countries, where market integration means that researchers continually face the challenges of conducting research spanning multiple cultures and countries. At the same time, as firms continue to expand operations in Asia and Latin America, the need for information to plan or adapt strategy to these markets is growing. Progress in academic research, on the other hand, has been hampered largely by the complexity and higher costs associated with the conduct of international research. In the short term this disparity between commercial and academic international marketing research seems likely to continue. As the internationalization of business continues unabated, collection of accurate and timely data, to guide decision making and to keep pace with the accelerating rate of change in markets around the globe, is even more critical. Commercial research suppliers must respond to this and be able to provide the types of information that businesses require to make accurate and timely decisions.

For academic researchers, with limited funding to support research and sparse resources to assist with research projects, the addition of another research context greatly increases the time required to complete the research and the complexity of the research process. This is a cost that many academic researchers do not want or cannot afford to incur. Fortunately, this is gradually changing as the potential of multi-country studies for making seminal contributions to knowledge and deepening understanding of behavior is recognized. Academic researchers are increasingly extending the boundaries of research inquiry by exploring and questioning the applicability and suitability of indigenous research paradigms, notably those developed in the US, to other countries and cultures.

When constructs and theory are found to hold in more than one country, confidence in the basic theory is enhanced. Understanding is also gained when a theory does not hold in another context. This establishes the limits of its applicability or suggests that the theory needs to be modified to incorporate the new context. In order to cover progress in this area a chapter has been added that deals with conceptual and methodological issues in designing and executing research.

Current advances in communications technology and particularly the bewildering speed of Internet growth is rapidly revolutionizing the way in which information is collected, processed, and disseminated. This has vast potential for enhancing the scope of international marketing research. Since this revolution is only in its infancy, it is difficult to discern exactly how it will change data collection, sampling, questionnaire administration, analysis, etc. While the Internet improves the speed and scope of data collection, attention still must be paid to the critical issues underlying the research design and its execution.

# Purpose

The purpose of this book is twofold. First, the book aims to assist academic researchers in conducting multi-country research. The book is designed to help researchers create sound research designs that will allow for valid and meaningful inferences to be made. Attention is paid to how comparability and equivalence of results in different countries can be established. Consideration is given to the conceptual framework that guides research as well as the methodological foundations. Consequently, the third edition pays greater attention to issues such as decentering of the research design, scale development, measurement equivalence and reliability, and multi-country data analysis. As a result, it is hoped that it will effectively serve academic researchers interested in the theoretical issues relating to international and cross-cultural research in marketing.

Second, it aims to provide some direction in conducting commercial research for international marketing decisions. International marketing research is here defined as research conducted to aid in making decisions in more than one country. These may include decisions concerning which countries or markets offer the most attractive opportunities for entry or expansion, as well as whether to standardize strategies across countries as opposed to adapting these to local market differences. Comparability in findings is thus required, since these decisions imply the integration or coordination of strategies across countries. Such research can be conducted simultaneously in all countries being investigated.

Many of these decisions, especially those concerned with foreign market entry, are intrafunctional in character. Thus, they have not only marketing but also financial or production aspects. Decisions to invest or establish a plant in a foreign country, for example, necessitate evaluation of foreign market risks, and the costs of producing from a foreign location. Some of the types of information required for such evaluations are covered here, but primarily insofar as these interact with marketing decisions. Emphasis is thus placed on the collection of information to aid in developing global marketing strategy and in integrating strategies across countries and product markets.

# Audience

This book is intended to have four main uses. First, it can serve as a text for specialized courses in international marketing research. It provides comprehensive coverage of the various issues involved in international marketing research of both a qualitative and quantitative character. Furthermore, it is applicable to problems encountered in the emerging market countries of the Far East and Africa, as well as industrialized countries such as the European nations or Japan. Second, it is suitable when supplemented with research articles, as a resource for a seminar on international marketing research. Third, it can be used as a supplementary text in marketing research or international marketing management courses to round out material and topics relating to international marketing research. Fourth, it may prove useful to practitioners of international marketing research, particularly in relation to issues of instrument design and scale development. It should be particularly valuable to those who are just beginning to conduct research in multiple countries for their clients.

Regardless of the use, the discussion in the text assumes familiarity with the basic principles of marketing research as, for example, non-survey data collection techniques, sampling, questionnaire design and administration, and data analysis. The focus is thus on issues involved in applying those principles in an international research context. For the reader who is not familiar with marketing research principles, references are made in relevant sections throughout the book to standard sources and texts.

# Structure

The same underlying principles that guided the previous two editions are present in the third edition, namely that the basic principles of marketing research are the same whether research is conducted in an international or a domestic context. However, the international marketing researcher is likely to encounter greater difficulties than his or her domestic counterpart. These difficulties stem from operating across national boundaries and in a diverse range of socio-cultural environments. Examples of issues that may arise include how to obtain response from illiterate or semi-literate populations, how to develop a sampling frame in the absence of reliable census data or sampling lists, or simply how to find or train competent interviewers. Frequently, creativity and resourcefulness are required in coping with unexpected problems. In addition, an ability to manage, deal with, and organize researchers of different cultural backgrounds and value systems is essential to successful international marketing research.

To address these issues, the third edition has fifteen chapters. The first chapter provides an introduction to the topic. It acquaints the reader with the complexity of the global environment and sets up the key issues that the international researcher must deal with. Chapter 2 addresses the issues associated with the design of international marketing research with particular emphasis on those related to the organization of international marketing research, the choice of supplier, the determination of information requirements, the selection of information sources, the appropriate unit of analysis and the development of a research plan and its administration. The chapter also covers the research infrastructure and the major players around the globe. This chapter has been updated to reflect changes in the research infrastructure including the most recent data from ESOMAR.

Chapters 3 and 4 are concerned with secondary data sources. These are often more important in international marketing research, due to the high costs of primary data collection. Chapter 3 identifies the various sources of international data, and outlines the main types of data that are available. Chapter 4 looks at the uses of these data, as, for example, in making initial market entry decisions and establishing rough estimates of demand potential. Both these chapters have been updated extensively to reflect the consolidation of the services that provide the information and in particular their availability through the Internet.

While academic and commercial marketing researchers have different motivations, both require a strong conceptual foundation. Two chapters are devoted to this topic. In Chapter 5 the conceptual foundations for international marketing research are examined based on the unit of analysis. Building on the previous chapter, Chapter 6 examines the critical role that construct equivalence and construct measurement play in obtaining reliable and valid results. The emic-etic dilemma is discussed, namely the inherent conflict between adapting constructs and measures to specific socio-cultural contexts versus assuming that the constructs are universal and can be employed in all countries. Issues dealing with data equivalence are examined as well as cultural bias that may contaminate the research design and eventual interpretation of data.

Chapter 7 discusses various non-survey data collection techniques. These include observational and quasi-observational data, protocols, projective techniques, and depth interviews. Use of these techniques in the preliminary stages of research is advocated in order to identify relevant concepts to be examined in subsequent stages of research. Their administration using computerized techniques is also discussed as well as the combination of qualitative and quantitative approaches.

Chapters 8 and 9 cover instrument design, sampling and data collection in survey research. In Chapter 8, issues in instrument design, such as questionnaire formulation, instrument translation, appropriate scales, and response format are discussed, as well as potential sources of bias arising from the respondent, or the interviewer-respondent interaction. Chapter 8 examines problems in sampling, such as identifying an efficient sampling procedure. The advantage and disadvantages of various data collection procedures, such as mail, telephone, Internet or personal interviewing, in international marketing research are also discussed. The material in Chapters 8 and 9 has been updated to reflect recent changes, as for example the use of the Internet to administer surveys.

Chapter 10 discusses the development and use of scales to measure constructs in a multi-cultural or multi-country context. Issues relating to scale reliability and validity are addressed, including procedures for testing scales developed in one country or culture to see whether they are applicable in another country. In addition, approaches to developing hybrid scales with pan-cultural components as well as components to measure constructs unique to a particular country or culture are covered. The chapter has been updated and expanded to reflect recent developments.

Chapters 11 and 12 cover analysis of multi-country data. In Chapter 11 analytical techniques that are suited to determining whether there are significant differences in the *level* of a variable between countries are discussed. In Chapter 12, analytical techniques that are appropriate for examining differences in the *structure* and relationship of variables between countries are covered. These different techniques are illustrated with recent examples from the literature. One of the clear trends is the increased sophistication in the types of quantitative analysis that are being used to analyze cross-cultural data.

Chapter 13 examines the steps involved in the development of a global information system. This covers the design of a global system, and its various components, as well as how information is collected and fed into the system on a regular basis. Issues relating to data access and its use in management decision-making are also examined. This chapter has been updated with more emphasis placed on the role of the Internet in facilitating the dissemination of information.

Chapter 14 brings together many of the themes addressed throughout the book. It also tries to provide some insights into the challenges that researchers face as markets become increasingly integrated and diverse at the same time. The impact of technological advances and new analytical techniques is covered. Ethical issues are examined as well as some of the special challenges associated with conducting research in emerging market economies. This chapter is updated, but continues to follow the same structure.

Chapter 15 sets the stage for the future of international marketing research. For progress to be made in the international arena, three inter-related issues need to be addressed. First, greater attention needs to be paid to comparability and equivalence of the basic constructs being examined between countries. Second, more thought needs to be given to the research design that guides international marketing research. Finally, better cross-cultural measures and analytical techniques need to be developed and applied to multi-country data. These themes, first articulated in the second edition, are expanded upon.

# Acknowledgements

As in the case of the first and second editions, we would like to thank all those who through their writing and their comments inspired the revision of this book. We are particularly grateful to our many colleagues on different continents from different research traditions and interests who encouraged us to undertake this rather daunting task. We believe that had it not been for their interest, encouragement and prodding, we probably would not have embarked on what has proven for us to be a highly rewarding undertaking. In particular, our discussions with colleagues at EMAC, AIB and other international meetings have been both stimulating and thought provoking – leading us down new paths, inspiring us to investigate new lines of inquiry, and above all to question some of our assumptions about how to conduct cross-national research. We hope they will forgive us if we have not always followed their advice or responded adequately to their concerns.

A special note of thanks go to the executives in marketing research firms and consulting firms who generously gave their time and shared their knowledge and experience on the conduct of international marketing research. In particular we would like to thank:

Richard Auton, Auton & Co.; Peter Cooper, Cram International; Sandrine Mounier, Greenlight; Michel Olszewski, Research International; John Pawle, Cram International; Joseph Plummer, McCann Erickson; David Pring, IPSOS; Christine Restall, Research Business International; Paul Strang, Hi Europe; Martine Thiesse, Research International Qualitatif.

We also want to thank the many people at John Wiley & Sons who helped make this book a reality. Sarah Booth worked closely with us through to its completion and Rachel Goodyear helped keep us on track.

Work on the third edition has been an ongoing process over the last two years, often interwoven and sometimes halted by our other research activities. It has been a stimulating and rewarding undertaking for both of us. We hope that academics, students, and practitioners will find the third edition to be helpful in formulating and executing international marketing research. The progress since the first edition of this book appeared in 1983 has been phenomenal. We firmly believe that even more dramatic changes will occur in the first decade of the 21st century. While the world is getting smaller, it is also becoming more complex and dependent on technology. The role of sound international marketing research to guide decision-making and extend knowledge and understanding is increasingly critical. We hope that this book will contribute in some small way to help improve research that spans multiple countries and cultures.

C. Samuel Craig
Susan P. Douglas
*New York City*

# Chapter 1

# MARKETING RESEARCH IN A GLOBAL ENVIRONMENT

## Introduction

The explosive growth of world trade has unleashed a torrent of demand for information about markets throughout the world. Companies expanding into new and unfamiliar markets need information about market demand and market conditions. Managers seeking to expand and diversify operations need information to develop effective strategies in these markets. Information needs now extend from the mature industrialized markets of Europe, the US and Japan, the unstable but growing markets of Latin America, the politically uncertain markets of the Middle East and Russia, and the rapidly changing markets of South East Asia to the emerging African markets.

At the same time, increasing cultural diversity makes it important to collect information with regard to changing lifestyle and consumption patterns in different parts of the world. Increased travel, waves of migration and global communications are resulting in the blurring of cultural boundaries. Traditional notions of culture as defined by geographical territory are changing as cultural interpretation occurs, resulting in a deterritorialization of culture. Links are being established between geographically dispersed cultures, resulting in the introduction of new ideas, products and lifestyles from one culture to another. In some instances, this generates a process of cultural fusion, resulting in the emergence of new hybrid cultures and global patterning of culture. Research is needed to investigate the impact of these changing cultural dynamics on consumption and purchasing patterns worldwide.

Advances in communications and information systems technology are further accelerating the pace of change, linking markets through flows of information, images and ideas across national boundaries. This makes it increasingly critical for management to keep abreast of changes and to collect timely and pertinent information to adapt strategy and market tactics in expanding local markets. As markets become more integrated worldwide, there is a growing need to conduct research spanning country boundaries, to identify regional or global segments, examine opportunities for integrating and better coordinating strategies in world markets, launching new global brands and developing effective global branding strategies.

Effective and timely research is an essential tool for crafting strategy in a rapidly changing global marketplace. Research can aid in uncovering potential opportunities in international markets, in correctly positioning new products and formulating products for international markets, as well as in identifying appropriate advertising appeals and diagnosing potential issues in relation to other aspects of the marketing mix.

## Correctly Positioning New Products

Research can help in correctly positioning new products. In China, PepsiCo was initially unsuccessful in introducing its Frito-Lay brand of potato chips into the market. Sales were particularly low in summer months. Research revealed that Chinese shoppers associated fried foods with *yang*, believed to generate body heat in summer months (Fowler and Setoodeh, 2004). As a result, Lay's introduced a 'cool lemon' variety in pastel-colored packaging to reflect *yin*, a cool feeling. The product subsequently became Lay's most successful in China.

## Avoiding Product Formulation Errors

Research can also help in uncovering how to reformulate products for local palates. HJ Heinz, for instance, wanted to market its oat-based baby food in China. Research showed that the Chinese were not familiar with oats and hence it was unlikely to be a popular food for babies (Fowler and Setoodeh, 2004). On the other hand, whitebait, a tiny fish, was discovered to be a staple food for infants in China. Heinz reformulated its baby food and produced a whitebait–oats combination. This proved to be an instant success among Chinese consumers.

## Sensitivity to Geographical Differences

Costly mistakes can be avoided by consulting secondary data. Often it can be as simple as making sure that geography is politically correct. Microsoft launched Windows 95 in India with a color-coded map that did not show the disputed Jammu-Kashmir region as being part of India. As a result, Windows 95 was banned throughout India, leading to a substantial loss of sales. When Office 97 was launched, the color coding was eliminated and the company sold 100 000 copies. A similar problem was encountered when Microsoft employees were arrested in Turkey because Kurdistan had been shown as a separate entity on maps. Microsoft ended up removing Kurdistan from all maps as a result (Brown, 2004).

# Understanding Cultural Change

Rapid changes around the world make it imperative that firms understand what consumers are thinking and how values are changing. To help its clients, McCann Erickson, the large global advertising agency, conducts marketing research in more than 40 countries simultaneously. The research allows it to understand each country's values from the consumers' perspective. The survey results help the agency determine the structure of consumption in each country, brand choice, lifestyles and media influence. Comparisons are made between sets of countries. This information helps spot trends and facilitates the creation of advertising.

# Identifying Appropriate Advertising Appeals

The appropriateness of advertising appeals also needs to be assessed through research. An $800 000 research project in Brazil helped Coke identify a motherly female kangaroo as the advertising device mostly likely to appeal to women shopping for their families. In Brazil women account for 80% of Coke's $3.5 billion sales (*Advertising Age International*, 1997). The ads are themed 'Mom knows everything' and feature the kangaroo sporting sunglasses and toting Coke cans instead of a baby. Although there are no kangaroos in Brazil, the animal tested well among Brazilian women, who said they thought it represented freedom, but at the same time responsibility and care for children.

# Assessing Translation Errors

Research can also aid in assessing the need for translation. In entering Eastern Europe, Procter & Gamble (P&G) translated its detergent labels into Polish and Czech to adapt its products to the local market. However, consumers reacted negatively, perceiving this as an effort to dupe customers by passing the company off as a local Polish firm. Research revealed that labels should be written in imperfect Polish to show the company was trying to fit in, but was not quite adept enough to be fluent (*Business Week*, 1993).

Collecting information about international markets is, however, by no means a simple matter. While numerous sources of secondary data for international markets are readily available, issues of comparability from one country to another and reliability arise especially with regard to emerging country markets. Primary data collection is also more complex, since the research design has to be adapted to different cultural, linguistic, economic and social environments. Often, exploratory research has to be conducted in order to define the problem more clearly, to determine precisely what should be investigated, as well as by whom. Questionnaires have to be translated and the research instrument adapted to the new environment. Sampling frames comparable to those available in industrialized countries are often nonexistent, particularly in developing countries.

Administration of marketing research has to be scheduled and coordinated across national boundaries, often incurring delays, miscommunication and other frustrations. Analysis also poses the problem of interpretation of data from a different cultural context, which may introduce the possibility of bias on the part of the researcher (Lee, 1966). The complexity of international marketing decisions, which have to be made in relation to and across diverse and rapidly changing environments, adds further to the difficulties of designing and implementing marketing research in international markets.

# Complexity of International Marketing

Marketing on a global scale poses problems that are inherently more complex than those encountered in a firm's domestic market (Douglas and Craig, 1995). Operations take place on a much broader scale and scope, often involving a range of different types of activities and management systems, including licensing, strategic alliances and joint ventures. At the same time, international marketing entails operating in a variety of diverse environmental contexts. International markets are also characterized by rapid rates of change in the technological, economic, social and political forces that shape their development. Often these changes affect markets at differing rates and in different ways. Sometimes, events such as an economic meltdown in one country can have a ripple effect, cascading through markets worldwide. Change is not only rapid and all-pervasive, but also often unexpected and unpredictable, radically altering the character and nature of opportunities and threats in international markets.

In the complex, diverse and continually changing international environment, marketing research assumes a vital role in helping management keep abreast and in touch with developments in far-flung markets throughout the world. Research aids in assessing where the best opportunities lie, where and how to enter new markets and expand operations, how to develop the most effective marketing strategies to operate in these diverse environments, and how to tailor strategy to the continually changing global landscape.

# Diversity of the International Environment

In addition to the broad geographical scope of international operations, international marketing decisions are made more complex by the diversity of environments in which these operations are conducted. Diversity occurs in relation to consumer tastes, preferences and behavior, and to a lesser extent in business-to-business markets. Differences in the nature of the marketing infrastructure, for example the availability and reach of media, the banking system or the structure of distribution, add a further level of complexity to strategy development and implementation. This, in turn, is further compounded by government regulation of business operations, product formulation and packaging, advertising, promotion and pricing as well as trade barriers such as tariffs, import quotas etc.

In the first place, countries differ with regard to economic wealth and its distribution among the national population. Table 1.1 shows GNP per capita for the top ten and bottom ten countries in the world in 2002. This ranges from a low of $100 in Burundi and the Congo to $38 730 in Norway. Yet, such aggregate figures can be misleading when one considers purchasing power equivalents. Based on these equivalents, the range narrows from $630 in Burundi and the Congo to $36 690 in Norway. In addition, in some countries wealth is concentrated in the hands of a few, while agricultural economies have a higher living standard than might appear from income per capita as they grow their own food.

Levels of literacy also vary from country to country. While the level of literacy in industrialized countries is typically 99%, it is important to remember that is far from the case in other countries. Table 1.2 shows levels of literacy in selected countries (UNDP, 2003). Literacy rises with income, with the lowest levels of literacy occurring in the lowest-income countries. While it is not unexpected to discover that levels of literacy are low in many parts of the world, it is striking to note the difference in female and male literacy. In Niger only 9% of females are literate compared with 25% of males, while in Nepal the corresponding figures are 25% and 61%. Similarly, in Morocco only 37% females are literate compared with 63% males, and in Saudi Arabia the figures are 68% and 84% respectively. This seriously limits the effectiveness of written communication; that is, product labeling or print advertising. Illiteracy also affects the type of research or research tools that can be used, for example the feasibility of using mail or self-administered questionnaires.

**Table 1.1**  The top ten and bottom ten countries based on per capita income

| | Population (millions) 2002 | GNP per capita | | PPP estimates of GNP per capita | |
|---|---|---|---|---|---|
| | | Dollars 2002 | Rank | Dollars 2002 | Rank |
| Low-income economies | | | | | |
| Burundi | 7 | 100 | 201 | 630 | 199 |
| Congo Dem. Rep. | 52 | 100 | 201 | 630 | 199 |
| Ethiopia | 67 | 100 | 199 | 780 | 196 |
| Guinea–Bissau | 1 | 130 | 198 | 680 | 197 |
| Liberia | 3 | 140 | 197 | – | – |
| Sierra Leone | 5 | 140 | 197 | 500 | 201 |
| Malawi | 11 | 160 | 195 | 570 | 200 |
| Niger | 11 | 180 | 194 | 800 | 195 |
| Tajikistan | 6 | 180 | 194 | 930 | 194 |
| Eritrea | 4 | 190 | 192 | 1040 | 193 |
| | | | | | |
| High-income economies | | | | | |
| Austria | 8 | 23 860 | 10 | 28 910 | 5 |
| Finland | 5 | 23 890 | 9 | 26 160 | 9 |
| Hong Kong | 7 | 24 690 | 8 | 27 490 | 6 |
| United Kingdom | 59 | 25 510 | 7 | 26 580 | 8 |
| Sweden | 9 | 25 970 | 6 | 25 820 | 10 |
| Denmark | 5 | 30 260 | 5 | 30 600 | 4 |
| Japan | 127 | 34 010 | 4 | 27 380 | 7 |
| United States | 288 | 35 400 | 3 | 36 110 | 2 |
| Switzerland | 7 | 36 170 | 2 | 31 840 | 3 |
| Norway | 5 | 38 730 | 1 | 36 690 | 1 |

Source: World Bank Development Indicators, 2004.

**Table 1.2**    Levels of literacy in selected countries (2001)

| Country | Adult literacy rate (people aged 15 and above) | |
| --- | --- | --- |
| | % of males | % of females |
| Algeria | 77 | 58 |
| Bangladesh | 50 | 31 |
| Egypt | 67 | 44 |
| Ethiopia | 48 | 32 |
| India | 69 | 46 |
| Morocco | 63 | 37 |
| Nepal | 61 | 25 |
| Niger | 25 | 9 |
| Saudi Arabia | 84 | 68 |

Source: UNDP *Human Development Report*, 2003.

**Table 1.3**    Principal languages of the world

| | Total speakers (millions) |
| --- | --- |
| Mandarin | 874 |
| Hindi | 366 |
| English | 341 |
| Spanish | 322–58 |
| Bengali | 207 |

Source: *World Almanac*, 2003.

Linguistic heterogeneity is another factor adding to the complexity of international operations. International marketers have to deal with operations spanning countries where various languages are spoken. For example, 133 languages are spoken by at least two million people, while 9 are the primary language for more than 100 million, and another 12 are spoken by at least 50 million people. This includes Mandarin, which is spoken by 874 million people, Hindi by 366 million, English by 341 million and Spanish by 322 million (*World Almanac*, 2004). There is also often a diversity of languages within one country. In many countries and cultures there are regional differences and dialects, not comprehensible in other areas. In India, where Hindi is the official language, there are 15 regional languages recognized by the constitution and an estimated 180 local languages, not to mention 544 dialects. Similarly in China, Mandarin is the official language, and while six major language groups are typically identified, each of the 22 provinces speaks a different version, and in addition there are numerous local dialects.

Cultural values and orientation also vary markedly from one country to another. Hofstede (1980, 2001) has, for example, identified four different value orientations (power distance, uncertainty avoidance, individualism–collectivism and masculinity–femininity), which he argues characterize differences in national culture. Subsequently a fifth dimension was added, which represented the long- versus short-term orientation found in Asian societies. According to Hofstede (1980), these dimensions define the collective mental programming that members of a nation, region or group share with each other, but not with members of other nations, regions or groups. Characterizing societies on these dimensions showed China to score high on power distance and long-term orientation, low on individualism, and moderately on uncertainty avoidance and masculinity. The US profile is below average on power distance and uncertainty avoidance, but scores high on individualism, and moderately on masculinity and short-term orientation. The Netherlands is similar to the US on the first three dimensions, but strongly feminine and moderately long-term oriented.

Individual value profiles also vary from one country to another. Schwartz (1992) has, for example, identified motivational domains of values such as enjoyment, security, social power, achievement, self-direction, prosocial restrictive conformity and maturity, based on the terminal and instrumental values of the Rokeach Value Survey. These domains have been mapped in different countries, revealing differences in the relative importance attached to these value domains.

Such differences in economic wealth and levels of literacy, coupled with the linguistic heterogeneity and cultural diversity in marketing environments throughout the world, imply that management cannot assume that a strategy that works in its domestic market will be equally effective in international markets. Customer needs and interests will vary and people may respond in different, often unexpected ways to marketing stimuli. Differences in the marketing infrastructure, in the availability and reach of communication media, the level of technology, ownership of computers, as well as linkages across markets through satellite television or linkages to the Internet, as well as travel or movement of goods and services, further complicate the development of strategy for international markets.

# *Continually Changing Environment of International Markets*

In addition to cultural and economic diversity, international markets are characterized by rapid rates of change (Craig and Douglas, 1996a). Change pervades all aspects of human life and business activity. Not only are rates of technological change and knowledge obsolescence accelerating and transforming the competitive landscape, but also unforeseen events are changing the political and economic context of international markets. At the same time, rapid social and economic change is taking place, fueled in part by advances in communication technology, which shrink distances and stimulate greater awareness and cross-fertilization of ideas, attitudes and lifestyles across the mosaic of the international market place.

Technological change makes product development, production processes and experience rapidly obsolete and contributes to heightened competitive pressures as well as social change. In the notebook segment of the personal computer market, for example, the cycle of new product introduction has shrunk to less than three months, rendering models rapidly obsolete. This requires constant vigilance in product development and in monitoring new sources of competition. One indication of the level of technological development is the number of Internet users per 1000 population. This varies considerably from country to country and region to region, and is not unsurprisingly closely related to the level of economic development. In high-income countries, Internet access levels average 445 users per 1000, compared with 60 users per 1000 in middle-income countries and 13 per 1000 in low-income countries (UNDP, 2004). Yet even among these groupings of countries there is considerable variation. For example, in Greece there are 157 Internet users per 1000 compared with 573 in Sweden. Similarly, in Malaysia there are 323 Internet users per 1000 compared with 46 in China.

The rapid pace of change is further complicated by its increasingly discontinuous nature. Until the late 1980s, change was relatively predictable and linear. Today, in many instances established models for predicting trends and forecasting sales no longer work due to the discontinuity of change. At one time, market trends and growth in an emerging market could be predicted on the basis of trends in more advanced countries 10 years earlier. For example, development of telecommunications networks within a country progressed slowly and required massive investment in wire and cables to connect customers. Today, cellular technology makes it possible for a country to develop a modern telecommunications system quickly and 'leapfrog' the wire stage.

The diffusion of new products and innovation is also taking place more rapidly, fueled by advances in communications technology. Rather than first being adopted by opinion leaders and then trickling down to other members of society, innovations are now spreading horizontally across countries and societies. No sooner does a new trend or fashion emerge in one country than it spreads rapidly to another. Global marketers have to keep abreast of these developments. Not only are they agents of change in introducing new products and services into other countries, at the same time global marketers must also respond to the tidal waves of change as new modes of communication link customers and businesses across vast geographical distances.

While the pace of change is accelerating, pushed by the engine of technology and global communication, it is becoming increasingly uncertain or unpredictable, occurring in unexpected ways from unexpected sources. With the disintegration of the former Soviet Union, markets in Eastern Europe such as the Ukraine are becoming engines of growth in that region, but markets in other parts of the world such as the Middle East and Latin America remain volatile and uncertain. The explosive growth of China is opening up potential markets for oil, energy, automobiles and other consumer products. Yet at the same time the fragility of the financial infrastructure and massive bank loans provide insecure underpinnings to this boom.

As a result, the spatial configuration of markets is changing and new patterns are emerging, giving rise to new opportunities and new markets, as well as the growth of new market segments. These changing patterns are fraught with uncertainty and risk, as the forces that swell up and foster one trend can suddenly ebb and lose their momentum, dampened by the flood of events in another part of the world.

# Importance of Research for International Marketing Decisions

The diversity and complexity of the international environment, coupled with management's frequent lack of familiarity with a foreign market, underscore the importance of undertaking research prior to making decisions and laying out marketing strategy. This is true whether with regard to decisions on initial market entry, product positioning or marketing mix, or subsequent expansion. Research is necessary to avoid the costly mistakes of inappropriate strategy and the possibility of lost opportunities in international markets. In the later stages, research is needed to determine how far international operations can be coordinated across countries to take advantage of potential synergies arising from marketing in a global environment. Research is also needed to determine when and whether new global brands can be launched and whether global strategies can be developed for existing brands.

# Information Needs

Information needs vary depending on the firm's experience and degree of involvement in international markets (Craig and Douglas, 1996b). In the initial phase of entry into international markets, information is needed to assess opportunities and risks in different countries throughout the world and to plan international market entry and mode of operation. Once initial entry decisions have been made, attention shifts to issues relating to marketing mix decisions such as new product development and testing, advertising copy and media research and price sensitivity. As experience in international markets develops and operations become more widespread, greater emphasis is likely to be placed on building global information systems to improve resource allocation across markets and countries and to take advantage of potential synergies through improved integration and co-ordination of international strategies.

## Phase 1 – Information for International Market Entry

In collecting information for initial market entry decisions, management requires data at two different levels. In the first place, management needs information relating to the general business environment in a country or region, for example the political situation, financial stability, the regulatory environment, market size and growth as well as the market infrastructure. This is information that is taken for granted in a company's domestic market, as management is typically aware of, and in touch with, the local business environment. In entering international markets, information on the business environment is of paramount importance in order to determine the most attractive market opportunities and appropriate mode of entry or operation in the market. Secondly, management needs information relating to the specific product market or service industry the company plans to enter. This includes information on sales potential and rate of market growth, product market structure and sources of direct and indirect competition, as well as the competitive situation.

Once the information required to make market entry decisions has been determined, management needs to establish procedures to analyze this, assess country market attractiveness and make estimates of market demand. Here, a wide variety of procedures can be adopted, depending on the volume of data, level of precision and analytical sophistication required. Approaches range from qualitative evaluation and ranking of data, to the development of elaborate simulation models. The appropriate procedures depend to a large extent on the budget and time available for collecting and evaluating information, as also on the role of management in the evaluation process.

## Phase 2 – Information for Local Market Planning

Limited management knowledge and experience outside the domestic market often mandate a preliminary phase of information collection in researching international markets. This is intended to help formulate research specifications and research design. Qualitative research is frequently helpful in providing input for the design of a market survey. Such research enables identification of constructs, product class definitions or relevant attitudes and behavior to be examined in subsequent phases of research. Preliminary research may also include the collection of background information, relating for example to the product market, complementary or substitute products, existing attitudinal studies, competitive analyses etc.

Research on local markets is likely to focus primarily on assessing various elements of the marketing mix. Research is required to assess how far products and positioning strategies developed in relation to a domestic market need to be modified for foreign markets. Products may appeal to different customer segments, and desired customer benefits and preferences may differ from country to country. For example, in the automobile market, the relative importance attached to gas mileage, road handling and safety features varies from country to country. Similarly, tastes, preferences and consumption scenarios for food products often vary. Research helps to assess how product modification or changing positioning is likely to increase sales, either by broadening the customer base or by increasing market penetration.

Promotional themes, advertising copy and packaging also need to be tested to assess their effectiveness in local markets. Again, differences in levels of literacy, cultural norms relating to sex and humor, aesthetic tastes, color associations and interpretation of symbols affect customer interpretation and response to different types of visual stimuli, emotional appeals and promotional arguments.

Price sensitivity also needs to be examined, as this will vary from country to country depending on income levels, customer segments, competing and substitute products, price perception etc. Research may also be required to determine appropriate distribution channels. Again, factors such as interest in service, delivery or convenience, customer brand and store loyalty, time available for purchasing and preferences for different modes of distribution vary from country to country and influence the effectiveness and reach of alternative distribution channels.

Research can also be conducted to identify opportunities for new products and services. This may range from monitoring environmental and technological trends and conducting lifestyle or consumer satisfaction surveys, to in-depth interviews with consumers, brainstorming, focus groups etc. The new product or service concepts generated require further testing. Those that show the greatest promise will go on to be market tested.

## Phase 3 – Information for Global Rationalization

As the firm moves into the phase of global rationalization, it faces new information requirements as well as the need to make more effective use of data already collected. Secondary data that helped guide country entry decisions should now be used to monitor changes in the firm's operating environment and assess the degree of market integration and interlinkage. Countries that were stable politically or welcomed foreign investment at one time can become unstable or hostile to foreign investment. Economic growth can slow down or alternatively accelerate. Inflationary pressures may rise and foreign exchange rates fluctuate. Data on trade flows and communication linkages can be used to assess the extent to which market boundaries are changing and markets becoming more interconnected, requiring reassessment of global strategy.

While emphasis on local market expansion generates a need for primary data to examine local market characteristics and to assess response to products and marketing stimuli, concern with improved coordination and integration of strategy across countries requires collection of information on a global basis. The firm needs to consider the spatial configuration of its assets and resources to build a strong, global competitive position and provide strategic flexibility in the light of changing market dynamics and resource conditions (Craig and Douglas, 2000). At the same time mechanisms need to be developed to facilitate transfer of information, experience and ideas from one market to another, and enable the firm to utilize the diversity of its experience to craft an effective strategy in international markets.

Similarly, information about consumer tastes and preferences gathered on a country-by-country basis needs to be consolidated, to identify commonalities across countries as well as emerging trends. This provides the basis for planning global marketing strategy, for example whether and how to launch new global brands and how far to coordinate strategy relating to local, national and regional brands across markets. Here, depending on the degree of commonality across markets, the firm will need to determine the relative importance attached to global brands as opposed to regional and local brands responding to specific local needs. In essence, management will need to develop an effective global brand architecture to build a strong and coherent identity in international markets (Douglas *et al.*, 2001).

At the same time, internal company data relating to performance for each product business or marketing function should be collected and coordinated across countries. This needs to be integrated with external secondary data relating to national and global market conditions. The need to integrate data from various internal and external sources suggests the desirability of designing a global information system to monitor performance and determine how best to allocate resources on a global basis.

The sheer volume and complexity of information required to build a global information system pose a major challenge. Not only does information have to be collected from the far reaches of the globe but, in addition, it has to be examined and analyzed relative to widely differing operating conditions if it is to be of value in decision making. Advances in communications technology have substantially expanded capability to collect, transfer and evaluate information on a global scale, facilitating control and coordination of operations worldwide; as a result, greater attention must be paid to the utility and value of information collected in order to avoid problems of information overload.

Systematic collection of information is critical to successful strategy development in international markets. Although the difficulties and costs of collecting information from different countries throughout the world are often a deterrent, the consequences of not doing so can be disastrous. Information is needed to assess which countries or markets offer the most attractive opportunities for entry or expansion, to determine how to enter or develop in these markets, how far to adapt product positioning or marketing tactics to specific local market conditions, as well as to monitor performance, and take advantage of and transfer ideas and successful 'best practices' from one part of the world to another.

# Issues in International Marketing Research

The task facing the international manager is a complex and challenging one. Correspondingly, the challenges facing the international researcher are equally daunting. In particular, there are a number of conceptual and operational issues to consider that do not arise, or at least not in the same magnitude as in domestic marketing research.

Research design and implementation issues hamper the collection of data and the conduct of research across multiple markets. These stem essentially from the diversity of international operations and the synergies arising from coordination of these operations. In particular, the need to conduct research in a multicountry, multicultural and multilinguistic environment and to establish comparability and equivalence of data collected in these different environments poses a major challenge.

# *Complexity of Research Design*

In the first place, designing research for international marketing decisions is more complex than where a single country is concerned. The conduct of research in different countries implies that much greater attention is required to defining the relevant unit and level of analysis; that is, countries versus groups of countries or regions, or national markets versus global market segments, as well as the scope of the research. This includes the need to examine issues at different levels – i.e. within versus across countries – as well as the extent to which the relevance of a given unit of analysis, for example the country, is changing. In addition, the definition of the problem needs to be assessed and whether this is similar in structure and relevant parameters, for example whether products are the same across countries.

While countries are convenient and the most commonly used units of analysis due to the existence of political and organizational boundaries, as well as because much secondary data are available on a country-by-country basis, these may not be the most appropriate units from a marketing standpoint. Management might prefer to target teenagers throughout the world, hence the relevant unit of analysis would be a 'culti-unit'; that is, a subgroup or segment with similar needs, interests and response patterns throughout the world (Douglas and Craig, 1997).

Similarly, the relevant respondent may differ from country to country. While in the US and many European countries children play an important role in decisions related to the purchase of chocolate or cereals, in other countries that are less child oriented the mother may be the relevant decision maker. Equally, the role of women in financial and insurance decisions or traditional male purchases such as automobiles may vary from country to country. Again, while in western societies women often have a key role in such decisions and in some cases may be sole purchasers of such items, in other societies, for example Arab countries, this is rarely the case.

Analysis can become yet more complex where attention is focused on the examination of similar subgroups and entities across countries. This requires implicit or explicit identification of the comparability of groups in each country, followed by comparison across countries. Both aspects suggest the need for a multistage approach to research design and analysis, as well as the importance of establishing the equivalence and comparability of the units examined in the different countries.

# Difficulties in Establishing Comparability and Equivalence

Considerable difficulties are likely to be encountered in establishing equivalence and comparability of research in different countries, both with secondary and primary data and with methods of data collection. For example, secondary data on motor vehicle registrations may not provide equivalent data between countries. In many industrialized countries, a company car is provided to sales people and is counted as a commercial vehicle. It may, however, also be used extensively for personal transport. Thus, data on noncommercial registrations would understate the actual extent of personal cars.

Similarly, many of the concepts, measurement instruments and procedures for primary data collection have been developed and tested in the US and Western Europe. Their relevance and applicability in other countries are far from clear. Concern with equivalence and comparability as well as accuracy may be particularly critical where secondary data are collected from the Internet. Often data available on the Internet are from diverse or unsubstantiated sources and hence their accuracy and reliability need to be carefully checked. Explicit administrative and analytical procedures for modifying concepts and measures developed in one country, and testing their relevance in another, should thus be incorporated into the research design. In addition, such procedures should enable identification of concepts and measures unique to a specific country or culture (Wind and Douglas, 1982).

Establishing the comparability of data administration procedures poses further difficulties. In one country a certain method of data collection, for example mail questionnaires, may be known to have a given level of reliability. In another country, personal interviews rather than mail questionnaires may have an equivalent level of reliability. Levels of reliability associated with comparable research techniques differ and suggest the desirability of using techniques with equivalent levels of reliability rather than techniques that are strictly comparable.

# Coordination of Research and Data Collection across Countries

The conduct of research in the international environment not only adds considerably to the complexity of research design and data collection, but also gives rise to a number of issues relating to the organization and administration of research in different countries.

Concern with the coordination, design and execution of research across different countries implies that agreement has to be reached with regard to research design in every country where research is conducted. The research instruments and data collection procedures also have to be harmonized. This can result in substantial difficulties and coordination problems, particularly where the research task is outsourced to a local research agency. These can add considerably to research costs and also lead to considerable time delays.

The types of coordination problem encountered are likely to be closely related to the organizational structure of the company and, specifically, where research is commissioned. When research is commissioned centrally, by an international division, corporate or regional headquarters, interactions with the research agency are likely to be centralized and coordination problems minimal. If, on the other hand, research is commissioned locally, problems typically occur related to not only coordination but also lack of comparability or duplication of research in different countries.

Such factors suggest the need for skill in the organization of research design and management, balancing the need for knowledge of and familiarity with the local market with the need for coordination across countries in order to develop strategy across markets.

# Intrafunctional Character of International Marketing Decisions

The intrafunctional character of many international decisions – especially in selecting countries to enter, where to expand, or what methods of operation to use – suggests the need for intrafunctional research. In selecting countries, for example, an important issue is not only the existence of market opportunities and market potential, but also possible sources of supply. This suggests that marketing research should be coordinated with research to identify and evaluate alternative suppliers or sources of supply. Similarly, decisions about the mode of operation also entail decisions about the degree of equity exposure and location of foreign production. Consequently, analysis of political risk, foreign exchange rates and financial markets is required, as well as assessment of the production and shipment costs associated with alternative production locations. Similarly, pricing decisions need to take into consideration currency fluctuations, foreign exchange risk and market factors.

Some difficulties are likely to be encountered in coordinating intrafunctional research. For example, the accounting or finance department might want to focus on measures of profitability such as cash flow or return on investment (ROI), while the marketing and sales departments are more concerned with market share and sales. An intrafunctional orientation provides a stronger conceptual and methodological foundation for research. Greater precision is introduced in the conceptual and operational definition of the variables and constructs to be studied, and these are more closely linked and integrated with the specific decisions to be made. This should also lead to improved coordination of strategic decisions made by different departments and also of information collection relative to international markets. Duplication of research effort in international markets can be avoided and economies of scale in research costs achieved by organizing and conducting research at the corporate or divisional level.

## Economics of International Investment and Marketing Decisions

A final factor to be considered is the economics of international investment and marketing decisions. The time horizon required for making such decisions is typically considerably greater than that required for comparable domestic decisions. This is due in part to the much more rapid rate of growth and change in many international markets, as for example Asia or Latin America. In particular, it is important to take a long-term view of market potential, and to consider entry at an early stage of market development, to avoid pre-emption of the market by competitors. The rapid pace of change in many industries, such as telecommunications, consumer and industrial electronics, means that market trends need to be monitored worldwide, as does the impact of different environmental scenarios on these trends.

Such considerations imply that the payout period for evaluating the costs associated with the conduct of international marketing research needs to be considerably longer than that in relation to comparable domestic research. While in the domestic market a payout period of one year might be appropriate, in international markets a period of five years might be more relevant. Similarly, the lack of familiarity with foreign environments, and with operations within these environments, implies that much research, especially in the initial entry stages, should be viewed as an investment rather than a current expense. This can help to avoid costly entry mistakes and enables the development of more effective long-run international expansion strategies.

# Scope of the Book

While the basic principles of marketing research are the same whether research is conducted in an international or a domestic context, the international marketing researcher is likely to encounter greater difficulties than his or her domestic research counterpart. These difficulties stem from operating across national boundaries and in a diverse range of sociocultural environments. Examples of issues that may arise include how to obtain responses from illiterate or semi-literate populations, how to develop a sampling frame in the absence of reliable census data or sampling lists, or simply how to find or train competent interviewers. Frequently, creativity and resourcefulness are required in coping with unexpected problems. In addition, an ability to manage, deal with and organize researchers of different cultural backgrounds and value systems is essential to successful international marketing research.

In the following 14 chapters, the various stages typically involved in the conduct of international marketing research are examined. In Chapter 2 the issues associated with the design of international marketing research are considered, focusing in particular on those related to the organization of international marketing research, the choice of supplier, the determination of information requirements, the selection of information sources, the appropriate unit of analysis and the development of a research plan and its administration.

Chapters 3 and 4 are concerned with secondary data sources. These are often more important in international marketing research, due to the high costs of primary data collection. Chapter 3 identifies the various sources of international data and outlines the main types of data that are available. Chapter 4 looks at the uses of these data, for example in making initial market entry decisions and establishing preliminary estimates of demand potential.

Chapter 5 discusses issues relating to the structure of the research design in international markets. This includes the definition of the unit of analysis in international markets, as well as the number and location of the sites at which research is conducted and whether the impact of internal and external influences on behavior is examined. The composition of the research team and potential communication problems arising from interaction between researchers from different research backgrounds and cultural perspectives are also discussed.

Chapter 6 examines various issues in primary data collection, focusing in particular on the need to establish the equivalence of the constructs studied, of the measurement of these constructs and of the samples from which data are drawn in different countries and sociocultural contexts. The emic–etic dilemma is discussed, namely that constructs and measures adapted to specific sociocultural backgrounds are unlikely to be comparable across countries, and equally that use of identical constructs or measures is unlikely to provide an optimal measuring instrument for all countries and cultures.

Chapter 7 discusses various nonsurvey data collection techniques. These include observational and quasi-observational data, protocols, projective techniques and depth interviews. Use of these in the preliminary stages of research is advocated in order to identify relevant concepts to be examined in subsequent stages of research.

Chapters 8 and 9 cover instrument design, sampling and data collection in survey research. In Chapter 8, issues in instrument design are discussed, such as questionnaire formulation, instrument translation, appropriate scales and response format, as well as potential sources of bias arising from the respondent or the interviewer–respondent interaction. Chapter 9 examines problems in sampling, such as identifying an efficient sampling procedure. The advantages and disadvantages of various data collection procedures, such as mail, telephone or personal interviewing, in international marketing research are also considered.

Chapter 10 discusses the development and use of scales to measure constructs in a multicultural or multicountry context. Issues relating to scale reliability and validity are addressed, including procedures for testing scales developed in one country or culture to see whether they are applicable in another. In addition, approaches to developing hybrid scales with pan-cultural components as well as components to measure constructs unique to a particular country or culture are covered.

Chapters 11 and 12 cover analysis of multicountry data. In Chapter 11, analytical techniques that are suited to determining whether there are significant differences in the *level* of a variable between countries are discussed. In Chapter 12, analytical techniques that are appropriate for examining differences in the *structure* and relationship of variables between countries are covered. These different techniques are illustrated with examples from the literature.

Chapter 13 examines the steps involved in the development of a global information system. This covers the design of a global system and its various components, as well as how information is collected and fed into the system on a regular basis. Issues relating to access to data and its use in management decision making are also examined.

Chapter 14 brings together many of the themes addressed throughout the book. It also tries to provide some insights into the challenges that researchers face as markets become both integrated and diverse at the same time. The impact of technological advances and new analytical techniques is covered. Ethical issues are examined, as well as some of the special challenges associated with conducting research in emerging market economies.

Chapter 15 sets the stage for the future of international marketing research. For progress to be made in the international arena, three interrelated issues need to be addressed. First, greater attention needs to be paid to the comparability and equivalence of the basic constructs being examined between countries. Second, more thought needs to be given to the research design that guides international marketing research. Finally, better cross-cultural measures and analytical techniques need to be developed and applied to multicountry data.

# References

*Advertising Age International* (1997) Coke Taps Maternal Instinct with New Latin American Ads, January.

Brown, P. (2004) Microsoft Pays Dear for Insults through Ignorance. *The Guardian*, 30 August.

*Business Week* (1993) Colgate-Palmolive Is Really Cleaning up in Poland, 15 March.

Craig, C.S. and Douglas, S.P. (1996a) Responding to the Challenges of Global Markets: Change, Complexity, Competition and Conscience. *Columbia Journal of World Business*, Winter, 7–18.

Craig, C.S. and Douglas, S.P. (1996b) Developing Strategy for Global Markets: An Evolutionary Perspective. *Columbia Journal of World Business*, Spring, 70–81.

Craig C.S. and Douglas S.P. (2000) Configural Advantage in Global Markets. *Journal of International Marketing*, **8**(1), 6–26.

Douglas, S.P. and Craig, C.S. (1995) *Global Marketing Strategy*. McGraw-Hill, New York.

Douglas, S.P. and Craig, C.S. (1997) The Changing Dynamic of Consumer Behavior: Implications for Cross-cultural Research. *International Journal of Research in Marketing*, **14**, 379–395.

Douglas, S.P., Craig, C.S. and Nijssen E.J. (2001) Integrating Branding Strategy across Global Markets: Building International Brand Architecture. *Journal of International Marketing*, **9**(2), 97–114.

Fowler, G.A. and Setoodeh, R. (2004) Outsiders Get Smarter about China's Tastes. *Wall Street Journal*, 5 August, B1–2.

Hofstede, G. (1980) *Culture's Consequences: International Differences in Work-related Values*. Sage, Beverly Hills, CA.

Hofstede, G. (2001) *Culture's Consequences: Comparing Behaviors, Institutions and Organizations*, 2nd edition. Sage, Thousand Oaks, CA.

Lee, J.A. (1966) Cultural Analysis in Overseas Operations. *Harvard Business Review*. March/April, 106–111.

Schwartz, S.H. (1992) Universals in the Content and Structure of Values: Theoretical Advances and Empirical Tests in 20 Countries. In Zanna, M. (ed.) *Advances in Experimental Social Psychology*, 25. Academic Press, Orlando, FL.

Wind, Y. and Douglas, S.P. (1982) Comparative Consumer Research: The Next Frontier. *Management Decision*, **20**, 24–35.

*World Almanac* (2004) World Almanac Books, NJ.

UNDP (2003) *Human Development Report*. United Nations, New York.

UNDP (2004) *Human Development Report*. United Nations, New York.

# Chapter 2

# DESIGNING INTERNATIONAL MARKETING RESEARCH

## Introduction

Broadly speaking, international marketing research can be defined as research that crosses national borders and involves respondents and researchers from different countries and cultures. Most commonly, it will involve collecting information and making inferences about respondents, or business activities, in two or more countries within the context of a single research project. The marketing research may be conducted simultaneously in multiple countries or sequentially over a period of time. In some cases, international marketing research may also involve collection of information in a single country by an academic researcher or by a commercial organization from another country, with a view to understanding differences and similarities with regard to their home market. In some instances, international marketing research may also include studies of immigrant populations, especially where emphasis is placed on understanding changes in attitudes and behavior as members of one culture or nationality move to another country or culture.

In general, two broad types of international marketing research can be identified: academic research and commercial research. Academic research includes research conducted by individuals at academic institutions with the objective of further understanding the behavior of consumers and organizations in other countries or in relation to their activities in other countries, or testing the applicability of concepts and theories in a range of countries and cultural contexts. Commercial research, on the other hand, is conducted for a profit by an organization, and is concerned with collecting information to aid management in making decisions relative to international markets. This includes decisions relating to international marketing strategy and marketing mix decisions within and across markets.

The two types of research share some common ground. Academic research, particularly that conducted by faculty at business schools, often addresses issues that are of importance in making business decisions. For example, studies examining similarities and differences in consumers' attitudes, behavior and purchase decisions in different countries can help to guide international segmentation decisions. Similarly, research on differences in customer response to marketing stimuli, such as packaging, price, advertising or promotion, may aid in formulating marketing tactics in different markets. Research conducted more broadly by other academics, primarily psychologists, anthropologists and sociologists, contributes to the understanding of theoretical constructs and behaviors that underlie and influence the behavior of consumers. These fundamental contributions to knowledge help guide research in more applied areas.

Commercial research focuses on applied problems. However, researchers will often apply academic theory as a guide to research design, or in the development of research products and models. Research models and procedures developed to assess international market opportunities and risks or to estimate demand in international markets have, for example, been applied commercially. New product diffusion and adoption models are also used to predict new product adoption rates, while communication models underlie measures of effective communication. In addition, each type of research benefits from methodological advances in the other. Developments in statistical analysis, such as covariance structure modeling (LISREL and EQS), have slowly filtered into commercial research. Advances in sampling and interviewing techniques are often first applied by commercial organizations and eventually influence academic data collection.

Academic research on international marketing issues has expanded considerably in recent years. Particularly marked has been the increase in research comparing consumer attitudes and behavior in different countries and cultures. As awareness and understanding of customer behavior and market environments in different countries and regions have increased, attention has shifted from descriptive and comparative studies of behavior to theory testing and development. These range from studies assessing the validity of constructs and models of behavior developed in one country, often the US, in other countries and cultural contexts, or applications of statistical techniques, to studies examining the factors underlying differences in behavior or market response patterns or in the strategies pursued by firms in international markets.

Commercial research has also increased considerably with the growing involvement of firms of different national origins and industries in international markets. As in domestic research, management decisions provide the basis for determining information needs and research design. In the international environment, however, the decisions facing management are more complex since decisions are often hierarchical, spanning different geographical regions or countries. Consequently, factors have to be considered at two different levels: (1) those relating to the macro country or regional environment; and (2) those relating to the specific product market or customer grouping. At the strategic level, decisions relating to international market entry and expansion span several countries and consequently require information relating to a number of different countries and environmental contexts. Increasingly, these concern markets in emerging countries where market potential is becoming increasingly significant. Similarly, tactical decisions relating to product positioning, global branding or standardizing marketing mix tactics across countries require information that is comparable and consistent from one country to another. This also entails coordination of research across these country units and gives rise to a number of design and organizational issues.

The distinction between academic and commercial research lies on a continuum. While the purpose of the research and the specific research questions may differ, as may the role of theory and theory testing, many of the same problems arise both in research design and organization and in the implementation of the research plan. The purpose of this chapter is to examine these issues, focusing on the various stages in the design and implementation of a marketing research plan. The different stages outlined are then covered in more detail in subsequent chapters.

# The International Marketing Research Plan

The complexity of conducting research in international markets and the increasingly wide range of countries in which it is conducted frequently require a multistage approach. Rarely can a detailed research plan be designed at the outset of the project. Rather, some exploratory investigation will need to be conducted to pinpoint the relevant dimensions of the decision problem and to determine the relevance of specific constructs or underlying assumptions about customer or management behavior or the nature of the market infrastructure. In the case of commercial research, a preliminary phase to determine the availability of existing information from secondary data sources is essential. In the case of academic research, it is important to review previous research relating to similar issues, in the same or related countries and cultures, as well as to examine the theoretical constructs in marketing and other social sciences, before a research design can be developed. In addition, some preliminary research will be needed to provide input into elements such as instrument design, the sampling plan or data collection procedures, as well as how best to organize the research process.

# *Preliminary Steps*

The time and effort devoted to exploratory research depend on the research budget, as well as on the level of experience in conducting research in a given country environment. As a firm gains experience in operating and conducting research in a given country environment, it is less necessary to conduct extensive preliminary research, particularly where the research concerns a product category with which management is already familiar. Preliminary research is necessary where research involves a new product category, consumption situation or market segment, or where the firm is considering introducing a product in a category that is not currently available and would radically change existing behavior patterns.

In the case of commercial research, this preliminary phase will involve some desk research based on secondary data. In selecting which markets to enter, investigation of trends in different countries, for example growth in GNP, political or financial stability, may help to narrow the choice and to select those to be investigated in more depth. Qualitative research, personal or depth interviews, focus groups or observational research may also be conducted to determine relevant questions to be examined in subsequent phases of research. In deciding whether or not to market and, if so, how to market in a given country or set of countries, qualitative research can provide some initial indication as to likely responses, as well as to attributes used in evaluating products and different scenarios in which products might be used. In addition, qualitative research may be useful in determining the relevant competitive product set or in defining the target market, and in providing guidelines for the sampling plan.

Organizational and administrative issues also need to be examined in the preliminary phase of research. These might include, for example, consideration of whether to conduct research in-house or which outside supplier to use. The availability and quality of research services in the various countries where research is to be conducted, as well as the costs of these services, need to be examined. Initial estimates of the costs of alternative procedures may also be obtained to determine which is likely to be the most cost efficient and to draw up the budget for the research. Some specific costs to conduct marketing research are shown at the end of this chapter. More complete information can be found in an ESOMAR (2003) study of marketing research prices.

# *Designing the International Marketing Research Plan*

Once the preliminary phase of the research has been completed, the next step is the design of the international marketing research plan. This may involve a number of stages and is frequently considerably more complex than domestic marketing research. This process is outlined in Figure 2.1.

First, the key research questions need to be determined. In the case of commercial research, formulation of a problem statement provides the basis for determining management information requirements and the structure of the research design. In the case of academic research, the research questions also establish guidelines for determining what theoretical constructs or models underlie the research design. Next, previous research and existing information sources need to be examined in order to determine what additional information has to be collected. Either secondary data sources may be consulted or primary research may be conducted.

Where primary research is conducted, an important consideration for management is whether this is purchased from outside sources and specifically from whom, or designed in-house and executed by a field organization. Similarly, academic researchers need to determine whether to rely solely on secondary data sources or to collect primary data and, if the latter, whether to collaborate with other researchers or research organizations. In general, this is likely to depend on the size of the organization and its research staff, as well as the degree of the organization's involvement and experience in international operations.

The design of the research plan entails specification of the data to be collected, as well as the research techniques and instruments to be used, the sampling plan, and research administration procedures and analyses to be conducted. This plan has then to be implemented and procedures for fieldwork put in place for the coordination of the roles of the various participants in the research process.

The final step is the analysis of the information collected and its presentation in verbal or written form. The findings have to be examined, some conclusions drawn and recommendations made with regard to managerial implications as well as future research. A key problem in commercial research is presentation of findings to management so as to maximize the likelihood of their acceptance and use in the decision process. Procedures to incorporate findings into the information system also need to be considered to ensure that the findings become part of the stock of accumulated knowledge and experience in international markets. This is covered in detail in Chapter 13.

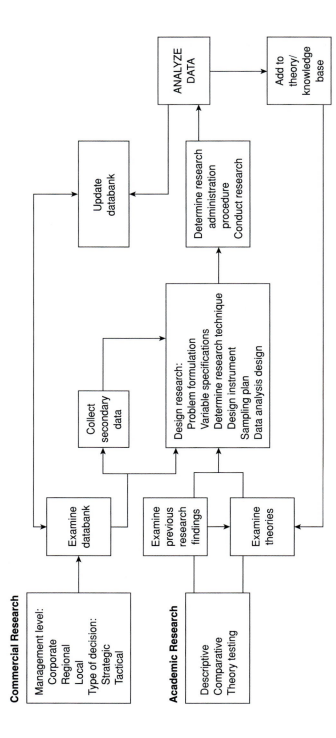

**Figure 2.1** The international marketing research process

# The International Marketing Research Process

The first step in the international marketing research process frequently incorporates a preliminary phase of assessing information needs and availability. Some exploratory investigation will have to be conducted to pinpoint more precisely the relevant dimensions of the decision problem and to relate it to information needs. In addition, some preliminary research will be required to provide input into elements such as instrument design, the sampling plan or data collection procedures, as well as how the research process is best organized.

## *Determining Key Research Questions*

Once the problem statement has been clearly articulated, following preliminary research, the specific research questions to be answered need to be formulated. In academic research this hinges to a substantial degree on the type of research. In commercial research, it depends on the level and type of decisions for which research is being conducted.

## *Types of Academic Research*

For the purposes of simplicity, three types of academic research can be identified: descriptive, comparative and theoretical. These differ primarily in terms of the purpose of the research and the key research questions, as well as the structure of the research design. *Descriptive* research typically focuses on understanding behavior and the market environment in a single country. *Comparative* research focuses on comparing attitudes and behavior of consumers, firms or other organizations in two or more countries or regions of the world. *Theoretical* research is concerned with the applicability of attitudinal and behavioral models and constructs in different countries and cultural contexts.

### *Descriptive Research*

Descriptive research is generally conducted in the initial phase of a project, when a researcher has little knowledge about a country or area of the world and needs to broaden understanding of the market and its parameters. While this type of research was popular in the 1960s and 1970s, when academic research on international markets was in the relatively early stages, it is now considerably less common. Increasingly, the availability of the Internet and the ease of collecting information from different sites, using search engines to identify relevant sources, facilitate rapid assembly of information from a variety of sources to develop a picture of a particular international research problem or issue.

## Comparative Research

Comparative research is the most frequently conducted type of research. The primary purpose is to compare consumer behavior, or to examine how markets function in two or more countries, or to assess different cultural environments, typically with a view to identifying differences and similarities. Often these are attributed to differences in the macroeconomic or cultural environment. Here, research varies in terms of the extent to which it incorporates an explicit model with research hypotheses to explain or account for findings of differences or similarities. In the simplest type of design, no explicit model is included and often observed differences and similarities are rationalized *ex post*, based on factors such as level of economic development, linguistic differences, or purely 'culture'.

An alternative approach is to develop a model that explicitly hypothesizes the various factors, relationships and intervening variables, which may account for similarities and differences. The model might, for example, include macrocultural variables, individual attitudes and values, patterns of social communication and so on. This helps to generate a deeper understanding of the factors that underlie observed differences in patterns of behavior in international markets.

## Theoretical Research

The primary purpose of theoretical studies is to examine the extent to which theories, models and constructs developed in one country are valid and applicable in other countries and cultural contexts. These types of studies are related to comparative studies that rely on a conceptual model, except that in this case the primary emphasis is on testing the validity or applicability of a model or construct, while in the former case the validity of the model is assumed, and it is used to explain or understand differences in patterns of behavior between countries and cultures.

# Organizational Research

Another type of academic research, which is related to commercial research, focuses on examining the strategy and tactical decisions of firms in international markets. Often it centers around examining the effectiveness of alternative strategies or marketing mix tactics. Much of this research has, for example, focused on assessing the relative effectiveness of standardized strategies as opposed to strategies adapted to local market conditions. This has been examined in relation to both competitive strategy and specific elements of the marketing mix. Another area of interest has been the comparison of strategies adopted by firms of different national origins, especially European, Japanese and US. Sourcing and international market expansion strategies have also been examined.

# Management Information Requirements

In commercial research, the key research questions and information to be collected depend on the level and type of decision for which the research is being conducted. As in domestic research, information may be required for decision making at different levels in the organization, from the *corporate* level relating to strategic issues, down to local operating units where concerns are often more tactical. Such decisions vary in focus and scope, from corporate decisions – relating to the long-run direction of the company and choice of which countries to enter and where to expand – to operational decisions, such as whether or not to modify advertising copy or packaging for a given country, whether to launch a new product and how to position it.

A company's organizational structure will determine to a large extent where responsibility for different decisions is located in the organization and specific problems investigated. In companies organized by product division, new product research and development is likely to be conducted within that division or product development unit. This is often centralized worldwide or on a regional basis. In companies where local operating units have greater responsibility, research is more likely to be conducted locally within each individual country.

In general, however, irrespective of the level at and location where research is conducted, two major types of decisions can be identified: strategic and tactical decisions. These differ in terms of their information requirements and in the types of data most commonly used to make decisions. Strategic decision making in international markets relies heavily on secondary data sources and on macroeconomic data, in addition to management experience accumulated through operating in different countries and marketing environments. In some cases, primary data collection may also be required. Tactical decisions, on the other hand, are likely to require primary data collection and research tailored to the specific decision to be made.

# *Information for Strategic Decisions*

Global strategic decisions are made primarily at the corporate or regional level. These relate to the long-run direction and goals of the firm, for example international market entry, market expansion and development strategies; that is, whether and which new countries or product markets should be entered and what portfolio of countries provide the appropriate balance for future growth. In addition, decisions have to be made regarding the segmentation of markets, for example whether markets are segmented on a country-by-country or on a transnational basis. Directly related to this are decisions concerning global branding strategies, for example organizational level, corporate, product division or product, and what positioning strategies should be used relative to each target segment.

Such decisions imply determining the overall allocation of company resources across countries, product markets and target segments. As such, they go beyond the marketing function, encompassing other functional areas such as financial and production management, and entail decisions relating to capital budgeting, accounting procedures and production scheduling. Different modes of entry, for example, imply different levels of financial and resource commitment and operational involvement.

Given limited resources, decisions to enter different countries or product markets are interrelated, since decisions to develop new products, to expand existing product lines or to extend them to other countries and product markets involve commitment of resources to specific countries or product markets. The potential for economies of scale and scope associated with multiple product operations in a given country, or in multiple countries, suggests the need for an integrated perspective in making such decisions, coordinating international operations across product lines and across geographical or regional areas. Evaluation of entry into new countries or product markets or target segments should be made relative to expansion and development (or divestment) of existing operations in other countries and product markets.

Adoption of a global perspective in making such decisions implies that information is required at different levels in the organization – that is, corporate, SBUs or product line – at which decisions have to be made, as well as relative to different geographical or market units – that is, regions, countries, product markets and target segments. Information is also needed relating to the degree of interconnectedness or linkages between markets relating, for example, to trade flows between countries or geographical regions, transportation and communication links across countries, movement

**Table 2.1**    Sample indicators for assessing risks and opportunities

|  | Types of indicators | Sample indicators |
|---|---|---|
| Country entry decisions | Political risk | Number of expropriations, expert ratings of stability |
| Risks | Financial risk | Rate of inflation, foreign exchange risk, restrictions on capital flow |
|  | Legal risk | Import–export restrictions, restrictions on ownership |
| Opportunities | Macromarket potential | GNP per capita, growth of GNP, ratio of investment to GNP, population size, density, urbanization, educational level |
| Modes of entry decisions | Production and marketing costs | Electricity, energy costs, labor skills and costs, management training, capital and technology availability and costs, rates of interest |
| Product market decisions | Product market size | Sales volume of product, ownership of product, sales of complementary and substitute products, number, and size of competing firms |

*Source*: adapted from Douglas and Craig, 1988.

of people and ideas, organizational and political linkages and so on. Information is required for marketing factors such as sales volume or product ownership, but also for financial variables such as rates of inflation and foreign exchange risk, legal factors such as product or advertising regulation, and political factors such as expropriations.

Some illustrations of the type of information likely to be required at each of these levels are summarized in Table 2.1. It should be noted that these examples are illustrative. The specific information to be collected by management needs to be determined in each case, depending on management and corporate objectives, company resources, and the relevant product market and target segment.

At the country level, two major dimensions need to be taken into consideration in making resource allocation decisions. These relate to the *risks* and the *opportunities* associated with operating in different countries. Surrogate indicators of these can be developed. As indicated in Table 2.1, risks might be assessed based on factors such as political instability, rates of inflation and foreign exchange risk; and opportunities based on indicators such as GNP per capita, total GNP and population size and density.

Different modes of operation and marketing strategies entail different costs. The costs associated with these can be estimated based on factors such as costs of electricity, energy, water and labor, retail margins, media costs and transportation rates. At the product market level, information relating to current and projected performance levels, for example ROI or market share, is likely to be required. However, this information will only be available in relation to product markets in which the firm is currently operating. In product markets where the firm is not currently involved, surrogate indicators can be developed, such as sales volume of products, product ownership, sales of complementary products and number of competing firms.

Once this information has been collected, it can then be integrated into an international database and updated on a regular basis. This will facilitate integration of information into the management decision process. Some problems are likely to be encountered due to lack of comparability in data collected in countries and different environmental contexts, and differences in product market definitions. Management issues relating to access and retrieval of information also have to be considered. These are discussed further in Chapter 13.

## Information for Tactical Decisions

The second type of information required relates to the specific tactics to be used in and across different countries and product markets. These are closely linked to market segmentation and positioning decisions. For example, given a specific brand positioning, research may be required to determine what advertising copy to use, how far a standardized theme can be used, or whether adjustments to a standard prototype campaign will be required. Examples of the types of decisions and related research are shown in Table 2.2.

Decisions with regard to new product development, for example, can require product benefit and attribute research, concept testing, and test marketing in all the countries in which the product is to be marketed. Questions may arise as to whether products should be adapted to meet differing environmental and market conditions, such as differences in customer tastes, needs and interests in other countries. Equally, branding strategies and brand names will need to be assessed. New products may be developed in response to specific market conditions and tested in single or multiple country markets.

**Table 2.2**    Tactical international marketing decisions requiring international marketing research

| Marketing mix decision | Type of research |
| --- | --- |
| Product policy decision | Focus groups and qualitative research to generate ideas for new products |
| | Survey research to evaluate new product ideas |
| | Concept testing, test marketing |
| | Product benefit and attitude research |
| | Product formulation and feature testing |
| Pricing decisions | Price sensitivity studies |
| Distribution decisions | Survey of shopping patterns and behavior |
| | Consumer attitudes to different store types |
| | Survey of distributor attitudes and policies |
| Advertising decisions | Advertising pre-testing |
| | Advertising post-testing, recall scores |
| | Surveys of media habits |
| Sales promotion decisions | Surveys of response to alternative types of promotion |
| Salesforce decisions | Tests of alternative sales presentations |

The effectiveness of using the same advertising theme or similar sales promotion tools in different countries or cultures also needs to be tested to determine whether these should be applied, or whether specific appeals and promotional tools geared to the particular market environment need to be developed. Research may also be desirable to assess whether price elasticities are similar in different countries, and whether similar pricing strategies can be used. Equally, distribution decisions need to be examined and adapted to different distribution channels in different countries and regions of the world.

The type of information required in relation to these decisions is essentially the same as that required in comparable domestic marketing research and often entails similar research procedures. Greater use may, however, be made of qualitative research techniques, especially in the initial stages of market entry, or where the researcher has little familiarity with the environment. The research process tends to be more complex since it is conducted in a variety of different cultural and environmental contexts and there is a need for comparability across these different contexts.

# Structuring the Unit of Analysis

Once the key research questions and information requirements have been determined, the next step is to decide on the relevant unit for data collection. The geographical scope of the unit can range from cities, regions or country groupings to the world. Data can then be collected from specific types or groups of customers or organizations or all customers and organizations within the geographical unit, or relative to the unit itself, for example sales consumption, patterns of expenditure and pricing patterns. The way in which data collection is structured will depend on the specific research problem, the type of information required and the size of the research budget.

## *The World*

The broadest type of geographical unit in relation to which data can be collected is the world. As yet, relatively little secondary data are available related to global units, other than data relating to global industries such as aerospace or pharmaceuticals or sales data for large multinationals with worldwide operations. With the shrinking of distances and increasing integration of markets, a growing volume of primary research is conducted relative to world markets. For example, surveys may be conducted of firms or managers in an industry worldwide, or of specific market segments or types of consumers.

## *Region or Country Grouping*

The next unit in relation to which data may be collected is that of the geographical region or groups of countries. Secondary data are sometimes available for regional units, for example the European Union or ASEAN (Association of South East Asian Nations). In general, however, such data are more commonly broken down by country, although the same measurement units are used throughout the region.

## *Country*

The geographical unit most commonly used in international marketing research is the country. Most secondary data are collected at the country level, for example Gross National Product (GNP), population, steel or energy consumption, price trends and private consumption expenditures. Many market reports and industry studies are also conducted relative to a given country. In primary data collection, research organizations and networks are often organized on a country-by-country basis.

## Cities

In some instances, cities may provide the appropriate geographical unit for data collection. This occurs where interest is focused on a specific market segment, for example young urban professionals, more affluent consumers, or organizations such as restaurants and department stores. In emerging markets, cities may be the appropriate unit, as customers in rural areas may not be sufficiently affluent or be too geographically dispersed to provide an attractive market opportunity.

The complex and hierarchical character of many international marketing decisions implies that the research design will make use of a multi-tier structure incorporating units at different levels. For example, the geographical units might be defined in terms of a region, a group of countries and data collected from specific customer groups, such as senior citizens or ecologically concerned consumers within that unit. Alternative types of units are discussed in more detail in Chapter 5.

In contrast to domestic marketing research, which typically entails use of a single level or unit of analysis, selection of appropriate units for data collection in international marketing research is likely to follow a complex multistage structure. This is discussed in greater detail in Chapter 5. This structure in essence provides the framework for the research design and the organization of the research plan and, more specifically, for the determination of the sampling frame and subsequent data analysis (Chapters 9, 11 and 12).

## Selecting Information Sources

The next stage in the research process is to examine previous research and then investigate alternative data sources for the required information. First, previous research needs to be studied relating to the topic and research questions of interest, both in general and in the particular countries or geographical regions. Then data relating to the research questions needs to be examined. Here, as in domestic research, two major types of data may be identified, secondary and primary data. They can be obtained from external sources – that is, outside the company – or internal – that is, intracompany sources. Each has a number of advantages and limitations relating primarily to their cost relative to their availability, reliability and applicability to the problem at hand.

# Prior Research

First, it is important to examine prior information relating to the key research questions and the specific countries and markets to be examined. In the case of academic research, theoretical research may be helpful, particularly in developing a conceptual framework for study and research hypotheses relating to underlying variables. In addition, prior research relating to the product market and the countries or geographical areas to be studied can be helpful in providing background for the study. Information on the country is useful in determining the scope of the study and various aspects or questions that need to be considered, as well as providing input into the research design. Such information may also be useful in planning the study, developing a sampling plan, selecting appropriate research administration procedures and interpreting research findings. Once previous research has been examined, the next step is to determine whether to use secondary data, or whether primary data will be required.

# Secondary Data

Secondary data play an important role in international marketing research, particularly in initial entry into international markets. In some cases, secondary data may be adequate to answer the research questions of interest. A wide range of different types of secondary data are available at various levels of aggregation as well as geographical scope. Data at the macroeconomic level include government, economic and social statistics as well as data published by regional and world organizations such as the European Union, the World Bank, the United Nations and commercial organizations such as the Economist Intelligence Unit. Trade associations, financial analysts and other organizations such as Euromonitor publish data at the industry or product market levels. Most of these sources are available on the Internet, but some charge a fee. The specific sources of such information are discussed in Chapter 3.

Internal company data relating to sales and costs provide information at the firm level. These data are useful in providing information about profitability and growth trends for specific products, product lines, geographical regions and channels of distribution, as well as the effectiveness of different marketing tools such as advertising, merchandising, sales promotions, personal selling or price discounts. Differences in national accounting systems and procedures, fiscal and taxation systems mean that these data are seldom comparable from one country to another. As a result, multinational corporations often keep two sets of books, one consistent with national accounting and fiscal procedures, the other meeting international accounting standards (Choi and Meek, 2005).

# Primary Data

Where secondary data do not provide adequate information input for management decision making, primary data collection will be required. Collection of such data often entails high costs relative to its perceived value. This stems from the difficulties encountered in international marketing research and the lack of experience in many markets, which may mean that more background data will need to be collected and that data are less accurate or reliable than in comparable domestic studies.

Collection of primary data is important for many strategic and tactical marketing decisions. It is essential in testing new products or concepts or advertising copy, or in evaluating price sensitivity. In conducting such research, different types of data collection techniques may be used, ranging from qualitative techniques such as focus groups or in-depth interviews, which require small sample sizes, to survey techniques that entail large sample sizes.

Qualitative data collection techniques are useful in the initial phases of research in identifying constructs, product class definitions or relevant attitudes and behavior to be examined in subsequent phases of research. In international marketing research this is advantageous insofar as the researcher may be unfamiliar with the market environment and need to obtain information about relevant parameters to structure the research problem. Qualitative research avoids the imposition of a cultural bias, since the researcher imposes no prespecified conceptual model a priori. On the other hand, the burden of interpretation is placed on the researcher, resulting in potential for cultural self-referent bias.

Where more precise estimation is required, survey research is likely to be desirable. Survey research is the most commonly used method of data collection in international marketing research and has the advantage that data can be collected and processed from large samples. Use of the survey in international marketing research is fraught with a number of difficulties, arising from collection of data in a range of diverse sociocultural and linguistic environments. Consequently, considerable care needs to be exercised in instrument design to avoid errors of interpretation on the part of respondents, particularly among those with low levels of literacy or education. Sampling and survey administration procedures need to be designed to avoid bias arising from nonresponse or respondent–interviewer interaction.

Internal resources can also be utilized to collect primary data. This is likely to be appropriate in business-to-business markets where sales representatives can serve as a valuable source of information with regard to potential customers and the needs and interests of existing customers. Sales persons' opinions can be used to provide input for new product development and product modification decisions, as well as changes in promotional or delivery policies. Such procedures are low cost but must be used with caution, especially if sales representatives anticipate that information supplied will influence their sales quotas.

Opinions and attitudes of management at local subsidiaries, sales or marketing organizations towards current trends and developments in local national markets can be surveyed. These might, for example, provide insights into changes in customer needs and interests, receptivity to new products, responses to changes in marketing strategy and tactics, as well as likely reactions and retaliatory strategies by competitors and distributors. A variety of different data sources can be used to obtain information on international markets. Procedures for collecting these data are examined in more detail in Chapters 7, 8 and 9.

# Research Plan

Drawing up a plan for primary data collection in international markets involves essentially the same steps as designing domestic marketing research. However, in international marketing research the plan will be more complex than in domestic research, entailing a number of successive stages and integrating secondary data with the collection of primary data.

First, the specific variables or factors to be examined and how these are categorized or defined in each country or research context have to be specified. Then, relevant relationships between these variables are hypothesized. Appropriate research techniques have then to be determined, for example whether qualitative or survey research should be conducted to examine the hypothesized relationships. Research instruments suitable for use in all the countries or cultures covered have to be developed, sampling procedures determined, and appropriate administration procedures selected.

Once the data have been collected, they have to be analyzed and, in the case of commercial research, findings need to be presented in a form that can be clearly understood by management.

A critical feature of international marketing is that it is conducted in a multicountry, multicultural and multilinguistic environment. This gives rise to a number of issues relating to the comparability of data collected in diverse research environments. A critical issue is whether the same or a similar research instrument and procedures are equally adapted or suitable, and will yield comparable results in each environment. The initial phase of problem formulation, data specification and instrument design is critical and poses a number of issues different from those encountered in domestic marketing research.

# Problem Formulation, Variable Specification and Categorization

In the first place, problems are not always couched in the same terms in different countries or cultural contexts. This results from differences in socioeconomic conditions, levels of economic development, cultural factors or competitive market structures. For example, the relevant set of competing products and services, or relevant product attributes, may vary from country to country. In emerging market countries, for example, a car is a luxury item and small compact cars compete with scooters or mopeds. Similarly, products such as washing machines may compete with low-cost laundry services or in-home help.

Even more complex differences occur in relation to attitudinal data due to differences in values, sociocultural and lifestyle factors that may affect preferences for different products or desired product benefits. The significance and prestige value attached to brand names such as BMW, Rolex or Armani, or the possession of items such as cars, designer clothing or high-tech household appliances, may vary. Similarly, the importance attached to saving time or to product quality and reliability varies, resulting in differences in customer interest in products such as instant noodles or Minute Rice, or the concern with product quality and engineering.

Such factors imply that, in specifying the scope and nature of the research design, careful attention needs to be paid to the equivalence of consumption and purchase behavior as well as the context in which this takes place and hence the underlying determinants of behavior. The way in which comparability is examined needs to be considered. Here, two alternative research designs may be adopted, an *adapted etic* design, which starts from a research design developed in a base country that is then adapted to other contexts, or a *linked emic* approach, which starts with research designs established in different countries or contexts and seeks to harmonize these across contexts. Comparability also needs to be examined in relation to the functional, conceptual and category equivalence of constructs, as well as the linguistic and metric equivalence of the measurement instruments and the equivalence of data collection and survey administration procedures. These issues are addressed in Chapter 6.

# *Choice of Research Techniques*

Selection of appropriate research techniques gives rise to a number of questions about their comparability and cost effectiveness in different countries and cultural contexts and their appropriateness to specific research problems. Essentially, the researcher has to decide whether to conduct a survey; make use of experimental techniques; collect data by observation or other qualitative procedures, for example focus group or projective techniques; or use some combination of these.

Survey research is widely used in multicountry research. Use of a survey assumes the existence of a population with a certain minimal level of education, able to understand and respond to oral or written questions or pictorial stimuli. Where a national or representative sample is required, it also entails ensuring the availability of sampling lists or profile data from which to draw samples. These conditions are not always met, particularly in emerging markets. Among largely illiterate populations and in certain cultures, considerable ingenuity may be required in devising research instruments and procedures to overcome potential communication and comprehension problems.

Experimental techniques are, at least in theory, applicable to all cultural and socioeconomic backgrounds. In practice, however, it is difficult to design an experiment that is comparable or equivalent in all respects in each country or sociocultural context. Field experiments, such as market tests, are typically embedded in the sociocultural context in which they are conducted. As a result, it is likely that differences in the structure of distribution, in the competitive context or the nature of response make strict comparability of such tests problematic.

Observational and projective techniques avoid some of the problems associated with survey techniques, since they do not impose on respondents any prestructured frame of reference that may reflect the specific cultural referents of the researcher. On the other hand, the lack of structure implies that the onus of data interpretation lies on the researcher, and hence cultural bias may occur at the analysis stage. Various types of nonsurvey research techniques are covered in Chapter 7.

# Instrument Design

Care is also needed in instrument design to ensure fit with the specific sociocultural context. It is important to try to avoid potential problems of miscommunication between respondents and researcher. A key issue is translation of the research instrument into concepts and terms that have equivalent meaning and relevance in all contexts and cultures studied.

Translation into another language gives rise to considerable difficulties due to the language- or culture-bound nature of many terms and concepts. Use of nonverbal, as opposed to verbal, stimuli or response measures can help to facilitate understanding, but does not totally eliminate miscommunication problems, since nonverbal stimuli will also require 'translation' or adaptation to ensure that they have the same meaning in each cultural context.

Different types of response bias, such as yea-saying, nay-saying, social acquiescence or cultural stereotyping, need to be assessed. These can be reduced by careful design of the research instrument and use of different response formats, since different types of formats tend to be prone to different types of response bias. These issues are discussed in Chapter 8.

# Sampling and Survey Administration Techniques

Another consideration in international marketing research concerns sampling and survey administration procedures. Difficulties of obtaining sampling lists in many countries, achieving comparability in sample composition and representativity, as well as differences in the feasibility and cost effectiveness of using various data collection procedures, may need to be resolved.

The absence of population lists and other lists commonly used as sampling frames means that it can be difficult to use random sampling techniques in many countries. Consequently, use of nonrandom procedures may be preferable and more cost efficient. Sampling procedures, such as random walk, cluster or area sampling, vary in reliability and accuracy from one country to another and a mix of different procedures may need to be used in order to obtain comparable samples.

Data collection techniques such as mail or telephone surveys and personal interviewing also vary in relative cost, feasibility and coverage of the population from one country to another. In some countries, low levels of literacy or telephone ownership may preclude the use of mail surveys or telephone surveys respectively. Often, especially outside industrialized countries, heavy reliance may be placed on personal interviewing. This requires the availability of trained interviewers fluent in the relevant language. These issues are discussed in more depth in Chapter 9.

## *Data Analysis*

Data analysis also poses certain unique problems in international marketing research. The specific analytical techniques used depend on the problem and the nature of the data collected. Procedures to test for reliability and measurement error in each country or context need to be incorporated in the research design.

Normalization or standardization of data is typically desirable to adjust for differences in cultural referent points and response biases in different countries. This is important for attitudinal and opinion variables where tendencies for specific response set biases are prevalent. Where scales are developed to measure specific constructs, certain additional steps beyond those followed in domestic research will have to be followed, to ensure construct and measure equivalence. These issues are covered in Chapter 10.

The multi-tier character of international marketing research suggests that it may be desirable to follow a sequential procedure in analyzing multicountry data. Data are examined first for each country or other relevant unit independently and cultural biases are identified. Issues of equivalence and comparability are examined and data are then compared and analyzed across different countries. This is further discussed in Chapters 11 and 12.

## Issues in Administering International Marketing Research

Once the research plan has been established, there are still a number of organizational and administrative issues that need to be resolved to carry out the plan. While these are mostly procedural details, they are nonetheless important for successful international marketing research and plan implementation. Three major issues in this regard are how the research effort is organized and coordinated, who actually conducts the research, and the costs. Each of these is further discussed in this section.

# Coordination of Research

An important issue is how international market research is organized and coordinated across countries and markets. Where research is conducted for the firm depends to a substantial extent on the organizational structure of the company and at what level (where) the research is conducted. In international operations, companies vary considerably in structure and with regard to the degree of local autonomy. In some cases, research is conducted or commissioned by corporate or regional headquarters or by a global or regional new product development unit. In this case, research is likely to be centrally designed and coordinated, although the design and fieldwork are carried out locally. In other cases, where local operating units or country managers have greater autonomy, local units may play a greater role in the research design and implementation. Consequently, attention will need to be paid to coordination of research across countries or regions and use of standardized procedures for conducting research and reporting results.

## Centralized Organization

Where research is centrally designed, management at corporate headquarters or at a global or regional product development unit establishes the specifications for the research. In general, few companies have adequate staff to handle such research projects. Consequently, even where research specifications are established in-house, details of the research design and data collection will be handled by an international research agency.

This approach ensures comparability in design, data collection and analysis across countries. Some cost efficiencies may be obtained, enabling costs to be controlled. There is, however, some danger of lack of attention to specific local issues, nuances or market conditions. Problems may arise in communicating findings to local operating units, including the implementation of research conclusions, if the units have not participated in the research process.

## Decentralized Organization

Another option is a decentralized approach. Corporate headquarters establishes research objectives in broad terms, but leaves the detailed specifications of the research design and management of the research process to the local country operating units. Local management is responsible for handling relations with research agencies and for interpreting and implementing findings. This approach is likely to be most appropriate where research is intended as an input to tactical, as opposed to strategic, decisions.

This type of approach provides optimal adaptation to differences in local market conditions and in research capabilities and services in different countries. On the other hand, there may be an emphasis on country-specific issues and concepts. Consequently, attention has to be paid to establishing key research questions as well as guidelines for fieldwork, data analysis and reporting. This becomes especially critical where research is conducted in markedly different research environments, for example emerging markets.

## Coordinated Organization

The limitations of both centralized and decentralized approaches suggest the desirability of an intermediate or coordinated approach. Corporate headquarters or a central new product development unit establishes overall research objectives, but local country managers provide input into these objectives, as also into the specifications of research design. In some cases, international or regional coordinating committees can be established, though this may be cumbersome and time-consuming. This approach allows local managers to indicate their opinion on proposed research, based on their experience with previous research, knowledge of local market conditions and the suitability and likely cost efficiency of the proposed plan. This helps to minimize local management objections to the research. However, it may result in some problems with regard to lack of data comparability, especially if modifications are made locally in research design or data collection procedures.

Ideally, the organization of international research should strike a delicate balance between centralization and direction of research from the central administrative unit and local input in research design and implementation. Too much centralization may result in lack of attention to specific local idiosyncrasies and problems of implementation, but too much local autonomy will lead to research and data that are not comparable across countries. While coordination of research across countries is essential to ensure comparability and equivalence of data, input from local operating units is critical to ensure their cooperation and implementation of plans based on research.

# Choosing a Research Supplier

A second issue concerns the choice of research supplier. As noted previously, it is unlikely that many companies have the expertise in-house to design, and still fewer to implement, all the types of research required in all international markets. This is particularly the case where primary data collection is involved. The need for familiarity with the local research environment and for multiple linguistic competencies is typically critical for effective field research. Consequently, unless a study consists predominantly of desk research, purchase of outside services is likely to be necessary.

## Global Marketing Research Firms[1]

The 25 largest research organizations are shown in Table 2.3. Of the top five, one is headquartered in the Netherlands, one in the US and three in the UK (see Honomichl (2004) for more details). More broadly, of the top 25 research organizations, twelve are US based, five are in the UK, four are located in Japan and one each in the Netherlands, Germany, Italy and France. As firms have expanded internationally, there has been a tendency towards concentration through acquisition and the formation of large marketing research groups. Typically, companies within a group operate independently and compete with each other. Of the five largest organizations, three (VNU, IMS and GfK) offer primarily syndicated services. AC Nielsen, the largest research organization, is owned by VNU and has 33 073 employees worldwide and customers in 81 countries. Nielsen provides five principal research services: retail audit in over 80 countries; consumer panel services in 22 countries; media measurement services; Internet measurement through Netratings Inc.; and customized research services provided through wholly owned subsidiaries or joint ventures.

Taylor Nelson Sofres (TNS), the second-largest research organization, was formed in 1997 when Taylor Nelson AGB (UK) acquired the Sofres Group (France). The recent acquisition of the NFO Worldwide Group by TNS moved it from the number eight place to number two. TNS has offices in 70 countries and provides services in more than 110 countries. It has a number of branded services, including AdEval, an advertising pre-testing system; Conversion Model, which measures consumer commitment to a brand and predicts market share; and Optima, a brand portfolio management system.

[1] The material in this section is based on Honomichl (2004).

**Table 2.3** Top 25 global research organizations

| Rank 2003 | Rank 2002 | Organization | Headquarters | Country | No. of countries with subsidiaries/ branch offices | Research-only full-time employees | Global research revenue (US $ millions) | Percent change from 2002 | Revenue from outside parent company (US $ millions) | Percent of global revenue from outside home country |
|---|---|---|---|---|---|---|---|---|---|---|
| 1 | 1 | VNU N.V. | Haarlem | Netherlands | 81 | 33 073 | $3048.3 | −7.5 | $3017.8 | 99.0% |
| 2 | – | Taylor Nelson Sofres plc | London | UK | 70 | 13 150 | 1565.1 | 2.8 | 1306.3 | 83.5 |
| – | 4 | *Taylor Nelson Sofres* | London | UK | 54 | 9100 | 1050.5 | 3.4 | 825.2 | 78.6 |
| – | 8 | *NFO WorldGroup Inc.* | Greenwich, CN | US | 40 | 4050 | 514.6 | 1.5 | 481.1 | 93.5 |
| 3 | 2 | IMS Health Inc. | Fairfield, CN | US | 75 | 6100 | 1381.8 | 13.3 | 843.9 | 61.1 |
| 4 | 3 | The Kantar Group | Fairfield, CN | US | 61 | 6000 | 1002.1 | 6.7 | 662.3 | 66.1 |
| 5 | 6 | GfK Group | Nuremberg | Germany | 48 | 5065 | 673.6 | 3.7 | 422.7 | 62.8 |
| 6 | 7 | Ipsos Group S.A. | Paris | France | 36 | 4181 | 644.6 | −0.8 | 541.8 | 84.1 |
| 7 | 5 | Information Resources Inc. | Chicago | US | 18 | 3400 | 554.3 | −0.1 | 166.3 | 30.0 |
| 8 | 9 | Westat Inc. | Rockville, MD | US | 1 | 1700 | 381.6 | 11.6 | NA | NA |
| 9 | 11 | Synovate | London | UK | 46 | 3446 | 357.7 | 0.9 | 326.7 | 91.3 |
| 10 | 10 | NOP World | London | UK | 6 | 1473 | 335.6 | −4.6 | 270.3 | 80.5 |
| 11 | 12 | Arbitron Inc. | New York | US | 3 | 850 | 273.6 | 9.5 | 7.9 | 2.9 |
| 12 | 13 | Maritz Research | St. Louis | US | 4 | 685 | 188.8 | 3.0 | 65.9 | 34.9 |
| 13 | 14 | Video Research Ltd. | Tokyo | Japan | 4 | 379 | 166.7 | 1.6 | 1.9 | 1.1 |
| 14 | 16 | J.D. Power and Associates | Agoura Hills, CA | US | 6 | 623 | 144.8 | 9.6 | 25.8 | 17.8 |
| 15 | 17 | Harris Interactive Inc. | Rochester, NY | US | 4 | 750 | 137.0 | 13.3 | 26.0 | 19.0 |
| 16 | 15 | Opinion Research Corp. | Princeton, NJ | US | 6 | 1125 | 131.2 | −1.1 | 46.5 | 35.4 |
| 17 | 18 | INTAGE Inc. | Tokyo | Japan | 2 | 320 | 122.3 | 7.5 | 1.2 | 1.0 |
| 18 | 19 | The NPD Group Inc. | Port Washington, NY | US | 11 | 705 | 117.6 | 19.2 | 20.8 | 17.7 |
| 19 | 21 | AGB Group | Milan | Italy | 19 | 941 | 81.6 | 2.6 | 64.5 | 79.0 |
| 20 | 23 | Market & Opinion Research Int'l | London | UK | 2 | 391 | 64.4 | 8.5 | 1.8 | 2.8 |
| 21 | 25 | Lieberman Research Worldwide | Los Angeles | US | 1 | 260 | 63.2 | 19.9 | 5.5 | 8.7 |
| 22 | 20 | Dentsu Research Inc. | Tokyo | Japan | 1 | 101 | 57.0 | −14.9 | 0.6 | 1.1 |
| 23 | 23 | Abt Associates Inc. | Cambridge, MA | US | 3 | 330 | 54.0 | 0.4 | 2.3 | 4.3 |
| 24 | – | Nikkei Research Inc. | Tokyo | Japan | 4 | 157 | 52.1 | 9.0 | 1.8 | 3.5 |
| 25 | 22 | Wirthlin Worldwide | McLean, VA | US | 4 | 266 | 52.0 | −5.6 | 11.9 | 22.9 |
| | | TOTAL | | | | 85 471 | $11 651.0 | 1.4% | $7842.5 | 67.3% |

*Source:* Honomichl, 2004.

IMS International, the third-largest research firm, specializes in pharmaceuticals and healthcare information and provides services in more than 100 countries. IMS is the main source of market information for pharmaceutical companies. In addition it provides a wide range of services to the pharmaceutical industry. These services include Portfolio Optimization, which helps identify the optimal mix of products in the firm's global portfolio; Launch Management, which helps with product launch plans and execution; Brand Management, which helps maximize sales of existing products; and Sales Force Effectiveness, which helps managers make decisions about sales force allocation. IMS has continually expanded its range of services to cover IT needs, consulting services, and longitudinal data on prescription drugs.

The Kantar Group is owned by WPP, a major advertising and marketing services holding company, and has more than 160 offices in 61 countries. Its two major components are Research International and Millward Brown. Research International (RI) is the largest ad hoc research organization and has offices in 57 countries. RI's Qualitatif is the world's largest qualitative research service. According to Honomichl (1998), RI has an ethos of multiculturalism, employing individuals with an understanding of the local culture as well as some sense of internationalism. As a result, RI can provide local knowledge and expertise combined with a fully globally integrated service. The company also has a number of global research products such as Micro Test (new product development and sales forecasting), Equity Engine (brand equity management), Locator (brand positioning optimization) and Loyalty Driver (evaluating and managing customer loyalty). Millward Brown, also a member of the Kantar Group, conducts research worldwide in 40 countries, and has a number of research products that focus on the effect of marketing communications on brands.

GfK is the fifth-largest research organization and provides syndicated tracking services through a network of 120 subsidiaries in 51 countries. Established in 1934, it was Germany's first marketing research company. Currently it generates 63% of its revenue outside Germany. Its main services involve tracking consumer products and nonfood products. In addition it has a healthcare division, a media division and an ad hoc research division that provides services in 88 countries.

Research companies also vary in the amount of their revenues that they derive from outside their home market, which for the top 25 research organizations ranges from 99% to zero. The average for all research organizations is 67%, which represents a dramatic increase from 1998 when it was only 45%, suggesting that research organizations are expanding internationally to meet changing client needs. It should be pointed out that some of this increase simply reflects a shift in ownership. AC Nielsen, which accounts for 25.8% of the top 25 total revenue, was a US-owned firm and derives a sizable portion of its revenues from the US market. In 2001 it was purchased by VNU, a Dutch company, changing its home country for reporting purposes to the Netherlands. However, all but 1% of its revenues are from outside the Netherlands. More information about each of the research organizations can be obtained by visiting the web sites shown in Table 2.4. The web sites

**Table 2.4**  World Wide Web addresses (URLs) of the top global marketing research organizations

| Firm | Address |
| --- | --- |
| VNU N.V. | www.vnu.com |
| Taylor Nelson Sofres plc | www.tns-global.com |
| IMS Health Inc. | www.imshealth.com |
| The Kantar Group | www.kantargroup.com |
| GfK Group | www.gfk.com |
| Ipsos Group S.A. | www.ipsos.com |
| Information Resources Inc. | www.infores.com |
| Westat Inc. | www.westat.com |
| Synovate | www.synovate.com |
| NOP World | www.nopworld.com |
| Arbitron Inc. | www.arbitron.com |
| Maritz Research | www.maritzresearch.com |
| Video Research Ltd. | www.videor.co.jp |
| J.D. Power and Associates | www.jdpower.com |
| Harris Interactive Inc. | www.harrisinteractive.com |
| Opinion Research Corp. | www.opinionresearch.com |
| INTAGE Inc. | www.intage.co.jp |
| The NPD Group Inc. | www.npd.com |
| AGB Group | www.agb.com |
| Market & Opinion Research Int'l | www.mori.com |
| Lieberman Research Worldwide | www.lrwonline.com |
| Dentsu Research Inc. | www.dentsuresearch.co.jp |
| Abt Associates Inc. | www.abtassociates.com |
| Nikkei Research Inc. | www.nikkeiresearch.com |
| Wirthlin Worldwide | www.wirthlin.com |

are informative and some offer summaries of research studies conducted by the firm. They also provide an in-depth look at the organizations and their key services.

## Size of the Research Market

The world market for commercial research was estimated at approximately €17.8 billion in 2001 ($15.9 billion; Table 2.5). Of this, approximately 40% is conducted in Europe (37% within the EU), 39% in the US and 13% in Asia Pacific (7% in Japan). These three geographical areas account for all but 6% of total spending on marketing research. Within Europe, the UK is the largest market followed by Germany and France (Table 2.6). Together these three markets account for two-thirds of the research volume in Europe. Based on the 2001 ESOMAR study of the market research industry, most research expenditures (80%) are for consumer research. The same study also found that 80% of marketing research is conducted for domestic clients and only 20% for international clients.

| **Table 2.5**   Market research markets, 2001 | | | | | |
|---|---|---|---|---|---|
| | Turnover *2001 | | | % Increase 2001/2000 | |
| | US$ million | Euros million | % Distribution | US$ | Euros |
| World total | 15 890 | 17 756 | 100 | 2.8 | 5.8 |
| Europe | 6316 | 7058 | 40 | 4 | 7.1 |
| EU 15 | 5842 | 6528 | 37 | 4.2 | 7.3 |
| North America | 6577 | 7349 | 41 | 3.3 | 6.3 |
| USA | 6159 | 6882 | 39 | 4 | 7.1 |
| Central/South America | 775 | 866 | 5 | 3.3 | 6.4 |
| Asia Pacific | 2027 | 2265 | 13 | (−4.8) | (−2.0) |
| Japan | 1070 | 1196 | 7 | (−11.3) | (−8.6) |
| Middle East and Africa | 195 | 218 | 1 | NA | NA |

* Based on average exchange rates: 2000: 1 Euro = $US 0.9213; 2001: 1 Euro = $US 0.8949 (IMF International Financial Statistics, May 2002)

NB: The estimates are not adjusted for inflation.

Source: ESOMAR, 2002.

**Table 2.6**   European market research markets, 2001

| Europe | Turnover US$ million |
| --- | --- |
| UK | 1652 |
| Germany | 1376 |
| France | 1141 |
| Italy | 430 |
| Spain | 275 |
| Netherlands | 234 |
| Sweden | 219 |
| Belgium | 130 |
| Switzerland | 123 |
| Denmark | 90 |
| Austria* | 79 |
| Poland | 79 |
| Finland | 75 |
| Norway | 71 |
| Russia | 53 |
| Portugal | 50 |
| Greece | 46 |
| Ireland | 43 |
| Turkey | 42 |
| Czech Republic | 34 |
| Hungary | 33 |
| Romania | 11 |
| Slovenia* | 6 |
| Croatia | 4 |
| Slovakia | 4 |
| Estonia | 4 |
| Bulgaria** | 3 |
| Cyprus | 2 |
| Luxembourg** | 2 |
| Other Europe | 5 |
| **Total Europe** | **6316** |

* = 2000 figure    ** = 1999 figure

Source: adapted from ESOMAR, 2002.

Structurally, marketing research expenditures are split between 'continuous/panel' research, which accounts for about 40%, and 'custom/survey ad hoc' research, which accounts for the remaining 60%. Continuous research consists mainly of syndicated market and media measurement involving panels of households, stores and doctors. In recent years it has expanded considerably with the growth of scanner technology, TV/people meters and the increase in computer power. Substantial investment has been required to establish and sustain this technology and has resulted in domination of this type of research by a small number of large organizations that operate in all major industrialized countries. While syndicated research is typically purchased on a country-by-country basis, large multinational organizations buy from the same supplier in each market, and hence suppliers are increasingly seeking to harmonize procedures and product categories across country markets.

Of the ad hoc customized research approximately 80% consists of quantitative research, with the rest being qualitative research. There are no significant barriers to entry so there are many small firms, which operate only on a national or regional basis. Furthermore, since the bulk of the research is conducted for domestic firms, there is no advantage to having a global presence for these clients. Only RI, Millward Brown, Taylor Nelson Sofres and GfK have a significant global presence. Other organizations offering global research capabilities typically operate as part of a network, which allows them to align with other suppliers to provide services on a particular project. Also, in the industrialized countries, the marketing research infrastructure is well developed so that necessary services such as mall intercept interviewing, focus groups or phone interviewing can be purchased locally to support a multicountry research project.

## Locating a Research Firm

Choice of research organizations depends to a large extent on the type of research required and the number of countries in which research is to be conducted. Where the research is exploratory in nature or a firm is concerned with understanding changes in consumer needs and preferences, qualitative research may be preferable. If more extensive ad hoc market surveys are required, use of one of the large international research organizations with offices and experience in the countries to be investigated is desirable. Similarly, if highly specialized research is required such as in pharmaceuticals, use of organizations specialized in the product market is essential.

Other considerations include the size and resources of the service provider and its experience in different countries or types of research, especially qualitative research and proprietary research products. Technical capability and experience with more sophisticated research techniques such as conjoint analysis, simulation, preference modeling or neural networks may be important. Experience in international marketing research and in the specific countries to be investigated is also extremely important.

In purchasing outside services, another issue is whether to purchase all services from the same supplier or 'patch together' services from different suppliers in different countries. Use of a single supplier helps in building a working relationship and minimizes the administrative effort required. However, as noted earlier, only a limited number of companies provide a complete range of services and global coverage. An alternative is to purchase services from different suppliers in each country; that is, medium-sized and small ad hoc agencies. However, this may entail higher costs and give rise to issues of comparability together with difficulties in the organization and coordination of the research.

Information about local research suppliers around the world can be obtained from the web sites of marketing research associations. The European Society for Opinion and Marketing Research publishes the *ESOMAR Directory of Research Organizations*. This is available online at www.esomar.org and can be searched by country to find local organizations that provide research services. Searches can also be performed by methods and techniques used as well as by operational fields of research. The New York Chapter of the American Marketing Association (AMA) publishes the *Worldwide Directory of Marketing Research Companies and Services*. This is also known as the Green Book and is available online at www.greenbook.org. The online version allows searches based on country, company, types of research, research services, industries/market specialties, online research tools and services, and computer programs used in research. The New York AMA also publishes the *Worldwide Directory of Focus Group Companies and Services*, which provides detailed information about companies that conduct qualitative research. This directory can also be searched online at www.greenbook.org. All three web sites provide a quick and easy means of locating research suppliers anywhere in the world.

# The Cost of International Marketing Research

The cost of conducting research in international markets is often higher related to expected market size as compared with the domestic market. This stems from the need for exploratory research to develop greater understanding and familiarity with the market, as well as differences in the development of the marketing research infrastructure, and the availability, efficiency and experience of marketing research organizations. Costs will vary depending on the nature and quality of the data collected and the difficulties of data collection.

These costs may constitute a psychological barrier to undertaking international marketing research, especially for small and medium-sized companies in the initial stages of international market expansion. As a result, research is often conducted too late, when some blunder has been made, rather than prior to making a strategic or tactical decision. In addition, most research is concentrated in the major industrialized nations where expected market size is sufficiently large to justify the expenditure. As Table 2.5 indicates, of the almost €18 billion spent on marketing research in 2001, 79% was conducted in North America or Western Europe. Little research is conducted in certain parts of the world, such as Central and South America, Africa and the Middle East. However, these are markets where management has less experience and is more prone to make mistakes.

Comparisons of expenditure levels are somewhat misleading, since the costs of conducting research in various parts of the world vary (Table 2.7). These costs do not always parallel wage and salary levels in each country, but depend on the efficiency and experience of marketing research organizations. Using psychologists to conduct focus groups or qualitative research will result in higher costs than if a marketing researcher is used. Similarly, social costs can add considerably to field interviewing expenses. For example, in France an additional 50% must be added to the basic interviewer fee for social costs.

In examining the cost of conducting research, ESOMAR (2003) examined the prices that research suppliers would charge for six different types of research projects. These covered a range of different types of research, from attitude and usage studies, consumer focus groups, web-based surveys and in-depth interviews to business-to-business research, and are indicative of the kinds of research that firms typically conduct. The most expensive places to conduct research for all types of projects were the US and Japan, where research costs are more than double the averages elsewhere. The least expensive countries to conduct research are India and Bulgaria, where costs are approximately one-third the average (Table 2.7). There is substantial variation within Europe. The costs of research in Sweden and the UK are more than twice those of research conducted in Greece and Portugal. The price differentials do suggest that in planning research expenditures differing amounts need to be budgeted to accomplish the same research objectives in different countries. For example, a research project that cost the equivalent of $20 000 in Portugal would cost approximately $46 700 in Sweden.

**Table 2.7**  Project price indices based on the average of six projects

| Countries: | Average Cost |
|---|---|
| | 149 333* |
| Expensive: | |
| USA | 242 |
| Japan | 230 |
| High Cost: | |
| Sweden | 180 |
| UK | 170 |
| Australia | 166 |
| France | 158 |
| S. Africa | 157 |
| Germany | 152 |
| Average Price +: | |
| Belgium | 138 |
| Netherlands | 137 |
| H. Kong | 123 |
| Finland | 116 |
| Spain | 115 |
| Austria | 105 |
| Average Price −: | |
| S. Korea | 96 |
| Italy | 92 |
| Brazil | 88 |
| Mexico | 84 |
| Greece | 81 |
| Portugal | 77 |
| Czech Republic | 76 |
| China | 70 |
| Turkey | 70 |
| Low Cost: | |
| Poland | 52 |
| Russia | 50 |
| Ukraine | 48 |
| Argentina | 47 |
| India | 37 |
| Bulgaria | 29 |

* US $

Source: adapted from ESOMAR, 2003.

In addition to the differences between countries in the cost of marketing research, there is also substantial within-country variation (ESOMAR, 2003). The product specification for one of the six studies outlined a national usage and attitude study conducted with in-home face-to-face interviews. The product was a chocolate confectionery product and required a quota sample of 500 regular users. The highest average price quote, $66 400, and the greatest variability occurred in the US, with the upper quartile $93 800 and the lower quartile $36 000 (see Table 2.8). For Japan, the second most expensive country, the within-country variation was less. The average price quote was $57 300; the upper quartile was $64 000 and the lower quartile was $51 100. These cost variations need to be incorporated into the overall planning and research budget of a multicountry research project. Given such cost differences, where research organizations have the capability to conduct research in several countries, it may be desirable to use an organization from a country where executive and management costs are lower to conduct international marketing research.

A factor underlying some of the within-country variability is the degree of experience a firm has with a particular type of research. For the usage and attitude project, firms that conducted this type of study *frequently* gave the lowest average price quote. Firms that conducted usage and attitude studies *occasionally* provided a quote that was 43% higher. Further, firms that indicated that they *hardly ever* conducted usage and attitude studies provided a quote that was 62% higher than the firms that frequently conducted usage and attitude studies. The same pattern of higher price quotes from less experienced firms was evident for the other five research projects as well.

The ESOMAR (2003) study also looked at the cost research firms charge for various types of personnel. Three types of positions were examined: (1) a junior researcher, (2) a senior researcher, and (3) a senior data analyst. The average price that a junior researcher was billed out at in the US was $500. Sweden and Germany were $760 and $720 per day, while Argentina and Bulgaria were $60 and $20 per day. Senior researchers were most expensive in Germany ($1100) and the UK ($1040), while Argentina and Bulgaria were the lowest at $110 and $40. The US was $980 per day for a senior researcher. Senior data analysts had some of the highest daily rates, with the highest being in the US at $1500 per day followed by France at $1170 per day. Again, Argentina and Bulgaria were the lowest at $90 per day. These differences in costs of personnel are responsible for much of the difference in the cost of conducting marketing research. With the exception of senior data analysts, personnel costs were highest in the EU followed by the US, Asia (excluding Japan), and Eastern Europe and Latin America.

**Table 2.8**  Price quotes for usage and attitude survey[a], chocolate confectionery product

| | Median Quote | Upper Quartile | Lower Quartile | Average |
|---|---|---|---|---|
| USA (7)[b] | 61.0 | 93.8 | 36.0 | 66.4 |
| Japan (10) | 51.5 | 64.0 | 51.1 | 57.3 |
| Australia (7) | 46.8 | 55.5 | 29.9 | 42.3 |
| South Africa (7) | 44.6 | 45.2 | 22.2 | 36.7 |
| Sweden (5) | 43.9 | 44.8 | 42.2 | 44.9 |
| Netherlands (5) | 39.0 | 48.8 | 27.8 | 36.6 |
| France (10) | 35.9 | 41.3 | 31.7 | 39.1 |
| UK (15) | 34.1 | 39.4 | 28.3 | 35.8 |
| Germany (25) | 29.3 | 43.9 | 24.0 | 33.3 |
| Belgium (8) | 28.5 | 33.0 | 22.0 | 29.8 |
| Hong Kong (5) | 27.5 | 29.6 | 26.5 | 27.2 |
| Spain (12) | 23.1 | 26.8 | 18.6 | 21.5 |
| Italy (13) | 21.9 | 28.5 | 20.9 | 23.8 |
| Portugal (7) | 20.9 | 24.0 | 12.2 | 19.3 |
| Austria (6) | 20.0 | 23.6 | 18.4 | 21.5 |
| Greece (11) | 18.3 | 20.3 | 14.1 | 16.7 |
| Korea (6) | 16.8 | 17.0 | 16.4 | 17.4 |
| Brazil (10) | 16.0 | 19.4 | 11.8 | 16.5 |
| Mexico (10) | 14.8 | 17.1 | 10.8 | 15.2 |
| Czech Republic (7) | 13.4 | 18.2 | 8.5 | 13.4 |
| Turkey (13) | 12.5 | 14.0 | 11.0 | 12.9 |
| Poland (10) | 9.9 | 11.8 | 8.3 | 9.9 |
| China (7) | 9.8 | 13.0 | 8.4 | 11.0 |
| Argentina (6) | 9.1 | 12.0 | 7.3 | 10.2 |
| Russia (8) | 8.0 | 9.2 | 7.5 | 8.0 |
| Romania (5) | 7.4 | 7.5 | 6.5 | 7.1 |
| Ukraine (8) | 6.5 | 11.4 | 3.8 | 10.4 |
| India (6) | 5.7 | 6.5 | 4.7 | 6.2 |
| Bulgaria (7) | 4.6 | 6.0 | 4.3 | 4.9 |

[a] All data are in thousands of US$

[b] Number in parenthesis indicates number of respondents

*Source*: adapted from ESOMAR, 2003.

Another factor that influences the overall cost of research is the cost of utilizing research facilities. The ESOMAR study (2003) included data on the cost of one hour of call center time, including telephone line charges. Germany was the highest at $70 per hour, followed by Sweden, Belgium and Brazil at $50 per hour. The US was grouped with the majority of countries with a rate of $30 per hour. The average for the EU was $40.

Despite the variation in research costs, the choice of supplier should not be based solely on the lowest bid at the expense of research quality. Careful examination of the relation between costs and delivered product, research expertise and quality controls should be made before a supplier is selected. One key factor is to find a research organization that frequently conducts the type of research sought. More experienced firms quote lower prices on average and the greater experience they have with a particular type of work helps ensure higher-quality results.

While the absolute level of marketing research costs varies by country, the cost relative to the level of sales in each country may vary even more dramatically. In particular, given that sample size requirements do not vary directly with the size of the population being sampled, smaller countries may account for disproportionately high marketing research costs. The cost of the surveys as a percentage of sales varies considerably. In some countries the level of sales does not justify the survey costs and management may prefer to extrapolate findings from a similar country or rely on executive judgment or secondary data.

Fluctuating foreign exchange rates and differing rates of inflation can have a dramatic impact on international research costs, particularly when research is being conducted in countries that are politically or economically unstable. This issue becomes important when the research project is a major one involving a number of countries and is spread out over one or two years. Typically, cost escalation clauses have to be built into contracts to account for these types of contingencies.

# Summary

As with domestic commercial marketing research, the decisions facing management provide the basis for determining information requirements and for the conduct of international marketing research. Yet, while the management decision problems provide direction for marketing research, the complexity of the international environment, and in particular its linguistic and sociocultural diversity, gives rise to a number of conceptual, methodological and organizational problems in the conduct of that research. The first stage in the process is an assessment of information needs and availability. Second, the key research questions and type of decisions for which information is to be collected need to be determined. In commercial research, information may be collected for both strategic and tactical decisions. Strategic decisions are based primarily on secondary data, which can be included in a global information bank combining both external and internal sources. This can then provide the basis for aligning strategy with competitive developments and market trends, making resource allocation decisions or monitoring customer trends. Tactical decisions, on the other hand, are more likely to require the collection of primary data.

A key consideration in the overall design of international marketing research is the geographical scope of the unit of analysis; that is, world, regions, country groupings, countries. This provides the framework for establishing the research plan. The first step in this plan involves problem formulation, variable specification and categorization. Next, the appropriate research technique has to be selected. Here, nonsurvey exploratory research techniques are helpful in the initial phases of research and may provide guidelines for the design of survey research in the latter stages of the research process. Where a survey is conducted, the instrument must be designed and adapted to each country or cultural context in which it is administered. Appropriate sampling techniques and survey administration procedures – that is, personal interview, telephone interview or mail – have to be selected. Finally, the data must be analyzed to provide some insight into the questions initially posed.

Related to design issues are those concerned with how international research is administered. Here, the firm must decide whether it has the in-house capability to design and coordinate all phases of the research or whether this should be delegated to outside suppliers. Frequently, some balance between in-house control and input into design and purchase of outside services is needed. Another important consideration is the cost of conducting international marketing research, since this may vary considerably from country to country.

# References

Choi, F. and Meek, G. (2005) *International Accounting*, 5th Edition. Prentice Hall, Upper Saddle River, NJ.

Douglas, S.P. and Craig, C.S. (1988) Information for International Marketing Decisions. In Walter, I. (ed.) *Handbook of International Management*. John Wiley & Sons Inc., New York.

ESOMAR (2002) *Annual Study of the Market Research Industry 2001*. ESOMAR, Amsterdam.

ESOMAR (2003) *ESOMAR 2003 Prices Study*. ESOMAR, Amsterdam.

Honomichl, J. (1998) Honomichl Global 25. *Marketing News*, **32**(August), 4.

Honomichl, J. (2004) Honomichl Global Top 25. *Marketing News*, **38**(August), 15.

www.esomar.org

www.greenbook.org

# Chapter 3

# SECONDARY DATA SOURCES

## Introduction

Secondary data are a key source of information in international marketing research due to their ready availability, their low cost relative to primary data and their usefulness in providing background information relating to a specific country or industry. Secondary data sources are valuable in assessing opportunities in countries with which management has little familiarity, and in product markets at an early stage of market development, such as emerging market countries.

Secondary data sources provide an easy means of rapidly gaining some insights into the market environment in a foreign country. They are available either in libraries or at low cost from the organization or institution that publishes them. An increasing number are available on the Internet, accessible in some cases at no cost, in other cases for a fee. They can be quickly consulted to provide general background and an overview of the context in which the company's products and services are to be marketed.

Secondary data are relatively inexpensive to collect or access. Where a good business research library is available, it merely requires the time of a research assistant to consult relevant sources and to assemble the desired information. The increasing availability of many sources in electronic form or on the Internet also facilitates access. Search engines such as Google can assist in finding data. However, the sources found may not always relate to the topic or be in the right form. As a result, data locator services have been set up. These index information and group relevant information and databases by topic or geographical area, for example by country or region.

The high costs and difficulties of collecting primary data in foreign countries make secondary data especially valuable. This is the case for countries where market potential is small and does not warrant an elaborate full-scale study, or where markets are not well developed and management has little experience or prior information.

Secondary data are useful where a two-step approach to international marketing research is adopted. Secondary data can be used to identify areas of potential concern that merit in-depth investigation based on primary research. For example, secondary data might be used to identify which of the 200 or so countries in the world appear likely to offer the most attractive prospects, or potential, for entry or market expansion and should be examined in depth.

The objective of this chapter is to provide some indication of the types of secondary data that are available and their specific advantages and limitations. The focus here is on *external* – that is, publicly available – secondary data sources. *Internal* sources – that is, company-specific data, which are also important – are discussed in Chapter 13. Some illustrative examples of the major external sources are provided, focusing in particular on sources that provide data for all or major markets in the world. Chapter 4 then discusses how these data may be used. An extensive list of types of information and assistance can be found in sources such as Dun and Bradstreet, Gale, Economist Intelligence Unit and Euromonitor as well as on a number of web sites such as www.ibrc.business.ku.edu/ at the University of Kansas, www.ciber.bus.msu.edu at Michigan State University, and www.rba.co.uk./sources/index.htm at RBA Information Services.

# Locating the Appropriate Information

## *Accessing Secondary Data Sources*

Secondary data sources are available in a variety of different formats, ranging from print and CD-ROM to various Internet-based sources and web sites. Often data are available in multiple formats to suit the user's preferences, usage needs and access capabilities. For example, the Economist Intelligence Unit makes available many of its publications in print, CD-ROM and online through its web site.

## *Alternative Data Formats*

Each of these different formats has its strengths and weaknesses. Print forms are most readily accessible to the population at large but are costly to produce and to distribute. They are also cumbersome to store. CD-ROMs, on the other hand, provide a compact means of storing large amounts of data. With an appropriate software package, a user can search for relevant information based on selected criteria and customize and manipulate data in creating tables, making calculations on selected data, adding new data, or downloading data for use in other applications.

Similarly, Internet-based formats enable the user to access and manipulate data with appropriate software. They can be made available to selected users, for example on a subscription basis. They can be readily integrated into internal company information systems or other databases. The primary advantage of Internet-based formats is that they can be updated on an ongoing basis as new information is obtained or entered into the database. Updating does, however, entail substantial costs making this type of format more appropriate for internal organization use, government information or subscription-based databases.

Internet-based formats can also be accessed anywhere in the world via an Internet connection, so they are well suited to users who travel and require access from different geographical locations. They are also better suited to information stored in graphic or visual form, and to multimedia formats. In addition, Internet-based formats can be readily linked to other Internet-based sites. Their primary limitations for an organization are the costs of converting information to the Internet-based format, maintaining the web site and keeping the content and format up to date.

# Global Data Locators

The increasing volume of information available in different regions, countries and markets throughout the world has led to the establishment of data locators. Given the need to keep information up to date and the rapidity with which information sources are changing, these are mostly available through web sites. A data locator provides an index to information relating to a specific topic; that is, country, region or product market. In some cases these relate to information from a particular source, for example UN documents or the US National Trade Data bank. More commonly, they cover information from a variety of sources. A number of the more comprehensive data locators are briefly discussed below. This should not be viewed as either an exhaustive or an up-to-date listing, as these are continually changing.

## The MSU-CIBER Web Site (ciber.msu.edu)

The GlobalEDGE section of the MSU-CIBER web site provides an extensive listing of information sources on global business. This is divided into six principal sections (Table 3.1): *global resources*,

**Table 3.1** Index for GlobalEDGE web site – Michigan State University, CIBER Center, East Lansing MI, www.ciber.msu.edu

## The MSU-CIBER Home page:
http://ciber.msu.edu/ or http://www.globaledge.msu.edu

## GlobalEDGE Contains:

Resource Desk

- Resource Desk Home Page
- Country Insights
  - Country Comparisons
  - Rank Countries
  - CAPITALize your Memory Game
- Market Potential Indicators
- Glossary of International Business Terms
- Feedback and New Site Submissions

Community

- Discussion Forum
- GINList

Knowledge Room

- Knowledge Room Home Page
- Webcasts
- Featured Insights
- Media Update
- Selected Articles
- Special Reports

Academy

- Academy Home Page
- Course Content
  - Textbook Publishers
  - Video Depositories
  - Case Depositories
  - Exercises & Simulations
- Announcements
  - Job Postings
  - Conferences
  - Call for Papers
  - Grant Opportunities
- Research
  - Academic Publishers
  - Paper Depositories
  - Journals
  - Professional
  - Organizations
  - Mailing Lists
- Academic Discussion Forum

Diagnostic Tools

- Diagnostic Tools Home Page
  - Company Readiness To Export (CORE)
  - Partner
  - Distributor
  - Freight
  - Benchmark Survey

which lists more than 2000 online resources categorized by research, news and periodicals, trade, money, reference and current topics in international business; *country insights*, which provides a wealth of information for 196 countries; *community*, an interactive forum for business professionals; *knowledge room*, which covers the latest issues in international business; *academy*, which contains extensive research and teaching resources; and *diagnostic tools*, decisions support tools for managers. The *global resources* section of the site contains an impressive list of sources, including some sites not as readily accessible or covered in other sources. A useful feature of this section is a search engine to search by key word. The site is free and information is updated on an ongoing basis.

## The University of Kansas International Business Resource Center Web Site (www.ibrc.business.ku.edu)

The University of Kansas International Business Resource Center web site provides a comprehensive listing of web sites relating to world and trade statistics and international business resources. It lists the top nine international trade sites on the web (Table 3.2). The site is comprehensive, providing information on embassies, exchange rates, government agencies, legal issues and small business resources. In addition, other business resources such as international news services and articles on trade can be accessed via the site. Lists of consulates and embassies are also provided. This site is supported by a grant from the US Department of Education's Business and International Education program. It also provides links to many of the sites listed, and is updated on an ongoing basis.

## VIBES: Virtual International Business and Economic Sources Web Site (www.libweb.uncc.edu/ref-bus/vibehome.htm)

This web site is at the University of North Carolina. It provides links to sources of international business information, including text files and statistical tables. It does not cover telnet sites, fee-based services or business directories. VIBES provides links to a range of sites, including comprehensive sites covering the world on topics such as agriculture, business and marketing, foreign exchange rates and taxation, as well as to sites for regions such as Western Europe, Latin America and country-specific sites. The site also lists metapages (links to home pages with several international links). It is comprehensive, practical and easy to use.

**Table 3.2**   IBRC's 'Top 9' business resource list – University of Kansas,
www.ibrc.business.ku.edu

| | |
|---|---|
| **1.** | **International Trade Administration** |
| *site* | http://www.ita.doc.gov/ |
| *summary* | Key international trade related links and press releases. |
| *affiliation* | U.S. Department of Commerce. |
| **2.** | **Center for International Business Education & Research – Michigan State University (MSU-CIBER)** |
| *site* | http://ciber.msu.edu/ |
| *summary* | Sponsored by the U.S. Department of Education, one of the first and best trade resource sites on the Internet. |
| *affiliation* | Michigan State University. |
| **3.** | **The Global Connector** |
| *site* | http://www.globalconnector.org |
| *summary* | Offers two streamlined country and industry search engines that provide links to specific resources. |
| *affiliation* | Indiana University. |
| **4.** | **TradePort** |
| *site* | http://www.tradeport.org |
| *summary* | Assistance centers, global trade tools, international trade tutorial, market research, buyers & trade leads, and a trade library. |
| **5.** | **The Federation of International Trade Associations** |
| *site* | http://www.fita.org/ |
| *summary* | Provides trade leads, market research, and their global trade shop which features goods and services that those involved with international trade may require. |
| **6.** | **Economist.com: Country Briefings** |
| *site* | http://www.economist.com/countries/ |
| *summary* | Country news, country profiles, forecasts, statistics, etc. |
| **7.** | **World Trade Organization – Trade Policy Reviews** |
| *site* | http://www.wto.org/english/tratop_e/tpr_e/tpr_e.htm |

| Table 3.2 | (continued) |
|---|---|
| 8. | **USDA's Foreign Agricultural Service (FAS) Online** |
| *site* | http://ffas.usda.gov/ |
| *summary* | Export assistance and programs, trade data, import programs, trade policy and negotiations, etc. |
| *affiliation* | U.S. Department of Agriculture. |
| 9. | **Stat-USA** |
| *site* | http://www.stat-usa.gov/ |
| *summary* | Business, trade and economic information. |
| *affiliation* | U.S. Department of Commerce, Economics & Statistics Administration. |

*Source*: http://www.ibrc.business.ku.edu/bus_res/top_ten.html (accessed 1 October 2004).

## Business Information on the Internet (www.rba.co.uk/sources/index.htm)

Another useful website maintained by Karen Blakeman (Rhodes Blakeman Associates) is Business Information on the Internet (Table 3.3). This is an annotated guide to Internet sites with business information and sources of business information, focusing in particular on financial information, stock market and share prices. It covers many sites and sources (especially UK, European and other non-US sources) useful for international business. The site lists ten top sites compiled by delegates attending RBA Business Information on the Internet workshops. There is an annotated guide to Internet business sources and those with wide coverage of business information. Sites of company directories for the UK, North America and worldwide are listed, as well as company profiles and financial information. In addition, Business Information on the Internet lists sites containing country information, worldwide, by region and by country, as well as sites with economic, market and statistical information. Another list covers UK and non-UK news sources and electronic bulletins. The site is well maintained and current. It provides a good starting point for locating information via the Internet, especially for a company or researcher not familiar with information sources available on the web.

## Other Data Locators

A number of other data locators are source based. For example, the UN has a data locator indexing the myriad of documents and databases that it compiles (UNSTAT). Stat-USA provides access to 50 000 documents in the National Trade Data bank. Others are topic based. For example, *The International*

**Table 3.3**  RBA Business information on the Internet – www.rba.co.uk

# _RBA_ Business Information on the Internet

The following links will take you to a selection of key business information sites on the Internet. If you have any comments or suggestions, or would like to recommend a site for inclusion (see our **Selection Criteria** for more information) please contact **Karen Blakeman**. Details of changes to the listings are announced in **What's New**

**General Listings & Key Starting Points**
(Updated 14th September, 2004)

**Support for SMEs**
(Updated 23rd September, 2004)

**Stock Market & Share Prices**
(Updated 14th September, 2004)

**Financials & Annual Reports**
(Updated 15th September, 2004)

**Mergers and Acquisitions**
(Updated 1st April, 2003)

**Directories**
(Updated 3rd October, 2004)

**Trade & Service Directories**
(Updated 2nd July, 2004)

**Miscellaneous Essentials**
(Updated 5th August, 2004)
Currency exchange rates and abbreviations, the Euro, offshore interest rates, industry classification codes, biographies, street maps, post codes, UK postal services, rail travel, UK flight arrivals, online bookshops, weather, translations.

**Further Reading & Keeping up to Date**
(Updated 3rd October, 2004)

**Search the RBA site**

[                    ]

[ All of RBA Information Services ▼ ]

[ Search ]

**Government & Politics**
(Updated 21st September, 2004)

**Market & Industry Research**
(Updated 1st July 2004)

**Statistics**
(Updated 24th June 2004)

**Direct Marketing**
(Updated 23rd November 2003)

**News**
(Updated 3rd October, 2004)

**Country Specific Information**
(Updated 2nd July, 2004)

**Information Brokers**
(Updated 17th January, 2004)

**Top 10 Sites** – a list of business sites compiled by delegates attending the Business Information on the Internet workshops.

Economy
► **Market Data**
**Dollar continues record declines**
**Oil prices rise on heating fears**
**Retail sales retreat in October**
Companies
► **Market Data**
**BT told to open network to rivals**
**Increased profits for Royal Mail**
**Nationwide boosted by mortgages**
E-Commerce
► **Market Data**
**Google warns sales growth to slow**
**BT told to open network to rivals**
**Microsoft 'warns of Linux claims'**
Search BBC News

[              ] [ Go ]

BBC News is editorially independent. Its appearance on this site should not be taken as an endorsement.

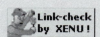

*Financial Statistics Locator* (Barbuto, 1995) lists by country where financial statistics may be found in one or more of 20 sources such as the *Federal Reserve Bulletin, International Financial Statistics* and the *UN Statistical Yearbook*. These sites are discussed below in relation to the specific sources.

# Information Sources

In this section, information sources are discussed that are useful in examining markets in different countries, and in making decisions relating to market entry and expansion strategies. Primary emphasis is placed on sources that are widely available and provide worldwide or regional coverage. Other sources relating to specific countries are available. These are most readily accessed via the web, for example through the University of Kansas web site, Stat-USA or a country-specific source. These provide more detailed or in-depth information and are highly valuable for making initial country entry and investment decisions.

A wide variety of secondary data sources is available. These range from sources that provide general economic, social and demographic data for most countries in the world, such as the *Human Development Report*, the *World Bank Development Report* or the *United Nations Statistical Yearbook*, to detailed reports on markets in a particular country, such as Euromonitor's *Consumer Asia* or *Market Research Europe* and Corporate Intelligence on Retailing's *Marketing in Europe* series. These provide general background information relating to business information and the likely costs of entering or doing business in a country. The market reports provide more detailed information relating to a specific product market. Sources vary in coverage, accuracy, the format in which they are available and the frequency with which they are updated. The principal sources and web sites where information is available are indicated, though as noted earlier, this is far from a comprehensive listing.

## *Macroeconomic Data*

A host of macroeconomic data sources are available, ranging widely in the number of countries or regions covered and the format in which they are available; that is, print, CD-ROM, online, or Internet based. Many of these are based on, or derived from, United Nations and World Bank data. Some databases combine statistics from different sources. For example, the Statistical Masterfile on CD-ROM is a combined set of databases from international organizations such as UN, OECD, World Bank, publications by the US government, as well as professional and trade associations and business organizations. The databases include social, economic, demographic, business and industrial statistics. The sources covered here are merely intended to illustrate the principal sources available, rather than to provide exhaustive coverage.

## United Nations (www.un.org)

The UN and its specialized agencies such as IMF, UNESCO, UNIDO and FAO publish statistics and other information on member nations. These are detailed, carefully compiled and collected. They consist primarily of demographic, social and general economic indicators. The UN data locator, the UNSTAT database, classifies these into four major categories: general statistics, demographic and social statistics, economic statistics and other.

These data are the source of many demographic, economic and social statistics and provide a useful starting point for gaining understanding about a country or region of the world, and in particular its position relative to other countries. The *Human Development Report*, published annually by UNDP, for example, provides a range of information relating to literacy, education, communication media and gender development, in addition to demographic and economic statistics (sample information for the top 12 and bottom 12 countries is contained in Table 3.4). The *UNESCO Statistical Yearbook* is the most reliable source of statistics on education, science, culture and communication. Similarly, the IMF publishes the most comprehensive and authoritative international financial statistics. These are published annually in *International Financial Statistics* and updated on a monthly basis. The *International Yearbook of Industrial Statistics* published by UNIDO provides information on manufacturing value-added (net contribution of the manufacturing sector to GDP) and the annual growth rate for different countries and regions of the world. Information is also provided by country on the number of establishments, persons employed, wages and salaries, output, value-added and gross fixed capital formation by sector.

The primary limitation of all of these sources, from a marketing standpoint, is that their focus is on economic and social issues, emphasizing historical trends rather than likely future developments.

## World Bank (www.worldbank.org)

The World Bank is another important source of information on economic, social and natural resource indicators for over 200 countries and territories. The *World Development Indicators*, published annually, includes over 800 indicators covering population, GNP per capita and its annual growth, purchasing power estimates, as well as economic statistics including growth of

**Table 3.4** Top 12 and bottom 12 countries on human development index

| HDI rank | Life expectancy at birth (years) 2002 | Adult literacy rate (% ages 15 and above) 2002 | Combined gross enrolment ratio for primary, secondary and tertiary schools (%) 2001/02 | GDP per capita (PPP US$) 2002 | Life expectancy index | Education index | GDP index | Human development index (HDI) value 2002 | GDP per capita (PPP US$) rank minus HDI rank |
|---|---|---|---|---|---|---|---|---|---|
| High human development | | | | | | | | | |
| 1 Norway | 78.9 | — | 98 | 36 600 | 0.90 | 0.99 | 0.99 | 0.956 | 1 |
| 2 Sweden | 80.0 | — | 114 | 26 050 | 0.92 | 0.99 | 0.93 | 0.946 | 19 |
| 3 Australia | 79.1 | — | 113 | 28 260 | 0.90 | 0.99 | 0.94 | 0.946 | 9 |
| 4 Canada | 79.3 | — | 95 | 29 480 | 0.90 | 0.98 | 0.95 | 0.943 | 5 |
| 5 Netherlands | 78.3 | — | 99 | 29 100 | 0.89 | 0.99 | 0.95 | 0.942 | 6 |
| 6 Belgium | 78.7 | — | 111 | 27 570 | 0.90 | 0.99 | 0.94 | 0.942 | 7 |
| 7 Iceland | 79.7 | — | 90 | 29 750 | 0.91 | 0.96 | 0.95 | 0.941 | 1 |
| 8 United States | 77.0 | — | 92 | 35 750 | 0.87 | 0.97 | 0.98 | 0.939 | −4 |
| 9 Japan | 81.5 | — | 84 | 26 940 | 0.94 | 0.94 | 0.93 | 0.938 | 6 |
| 10 Ireland | 76.9 | — | 90 | 36 360 | 0.86 | 0.96 | 0.98 | 0.936 | −7 |
| 11 Switzerland | 79.1 | — | 88 | 30 010 | 0.90 | 0.95 | 0.95 | 0.936 | −4 |
| 12 United Kingdom | 78.1 | — | 113 | 26 150 | 0.88 | 0.99 | 0.93 | 0.936 | 8 |
| 166 Angola | 40.1 | 42.0 | 30 | 2 130 | 0.25 | 0.38 | 0.51 | 0.381 | −38 |
| 167 Chad | 44.7 | 45.8 | 35 | 1 020 | 0.33 | 0.42 | 0.39 | 0.379 | −8 |
| 168 Congo, Dem. Rep. of the | 41.4 | 62.7 | 27 | 650 | 0.27 | 0.51 | 0.31 | 0.365 | 4 |
| 169 Central African Republic | 39.8 | 48.6 | 31 | 1 170 | 0.25 | 0.43 | 0.41 | 0.361 | −15 |

## Table 3.4 (continued)

| HDI rank | Life expectancy at birth (years) 2002 | Adult literacy rate (% ages 15 and above) 2002 | Combined gross enrolment ratio for primary, secondary and tertiary schools (%) 2001/02 | GDP per capita (PPP US$) 2002 | Life expectancy index | Education index | GDP index | Human development index (HDI) value 2002 | GDP per capita (PPP US$) rank minus HDI rank |
|---|---|---|---|---|---|---|---|---|---|
| 170 Ethiopia | 45.5 | 41.5 | 34 | 780 | 0.34 | 0.39 | 0.34 | 0.359 | −1 |
| 171 Mozambique | 38.5 | 46.5 | 41 | 1 050 | 0.22 | 0.45 | 0.39 | 0.354 | −14 |
| 172 Guinea-Bissau | 45.2 | 39.6 | 37 | 710 | 0.34 | 0.39 | 0.33 | 0.350 | −1 |
| 173 Burundi | 40.8 | 50.4 | 33 | 630 | 0.26 | 0.45 | 0.31 | 0.339 | 0 |
| 174 Mali | 48.5 | 19.0 | 26 | 930 | 0.39 | 0.21 | 0.37 | 0.326 | −11 |
| 175 Burkina Faso | 45.8 | 12.8 | 22 | 1 100 | 0.35 | 0.16 | 0.40 | 0.302 | −20 |
| 176 Niger | 46.0 | 17.1 | 19 | 800 | 0.35 | 0.18 | 0.35 | 0.292 | −8 |
| 177 Sierra Leone | 34.3 | 36.0 | 45 | 520 | 0.16 | 0.39 | 0.28 | 0.273 | −1 |
| High income | 78.3 | — | 92 | 28 741 | 0.89 | 0.97 | 0.94 | 0.933 | |
| Middle income | 70.0 | 89.7 | 71 | 5 908 | 0.75 | 0.84 | 0.68 | 0.756 | |
| Low income | 59.1 | 63.6 | 51 | 2 149 | 0.57 | 0.59 | 0.51 | 0.557 | |
| World | 66.9 | — | 64 | 7 804 | 0.70 | 0.76 | 0.73 | 0.729 | |

*Source*: UNDP, 2004.

production by sector, consumption growth, trade and capital movements and demographic and social statistics such as adult literacy. Data are presented for 151 industrialized and developing countries with a population of 1 million or more as well as for 56 countries with a population of less than 1 million. These data are available in print, on CD-ROM and online. The WDI CD-ROM database contains over 550 time series indicators for 208 countries and 18 country groups from 1960–2002 and provides mapping, charting and data export formats.

The *World Development Report*, published annually, focuses on a different topic each year and contains a set of selected indicators for more than 200 countries. This is available on CD-ROM. The World Bank publishes other statistics (primarily financial), such as *Global Development Finance* (formerly *World Debt Tables*), the *World Bank Mini Atlas* and *African Development Indicators*. The *Atlas* contains color maps, charts and graphs, representing the main social, economic and environmental indicators for 210 countries. Detailed reports on topics of related interest are published, such as *Major Trade Trends in East Asia*. These data are supplemented by other publications including reports and working papers, which are available through the World Bank web site.

The main advantage of these data is that they are comprehensive and cover a large number of countries. They are compiled based on primary data collected by the World Bank and statistical publications of member countries, together with those of other international organizations such as the United Nations and Organization for Economic Co-operation and Development (OECD), and are highly reliable. However, they suffer from the same limitations as the United Nations data: the latest figures are approximately two years old and the primary focus is on the analysis of past trends rather than on future developments.

## OECD (*www.oecd.org*)

OECD publishes statistics and other information relating to member nations. These include *Main Economic Indicators*, which contains statistics such as industrial production, domestic trade, labor and wage rates for the 30 member nations. National accounts data are published for member countries, as well as country economic surveys, which provide useful background data on each country.

## The European Commission (*www.europa.eu.int*)

The European Commission publishes an extensive range of statistics and reports relating to the European Union and member countries. These include basic statistics and comparisons with principal partners of the Union as well as Green Papers and White Papers. Green Papers are discussion papers published by the Commission on a specific policy area for those individuals and organizations interested in the area. White Papers are documents containing proposals for EU action in a specific area. While Green Papers set out a range of ideas for public discussion, White Papers contain an official set of proposals in specific policy areas.

In addition, the Commission publishes basic statistics and indicators relating to member countries. These include long-term indicators relating to population, the economy and ecology, structural indicators relating to employment, innovation and research, and the environment, and short-term indicators such as the balance of payments, consumer prices, monetary and financial indicators as well as business and consumer surveys. The *Eurostat Yearbook* gives an overview of basic statistics on Europe and each country within the EU, while *Regions: Statistical Yearbook* contains detailed statistics by regions. These are also to be found in the Eurostat online database.

In addition, the EU publishes an extensive range of information and reports relating to issues such as external trade, population and social conditions, laws, agriculture and fisheries, transport, finance, environment and energy competition, science and information technology (http://europa.eu.int/comm/eurostat/).

## Government Sources

Government agencies and organizations in different countries are also a valuable source of economic, demographic and social statistics for a specific country. For example, most developed countries have National Statistical Offices, which publish country yearbooks and other statistical information on the country. Some of these are available on the Internet. Central banks also often publish financial information on their country, which are available on the Internet. In most cases these are published in the official national language, though in some cases summary versions in other languages, typically English, are available. For example, the Japan Statistics Bureau and Statistics center (http://www.stat.go.jp/english/index.htm) provides economic and financial data, population census data, consumer and business surveys, the consumer price index as well as guides to other statistical research in Japan. JETRO (the Japanese External Trade Organization) also publishes an *Economic Yearbook* as well as market reports and other information in English. Statistics Netherlands, http://www.cbs.nl/en/, provides Economic Monitor as well as links to other research and statistical information on the Netherlands. The German Statistical Office, http://www.destatis.de/e_home.htm, provides an array of information on topics such as population, geography, environment, domestic trade, money and banking services and national accounts as well as various sources of international data.

## US Government

Various US government agencies and departments are important sources of information on international markets. Much of this information consists of international trade data or export-related data and information, designed to assist US firms interested in exporting or doing business in international markets. Consequently the focus is on key target markets and opportunities for US firms, but some sources are of more general interest. The US Office of Documents maintains an Internet-based data locator, Stat-USA, at www.stat-USA.gov, which provides access to the more than 40 000 documents in the National Trade Data bank. This is one of the most extensive international sites on the web and is part of a US Department of Commerce site.

In-depth country and industry reports are a key feature of this site. In the Market and Country research section there are the following types of information:

- International Marketing Insight Reports (IMI)
- Industry Sector Analysis Reports
- Best Market Reports (BMRs)
- Global Agricultural Information Network (GAIN)
- Country Commercial Guides
- Country Background Notes
- Multilateral Development Bank (MDB)

The Country Commercial Guides provide overviews of leading sector product markets for US exports and investments. The Best Market Reports identify key market opportunities for over 50 markets, ranging from telecommunications, drugs and pharmaceuticals to architecture, construction and engineering. The Market Research Reports provide in-depth comprehensive information on particular industries within a country, for example the pharmaceutical industry in India. The reports provide detailed information and comprehensive analysis and are extremely valuable for a firm looking to enter a particular market. They may not exist for a specific product market or country and focus only on industries identified as prime export potential for US companies. In instances where an appropriate report is found, it will save countless hours of research.

Other government agencies maintain their own web sites, some of which contain information of interest to international marketers and exporters. For example, the International Trade Administration maintains a web site, www.ita.doc.gov, designed to help US businesses compete in international markets. The US Department of Agriculture also maintains a web site on foreign markets: Foreign Agriculture service online, www.ffas.usda.gov.

The CIA publishes the *World Factbook*, which provides a snapshot of the world including country profiles on 141 nations covering geography, people, government, the economy, communications, transportation, military and transnational issues. This is available in print and online versions and is updated weekly throughout the year. It provides an excellent and up-to-date database for the marketing researcher.

# Commercial Data Sources

In addition to international and government sources of information, there are a substantial number of commercial sources. These vary in terms of the scope of the information – that is, macroeconomic compared with industry specific – as well as its accuracy, timeliness and accessibility. The Economist Intelligence Unit, for example, provides a broad range of services from country risk assessment and country reports to reports on specific industries and product markets. Euromonitor, on the other hand, specializes in marketing data, relating especially to consumer markets and retail trade. Some of the principal sources are outlined here to illustrate the type of information available. Again, this is not intended to provide a comprehensive listing and is selective in character.

## The Economist Intelligence Unit (www.eiu.com)

The Economist Intelligence Unit (EIU) is another key source of international economic and market information relating to general country- and product market-specific data. Much information is available in a range of formats, including print, CD-ROM, online databases and through the EIU web site, www.eiu.com. There is a fee for access to this information and it is available on a subscription basis.

The EIU web site lists data available by five geographical regions (the Americas, Africa/the Middle East, Asia and Australia, Eastern Europe and Western Europe) and globally. *The Country by Country Report*, published annually, covers political and economic trends for over 190 countries and provides regional and global forecasts for key macroeconomic indicators influencing world trade based on five-year historical data. Country Forecasts update five-year macroeconomic projections for 60 of the world's largest economies. They provide an in-depth, medium-term policy and political outlook as well as forward-looking assessments of the business environment. Market opportunities with five-year demand-side forecasts are provided for the automotive industry, consumer goods and retailing, energy, food, beverages and tobacco, healthcare and pharmaceuticals, telecoms and technology, travel and tourism, and financial services. The EIU weekly newsletter provides up-to-the-minute intelligence and analysis on key issues around the world, selected from ViewsWire, Risk Wire, Executive Briefing and Ebusiness forum websites.

Detailed reports by region and specific country are published for nearly 200 countries, including Country Profiles and Country Reports, which analyze and forecast political, economic and business trends for a five-year period. *Country Commerce* provides a practical reference guide to operating conditions, commercial laws and business regulations in 55 countries worldwide, designed for companies that export directly or have established subsidiaries, joint ventures or licensing arrangements abroad. The EIU undertakes customized analysis and publishing, tailored to individual client needs.

## Euromonitor (www.euromonitor.com)

Euromonitor, headquartered in London, is another important source of data on international markets, focusing in particular on data on consumer and business markets. Its books and databases are excellent starting points for researching international markets. Euromonitor researches countries, markets, companies and consumer lifestyles and publishes statistics, forecasts, company profiles and business information sources. These sources are now listed in three volumes: *Asian Marketing Information Sourcebook*, *European Marketing Information Sourcebook* and *Latin American Marketing Information Sourcebook*.

An extensive range of information on total and per capita consumption for a large number of product markets as well as other communications, population and economic statistics are now available in Euromonitor's online database. This is also available in CD-ROM and print form in *European Marketing Data and Statistics*, *Asian Marketing Data and Statistics* and *Latin American Marketing Data and Statistics*, as well as *International Marketing Data and Statistics*. The information and data available for the European markets are more detailed, though the principal categories are the same. In some cases the statistics are taken from official sources or from trade association sources; in others the estimates are compiled by Euromonitor. More detailed information on consumer markets in specific regions is published in, for example, *Consumer Asia* (see Table 3.5),

**Table 3.5** *Consumer Asia, representative data 1997–2002*

**a** Asia: sales of color televisions 1997–2002

'000 units/as stated

| | 1997 | 1998 | 1999 | 2000 | 2001 | 2002 | Per capita volume 2002 (Per '000 inhabitants) | Total value 2002 (US$) million | Per capita value 2002 (US$) |
|---|---|---|---|---|---|---|---|---|---|
| China | 16 842.0 | 18 188.0 | 19 462.0 | 21 318.5 | 22 727.1 | 23 851.0 | 18.43 | 6800.40 | 5.26 |
| Hong Kong, China | 475.0 | 438.0 | 440.3 | 473.9 | 483.6 | 493.4 | 68.36 | 133.08 | 18.44 |
| India | 2 004.0 | 2 298.7 | 2 841.7 | 3 133.2 | 3 251.0 | 3 369.6 | 3.25 | 912.83 | 0.88 |
| Indonesia | 1 599.0 | 1 343.0 | 1 471.0 | 1 612.0 | 1 688.4 | 1 836.8 | 8.50 | 326.96 | 1.51 |
| Japan | 7 818.9 | 7 562.0 | 7 346.0 | 8 280.7 | 8 104.7 | 7 924.1 | 62.37 | 2318.84 | 18.25 |
| Malaysia | 223.4 | 174.3 | 170.3 | 194.6 | 200.1 | 217.7 | 9.40 | 77.74 | 3.36 |
| Philippines | | | | | | | | | |
| Singapore | 149.1 | 144.8 | 148.8 | 169.4 | 175.7 | 183.2 | 54.85 | 39.60 | 11.85 |
| South Korea | 2 095.0 | 1 725.9 | 1 784.0 | 1 649.1 | 1 593.3 | 1 555.4 | 32.29 | 371.29 | 7.71 |
| Taiwan | 1 063.0 | 1 041.0 | 1 020.0 | 999.7 | 1 004.1 | 1 002.5 | 44.42 | 305.99 | 13.56 |
| Thailand | 1 985.0 | 1 486.4 | 1 608.9 | 1 720.0 | 1 721.3 | 1 766.9 | 28.38 | 152.98 | 2.46 |
| Vietnam | 775.0 | 870.5 | 982.0 | 1 046.0 | 1 056.8 | 1 079.4 | 13.09 | 307.58 | 3.73 |

*Source: Euromonitor.*

**b** Asia: sales of beer (off-trade) 1997–2002

Million litres/as stated

| | 1997 | 1998 | 1999 | 2000 | 2001 | 2002 | Per capita volume 2002 (Litres per capita) | Total value 2002 (US$) million | Per capita value 2002 (US$) |
|---|---|---|---|---|---|---|---|---|---|
| China | 11 929.6 | 12 895.0 | 13 871.9 | 14 769.4 | 15 656.5 | 16 660.0 | 12.88 | 9 972.03 | 7.71 |
| Hong Kong, China | 83.4 | 76.9 | 56.0 | 47.7 | 43.8 | 46.0 | 6.37 | 149.83 | 20.76 |
| India | 375.4 | 399.2 | 427.3 | 457.2 | 488.9 | 530.7 | 0.51 | 605.12 | 0.58 |
| Indonesia | 56.2 | 50.4 | 56.2 | 61.3 | 65.9 | 58.0 | 0.27 | 126.01 | 0.58 |
| Japan | 4 484.6 | 4 771.1 | 4 870.9 | 4 848.7 | 5 212.1 | 5 094.9 | 40.10 | 19 320.50 | 152.08 |
| Malaysia | 40.7 | 41.4 | 39.5 | 40.0 | 39.0 | 40.2 | 1.74 | 159.72 | 6.89 |
| Philippines | 674.8 | 731.2 | 746.4 | 762.0 | 749.1 | 775.8 | 9.78 | 760.05 | 9.58 |
| Singapore | 23.2 | 23.1 | 22.8 | 22.8 | 28.0 | 28.7 | 8.60 | 143.40 | 42.92 |
| South Korea | 972.5 | 819.2 | 861.0 | 915.2 | 967.0 | 1 018.0 | 21.14 | 3 004.00 | 62.37 |
| Taiwan | 341.5 | 351.9 | 335.2 | 321.9 | 313.3 | 302.4 | 13.40 | 677.76 | 30.03 |
| Thailand | 213.4 | 277.2 | 377.5 | 439.0 | 521.7 | 634.0 | 10.18 | 724.24 | 11.63 |
| Vietnam | 150.5 | 173.6 | 177.2 | 185.2 | 194.6 | 208.5 | 2.53 | 284.88 | 3.46 |

*Source:* Euromonitor.

**Table 3.6**   *Consumer Europe,* representative data, 1998–2003

**a** OTC healthcare – value sales

| EUR million | 1998 | 1999 | 2000 | 2001 | 2002 | 2003 |
|---|---|---|---|---|---|---|
| Austria | 325.1 | 340.3 | 348.2 | 357.8 | 371.3 | 386.5 |
| Belgium | 579.3 | 594.7 | 613.1 | 628.1 | 634.6 | 640.0 |
| Denmark | 256.2 | 267.2 | 278.3 | 287.9 | 295.8 | 302.8 |
| Finland | 290.7 | 302.3 | 310.8 | 323.8 | 336.1 | 346.6 |
| France | 2 260.4 | 2 309.6 | 2 375.2 | 2 427.2 | 2 442.0 | 2 499.6 |
| Germany | 4 054.1 | 4 232.8 | 4 441.8 | 4 470.2 | 4 449.9 | 4 494.5 |
| Greece | 108.1 | 113.6 | 120.7 | 129.1 | 140.1 | 149.8 |
| Ireland | 105.9 | 113.0 | 122.6 | 132.2 | 143.2 | 155.4 |
| Italy | 2 503.4 | 2 638.9 | 2 680.7 | 2 725.3 | 2 855.1 | 3 043.1 |
| Netherlands | 385.3 | 409.9 | 438.4 | 469.7 | 506.9 | 539.6 |
| Norway | 291.5 | 317.0 | 346.3 | 366.8 | 413.9 | 412.3 |
| Portugal | 201.6 | 208.8 | 213.7 | 223.3 | 242.7 | 258.9 |
| Spain | 928.2 | 987.4 | 1 047.4 | 1 086.3 | 1 138.0 | 1 198.4 |
| Sweden | 420.6 | 434.4 | 472.2 | 439.7 | 464.3 | 483.1 |
| Switzerland | 635.6 | 663.9 | 698.8 | 731.2 | 756.2 | 741.0 |
| Turkey | 708.9 | 789.5 | 978.9 | 912.5 | 1 024.7 | 1 066.3 |
| United Kingdom | 2 808.5 | 3 106.1 | 3 567.3 | 3 598.1 | 3 633.5 | 3 391.9 |
| **European Total** | **16 863.5** | **17 829.5** | **19 054.3** | **19 309.0** | **19 847.9** | **20 109.9** |

*Consumer Europe* (see Table 3.6) and *Consumer Latin America.* These provide more detailed breakdowns of products and annual growth rates.

The primary advantages of these data are the wealth of information contained and the breadth of coverage, as well as its relevance for marketing decisions. However, reliability varies depending on the specific data source, and data are frequently missing, especially for developing countries.

Euromonitor also publishes *Market Research International* and *Market Research Europe* on a monthly basis. These are available in print form and online and include reports on food and

**Table 3.6**   (continued)

**b** OTC healthcare – quick comparisons

| As stated | Market share 2003 (% EUR value) | % change 1998/2003 (value) | Total value 2003 (US$ million) | Total value 2003 (national currency million) | Per capita value 2003 (EUR) | Per capita value 2003 (US$) |
|---|---|---|---|---|---|---|
| Austria | 1.92 | 18.88 | 436.90 | 387 | 47.85 | 54.08 |
| Belgium | 3.18 | 10.48 | 723.45 | 640 | 61.81 | 69.86 |
| Denmark | 1.51 | 18.20 | 342.37 | 2251 | 56.22 | 63.56 |
| Finland | 1.72 | 19.21 | 391.76 | 347 | 66.49 | 75.15 |
| France | 12.43 | 10.58 | 2 825.34 | 2500 | 41.90 | 47.35 |
| Germany | 22.35 | 10.86 | 5 080.21 | 4495 | 54.45 | 61.54 |
| Greece | 0.74 | 38.60 | 169.29 | 150 | 14.09 | 15.93 |
| Ireland | 0.77 | 46.74 | 175.68 | 155 | 39.53 | 44.69 |
| Italy | 15.13 | 21.56 | 3 439.69 | 3043 | 52.34 | 59.16 |
| Netherlands | 2.68 | 40.05 | 609.91 | 540 | 33.32 | 37.67 |
| Norway | 2.05 | 41.43 | 466.44 | 3298 | 90.49 | 102.39 |
| Portugal | 1.29 | 28.46 | 292.67 | 259 | 24.91 | 28.16 |
| Spain | 5.96 | 29.11 | 1 354.52 | 1198 | 29.52 | 33.37 |
| Sweden | 2.40 | 14.87 | 545.94 | 4401 | 54.04 | 61.07 |
| Switzerland | 3.68 | 16.59 | 838.96 | 1128 | 101.62 | 115.06 |
| Turkey[a] | 5.30 | 50.41 | 1 207.63 | 1208 | 15.08 | 17.08 |
| United Kingdom | 16.87 | 20.77 | 3 833.19 | 2349 | 57.08 | 64.50 |
| **European Total** | **100.00** | **19.25** | **22 733.92** | | **43.52** | **49.20** |

Notes: (a) National currency data are in US$ million.
Source: Euromonitor.

nonfood markets for international, pan-European or specific country markets. For example, in June 2004 *Market Research International* contained reports on the Brazilian market for cigarettes, the Filipino market for spirits, the Malaysian market for travel and tourism and the US market for consumer foodservice. In June 2004, *Market Research Europe* carried a report on the Western

European market for sweet and savory snacks as well as reports on the Hungarian market for depilatories, the Spanish market for bottled water and the Swedish market for spirits.

## Other Data Sources: Country and Regional Guides

Numerous other sources specific to individual countries or product markets are available. Country handbooks, reports or economic surveys provide much valuable information with regard to the business environment in a given country. Where these handbooks or surveys are published by governmental or other official bodies within a country, as listed on the web sites discussed earlier, they may not be strictly comparable from country to country.

Various private sources publish regional and country handbooks. Europa Publications, for example, publishes a *World Yearbook*, which lists over 1650 major international organizations such as the UN, UN-related organizations and trade organizations, and provides up-to-date information on over 250 countries and territories, covering their history, an economic and demographic survey and other useful facts about government, education and industry and a directory of associations.

PricewaterhouseCoopers publishes information guides on over 80 countries, covering foreign invest-ment opportunities; that is, basic resources, major industries and growth areas, exchange controls and restrictions, trade regulations related to exporting and importing, product and packaging re-gulation, and transportation. The main focus is on information relevant to potential exporters to the country. It also publishes summaries of corporate and individual tax law for over 127 countries.

## Periodicals, Newsletters, Indexing and Abstracting Services

Newsletters and articles or reports on countries, regions or specific industries are also published by trade associations, banks, trade journals and other organizations such as the EIU and Euromonitor. The Political Risk Group publishes the *Political Risk Letter*, a monthly newsletter on the major events affecting the business climate in 100 countries, including summaries of economic reforms, political struggles, social unrest and so on. Each issue also contains the Political and Economic Forecasts Table, 18-month and five-year forecasts for turmoil and risk in all 100 countries. Euromonitor also publishes consumer market insights in its online database.

In addition, newspapers and periodicals such as *Business Week, The Times, The New York Times*, the *Financial Times, Advertising Age* and the *Economist* often publish special world, regional or country reports, which constitute valuable sources of information in assessing foreign market or industry potential. These sources are too numerous to be covered here.

Abstracts of these and other reports and surveys relating to a region, country or industry can be accessed through online indexing and abstracting services such as ABI/Inform or Predibriefs. Information on companies and market news in different countries and regions can be found in sources such as Lexis/Nexis, Dialog, Factiva, Proquest and Viewswire (EIU). The appropriate source will depend to a large extent on specific research objectives. The decision will also be influenced by the geographical area and the industry of interest, as well as whether the concern is with long-run trends or late-breaking news.

# Data Accuracy and Equivalence

Macroeconomic and industry data vary considerably in their accuracy and equivalence. This is particularly marked in the case of macroeconomic data for developing countries, where data are sparse and less systematically compiled. It may be a hidden danger, though less apparent, in relation to industry data.

Different sources often report different values for a given statistic such as GNP per capita, number of television sets or radios per household, vehicle registration or number of retail institutions, casting doubt on the accuracy of the data. In some cases, discrepancies result from differences in the way a measurement unit is defined. For example, GDP may include income of nationals in foreign countries in some cases and not in others. Similarly, the frequency with which estimates are updated often varies, for example whether estimates are made to update population figures or income is adjusted for inflation. In general, it is desirable to understand how a specific statistic is defined for each information source so that differences can be reconciled. Then the statistic best suited for the specific problem can be selected.

Accuracy of data also varies from one country to another. Data from highly industrialized nations typically have a higher level of accuracy than those from developing countries. This is largely due to the mechanisms for collecting data. In industrialized nations, relatively reliable and sophisticated procedures for collecting population or industry census, national accounting or other macrodata are utilized. In developing countries, where a substantial proportion of the population is illiterate and difficult to access, such data may be based on estimates or rudimentary data collection procedures that incorporate a high component of measurement error. In China, for example, the population census is based on personal interviews conducted with the head of the household. If it appears that the head of the household has not understood, the interviewer 'guesses' the number in the household.

Similarly, business statistics and income data are affected by the taxation structure and the level of tax evasion. In a number of EU countries, production and sales statistics are often inaccurate, especially for small family businesses, because business taxes are based on domestic sales figures. Consequently, businesses often underreport sales or production to reduce their tax burden. Similarly, income statistics frequently underestimate actual income, especially among self-employed persons.

Furthermore, comparability of data varies from country to country. Population censuses may not only be inaccurate, but also vary in the frequency and the year in which they are collected. While in the US a population census is conducted every 10 years, the last censuses in Afghanistan, the Congo and Liberia were taken before 1985. Consequently, population figures are not for the same year in each country, or where updated, for example by the EIU or the World Bank, are based on estimates of population growth. Similar issues arise regarding income or consumption statistics, where reporting systems, particularly in the developing countries, are not as efficient or up to date as in industrialized countries. The rapid rates of population growth and rise in living standards in Asia and other emerging market countries, as well as high rates of inflation in Latin American countries, make such problems particularly acute in these regions.

In addition, measurement units are not necessarily equivalent from country to country. In the case of income, for example, all salaried workers in France and Belgium are paid for a 'thirteenth month' as an automatic bonus. This is reported as part of annual income, producing a measurement construct different from that in other countries. Similarly, in Germany purchase of a television set is included as an expenditure for recreation and entertainment, while in the US this is included as furniture, furnishing and household equipment.

The definition of 'urban' used to establish the proportion of the urban population in the *UN Demographic Yearbook* varies substantially from country to country, depending largely on the population density. In Japan, for example, urban population is defined as a *shi* (city) with 50 000 inhabitants or more. In India it includes all places with 5000 inhabitants or more; in Ireland it includes cities and towns with 1500 or more inhabitants; in Canada places of 1000 or more inhabitants; and in Iceland localities of 200 or more inhabitants.

Interpretation of apparently equivalent measures poses a number of problems. Comparisons of GNP per capita may, for example, be misleading. Personal taxation structures and the provision of socialized services such as medicine or education, or retirement pensions or family allowances, vary from country to country. In Sweden, for example, high rates of personal taxation, coupled with socialized services, imply a lower standard of living than the country's high per capita income would suggest. Adjustment of national income statistics for purchasing power equivalence results in significant adjustments of apparent relative wealth, especially for emerging economies. Often subsistence requirements in terms of clothing are low and the provision of much food and services does not enter into the monetary economy.

A large number of secondary data sources are available. These vary in coverage and in accuracy, recency and timeliness. In general, there is a trade-off between the two. The UN and World Bank statistics, while highly reliable, are not as up to date as those provided by commercial services. Similarly, sources vary in the extent to which they focus on analysis of historical trends, or alternatively on the forecasting of future trends. Management has to select the most appropriate sources based on its specific objectives and concerns, as well as suitability of sources for the industry or product, and the particular decision concerned.

# Information Requirements

In making decisions about the mode of operation in a given country and the specific marketing strategy to employ, more specific sources of information will be required in addition to the general sources discussed earlier. This includes information not only directly related to marketing decisions but also to other aspects of the firm's operations, such as financial production or legal questions.

More specifically, four main types of information requirements can be identified. These are:

- *Political, financial and legal* data, which provide indicators of the risks associated with operation in a given country or region.
- *General market* data, which can be used to assess the business climate and long-run market potential.
- Data relating to the *infrastructure*, which are needed to estimate probable costs associated with alternative modes of operation.

- *Product-specific* data, which are required to develop more precise estimates of current market potential and profitability.

Each of these is further discussed in the next section.

# Political, Financial and Legal Data

In the first place, management is likely to be concerned with examining the risks associated with operating in a specific national or country environment. This requires the collection of political, financial and legal data to assess the risks involved in marketing in various countries. These can have a significant impact on both the short- and long-run profitability of operations in a given country.

## Political Factors

Collection of information relating to political factors such as attitudes toward foreign investment, internal political stability and turmoil is important in assessing the attractiveness and stability of the investment climate. This is critical in initial entry and market expansion decisions or in balancing the country portfolio, although monitoring on an ongoing basis is also necessary. Often countries or regions that offer attractive growth potential are politically or economically unstable, for example emerging market countries.

The significance of assessing this risk does vary with the company, the industry and the mode of entry envisaged. The extractive industries, such as oil refining or mining, as well as defense, utility and transportation, are particularly susceptible to such issues as they are capital intensive and have high-profile operations. Large multinationals, particularly of US origin, need to be sensitive to such issues due to the feelings of hostility and nationalism that these tend to arouse. This has been particularly acute in recent years because of US foreign policy and increasing involvement in military operations in other countries such as Afghanistan and Iraq.

A number of services for evaluating political and economic risk are available. As noted earlier, the EIU publishes a Country Risk service evaluating 100 countries in the world. This monitors emerging and highly indebted markets on a continuous basis, producing two-year forecasts for economic variables of most importance for risk assessment, such as current account balance, financing requirements, foreign reserves, short-term debt and 'hot money inflows'. The *Political Risk Year-book*, published by the Political Risk Group, assesses 100 countries based on three types of risk:

- *Financial transfer*: the flow of various financial instruments across the country's borders.
- *Direct investment*: the risk of maintaining operations such as manufacturing within the country.
- *Export markets*: risks to the business in exporting goods or services to the country.

The likelihood of economic disruption from turmoil (war, insurrection, demonstration or terrorism) is also assessed. All four factors are forecast for an eighteen month and five-year period. Data are also available for a number of financial and economic indicators. The Political Risk Group also publishes the *Political Risk Letter*, a monthly newsletter providing up-to-date information on the major events affecting the business climate in 100 countries, and a monthly International Country Risk guide for 145 countries quantifying risk on 22 variables in three subcategories: political, financial and economic (see Table 3.7 for ratings of countries in North Africa, the Middle East and Central Asia). These publications are available online and through the web sites www.countrydata.com and www.prsgroup.com.

## Financial and Foreign Exchange Data

Examination of financial and foreign exchange factors, such as the rate of inflation, currency depreciation, restrictions on capital flows and repatriation of earnings, is important as they have a critical impact on overall levels of profitability and expected ROI. Such factors are a major consideration in making international investment and resource allocation decisions.

Assessment of foreign exchange risk is critical where production is located in several different countries and goods or services move across national boundaries. For example, a manufacturer planning the location of a plant in the UK to supply European markets, will need to make a careful evaluation of the anticipated movement of the pound relative to the euro. Similarly, the movement of inflation and interest rates may be an important factor for companies with high credit exposure in other countries, such as consumer credit card companies or retailers.

Data on many of the relevant variables are to be found in *International Financial Statistics*, published by the IMF. Again, a number of commercial services specialize in assessing and predicting different types of financial risks. These include services for predicting foreign exchange rates in the long run, such as those provided by the major international banks, including Deutsche Bank, the

**Table 3.7**   Current risk assessments and forecasts

| Country | Current ratings | | | | Composite ratings | | | | |
|---|---|---|---|---|---|---|---|---|---|
| | Political Risk 09/03 | Financial Risk 09/03 | Economic Risk 09/03 | Year Ago 10/02 | Current Rating 09/03 | Forecasts | | | |
| | | | | | | One Year | | Five Year | |
| | | | | | | WC | BC | WC | BC |
| Algeria | 45.5 | 43.5 | 43.5 | 61.3 | 66.3 | 60.5 | 69.5 | 59.0 | 76.5 |
| Armenia | 61.0 | 31.0 | 32.5 | 60.3 | 62.3 | 57.5 | 63.0 | 55.5 | 71.5 |
| Azerbaijan | 64.0 | 38.5 | 35.0 | 67.3 | 68.8 | 58.0 | 69.0 | 54.0 | 70.5 |
| Bahrain | 77.0 | 44.0 | 38.5 | 80.3 | 79.8 | 76.0 | 81.0 | 67.0 | 79.5 |
| Egypt | 64.0 | 34.0 | 33.5 | 66.8 | 65.8 | 60.5 | 72.5 | 55.0 | 70.5 |
| Iran | 58.0 | 46.5 | 36.5 | 63.8 | 70.5 | 37.5 | 68.5 | 39.0 | 75.0 |
| Iraq | 41.5 | 22.5 | 20.0 | 45.5 | 42.0 | 39.0 | 53.3 | 37.5 | 72.5 |
| Israel | 67.5 | 39.5 | 38.0 | 65.3 | 72.5 | 60.0 | 72.0 | 58.0 | 77.5 |
| Jordan | 69.5 | 36.5 | 36.0 | 70.0 | 71.0 | 69.0 | 74.0 | 66.5 | 77.5 |
| Kazakhstan | 70.5 | 37.0 | 37.0 | 72.3 | 72.3 | 68.5 | 73.0 | 61.5 | 74.5 |
| Kuwait | 78.0 | 47.5 | 47.0 | 81.5 | 86.3 | 74.5 | 87.0 | 67.5 | 88.0 |
| Lebanon | 60.0 | 25.0 | 26.0 | 55.5 | 55.5 | 48.5 | 57.0 | 45.0 | 63.5 |
| Libya | 62.0 | 44.0 | 41.5 | 69.5 | 73.8 | 71.5 | 78.3 | 56.5 | 78.3 |
| Morocco | 73.5 | 40.0 | 37.0 | 72.5 | 75.3 | 69.0 | 76.0 | 62.5 | 77.5 |
| Oman | 75.5 | 42.0 | 42.0 | 79.8 | 79.8 | 70.5 | 74.0 | 65.5 | 74.5 |
| Qatar | 73.0 | 36.5 | 47.5 | 79.3 | 78.5 | 60.0 | 64.5 | 57.5 | 68.5 |
| Saudi Arabia | 67.0 | 45.5 | 41.0 | 73.0 | 76.8 | 61.0 | 72.5 | 60.0 | 78.0 |
| Sudan | 45.0 | 29.5 | 34.0 | 54.3 | 54.3 | 41.0 | 59.0 | 39.0 | 67.0 |
| Syria | 64.5 | 39.0 | 37.5 | 70.3 | 70.5 | 62.0 | 71.0 | 57.5 | 71.0 |
| Tunisia | 73.0 | 36.0 | 36.5 | 72.0 | 72.8 | 58.5 | 73.5 | 55.0 | 75.5 |
| Turkey | 65.5 | 31.5 | 26.5 | 57.3 | 61.8 | 57.5 | 65.5 | 60.5 | 73.0 |
| United Arab Emirates | 78.0 | 45.0 | 46.0 | 82.0 | 84.5 | 79.5 | 85.5 | 71.5 | 86.5 |
| Yemen, Republic | 62.5 | 35.0 | 36.5 | 66.0 | 67.0 | 62.0 | 66.0 | 57.5 | 71.5 |

*For historical risk ratings and key economic data on these and other countries in ICRG, please go to* www.CountryData.com.

*Source*: Political Risk Letter, www.prsgroup.com.

Union Bank of Switzerland, the Royal Bank of Scotland, ABN-Amro and HSBC, or specialized econometric forecasters, such as DRI or Wharton Econometrics. The accuracy and reliability of these services have been extensively investigated and show variation, depending on the currency and time horizon used (Levich, 1980). Summary indicators, such as the ranking of over 100 countries' creditworthiness by international bankers, are published by *Institutional Investor* and are available online.

## Legal and Regulatory Data

Information should be collected on legal and regulatory factors, such as import–export regulations, modes of operation, tariff barriers, taxation, and product regulation and environmental standards. Regulation often has a major impact on market entry and the modes of operation as well as affecting the extent to which products or marketing strategies will need to be modified.

Although, in general, restrictions on foreign investment and foreign trade have declined substantially with the growth of the global economy, some countries limit majority ventures or investment in strategic industries such as transportation or telecommunications. Others impose indirect controls by establishing a system of import licenses, product regulations or quality standards. The product standards for foods and pharmaceutical products established by the EU have limited imports of these products from various emerging country markets.

Information about such factors must generally be analyzed on a country-by-country basis for a specific product category and is to be found in sources such as PricewaterhouseCoopers' Information Guides, Dun and Bradstreet's *Exporters Encyclopedia* and the EIU's Country Commerce series.

# Marketing Data

Information is needed about key characteristics of the business and market environment in a country, such as demographic, economic, geographical, technological and sociocultural characteristics. These help to provide an indication of long-run market potential and growth and in some cases can be used as surrogate indicators of market size. Some illustrations of the types of indicators that might be used are provided here. It should, however, be emphasized that these are only examples, and that management will need to select the specific indicators relevant to the company's international objectives and to the specific industry, product market or market segment targeted.

## Demographic Characteristics

Information on demographic characteristics such as population size, rate of growth, age structure and composition provides an indication of potential market size. The estimated population of over one billion in the People's Republic of China is, for example, an important element encouraging entry into this market. Conversely, small countries such as Iceland and Antigua are rarely of interest to international marketers due to their small population size (< 300 000). For some products, such as baby foods, diapers or DVDs, demographic characteristics may be key indicators of market potential or target market segments. For companies in the recording business, the size of the population under 18 together with per capita GDP are good indicators of market potential.

## Economic Characteristics

Information about economic characteristics helps to evaluate the wealth of a country. While population delineates market size, expensive or large-ticket items such as designer clothing, high-end audio equipment, expensive household appliances or consumer services require moderate to high levels of GNP per capita. Where small affluent market segments are targeted, information will be required on aggregate income levels as well as on income distribution. For example, a marketer of expensive collagen skin products might identify an important target segment in Brazil or Argentina, although average per capita income is only $2830 in Brazil and $4220 in Argentina.

## Geographical Characteristics

The geographical characteristics of a country play a role in influencing the ability to exploit marketing opportunities and how easy that will be. A country's physical size and the nature of its terrain will affect distribution costs and ease of communication with potential target markets. For some products, such as snowboards, snowmobiles, fur coats or sunblock, geographical or climatic factors indicate market potential. Physical geography can also be an inhibitor in countries such as Nigeria, Indonesia or Peru, where considerable difficulty and high cost may be encountered in reaching the population in outlying rural areas.

## Technological Characteristics

Technological characteristics, such as the level of technological skills or education, affect the costs of alternative modes of operation in a country and are also indicators of market potential for products such as personal computers, Internet services, electronic games and so on. The sophistication of local production technology and availability of managerial and technological skills will, for example, influence decisions with regard to local production or sourcing, as well as having an impact on the requirement to transfer management or production technology. A company selling Internet services will need to identify not only the number of Internet users but also the availability of companies and personnel able to maintain Internet services.

## Sociocultural Characteristics

Sociocultural characteristics such as values, lifestyles, ethnic and linguistic groupings and the level of immigration are often important factors influencing the potential for certain products as well as the likely response to marketing stimuli and communications. This is particularly the case for culturally embedded products such as food and drinks, and certain personal items. A marketer of vegetarian foods might, for example, be concerned with obtaining data on eating habits at breakfast, the number of vegetarians, animal rights movements and activists, as well as interest in natural and organically grown foodstuffs. Cultural factors can also affect the cost of marketing in a country, especially where multiple languages require the development of multilingual packages or separate promotional and advertising appeals.

Studies of cultural values and lifestyles have been conducted in a number of countries and regions, for example the Euromonitor study of World Consumer Lifestyles (http://www.euromonitor.com/report_summary.asp?rcode=consumer+lifestyles&docid=i3274). This helps to understand national habits, spending patterns and lifestyle choices for 71 countries worldwide and covers a wide range of activities, ranging from leisure habits and crime patterns to income and expenditure trends and household characteristics, including education, eating habits, drinking habits, shopping habits, leisure, personal care and clothing, media, communications, transport and tourism. It provides an extremely comprehensive survey of lifestyles and can be helpful not only in understanding current lifestyle trends but also the potential response to marketing stimuli such as advertising, pricing and so on.

# Infrastructure Data

Information is also required relating to the market infrastructure. This includes the physical transportation structure, the retail distribution network and the communication infrastructure, as well as the availability and cost of certain basic resources such as electricity, work skills, management and capital. These affect the costs and difficulties of doing business in a country and the feasibility of adopting a given type of marketing program or entry strategy.

## Integrative Networks

Three major components of the market infrastructure need to be examined: the distribution system, which includes physical distribution and channels of distribution; communication networks, which underlie advertising and communication decisions; and organizational networks, such as market research or advertising agencies, banks or other financial and credit institutions that facilitate the organization and performance of marketing functions.

*Distribution Systems.*   Information is required in relation to both the physical distribution network and channels of distribution. The level of development and sophistication of the physical distribution infrastructure in a country is an important element affecting distribution efficiency. A poor physical infrastructure can add significantly to distribution costs. Delays in transporting goods may occur, adding to inventory carrying costs or resulting in lost sales and customer dissatisfaction. Similarly, the organization of the distribution structure, for example the importance of organized or mass distribution outlets, influences the efficiency of distribution and the ability to develop direct channels of distribution.

The development of the transportation infrastructure is critical in countries with a difficult terrain, or where a significant proportion of the market is in rural areas, as is the case in many emerging market countries. Some countries with a rugged topography, such as Switzerland, have a well-developed transportation infrastructure and distribution does not pose a major problem. In other countries, however, such as Peru, this is not the case. This can be critical for a company marketing perishable goods such as ice cream, which will require investment in establishing a cold supply chain. Similarly, in many African countries, access to the population living in remote hinterlands or in jungle areas is likely to pose problems. The development of the physical distribution infrastructure can be assessed using statistics such as kilometers of railroads, the network of paved roads, tons of freight per kilometer of road and railroad, or the volume of air freight. These can be found in many of the information sources cited earlier as well as from country almanacs and handbooks.

Information on the distribution system will be needed to assess the feasibility of alternative distribution channels or mass-merchandising techniques. In many emerging countries, for example, the distribution structure is fragmented, consisting largely of small family businesses open from early in the morning until late at night in a space little larger than a front room. As a result, distribution channels may be lengthy. For example, a cigarette manufacturer may have to sell in small units through kiosks and newspaper stands rather than selling in packs and cartons through supermarkets and vending machines.

Information on different channels of distribution is difficult to obtain, especially on a global basis. Some data sources, such as Euromonitor, provide information on the number of retailers or retail outlets as well as sales through different types of outlets such as hypermarkets, department stores or superstores. Reports by trade associations or consulting companies on distribution channels in a given sector such as fast-moving consumer goods are available for some regions or countries. These usually focus on the industrialized nations and are not available on a systematic basis. More detailed information is contained in country-specific sources such as national censuses of distribution, or in publications of national trade associations.

*Communication Infrastructure.*   The communication infrastructure needs to be examined, since this affects the feasibility and costs of alternative communication and promotional strategies. Here, a number of different aspects need to be considered. Communication media vary considerably in geographical scope and reach and the type of information carried. Mass media such as television, radio, magazines and newspapers are typically national in scope, though with the growth of satellite systems, regional or global media are becoming more widespread. Intrapersonal communication networks such as telephone, postal and computer systems are proliferating, though their spread varies considerably from one part of the world to another (see Table 3.8 for representative data from the UN *Human Development Report* on the communications infrastructure).

*Mass media.*   Reach, audience characteristics and costs of advertising in different media, as well as restrictions on advertising content, vary from one country to another. In many countries some television and radio channels do not permit advertising and in a number of countries the amount of advertising time is restricted.

In the developing countries, high levels of illiteracy and low levels of television ownership imply that both print media and television advertising will only reach a relatively limited upscale target segment. In countries such as Morocco and Algeria, which have high levels of illiteracy, print media can reach no more than a limited segment of the population. Similarly, levels of television ownership below six per hundred in countries such as Ghana, India and Nigeria imply limited television audiences.

**Table 3.8**    Components of the communications infrastructure

| HDI rank | | Telephone mainlines (per 1000 people) | | Cellular subscribers (per 1000 people) | | Internet users (per 1000 people) | |
|---|---|---|---|---|---|---|---|
| | | 1990 | 2002 | 1990 | 2002 | 1990 | 2002 |
| High human development | | | | | | | |
| 1 | Norway | 502 | 734 | 46 | 844 | 7.1 | 502.6 |
| 2 | Sweden | 681 | 736 | 54 | 889 | 5.8 | 573.1 |
| 3 | Australia | 456 | 539 | 11 | 640 | 5.9 | 481.7 |
| 4 | Canada | 565 | 635 | 22 | 377 | 3.7 | 512.8 |
| 5 | Netherlands | 464 | 618 | 5 | 745 | 3.3 | 506.3 |
| 6 | Belgium | 393 | 494 | 4 | 786 | (.) | 328.3 |
| 7 | Iceland | 510 | 653 | 39 | 906 | 0.0 | 647.9 |
| 8 | United States | 547 | 646 | 21 | 488 | 8.0 | 551.4 |
| 9 | Japan | 441 | 558 | 7 | 637 | 0.2 | 448.9 |
| 10 | Ireland | 281 | 502 | 7 | 763 | 0.0 | 270.9 |
| 11 | Switzerland | 574 | 744 | 18 | 789 | 5.8 | 351.0 |
| 12 | United Kingdom | 441 | 591 | 19 | 841 | 0.9 | 423.1 |
| 13 | Finland | 534 | 523 | 52 | 867 | 4.0 | 508.9 |
| 14 | Austria | 418 | 489 | 10 | 786 | 1.3 | 409.4 |
| 15 | Luxembourg | 481 | 797 | 2 | 1061 | 0.0 | 370.0 |
| 16 | France | 495 | 569 | 5 | 647 | 0.5 | 313.8 |
| 17 | Denmark | 567 | 689 | 29 | 833 | 1.0 | 512.8 |
| 18 | New Zealand | 434 | 448 | 16 | 622 | 0.0 | 484.4 |
| 19 | Germany | 441 | 651 | 4 | 727 | 1.4 | 411.9 |
| 20 | Spain | 316 | 506 | 1 | 824 | 0.1 | 156.3 |
| 21 | Italy | 388 | 481 | 5 | 939 | 0.2 | 352.4 |
| 22 | Israel | 343 | 453 | 3 | 955 | 1.1 | 301.4 |
| 23 | Hong Kong, China (SAR) | 450 | 565 | 24 | 942 | 0.0 | 430.1 |
| 24 | Greece | 389 | 491 | 0 | 845 | 0.0 | 154.7 |
| 25 | Singapore | 346 | 463 | 17 | 796 | 0.0 | 504.4 |

*Source*: UNDP, 2004.

Even in the developed countries, there are substantial differences in reach and audience characteristics from one country to another. In the US, print media are highly segmented and there are no national newspapers. In other countries such as Germany, France or the UK, there are national newspapers such as the *Bild Zeitung, France Soir* or the *Daily Telegraph*, which have a relatively broad-based circulation. In Europe, cinema advertising can be an effective way to reach young adults, particularly in Germany, France, the UK and Spain. Further, the importance of cable television varies substantially, even within Europe. For example, 88% of homes in Belgium and the Netherlands have cable, while Italy represents only 0.4% of the 30.2% of households in Europe with cable television.

General information about the number of television sets or radio ownership is contained in most information sources cited previously. More detailed information about costs of different media, audience characteristics, time and space availability and regulation is available in more specific sources such as the *Media Guide International for Business and Professional Publications and Newspapers*, or trade publications such as *Advertising Age's* international issues or Internet sites.

*Intrapersonal Communication Networks.*   The second type of communication network on which information is required concerns interpersonal communication. This includes factors such as the development of the telephone system, international satellite connections, availability of fax services and Internet connections, as well as the efficiency of the postal system and the cost and availability of postal and courier services. These have impacts both on the costs of doing business in a country and on the speed and efficiency with which communication can be maintained between operations in different countries.

In many emerging countries, telephone systems are not well developed and linkages are poor. For example, in Thailand in 2003 there were 10.55 phone lines per 100 people, and in Indonesia and the Philippines 3.65 and 4.17, respectively (ITU, 2004). Some countries have introduced cellular phone technology, expanding access to public telephones in rural areas. In countries with high urban density such as Singapore and Hong Kong, mobile cellular phone ownership is high at 791 and 942 per 1000, as is also the case in the Scandinavian countries. The number of Internet users varies by country, ranging from 551 per 1000 persons in the US, 573 in Sweden and 481 in Australia to 156 in Spain and 154 in Greece (UNDP, 2004; see Table 3.8).

Similarly, the development of the postal system varies. In Bolivia, for example, there were only 2.8 post offices per 100 000 people in 1997, in Thailand 7.3 and in Brazil 7.8 (UNDP, 1997). Yet, even where the postal system is well developed, its efficiency may vary. In countries such as Brazil, it has been estimated that approximately 30% of the mail is never delivered and consequently businesses in urban areas make extensive use of messenger services. Even in countries where the postal system is widespread, services such as express delivery or commercial mail metering may not be offered.

General information about factors such as the number of telephone lines, cellular telephones or facsimile machines in use is available in most standard information sources. However, since communications, particularly satellite and Internet accessibility, are changing very rapidly, this information is not always up to date.

*Service Organizations.*   The third component of the market infrastructure about which information is required relates to service organizations, such as banks, financial or credit institutions, advertising agencies and marketing research organizations. Information about the availability of banking and other financial or credit services can be obtained from international sources and associations such as the *Investor's Chronicle*. Alternatively, more detailed information about financial and banking services available and the existence of branches in different countries can be obtained from the major international banks such as HSBC, Citibank, Société Générale and Deutschebank. More detailed information about availability of different services can be obtained from specific country sources.

Similarly, information about advertising agencies in different countries can be obtained from the International Advertising Association. The major international advertising agencies, such as McCann World Group, BBDO, Grey Global, Young & Rubicam, J. Walter Thompson and Ogilvy & Mather, can provide listings of offices in different countries. More detailed information about specific local agencies and services provided can be obtained from regional or country-specific sources.

Association sources can be used to obtain information about the availability of marketing research organizations in other countries. As indicated in Chapter 2, the New York chapter of the American Marketing Association (www.greenbook.org) and ESOMAR (www.esomar.org) publish lists of market research organizations throughout the world. More detailed information can be obtained from ESOMAR or national marketing research organizations such as the Market Research Society of the UK or the South African Market Research Association. Furthermore, the major international research agencies, such as AC Nielsen, IMS, RI, Millward Brown and Taylor Nelson Sofres, can provide listings of offices in other countries, and of services and coverage of other countries.

# Resource Requirements

The second type of infrastructure data consists of data that are needed to assess the costs of operating in a specific country environment. This is of concern when management is considering establishing a production facility in a country, but may be of some importance if a sales or marketing organization is to be established within a foreign market. The factors that will be important include energy costs, wage rates, availability of labor skills, capital resources and technology.

Three major types of resources can be identified: physical, human and capital.

## Physical Resources

When establishment of a physical plant is being considered, examination of the availability and costs of physical resources such as electricity, oil, coal or water is important, especially in many heavy industries including steel and construction. Such factors are important if a sales or marketing organization is to be established in the country, but are less crucial in this context.

## Human Resources

Investigation of the availability and costs of different types of labor and management skills is another important consideration. For companies considering foreign-based production, wage rates and the availability of certain technological skills are frequently important factors. Low wage rates in Asian countries such as China and Indonesia have, for example, been an important factor inducing the movement of textile and electronics industries to these locations. Availability of technological skills is an important consideration for companies that require engineering skills, such as those in the construction industry, since otherwise expatriate engineers have to be employed, adding substantially to production costs. Availability of trained management and sales personnel may also be a significant factor, even in industries such as fast foods, because otherwise management or sales training programs have to be developed for franchisees to ensure uniform service and quality, adding substantially to costs.

## Capital Resources

Availability of capital and financial resources may be important to take into account, especially where a local production facility is contemplated. Factors to be examined include the availability of local capital; the cost and normal terms of borrowing, for example interest rates, government credit aids and tax incentives to new businesses; and the country's rating as a borrower by US, European or other sources. In addition, opportunities for reinvestment of earnings can be critical, especially where there are restrictions on the repatriation of earnings. In countries such as Ireland, for example, the government grants substantial tax relief in order to encourage foreign invest-ment and the development of employment opportunities by foreign companies. In India foreign investment requires approval, but certain types of investment qualify for automatic approval and exchange controls are being reduced. In China, repatriation of capital is subject to strict restrictions.

As noted earlier, information with regard to such factors is to be found in general sources such as *International Financial Statistics* (IMF, annual) country guides, or relevant business publications. These sources will only provide a general indication, since there is likely to be considerable variation in the extent to which such resources are readily available or can be negotiated, and also variation in relevant rates and terms from one industry or one company to another.

# Product Market Data

In addition, data relating to specific product markets should be collected. The type of data required varies depending on the type of product – that is, industry, commodity, manufacturing or services – its stage in the product life cycle and so on. In the case of industrial products, con-sumption and production data are desirable and, where possible, market share data as well as information relating to the end-user industries. For consumer products, product usage data or product market data should be collected, and information relating to complementary or substitute products and the competitive market structure. The ease of obtaining such data is likely to vary substantially, depending on the specific product category, its recency and rate of growth, and the country concerned.

## Industrial Products

For industrial products, many of these sources cited previously provide consumption and produc-tion data as well as market surveys. UNIDO's *International Yearbook of Industrial Statistics*, for example, provides detailed statistics on the performance and trends in the manufacturing sector in different countries and areas worldwide, and enables analysis of growth patterns, structural change and industrial performance in individual industries. Predicasts has a service, PROMT, that provides abstracts and full text from nearly 1000 business and trade journals, industry newsletters, newspapers, market research studies, news releases and investment and brokerage firm reports on companies, products, markets and technologies throughout the world. It is available in print form and via the Internet on InfoTrac Web.

Information with regard to end-user industries may be found in such sources, depending on the specific industry. Trade sources and trade publications provide useful information, particularly relating to industry conditions and competitive market structure, though typically these are likely to provide information for specific countries or by region. US government sources (such as Stat-USA) provide information relating to certain industries. Often government, industry or trade sources in a given country provide relevant information, but then comparability across countries is lacking.

## Consumer Products

Availability of product market data for consumer markets varies. While information for the major industrialized markets – that is, Europe, the US and Japan – is readily available, data tend to be sparse for emerging markets. It may pose problems with regard to products where the market is changing rapidly, for example home entertainment. In cases where a product is already marketed in other countries, information relating to current product usage or consumption patterns is useful to assess current levels of market saturation and future development potential. It provides some indication of the extent to which effort will need to be devoted to developing primary demand as opposed to emphasis on brand marketing or developing a more selective positioning. Where the product or specific product variant is not currently marketed in a given country, surrogate indicators may be required to assess potential demand.

*Product Usage Data.*   In the case of durable products, data relating to levels of product ownership, for example ownership of television sets, washing machines, personal computers and other durables, as well as annual sales is helpful to assess market penetration. A manufacturer of microwave ovens might be interested in levels of microwave oven ownership, as well as current sales. In some cases, such as automobiles, information on duration of ownership might be valuable. In addition, to the extent that purchase of household durables often follows a sequence – that is, oven, refrigerator, washing machine, dishwasher, microwave oven and so on – information on ownership of related durables may be useful. Data on durable ownership can be obtained from some of the information sources cited earlier such as Euromonitor.

For nondurable items, data relating to current sales trends and growth rates, repeat purchase rates and usage patterns need to be collected. Marketers of consumer packaged goods, or basic staples such as coffee, soups or detergents, are more likely to be concerned with trends in total and per capita consumption, repeat purchase behavior, sales of various product variants by market segment, retail outlet or price point, and other usage conditions for these products in different countries. In the case of soups, a manufacturer might be interested not only in per capita consumption, but in differences in consumption and usage of different product variants; that is, canned versus dehydrated soups as well as serving size and price point.

As noted earlier, information on total volume and per capita consumption of consumer products as well as growth rates are available in the Euromonitor consumer series. Product market surveys such as those to be found in *Marketing in Europe, Market Research International* and trade publications provide more detailed information, but are not available on a regular basis. As noted in Chapter 2, AC Nielsen tracks product movement through food, drug and other outlets in over 80 countries and also maintains household panels tracking packaged goods purchasing. IMS collects data on pharmaceutical and healthcare products in over 100 countries, and is the premier source of intelligence for pharmaceutical and biotech companies. In Europe a network of organizations form the Euro-Panel International, which collects data from continuous consumer panels run by GfK and TNS in over 40 countries. A number of national and regional store audits and panels are also available. Infratest, for example, has extensive panel and audit services in many European countries.

*Usage of Related Complementary or Substitute Products.* Information relating to usage of substitute, complementary or related products may be useful. A broad view of the structure of the product market is appropriate in cases where the product of interest is new and radically different, or where the market is rapidly evolving and there are not clearly established market boundaries. This raises a number of questions about the comparability and equivalence of product markets in different countries. For example, a marketer of an 'alcopop' might look at consumption of carbonated soft drinks, fruit juices, iced tea and mineral waters as well as beer, wine spritzers, shandies and other locally available soft drinks and alcoholic beverages. Similarly, a manufacturer of jellied cranberry sauce might want to look not only at sales of bottled or canned cranberry sauce, but also turkey consumption and sales data, as well as sales of other sweet or tart meat accompaniments such as mint jelly, crabapple jelly, chutneys or other relishes available in other countries and gelatin-based desserts or molds in which cranberry sauce might be used.

*Competition.* Examination of competition is important insofar as it will affect ease of market entry and potential profitability. The domination of a market by a few large companies may suggest difficulties in market entry and obtaining distribution. A more fragmented structure may pose fewer problems. In examining competition, a number of factors need to be considered. These range from the number and size of competitors, their sales volume, rates of growth or relative market share to the type of competitor; that is, multinational versus local and their relative resources.

The specific factors will depend to a large extent on the particular industry. In detergents, for example, the key factor may be the presence of a major multinational competitor with extensive financial and other resources, such as Procter & Gamble, Colgate or Unilever. Local competitors are not to be ignored, as they may have less administrative overhead, lower operating costs and greater competitive flexibility. In each case the feasibility of obtaining such data is likely to vary significantly with the specific product. Difficulties are likely to be encountered, particularly in obtaining worldwide marketing information. Nielsen and other audit data are available for a number of countries. In addition, national and international trade sources may be helpful, but in general information may be patchy.

# Summary

There is a wide variety of secondary data sources available for conducting international marketing research. In essence, the problem is not the scarcity of data, but rather the plethora of information available. Hence, it becomes important to be selective in picking information sources that provide up-to-date and accurate data relevant to the specific product or services and the decision problem concerned.

Secondary data provide a good starting point for many international marketing research projects. They are readily available, relatively inexpensive and can be quickly consulted. They are useful in pinpointing specific problems and key areas that need to be investigated in more depth, and should provide the major focus in subsequent research.

Secondary data provide information relating to different aspects of international operations. They cover, for example, economic, geographical, technological or sociocultural data relating to the general business environment in a country, specific industry data with worldwide coverage, as well as data relevant to specific marketing strategy decisions. They can provide information about political, financial, foreign exchange, legal and regulatory data; data relating to the availability and character of distributive and communication networks and service organizations; and data about other physical, human and capital resources that are needed in making market entry and investment decisions.

The specific sources that are selected and the degree of detail in which information is collected will depend on specific corporate objectives and resources. In particular, the degree of commitment to international market expansion and involvement is important, as is the size of the company and its experience in international markets. The relevant management decision problem also dictates to a large extent the time and resources allocated to secondary data collection. The uses of secondary data are discussed in a subsequent chapter.

# References and Bibliography

## *Web Sites*

www.cbs.nl/en/
www.ciber.msu.edu
www.countrydata.com
www.destatis.de/e
www.eiu.com
www.esomar.org
www.euromonitor.com
www.europa.eu.int
www.ffas.usda.gov
www.greenbook.org
www.ibrc.business.ku.edu
www.ita.doc.gov
www.oecd.org
www.libweb.uncc.edu/ref-bus/vibehome.htm
www.prsgroup.com
www.rba.co.uk/sources/index.htm
www.stat.go.jp/English/index.htm
www.stat-usa.gov
www.un.org
www.worldbank.org

# International Organizations

Eurostat (annual) *Panorama of E.U. Industry*. Office for Official Publications of the European Communities, Luxembourg,

OECD (annual) *Main Economic Indicators*. UNESCO, Paris.

OECD (annual) *National Accounts*. UNESCO, Paris.

United Nations (annual) *United Nations Statistical Yearbook*. United Nations, New York.

United Nations (annual) *International Trade Statistics*. United Nations, New York.

UNDP (annual) *Human Development Report*. Oxford University Press, New York.

UNESCO (annual) *Yearbook*. United Nations Publications, Washington, DC.

UNIDO (annual) *International Yearbook of Industrial Statistics*. United Nations, New York.

World Bank (annual) *World Development Report*. Oxford University Press, New York and London.

World Bank, *World Tables*. World Bank Publications, Washington, DC.

World Bank, *World Bank Atlas*. World Bank Publications Washington, DC.

World Bank, *Social Indicators of Development*. World Bank Publications, Washington, DC.

# Commercial Organizations

*Advertising Age* international issues.

Barbuto, D. (1995) *The International Financial Statistics Locator*. Garland, New York.

Cathelat, B. (1990) *Les Sociostyles Systèmes*. Editions d'organizations, Paris.

Dun and Bradstreet (annual) *Exporters Encyclopedia*. Dun and Bradstreet, New York.

Economist Intelligence Unit (www.eiu.com), London.

*City Data*
*Country Commerce*
*Country Forecasts*
*Country Reports*
*Country Risk Service*
*Industry Forecasts*
*Industry Wire*
*Market Indicators and Forecasts*
*Risk Wire*
*View Wire*
*World Data*

Euromonitor (www.euromonitor.com), London.

*Consumer Asia*
*Consumer Eastern Europe*
*Consumer Europe* (annual)
*Consumer Latin America*
*European Marketing Data and Statistics*
*International Marketing Data and Statistics*
*World Directory of Business Information Web Sites*

Euromonitor Online Databases

*Global Market Information Data Base*
*Global Market Share Planner*
*Market Research Monitor*
*Retail Trade International*
*World Consumer Lifestyles*
*World Consumer Markets*
*World Marketing Data and Statistics*
*World Marketing Forecasts*

Europa Publications (annual) *World Yearbook* (www.europe.eu.int).

Gale Research (annual) *Gale Country and World Rankings Reporter*. Gale Research, Detroit, MI.

Gale Research (triennial) *Gale Encyclopedia of Business Information Sources*. Gale Research, Detroit, MI.

GfK (2004) *The European Consumer 2004*. GfK AG, Nuremberg.

IMD (annual) *The World Competitiveness Yearbook*. IMD, Lausanne.

ITU (2004) International Telecommunications Union, Main telephone lines per 100 people (www.itu.int/ITU-D/ict/statistics/).

JETRO (annual) *Economic Yearbook*. Jetro, Tokyo.

Kurian, G.T. (1997) *Global Data Locator*. Bernan Press, Lanham, MD.

Levich, R.M. (1980) Analyzing the Accuracy of Foreign Exchange Advisory Services: Theory and Evidence. In Levich, R.M. and Wihlborg, C.G. (eds) *Exchange Risk and Exposure*. D.C. Heath, Lexington, MA, pp. 99–128.

*Media Guide International*. Directories International, New York.

Political Risk Group (annual) *International Country Risk Guide* (www.prsgroup.com).

PricewaterhouseCoopers Information Guides. *Doing Business in . . .* PricewaterhouseCoopers, New York.

The Nikkei Weekly (annual) *Japan Economic Almanac*. Nikon Keizai Shimbun, Tokyo.

UNDP (2004) *Human Development Report 2004*. Oxford University Press, New York.

# Chapter 4

# USES OF SECONDARY DATA

## Introduction

The vast store of secondary data described in Chapter 3 makes it possible to get preliminary answers to a wide range of questions. Executives can assess market potential and market risk without having to venture beyond a good reference library or by surfing the Internet from their own offices. Data compiled by the European Commission, the UN, the World Bank and other organizations include macroeconomic data that can serve as surrogate indicators of market attractiveness, market potential, economic growth and infrastructure conditions. Information available in the Economist Intelligence Unit and Euromonitor publications provides initial insights into a range of product markets throughout the world. These types of data can be used to provide guidance in three key decision areas:

- Selecting different markets to evaluate for initial entry.
- Estimating demand for a company's products or services in international markets.
- Assessing market interconnectedness to guide resource deployment across country markets or between and within regions.

In the first case, secondary data can be used systematically to assess the market potential, risks and the likely costs of operating in different countries throughout the world. Countries that appear to be the most attractive can then be investigated in greater depth. Additional data will have to be collected to evaluate attractive countries more fully. This step may involve direct market contact. However, before the more expensive step of collecting primary data locally, secondary data can be used to develop more precise estimates of demand.

As markets become more interrelated and links are established across national boundaries, firms need to understand the relationships between the different markets in which they conduct business. Secondary data can be used to understand the nature of these relationships. Through an understanding of market linkages, the firm is in a better position to develop a balanced portfolio of businesses and compete more effectively.

In this chapter, different methods of estimating likely demand are illustrated using the types of data described in Chapter 3. In addition to the approaches covered here, many firms have specific techniques that they have found to be useful for estimating demand. These are typically proprietary and not available in the literature.

# Market Entry

Companies entering international markets for the first time face the dual decision of selecting the appropriate country or countries to enter and determining the best mode of entry into these markets. Data have to be collected to assess the market potential and investment climate in all countries that are being considered, as well as the risks and costs of operating in these different environments. A major problem in the initial stages of international market entry is the bewildering array of countries and markets that can be entered. Since it is too time consuming to evaluate all possible countries in depth, the first step is to establish screening procedures to select those for further investigation.

For firms that already have some international operations, screening procedures and criteria are already established and routinized. To begin with, management does not have to overcome the initial uncertainty associated with operations outside of the home market. More importantly, the experience gained by operating in different country environments provides additional information to assess new country environments. Countries that provide operating environments similar to those where the firm has already been successful are likely to be attractive prospects.

In either case, secondary data are useful for this evaluation. They can be used to develop general procedures to categorize countries based on overall attractiveness or risk to suggest which countries should be eliminated from further consideration, and which should be investigated in more depth. Alternatively, secondary data can be incorporated into customized screening procedures that are geared to company objectives and specific industries.

## *Generalized Procedures*

At the broadest level, countries can be grouped together based on their similarities to each other. This provides some indication of what countries have common macroeconomic environments. The implicit assumption is that countries that are similar on these dimensions provide similar market opportunities. To examine this assumption in more depth, countries can be grouped based on market potential, attractiveness or growth, which allows choices to be made that more closely reflect demand for a product.

## Country Classification Schemes

Macro indicators can be used to classify countries according to their business environments. The Marketing Science Institute (Liander, 1967) conducted the classic study of this type. In addition to developing a regional typology, two approaches were adopted. The first was based on two dimensions: a country's degree of demographic and economic mobility and its domestic stability and cohesion. A country's position on the economic–demographic dimension was measured by 21 variables relating to development and industrialization, marketing orientation, communication, transportation, organization of population, education and health. The second dimension, internal stability and cohesion, was measured by four indicators: death from group violence, cultural homogeneity, fragmentation, and national identity duration. In the second approach, countries were first classified into Berry's five levels of technological development: most highly developed, developed, semi-developed, underdeveloped, and very underdeveloped. Similarity among countries within each level was examined, based on 12 environmental and societal characteristics including population growth, urban population, and religious and racial homogeneity.

This type of research continued to flourish during the late 1960s and throughout the 1970s. Additional classification schemes were developed by different researchers (Litvak and Banting, 1968; Sethi, 1971; Sethi and Curry, 1973; Sheth and Lutz, 1973; Johansson and Moinpour, 1977). These studies differed primarily in terms of the types and number of variables used as well as the range of countries examined, but tended to result in groupings related to the level of development and growth.

In the 1980s interest emerged in examining the cultural or psychic distance between countries, based on the notion that entry into countries with psychic or cultural affinity was likely to be easier than entry into culturally distant countries (Kogut and Singh, 1988). Consequently, measures of cultural proximity or distance such as Hofstede's measures of national culture were often included in the clustering or ranking of countries.

Craig et al. (1992) examined the issue of how groupings of countries change over time. Starting with 42 variables, the authors reduced them to a set of 15 variables, using a combination of judgment and factor analysis (Table 4.1). Using the 15 variables a dissimilarities matrix was calculated for

**Table 4.1**   Correlation of individual variables with dimension coordinates, 1960–1988

|  | Dimension[a] | | |
|---|---|---|---|
|  | 1 | 2 | 3 |
| Infant mortality | −0.64** | −0.21 | 0.06 |
| Male life expectancy | 0.53** | 0.31** | 0.12 |
| Cost of living | 0.26** | 0.93** | −0.12 |
| Real per capita income | 0.98** | −0.13 | −0.06 |
| Inhabitants per physician | −0.55** | −0.44** | 0.27* |
| Population density | −0.10 | 0.02 | 0.08 |
| Electricity production | 0.64** | −0.05 | 0.02 |
| Rail passengers | −0.00 | −0.10 | 0.06 |
| Passenger motor vehicles | 0.90** | 0.04 | 0.04 |
| Aviation passengers | 0.81** | 0.13 | 0.61** |
| Telephones in use | 0.90** | 0.05 | 0.08 |
| Students | 0.26* | 0.06 | 0.10 |
| Book production | 0.43** | 0.10 | −0.10 |
| Daily newspaper circulation | 0.37** | −0.42** | 0.01 |
| Radios in use | 0.81** | −0.04 | 0.26* |

[a] 1, standard of living; 2, cost of living; 3, aviation.
* $p < 0.05$, ** $p < 0.01$.
*Source*: adapted from Craig *et al.*, 1992.

four years (1960, 1970, 1980 and 1988). This served as input into a multidimensional scaling routine to allow mapping of the countries over time. Three dimensions were identified, with the first two, standard of living and cost of living, explaining most of the variance. The same procedure was conducted for each year to allow investigation of how the relationship between countries was changing over time. Their findings suggest that the relationship between countries, based on macroeconomic data, is a dynamic one that is changing, with countries becoming more dissimilar over time. Further, countries that are geographically proximate tend to be more similar to each other.

Building on the early clustering work, Helsen *et al.* (1993) have linked clusters based on macroeconomic data to product consumption. First, data on 23 macroeconomic variables for 10 European countries plus Japan and the US were factor analyzed. Their analysis resulted in six factors that explained 94% of the total variance. The factor scores were then used in a standard K-means clustering algorithm. In the two-segment solution, Japan, Sweden and the US formed the second segment with nine European countries forming the first segment. In the three segment solution, the US was in a segment by itself and Sweden and Japan were joined by the UK and the Netherlands (Table 4.2).

The unique aspect of this study is not so much the clustering, which produced dimensions and clusters similar to those obtained in earlier studies, but the direct comparisons of the clustering to the diffusion rates of consumer durables. Diffusion parameters for the Bass model (Bass, 1969) were estimated for color television sets, video cassette recorders (VCRs) and CD players for the same set of countries. The results suggested a lack of any relation between the clustering and diffusion of various durables, casting doubt on the utility of the clustering procedures to provide managerially relevant insights.

The above study highlights the major limitation to generalized classification schemes. They are based solely on macroeconomic data, social and political indicators and implicitly assume that the same indicators are equally relevant for all product markets and companies. While this may be true for some indicators such as GDP and population size, it is not for others. For example, political factors are likely to be important where a substantial investment is being considered, for companies in strategic industries, such as extractive industries, or high-technology industries such as telecommunications. For a company engaged primarily in export or dealing in consumer goods, political considerations are likely to be less important. Furthermore, the classifications do not contain information on specific industries except as they relate to the basic infrastructure of the country, for example air passenger traffic, electricity production and telephones in use. These classification schemes do help to group countries based on similarities and are of some value in the initial stage of assessing market attractiveness.

## Multiple-factor Indexes

Multiple-factor indexes are published by various commercial services. The Economist Intelligence Unit (EIU), for example, regularly publishes information on the global business environment for the 60 countries covered in its Country Forecasts. The information can be useful for businesses that are trying to assess the quality of the business environment, particularly for market entry and investment decisions. A summary of these analyses for the 10 most attractive business environments and the 10 least attractive markets is shown in Table 4.3.

**Table 4.2**    Macro-level country segments based on factor scores

A. Two-segment solution

| Segment 1 | | | Segment 2 | |
| --- | --- | --- | --- | --- |
| Austria | | | Japan | |
| Belgium | | | Sweden | |
| Denmark | | | US | |
| France | | | | |
| Finland | | | | |
| Holland | | | | |
| Norway | | | | |
| Switzerland | | | | |
| UK | | | | |

| Centroids: | Mobil. | Health | Trade | Life | Cosmo. |
| --- | --- | --- | --- | --- | --- |
| Segment 1 | −0.263 | −0.208 | 0.137 | −0.157 | 0.199 |
| Segment 2 | 0.788 | 0.623 | −0.410 | 0.470 | −0.597 |

B. Three-segment solution

| Segment 1 | Segment 2 | Segment 3 |
| --- | --- | --- |
| Holland | Austria | US |
| Japan | Belgium | |
| Sweden | Denmark | |
| UK | Finland | |
| | France | |
| | Norway | |
| | Switzerland | |

| Centroids: | Mobil. | Health | Trade | Life | Cosmo. |
| --- | --- | --- | --- | --- | --- |
| Segment 1 | −0.272 | 0.815 | −0.016 | −0.141 | −0.613 |
| Segment 2 | −0.288 | −0.438 | 0.058 | 0.027 | 0.379 |
| Segment 3 | 3.103 | −0.195 | −0.346 | 0.373 | −0.203 |

*Source*: Helsen *et al.*, 1993.

**Table 4.3** Business environment scores and ranks: Top ten and bottom ten countries

| | 1999–2003 Total score | 1999–2003 Rank | 2004–08 Total Score | 2004–08 Rank | Change in total score | Change in rank | 1999–2003 Grade | 2004–08 Grade |
|---|---|---|---|---|---|---|---|---|
| Canada | 8.55 | 2 | 8.65 | 1 | 0.10 | 1 | very good | very good |
| Netherlands | 8.54 | 3 | 8.62 | 2 | 0.08 | 1 | very good | very good |
| US | 8.61 | 1 | 8.57 | 3 | −0.04 | −2 | very good | very good |
| Finland | 8.26 | 8 | 8.54 | 4 | 0.28 | 4 | very good | very good |
| Singapore | 8.40 | 6 | 8.53 | 5 | 0.12 | 1 | very good | very good |
| Hong Kong | 8.51 | 5 | 8.51 | 6 | −0.01 | −1 | very good | very good |
| UK | 8.52 | 4 | 8.45 | 7 | −0.06 | −3 | very good | very good |
| Switzerland | 8.33 | 7 | 8.43 | 8 | 0.10 | −1 | very good | very good |
| Denmark | 8.00 | 12 | 8.40 | 9 | 0.40 | 3 | very good | very good |
| Ireland | 8.12 | 9 | 8.33 | 10 | 0.20 | −1 | very good | very good |
| Ukraine | 4.32 | 58 | 5.36 | 51 | 1.04 | 7 | very poor | poor |
| Azerbaijan | 4.47 | 56 | 5.34 | 52 | 0.86 | 4 | very poor | poor |
| Egypt | 5.05 | 48 | 5.27 | 53 | 0.22 | −5 | poor | poor |
| Vietnam | 4.71 | 55 | 5.24 | 54 | 0.53 | 1 | very poor | poor |
| Kazakhstan | 4.95 | 53 | 5.22 | 55 | 0.27 | −2 | very poor | poor |
| Algeria | 4.37 | 57 | 5.19 | 56 | 0.81 | 1 | very poor | poor |
| Venezuela | 4.98 | 52 | 5.18 | 57 | 0.19 | −5 | very poor | poor |
| Pakistan | 4.74 | 54 | 5.02 | 58 | 0.28 | −4 | very poor | poor |
| Nigeria | 3.94 | 59 | 4.58 | 59 | 0.64 | 0 | very poor | very poor |
| Iran | 3.69 | 60 | 4.45 | 60 | 0.76 | 0 | very poor | very poor |
| Average[a] | 6.40 | — | 6.91 | — | 0.50 | — | — | — |
| Median[a] | 6.57 | — | 7.08 | — | 0.51 | — | — | — |

Qualitative grades are assigned according to the following scale: very good, score more than 8; good, 6.5–8; moderate, 5.5–6.4; poor, 5–5.4; very poor, less than 5.

[a] Calculation for all 60 countries.

*Source:* Adapted from EIU Country Forecasts, 2004.

The model used to arrive at scores and ratings is based on the scores for 70 different indicators, which are a combination of quantitative data, business surveys and expert opinions. The quantitative data are obtained from a variety of sources, including many of those covered in Chapter 3. The indicators are grouped into 10 different categories: (1) political environment, (2) macroeconomic environment, (3) market opportunities, (4) policy toward private enterprise and competition, (5) policy toward foreign investment, (6) foreign trade and exchange controls, (7) taxes, (8) financing, (9) the labor market and (10) infrastructure. Each of the 70 indicators is converted to a 5-point scale, ranging from 1, very bad for business, to 5, very good for business. All the indicators receive equal weights and are converted to a 10-point scale. The results are used to create a five-year historical score and rank as well as a forecast for the next five years. In Table 4.3 the US was the most attractive business environment for the 1999–2003 period, but it is forecast to slip to number 3, behind Canada and the Netherlands, in the 2004–2008 period.

Scores on each of the components are available for the G7 countries, Western Europe, Eastern Europe, Asia, Latin America, and the Middle East and Africa. This provides a general indicator of the attractiveness of operating in different parts of the world. A firm could also weight the individual components according to how they affect the firm's business to come up with a more refined measure.

Michigan State University's CIBER center publishes its market potential indexes (EMPI) for 24 emerging market countries. These countries comprise more than half the world's population, have a large share of world output and have high growth rates. Eight dimensions – market size, market growth rate, market intensity, market consumption capacity, the commercial infrastructure, economic freedom, market receptivity and country risk – are weighted to develop the overall index (see Table 4.4). Each of the individual indexes is based on multiple indicators. For example, market size is based on urban population and electricity consumption and market receptivity is based on per capita imports from the US and trade as a percentage of GDP. Singapore has the highest overall market potential index and Colombia the lowest.

The *World Competitiveness Yearbook* (WCY) has been published annually by the International Institute for Management Development (IMD) since 1989. It rates 60 national and regional economies on their competitiveness and provides rankings and analysis of how a nation's environment creates and sustains competitiveness. The rankings are based on four factors that are developed from 323 criteria (numbers in parentheses indicate number of criteria for each factor): Economic Performance (83), Government Efficiency (77), Business Efficiency (69) and Infrastructure (94).

**Table 4.4** Market potential index for emerging markets, 2004

| Countries | Market size | | Market growth rate | | Market intensity | | Market consumption capacity | | Commercial infrastructure | | Economic freedom | | Market receptivity | | Country risk | |
|---|---|---|---|---|---|---|---|---|---|---|---|---|---|---|---|---|
| | Rank | Index | Rank | Index | Rank | Index | Rank | Index | Rank | Index | Rank | Index | Rank | Index | Rank | Index |
| Hong Kong | 21 | 1 | 10 | 80 | 1 | 100 | 12 | 54 | 2 | 98 | 2 | 92 | 1 | 100 | 2 | 8 |
| Singapore | 24 | 1 | 5 | 84 | 9 | 57 | 10 | 62 | 3 | 92 | 9 | 69 | 2 | 60 | 1 | 10 |
| S. Korea | 6 | 12 | 11 | 78 | 7 | 66 | 2 | 99 | 6 | 76 | 8 | 71 | 9 | 18 | 4 | 6 |
| China | 1 | 100 | 7 | 82 | 24 | 1 | 11 | 59 | 14 | 38 | 24 | 1 | 12 | 8 | 11 | 4 |
| Israel | 22 | 1 | 14 | 75 | 3 | 75 | 4 | 82 | 5 | 79 | 4 | 78 | 4 | 29 | 6 | 5 |
| Hungary | 23 | 1 | 22 | 50 | 2 | 76 | 1 | 100 | 4 | 81 | 5 | 78 | 5 | 24 | 3 | 6 |
| Czech Rep. | 20 | 2 | 21 | 51 | 17 | 51 | 3 | 97 | 1 | 100 | 3 | 83 | 6 | 24 | 5 | 6 |
| India | 2 | 47 | 2 | 96 | 19 | 40 | 6 | 77 | 22 | 14 | 16 | 46 | 24 | 1 | 14 | 3 |
| Poland | 10 | 5 | 23 | 34 | 5 | 67 | 5 | 80 | 7 | 66 | 7 | 73 | 18 | 4 | 8 | 5 |
| Chile | 18 | 2 | 12 | 78 | 10 | 56 | 22 | 13 | 8 | 54 | 1 | 100 | 11 | 11 | 7 | 5 |
| Mexico | 5 | 13 | 17 | 61 | 6 | 66 | 20 | 27 | 15 | 37 | 10 | 66 | 7 | 23 | 10 | 5 |
| Russia | 3 | 37 | 15 | 73 | 22 | 28 | 15 | 53 | 11 | 41 | 21 | 21 | 15 | 6 | 15 | 3 |
| Thailand | 14 | 4 | 8 | 82 | 21 | 38 | 13 | 54 | 16 | 33 | 12 | 61 | 8 | 22 | 12 | 4 |
| Malaysia | 17 | 3 | 1 | 100 | 23 | 15 | 18 | 42 | 12 | 38 | 19 | 33 | 3 | 46 | 9 | 5 |
| Turkey | 9 | 8 | 13 | 75 | 14 | 54 | 9 | 67 | 9 | 47 | 18 | 38 | 13 | 7 | 16 | 2 |
| Egypt | 13 | 5 | 3 | 90 | 4 | 74 | 8 | 70 | 19 | 22 | 23 | 14 | 19 | 4 | 17 | 2 |
| Indonesia | 7 | 12 | 6 | 83 | 16 | 51 | 7 | 72 | 20 | 18 | 20 | 30 | 14 | 6 | 22 | 1 |
| Philippines | 11 | 5 | 9 | 82 | 13 | 54 | 17 | 47 | 24 | 1 | 13 | 57 | 10 | 17 | 20 | 2 |
| Argentina | 12 | 5 | 4 | 84 | 12 | 55 | 19 | 39 | 10 | 41 | 15 | 52 | 21 | 3 | 24 | |
| Brazil | 4 | 26 | 18 | 58 | 20 | 38 | 23 | 13 | 13 | 38 | 14 | 56 | 23 | 1 | 18 | 2 |
| Peru | 19 | 2 | 16 | 62 | 8 | 62 | 14 | 53 | 21 | 15 | 11 | 62 | 22 | 2 | 21 | 2 |
| S. Africa | 8 | 8 | 20 | 51 | 11 | 56 | 24 | 1 | 23 | 13 | 6 | 74 | 17 | 5 | 13 | 4 |
| Colombia | 16 | 4 | 19 | 51 | 15 | 52 | 21 | 17 | 17 | 32 | 17 | 39 | 16 | 5 | 19 | 2 |
| Venezuela | 15 | 4 | 24 | 1 | 18 | 45 | 16 | 52 | 18 | 25 | 22 | 20 | 20 | 4 | 23 | |

**Table 4.4** (continued)

Dimensions and measures of market potential

| Dimension | Weight | Measures used |
|---|---|---|
| Market Size | 10/50 | Urban population (million) – 2003[1] |
| | | Electricity consumption (billion kwh) – 2002[2] |
| Market Growth Rate | 6/50 | Average annual growth rate of commercial energy use (%) – between years |
| | | Real GDP growth rate (%) – 2003[1] |
| Market Intensity | 7/50 | GNI per capita estimates using PPP (US dollars) – 2003[1] |
| | | Private consumption as a percentage of GDP (%) – 2002[1] |
| Market Consumption Capacity | 5/50 | Percentage share of middle-class in consumption/income (latest year available) |
| Commercial Infrastructure | 7/50 | Telephone mainlines (per 100 habitants) – 2003[3] |
| | | Cellular mobile subscribers (per 100 habitants) – 2003[3] |
| | | Number of PCs (per 100 habitants) – 2003[3] |
| | | Paved road density (km per million people) – 2002[1] |
| | | Internet hosts (per million people) – 2003[3] |
| | | Population per retail outlet – (latest year available) |
| | | Television sets (per 1000 persons) – 2003[1] |
| Economic Freedom | 5/50 | Economic Freedom Index – 2004[5] |
| | | Political Freedom Index – 2004[6] |
| Market Receptivity | 6/50 | Per capita imports from US (US dollars) – 2003[7] |
| | | Trade as a percentage of GDP (%) – 2003[1] |
| Country Risk | 4/50 | Country risk rating – 2004[8] |

Data used are those available for most recent year.

[1] Source: World Bank, *World Development Indicators* – 2003
[2] Source: US Energy Information Administration, *International Energy Annual* – 2003
[3] Source: International Telecommunication Union, *ICT Indicators* – 2003
[4] Source: Euromonitor, *European Marketing Data and Statistics* – 2004
[5] Source: Heritage Foundation, *The Index of Economic Freedom* – 2004
[6] Source: Freedom House, *Survey of Freedom in the World* – 2004
[7] Source: US Census Bureau Foreign Trade Division, *Country Data* – 2004
[8] Source: Euromoney, *Country Risk Survey* – 2004

*Notes*

1. The most recent version of the Market Potential Indicators can always be found on globaledge, http://globaledge.msu.edu/ibrd/marketpot.asp.
2. We also keep an archive of the Market Potential Indicators for the previous years. To find these archives, visit the Publications section of our MSU-CIBER web site.
3. For more information on methodology index, refer to S. Tamer Cavusgil (1997) Measuring the Potential of Emerging Markets: An Indexing Approach, *Business Horizons*, **40**(1), 87–91.

*Source*: Michigan State University, CIBER Center, Eart Lansing MI, www.ciber.msu.edu.

Each of these four factors is broken down into five equally weighted subfactors. For example, Infrastructure is broken down into Basic Infrastructure, Technological Infrastructure, Scientific Infrastructure, Health and Economic, and Education. Data for the 323 criteria include a combination of statistical indicators and perceptual evaluations along with an annual survey of business executives on the competitiveness of their countries. There are 129 hard data criteria that are based on statistical data obtained from international, national and regional organizations as well as private institutions and a network of over 50 organizations that partner with IMD. These hard data receive approximately two-thirds of the total weight. The other component of the WCY is over 4000 responses to 112 questions on a survey sent to executives in the 60 economies. The survey data account for the other one-third of the index.

The ranking of a country overall and on individual criteria can be helpful in assessing the business climate in that country. The information allows comparison of economies around the globe on various dimensions and provides insights into the strengths and weaknesses of various economies. Usefulness of different subfactors is likely to depend on the country or industry. High-tech companies might, for example, be interested in the Technological and Scientific Infrastructure, while service or labor-intensive companies would focus on the Employment and Labor Market. Finally, trends can be examined by looking at five years of data.

The World Economic Forum publishes its own index called the *Global Competitiveness Report*. The report, which is published annually, assesses the comparative strengths and weakness of 102 industrialized and emerging economies. The report contains three main parts: (1) analytical chapters related to competitiveness, (2) country profiles, and (3) data tables with country rankings for every indicator. In addition to the statistical data on each country, the report contains the responses of over 7000 business leaders who responded to the Executive Opinion Survey. This provides information on perceptions and observations from individuals in each country.

The principal limitation of these indexes is that they focus on macro country indicators. These are used as surrogate indicators or proxy variables for evaluating the general business climate. As such, they are useful as a first step in identifying countries that are likely to be attractive candidates for initial entry or expansion of international operations. Individual companies will need more detailed analyses, tailored to corporate objectives and the specific product markets in which they are involved. Consequently, the use of these types of indexes is limited, particularly for companies that wish to make a serious commitment to international operations.

# Customized Models

An alternative approach is to develop customized models using secondary data geared to specific company objectives and industry characteristics. The variables used to screen countries are selected by management based on objectives relative to international market operations and are adapted to the industry and product lines concerned. Some companies may, for example, attach greater importance to political risk than other factors, while other companies may be more concerned with the rates of inflation or future market growth. Similarly, the kinds of criteria that may be relevant for one industry may not be the same for other industries. Companies marketing snack foods might, for example, be concerned with the growth of consumption outside the home and the size of population aged 12–30. Agricultural equipment manufacturers, on the other hand, would be more concerned with agricultural production and the percentage of the population employed in agriculture.

A selection of such indicators can be used to make a subjective evaluation of countries and areas that appear to offer the best prospects for market entry. Alternatively, more systematic procedures can be developed, combining a selection of these variables with a screening or scanning routine to evaluate countries on the basis of relevant variables.

## Developing Customized Models

Given the number of variables that might be considered in assessing market potential, one procedure is to adopt a multistage screening approach. Management first establishes a number of initial screening criteria to eliminate countries from further consideration, such as minimum population size or minimal levels of GDP per capita. Other factors that would automatically eliminate a country from consideration can also be included. For example, a company selling snowboards or down parkas would eliminate countries with warm climates. Further, for snowboards, the percentage of the population under 20 as well as the number and size of ski resorts would enter into the model.

Next, macroeconomic indicators suggesting a high-risk or unfavorable business climate might be examined. These might include, for example, indicators of political risk or economic instability, rate of economic growth and the regulatory environment. Again, relevant indicators can be selected based on management objectives and risk orientation, and tailored to specific product markets and target segments or market positioning. At this stage, either minimal screening levels can be imposed, or relevant indicators weighted according to management judgment.

The third level might consist of indicators specific to the product market. These might include surrogate indicators of market demand, for example population of 15- to 25-year-olds for inline skating equipment or actual product sales, rate of market growth, sales of complementary or substitute products. For example, a marketer of pasta sauces might examine sales of packaged pasta as well as other ready-to-prepare sauces. Again, indicators might either be weighted to develop an overall ranking of market potential, or levels of each indicator can be compared to develop a general picture of potential in each country. The latter approach may be preferable if data are missing for some countries, or some data are not reliable or up to date, or where there is no clear consensus in assigning weights.

The final level might consist of indicators relating to the cost or ease/difficulty of marketing in a given country, or pursuing the same marketing/positioning strategy. For example, a company that currently sells its products through department stores might look at the availability of department stores, or a shoe company at the existence of specialty shoe chains. Equally, the cost and reach of mass media might affect promotional costs. Presence of competition might be another factor that could be a major barrier to entry.

This approach can be used as a template to assess market potential for country entry or expansion decisions. The template is then applied each time an entry decision is to be made and the data are collected and updated from relevant sources. Alternatively, if an international database contains information on each of these levels, software for evaluating and selecting countries can be developed. This might, for example, update and incorporate management weighting of different decision criteria. Equally, modules can be introduced changing the weighting and criteria depending on the mode of entry.

One approach to evaluating countries is shown in Figure 4.1. The flow chart depicts a model that uses managerial judgment to select countries to enter or the mode of entry to employ. Relevant variables are selected and weighted according to their perceived importance. A rank order of countries is then obtained, indicating priority for further investigation. This procedure involves three stages. First, criteria for examining countries are identified. Next, criteria for evaluating countries and the weights to be assigned to them under different modes of operation or entry are determined. Finally, countries are evaluated based on these criteria, utilizing information relating to the general business and investment climate and, where available, to the specific product market. The flow diagram provides a systematic approach to screening countries and can be modified to suit an individual firm's needs.

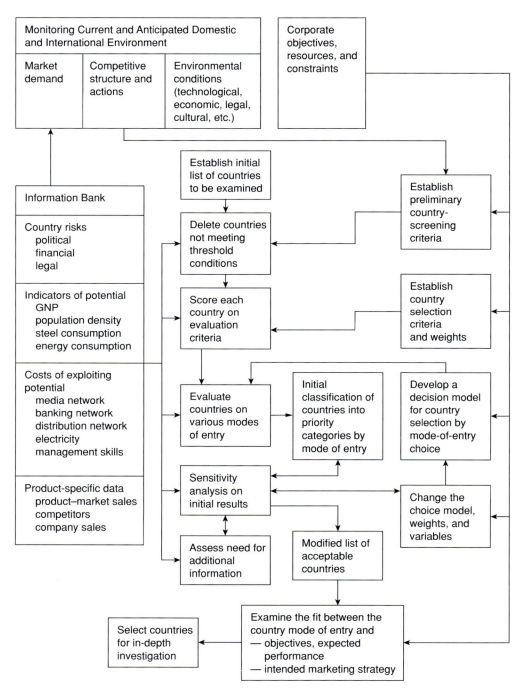

**Figure 4.1** Conceptual framework for country selection

Other procedures for evaluating target countries based on secondary data can be developed. These vary in their degree of complexity and sophistication, depending on company size and resources available for international market evaluation. Simple country-rating schemata may be used, or more intricate models developed incorporating political and financial risk analysis. In either case, careful selection of country indicators relevant to the specific company or product market and availability of appropriate information sources is crucial to effective country market assessment.

# Demand Estimation

The initial phase of estimating demand involves identifying appropriate countries and markets for in-depth investigation. This reduces the set of countries to a manageable number that can be examined further and paves the way for the next step, demand estimation. Estimating market demand makes possible a much more explicit evaluation of the attractiveness of the various markets. In doing so, management faces the dual task of estimating initial demand potential and projecting future market trends. Since the costs of initial market entry are high and there is considerable uncertainty concerning success, this is a critical step. Further, since some market entry decisions are predicated less on initial demand and more on establishing a presence to take advantage of future demand, the second task is also important.

Where the industry or product market is already well developed and historical sales data are available, procedures similar to those used in the domestic market can be followed. For example, time-series, trend or double exponential smoothing analysis can be used. Since their applications are identical to those used in the domestic market situation, these are not discussed here.

In situations where management is considering entry into new markets or is in the initial stages of market development, other procedures are required. This is further complicated by many small and fragmented markets, particularly in developing countries, and the limited secondary data that exist for such markets. Their small size, as well as the difficulty and high costs of undertaking research under such conditions, suggests that techniques commonly used in the domestic market, such as surveys of purchase intentions or test markets, are either infeasible or prohibitively expensive. Consequently low-cost rudimentary procedures may be the only tools available.

Data extrapolation techniques are very useful to estimate demand when limited data are available. Past experience and data collected in other countries can be used to develop estimates or forecasts of potential in other countries. However, there are a number of implicit assumptions concerning the relevance of data collected in one country and applied to another. First, the countries must be equivalent in certain relevant respects. For example, extrapolation between countries that have similar market structures or demand characteristics is likely to be the most successful. Second, the measurement units need to be comparable or equivalent for all countries. If monetary units are used, then the appropriate currency conversions have to be made. The adoption of the euro as the official currency of most European countries greatly facilitates comparisons. In other parts of the world, however, conversions will have to be made. While exchange rates are published daily, there are issues related to the difference between the 'official' and the 'unofficial' rates as well as whether the conversion is done using purchasing power parity. Third, some care has to be taken to be certain that the underlying relationship between demand determinants and sales is the same in all countries. Thus, a model may assume that if GDP is related to consumption of a particular product in one country, it is related to consumption of the product in another. Fourth, the product categories should be comparable and equivalent in all countries. For example, the comparability of laundry products or soft drinks between countries would have to be established. Finally, if projections over time are to be made, the rate of change in all markets should be approximately the same.

## *Lead–Lag Analysis*

One simple and straightforward method of data extrapolation is lead–lag analysis. This is based on the use of time-series data from one country to project sales in other countries. It assumes that determinants of demand in the two countries are identical and the only factor that separates them is time. Thus, for example, sales of televisions in the UK might be used to predict the sales of televisions in India, with a lag of $x$ years. This requires the assumption that the diffusion process and specifically the rate of diffusion is the same in all countries. Figure 4.2 shows the diffusion of room air conditioners, washing machines and calculators for the US, Japan, Taiwan and South Korea. While the diffusion process was modeled effectively for all cases, the coefficient of imitation differed between countries (Takada and Jain, 1991). Examination of the curves shown in Figure 4.2 suggests that while there is some similarity, there are also major differences. For example, the authors found that products introduced more recently diffused more quickly. This is a common phenomenon as rapid rates of change in international markets often mean that products introduced into new markets from other markets years later will diffuse more rapidly.

Another problem is illustrated by the work of Eliashberg and Helsen (1994) that looked at the diffusion of VCRs in Europe. They examined a reasonably homogeneous set of countries in Western

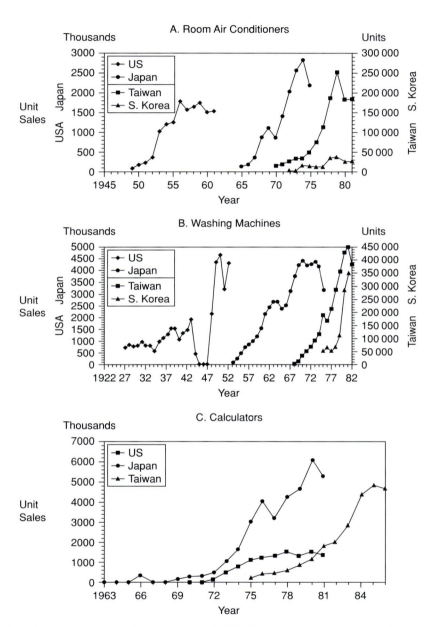

**Figure 4.2**  Lead and lag time relationships of diffusion processes among four countries

*Source*: Takada and Jain, 1991.

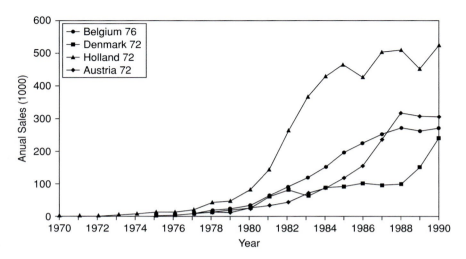

**Figure 4.3**　Diffusion of VCRs in pan-European market
*Source*: Eliashberg and Helsen, 1994.

Europe. As shown in Figure 4.3, even when the date of initial introduction of VCRs into the market was the same, as was the case for the Netherlands, Austria and Denmark, the rate of diffusion differed. This underscores the difficulty of taking experience in one country and accurately project-ing demand for another. Even where a product is successful in one country, the degree of success will depend on a host of factors that are often difficult to capture.

Lead–lag analysis is not frequently used as the accuracy of estimates is open to question. The difficulty of identifying the relevant lag period and the range of factors that affect demand make it all the more difficult to use the technique. However, the approach has considerable intuitive appeal to managers and is likely to guide some of their thinking. Management is prone to think, 'If we sold 120 000 units in Australia in the first three years, then we should be able to sell twice that when we enter Thailand.' Ultimately, the technique is likely to be most effective for new products that have similar underlying determinants of demand in different countries. Most often this is not the case. For a more complex application of lead–lag analysis, see Lindberg (1982).

## *Shift–Share Analysis*

The shift–share approach can be used to identify export opportunities (Green and Allaway, 1985). The technique has most typically been used to evaluate changes in employment, variations in economic growth and changes in regional production. The basic approach involves collecting data on imported products for a number of countries at the beginning and end of a time period, for example five years. The average growth in the import of the product is calculated for all countries. An expected growth rate is calculated for each country based on the average for all countries. The expected growth rate is then compared with the actual for each country. For countries gaining share of the particular import the net shift in share will be positive, and for those losing share the net shift will be negative. A percentage net shift can then be calculated to evaluate the relative change (country's net shift divided by total net shift times 100). According to Williamson (1980), the major advantages of shift–share analysis are that it is relatively simple and able to overcome problems associated with reliance on absolute or percentage measures.

Green and Allaway (1985) illustrate the technique using four-digit SITC (Standard International Trade Classification) data on high-technology products for 1974 to 1979. They show how it can be used to identify product categories with high export potential and to identify target markets. Their paper also compared results obtained using the shift–share approach with absolute and percentage measures. They point out that in applying shift–share analysis it is important to select a sufficiently long time frame for changes to occur and to examine the effect of outside economic forces. Further, the analysis is sensitive to the set of countries included in the analysis and the researcher must look beyond the percent net shift calculation to consider the absolute size of a market as well.

Wilson (2000) examined the export competitiveness of six Asian economies that export to the US, the EU and Japan. Rather than use the static shift–share analysis, he incorporated a dynamic shift–share model (see Barff and Knight, 1988) that allows continuous changes in the industry mix components to be taken into account. The static model only considers changes between the beginning and the ending year of the time period being considered. The dynamic model allows continuous changes throughout the period to be incorporated into the model.

# Surrogate Indicators

The use of surrogate indicators is similar to the use of general macro indicators, except that these are developed relative to the specific industry or product market. Data on these indicators can then be collected from surveys or secondary data sources. Two types of indicators can be used: (1) market potential indexes, for countries where survey data are available; and (2) macro surveys, where greater reliance has to be placed on visual indicators or observational measures.

## Market Potential Indexes

Indexes composed of a number of surrogate indicators hypothesized to be related to market potential for a product or industry can be developed. In a classic study, Dickensheets (1963) developed a market potential index for refrigerators with larger storage capacity, consisting of 11 indicators, including food shopping habits, number of supermarkets and self-service food stores, car ownership, consumption of frozen foods, per capita private consumption expenditure, employment of women, availability of domestic help, availability of consumer credit, cost of electricity for residential use, dwelling construction, size of new dwellings and refrigerator saturation in high-income families.

If either the rank order of importance of these variables or specific weights are developed, such indexes can be used to rank countries in terms of their relative attractiveness. Alternatively, they can be estimated for regions within a country and used to evaluate the sales potential of different regions within a country. Erickson (1963), for example, constructed an index for Brazil to rank submarkets within the country. This index was based on population, domestic income and retail store sales in each state as a percentage of the national total. This provided a measure of relative sales potential in each Brazilian state. However, such indicators tend to be unwieldy and it is not always clear to what extent similar indicators may be relevant from one country to another.

A more general approach has been developed by Samli (1977) to approximate market potential in Eastern Europe as a percentage of US market potential. The approach adjusts market size to reflect the quality of the market. Market quality is expressed in terms of eight general indicators that capture aspects of the degree of economic development (per capita income, manufacturing employment, steel consumption, kilowatt hours produced) and quality of life (motor vehicle registration, telephones, radios and television sets in use). The approach has not been validated, but it does suggest how secondary data might be used to obtain a rough estimate of market potential.

A variant of the shift–share approach can be used to develop a market potential index. Market potential is assumed to be a function of the trade-off between demand potential for a product in a given country and the barriers that would make it more difficult to import goods into that country. *Demand potential* is estimated based on *consumption* – that is, domestic production plus imports minus exports – *import penetration* – imports as a percentage of consumption – and *market share* of exporting country in imports of a target country and market share. *Import barriers* are estimated based on tariff barriers, nontariff barriers, geographical distance and exchange rates. Countries can either be grouped based on the relative score of these two factors, or alternatively each individual factor can be weighted and summed to derive an overall score for the country.

## The Macro Survey

An analogous procedure based on observational rather than survey data is the macro survey. This can be useful in developing countries, where there is low market potential that is widely dispersed in rural areas. A first step is to develop a scale consisting of several indicators, comprised of objects or indicators that can be observed. The presence of each of these is hypothesized to correspond to a given level of market potential. For example, the presence of a market square might be considered to indicate a potential market for piece-goods cloth and light agricultural implements, while the existence of a fiber mill, place of worship, an elementary school and some shops suggest markets for mopeds, hardware, school supplies and simple motorized agricultural equipment.

# Barometric Analysis

Barometric procedures can also be applied to cross-sectional data to predict likely demand. This assumes that if there is a direct relationship between the consumption of a product or service and an indicator in one country, the same relationship will hold in other countries. This relationship can be assumed to hold either at the aggregate level for the entire market, or for specific segments within the market.

## Aggregate Barometers

In markets where factors underlying demand are likely to be similar, barometric procedures can be used to extrapolate the relationship between an aggregate indicator and consumption or sales in one or more countries to other countries. This is likely to hold for basic commodities such as paper, sugar or cement and in industrial markets. In some cases the relationship will be as basic as between a commodity and levels of GDP. To illustrate this approach, regression analysis was conducted between sugar consumption and GDP for 65 countries at different levels of development. The adjusted $R^2$ was 0.25 and significant at the 0.01 level.

The results suggest the lack of a strong relationship between GDP and sugar consumption. To examine this relationship more closely, the sample was divided into two groups based on per capita

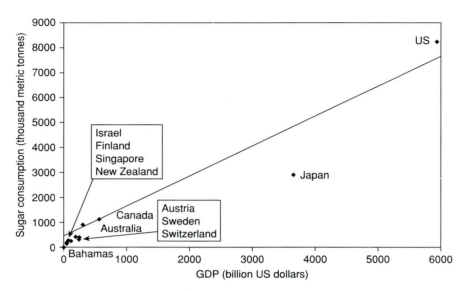

**Figure 4.4**   Sugar consumption and GDP

GDP. The 12 countries with GDP of $10 000 or more and the 53 with per capita GDP less than $10 000 were analyzed separately. The relationship was much stronger when the two groups of countries were analyzed separately. For the higher-income group the adjusted $R^2$ was 0.92, suggesting that for high-income countries GDP explains 92% of the variation in sugar consumption. This relationship is shown graphically in Figure 4.4. For the lower-income countries the relationship was weaker, with an adjusted $R^2$ of 0.60. The equation developed from these data can then be used to predict sugar sales based on the level of GDP in other countries. This suggests that as GDP increases, so will sugar consumption. Also, depending on the level of GDP, different models are required.

Rao and Steckel (1998) used the degree of urbanization and railway passenger kilometers per 100 people to predict the number of telephones per 100 people. To take into account the industrialized level of countries, they transformed the variables into logarithms. The results of their analysis are shown in Table 4.5. Twenty-seven countries were used to estimate the model, with an overall adjusted $R^2$ of 0.75. The coefficient for urbanization was 2.39 and for passenger kilometers 0.44. Both were highly significant.

Since the variables were transformed into logarithms, these coefficients can be interpreted as elasticities. For each 1% change in urbanization, there should be a 2.39% change in the number of

**Table 4.5** Forecasting of telephone penetration in various countries

Panel A: data used

| Country | Population thousands in 1988 | Telephones per 100 people in 1988 Y | Adjusted % urban (1988) $X_1$ | Railway passenger– km millions (1988) | Passenger– km per 100 people $X_2$ |
|---|---|---|---|---|---|
| Austria | 7 651 | 54.30 | 57.6 | 7 994 | 104 488 |
| Belgium | 9 845 | 49.90 | 95.7 | 6 348 | 64 479 |
| Bolivia | 7 002 | 2.80 | 50.0 | 369 | 5 270 |
| Brazil | 144 246 | 9.60 | 73.7 | 13 891 | 9 630 |
| Canada | 25 999 | 51.30 | 76.6 | 2 989 | 11 496 |
| Chile | 12 736 | 6.80 | 84.1 | 1 013 | 7 954 |
| Cuba | 10 400 | 5.20 | 72.6 | 2 627 | 25 260 |
| Czechoslovakia | 15 600 | 25.20 | 75.3 | 19 408 | 124 414 |
| Denmark | 5 130 | 88.20 | 84.6 | 4 850 | 94 547 |
| Finland | 4 956 | 49.90 | 59.7 | 3 147 | 63 496 |
| France | 55 880 | 45.20 | 72.8 | 63 920 | 113 261 |
| Germany | 62 356 | 68.20 | 85.0 | 41 760 | 66 970 |
| Greece | 10 008 | 43.10 | 61.3 | 1 963 | 19 614 |
| India | 796 502 | 0.60 | 25.0 | 263 731 | 33 111 |
| Indonesia | 173 356 | 0.50 | 27.3 | 7 863 | 4 536 |
| Ireland | 3 517 | 23.80 | 54.7 | 1 180 | 33 551 |
| Kenya | 23 290 | 1.50 | 22.0 | 2 608 | 11 198 |
| Malaysia | 16 967 | 9.70 | 41.3 | 1 518 | 8 947 |
| The Netherlands | 14 765 | 65.90 | 88.4 | 9 664 | 65 451 |
| Peru | 21 132 | 2.30 | 69.8 | 596 | 2 820 |
| Spain | 38 726 | 28.00 | 77.5 | 15 716 | 40 582 |
| Sweden | 8 474 | 66.20 | 83.8 | 6 081 | 71 760 |
| Switzerland | 6 619 | 88.20 | 60.5 | 12 391 | 187 203 |
| Tanzania | 24 023 | 0.60 | 19.5 | 855 | 3 559 |
| Thailand | 54 975 | 1.80 | 21.4 | 10 301 | 18 738 |
| Turkey | 55 211 | 11.70 | 58.6 | 6 708 | 12 150 |
| UK | 57 009 | 45.50 | 88.9 | 34 412 | 60 363 |
| USA | 245 535 | 49.60 | 74.9 | 9 156 | 3 729 |
| Venezuela | 18 747 | 9.30 | 89.6 | 29 | 155 |

**Table 4.5**   (continued)

Panel B: Regression results for the exponential model (regression of ($\ln Y$ on $\ln X_1$ and $\ln X_2$)) $R^2 = 0.77$; Adjusted $R^2 = 0.75$

Analysis of variance

|  | df | Sum of squares | Mean square | F | Significance of F |
|---|---|---|---|---|---|
| Regression | 2 | 58.14 | 29.07 | 43.37 | < 0.0005 |
| Residual | 26 | 17.43 | 0.67 | | |
| Total | 28 | 75.57 | | | |

|  | Coefficients | Standard error | t-statistic | P-value |
|---|---|---|---|---|
| Intercept | −11.40 | 1.51 | −7.52 | < 0.0001 |
| $\ln X_1$ | 2.39 | 0.33 | 7.21 | < 0.0001 |
| $\ln X_2$ | 0.44 | 0.10 | 4.22 | 0.0002 |

Panel C: Forecasts

| Country | $X_1$ | $X_2$ | Y | $\ln X_1$ | $\ln X_2$ | Predicted $\ln Y$ | Actual $\ln Y$ | % Error |
|---|---|---|---|---|---|---|---|---|
| Argentina | 85.6 | 32 609 | 11.50 | 4.45 | 10.39 | 3.845 | 2.442 | 53.34 |
| Japan | 76.9 | 290 865 | 40.20 | 4.34 | 12.58 | 4.441 | 3.694 | 20.23 |
| Sri Lanka | 21.3 | 11 248 | 1.10 | 3.06 | 9.32 | −0.0359 | 0.0953 | −137.6 |
| Norway | 74.1 | 62 187 | 47.80 | 4.31 | 11.03 | 3.682 | 3.867 | −4.78 |
| South Africa | 48.6 | 63 391 | 14.60 | 3.88 | 11.05 | 2.685 | 2.681 | 0.14 |

*Source*: Rao and Steckel, 1998.

telephones per 100 people. To account for saturation levels of telephones in industrialized countries, it was hypothesized that the relation between GDP and level of telephones would take the form of a logarithmic curve as telephone ownership reached saturation levels.

Despite the relatively good fit of the model for the initial 27 countries, its predictive ability varies over the five countries shown in Table 4.5 (panel C). Of the five countries in the predictive model, the best predictions are for South Africa and Norway while the poorest predictions are for Sri Lanka and Argentina. As the authors point out, there are other factors affecting telephone ownership that are not captured in the model. This underscores the importance of validating any model over a range of countries to assess the reliability and generalizability of results.

## Segment Extrapolation

Segment extrapolation is another type of barometric analysis. Barometric procedures assume that certain gross indicators are related to aggregate market potential. In some cases the factors underlying demand differ from segment to segment. In other cases the different segments simply have different rates of market penetration.

Where different factors drive demand from one segment to another, different indicators should be developed for each market segment. Diesel engines for small boats, for example, may have two potential markets, pleasure craft and fishing boats. Estimating the demand for pleasure craft in a country or region might be based on per capita disposable income as well as information on navigable waterways. Demand for engines for fishing boats should include information on the length of the coastline as well as estimates of the annual fish haul. Similarly, for hotels there are two potential segments, tourist and business travel. The first may be estimated using the number of tourists traveling to a given country and the second through the rate of growth in GDP or the amount of FDI (foreign direct investment).

Where different market segments have different rates of consumption or market penetration, barometric analysis should be conducted at the segment level. Each segment has a given level of demand as a function of another variable, such as income or age. If, for example, purchase of wrist watches varies by income strata in country A, the number of units purchased by different income groups can be identified. The number of household units in each income group is then identified in country B and multiplied by the relevant penetration rate to obtain potential market size by group. By aggregating all groups the total market potential can be determined. In Table 4.6, demand for wrist watches in two categories, below $75 and $75 and above, is examined as a function of income in country A. By applying these penetration rates to the distribution of income in country B, estimates of overall demand can be established. Since the income skews lower in country B, projected sales of watches selling for below $75 is greater than for watches selling for $75 or more.

Similarly for industrial markets, different user industries can be identified and the rates of penetration in each industry determined for one country. The market potential in each of these industries in a second country can be determined by using the relevant penetration rates to estimate demand. The approach taken by Orbital Communications Corporation to forecast demand for its ORBCOMM service illustrates this approach. ORBCOMM is a satellite-based mobile data communication system that was developed to offer a wide range of emergency, data acquisition and messaging services.

**Table 4.6**  Predicting sales of wrist watches

| Country A | | | Country B | | |
|---|---|---|---|---|---|
| | Household unit sales by price range | | Number of households (in thousands) | Potential unit sales volume (by price range) | |
| Household income | Under $75 | $75 and over | | Under $75 | $75 and over |
| Over $60 000 | 0.25 | 0.61 | 219 | 54 750 | 133 590 |
| $50 000 to 59 999 | 0.28 | 0.53 | 434 | 121 520 | 230 020 |
| $40 000 to 49 999 | 0.31 | 0.49 | 978 | 303 180 | 479 220 |
| $30 000 to 39 999 | 0.34 | 0.41 | 1 963 | 667 420 | 804 830 |
| $20 000 to 29 999 | 0.39 | 0.33 | 2 567 | 1 001 130 | 847 110 |
| $10 000 to 19 999 | 0.48 | 0.21 | 3 019 | 1 449 120 | 633 990 |
| Under $10 000 | 0.52 | 0.15 | 3 527 | 1 834 040 | 529 050 |
| | | | 12 707 | 5 431 160 | 3 657 810 |

To develop a forecast for the US market the company followed a three-step process: (1) vertical market definition; (2) aggregate market forecasts; and (3) detailed market forecasts. To help define the various industries over 300 potential end users were interviewed. Based on the interviews, 11 vertical market segments were identified (see Table 4.7 for the segments, excluding the government, which was used in the US). A top-down analysis was conducted to estimate the size of each vertical market. As a third step, a detailed bottom-up analysis was undertaken to provide a better understanding of each market. The data were used to provide a forecast of the average number of subscribers per year from 1994 to 2001.

Applying the US forecast to international markets presented a number of challenges. First, the government market was absorbed into the other ten sectors. Second, the number of new subscribers had to be forecast, rather than the average number of subscribers. Third, since service would not be available until 1996, the estimates had to be adjusted accordingly. To project demand in each foreign country the following procedure was used:

1. The ten vertical markets were placed in one of three groups depending on the type of services used. Group A covered applications for remotely located sensors, group B demand for mobile services, and group C demand for messaging services.

**Table 4.7**  Derivation of group factors for China

| Group | Markets | Relevant statistics | China stats | US stats | Ratios[a] | Group factors[b] |
|---|---|---|---|---|---|---|
| A | Environmental | | | | | |
| A | Agricultural | GNP ($ billions) | $424 | $5 686 | 0.075 ⎫ | |
| A | Energy | Area (sq. miles) | 3692 | 3 619 | 1.020 ⎬ | 0.276 |
| A | Oceanography | | | | | |
| B | Cargo tracking | Area | 3692 | 3 619 | 1.020 ⎫ | |
| B | Long-haul trucking | Vehicles (thousands) | 4172 | 45 106 | 0.093 ⎬ | 0.337 |
| | | Telephone density (no. lines/100 people) | 2 | 50 | 1.096 ⎭ | |
| C | Marine messaging | Area | 3692 | 3 619 | 1.020 ⎫ | |
| C | Commercial messaging | GNP/capita ($) | 370 | 22 563 | 0.016 | |
| C | Consumer messaging | Population (millions) | 1150 | 252 | 4.563 ⎬ | 0.434 |
| C | Emergency | Availability (%) | 86 | 92 | 0.935 | |
| | | Telephone density | 2 | 50 | 1.096 ⎭ | |

[a] Calculated by dividing US statistics by China statistics, except for the telephone density ratio which was calculated as 1.1–0.1 × (country telephone density/US telephone density). The ORBCOMM availability ratio reflected the 'average' system availability in a target country to that in the US.

[b] Calculated by taking the geometric average of the correlated ratios and then multiplying them by the uncorrelated ratios (telephone density and ORBCOMM availability). For example, group B factor = (telephone density ratio) × √((area ratio) × (vehicle ratio)).

Source: Narayandas and Quelch, 1997.

2. Next, macro country statistics influencing demand in each group were selected. In Table 4.7, GNP and land area were selected as factors for group A. For group B, area, number of vehicles and phone density were used. Finally, for group C, area, per capita GNP, population, availability and phone density were selected. Certain other variables such as miles of roads and the number of boats were considered but not used due to lack of comparability across countries.
3. The ratio of each country to the US for each variable was then computed. In Table 4.7 the ratio of China compared to the US is shown.
4. A total score was computed for each group. The specific procedure followed was idiosyncratic to the particular application. In this case the uncorrelated ratios (phone density and availability) were multiplied by the geometric average of the correlated ratios (all other variables).

For group B, it was the square root of $(1.02 \times 0.093)$ times 1.096. This gives a group factor of 0.337.

5. The group factor was used to estimate demand in China as a fraction of US demand (Table 4.7).

This approach can be further refined by breaking down companies within each of these industries by size, sales volume and factors that are indicative of sales volume. This example illustrates the complexity of estimating demand in another country. When the service is totally new, as was the case with ORBCOMM, the accuracy of the demand forecasts is unknown. However, the forecast provides an indication of the likely level of demand. This basic approach can be used in a variety of industries. Nevertheless, the specific variable used will need to be selected and tailored to the application. More information about ORBCOMM can be found at www.orbcomm.com.

## Cohort Analysis

In certain instances it may be desirable to refine segment extrapolation by looking at the dynamics underlying the cohorts of consumers that comprise the segments. Cohorts are groups of consumers, typically stratified by age. The value of cohort analysis is that it focuses on groups as their consumption evolves over time. As cohorts are most typically defined in terms of age, the key issue is whether consumption of a product or product category changes or differs from one age group to another, changes over time and how these trends affect projections of future demand.

Consumption of beverages in the US has changed dramatically. Coffee consumption has declined while soft drink consumption has increased. When consumption is broken down by age, it is apparent that while all groups are consuming less coffee, this trend is most pronounced for younger Americans. Even more alarming for the coffee industry, this suggests that in the future consumption will be even lower than at present. On the other hand, soft drink consumption is increasing, with much of the increase coming from younger Americans. The value of cohort analysis is that it examines the dynamics of consumption rather than the aggregate per capita rates. For example, Rentz and Reynolds (1991) show that a cohort analysis provides a more accurate estimate of penetration (percent of individuals in an age cohort consuming coffee) than a cross-sectional forecast.

Applying this technique to international markets requires that product consumption first be examined by age cohort in one country market. Second, the age distribution in a second country is examined to determine current market potential and provide the basis for estimating future

| Table 4.8 | Per capita consumption of soft drinks (gallons consumed per year per person) | | | |
|---|---|---|---|---|
| Age | 1960 | 1969 | 1979 | |
| 8–19 | 31.4 | 40.0 | 48.6 | |
| 20–29 | 30.2 | 42.1 | 48.3 | C8 |
| 30–39 | 21.1 | 34.7 | 42.1 | C7 |
| 40–49 | 17.3 | 28.4 | 34.8 | C6 |
| 50+ | 11.8 | 22.5 | 23.5 | C5 |
| | | C2 | C3 | C4 |

C2, cohort born prior to 1910; C3, cohort born 1911–1920; C4, cohort born 1921–1930; C5, cohort born 1931–1940; C6, cohort born 1940–1949; C7, cohort born 1950–1959; C8, cohort born 1960–1969.

*Source*: Rentz *et al.*, 1983.

demand. The premise is that as a particular cohort ages, it will continue to follow the consumption pattern that the group established, rather than reverting to behavior patterns exhibited by the cohort before it. Just comparing consumption by age category provides a result similar to segment extrapolation discussed earlier. Looking at cohort dynamics provides a much stronger basis for predicting future sales.

The first step in conducting a cohort analysis is to construct a cohort table for the base country. The example shown in Table 4.8 is from a study conducted by Rentz *et al.* (1983). It shows that consumers aged 20–29 consumed 30.2 gallons of soft drinks per year in 1960 and 48.3 gallons in 1979. However, following the same cohort from 1960 to 1979 indicates that its consumption was only 34.8 gallons per person, or 4.6 gallons more than it consumed in 1960. The difference between 1960 and 1979 for the 20–29-year-old age group is 18.3 gallons (48.3–30.2), suggesting that consumption patterns are changing dramatically for younger consumers. A similar cohort table would be constructed for the country for which projections are to be made.

After the cohort tables are constructed a constrained multiple regression can be used (see Rentz *et al.* (1983) for an example) to estimate cohort effects, effects of age and period effects. The results obtained in the base country and the 'projection' country are then compared. An assessment can be made of whether the same model is appropriate, or more specifically whether there is the same underlying dynamic. To compare the two regression models the Chow test can be used to see whether the same model can be employed or whether different equations are appropriate (Chow,

1960). If the same model can be used, then the researcher has greater confidence that the underlying dynamics of demand for the product are the same in the two countries.

In applying cohort analysis, there needs to be a recognition that certain behaviors do change over time. For example, younger consumers are more likely to participate in skateboarding and inline skating. If consumers start boarding or skating as teenagers, they are more likely to continue to participate in the sport. However, as they grow older they may be less likely to continue due to a variety of factors, for instance they engage in other activities, may be less able to participate, or may have broken a bone as a youth and stopped boarding or skating.

Cohort analysis can provide important insights into the underlying dynamics of consumer behavior and likely demand. To conduct a cohort analysis properly, one needs either cross-sectional or panel data. Since these data exist only in the most developed countries, it may as a general rule be difficult to perform cohort analyses broadly in international markets.

## *Analytical Models*

The role of secondary data in estimating market demand can be strengthened if it is combined with survey data. The addition of survey data from potential purchasers not only allows a better estimate of demand, but also helps to identify different segments. These segments may end up mapping into country markets, or more typically be evident in a range of countries. In addition, the use of survey data can also help to evaluate the attractiveness of the various segments, particularly with respect to their likelihood of response to various marketing mix elements.

Agarwal (2003) develops a comprehensive approach to identifying segments for a global satellite-based paging service across 22 countries. The new service was tested against two other competitors that offered paging services with different attributes. The primary differentiating features of the new service were that it offered worldwide coverage and availability and could be used in moving vehicles. As a first step, 27 country-level macro variables were factor analyzed to reduce them to a smaller set of variables that captured country differences. Six factors were identified: (1) consumption, (2) mobility, (3) telecommunications/newspaper infrastructure, (4) trade, (5) size and (6) consumer price index. These were similar to the factors identified by Helsen *et al.* (1993) discussed earlier in this chapter.

To provide information on likely demand and product preferences, survey data were collected from approximately 200 individuals in each country. To be eligible to participate, respondents' income level had to be in the top 5% within their country and they must have traveled abroad at least three times per year. Surveys were either conducted over the telephone, by mail or face to face, depending on the country. Respondents were presented with nine sets of three product profiles, out of a possible 27 different product profiles, and asked to indicate their choice within each set. The product profiles varied in terms of the paging services' geographical coverage, where it was capable of receiving a signal (e.g. in vehicles, indoors, near high-rise buildings), application (numeric or alphanumeric capabilities) and the size of the device. In addition to the capabilities of the services, the service descriptions differed on the cost of the pager, the monthly usage fee and the price per page.

A total of 3463 individuals responded. These were split into an estimation sample of 2777 and a validation sample of 685. The model was estimated using individual demographic data (age, occupation and income) and country macro variables. The factor scores on the six factors described earlier were the country-level variables. A latent class model was estimated for two to nine segments, with the best fit found for a seven-segment solution (see Lattin *et al.* (2003) and Agarwal (2003) for more details on latent class models). Two of the segments included almost 60% of the respondents, while the other five ranged between 7% and 12%. The segments differed in their price sensitivity with respect to the three elements, pager cost, monthly fee and usage fee. The least price sensitive was comprised primarily of respondents from Brazil, China, Hong Kong and South Korea. Another segment that was price sensitive to usage fees had approximately 20% of respondents from Australia and Canada.

This study illustrates a very sophisticated and systematic approach to demand estimation. The approach allows estimation of the total demand for a new service and the market share for each competing service. The price sensitivity information allows more precise estimates of demand by segment and ultimately in each country. For example, Agarwal found that in the highest price scenario, the percentage of respondents who would buy one of the services fell from 75% to less than 50%. Results also differ across the seven segments based on their price sensitivity. The results of the analysis can also be used to help position the new service in each segment or country, particularly with respect to the relative emphasis on the three price complements. It is useful not only because it helps estimate demand, but also because it identifies market segments that cut across multiple countries. Multicountry market segmentation has also been examined by ter Hofstede *et al.* (1999) and Cohen and Neira (2004).

In a much earlier study relying only on secondary data, Armstrong (1970) developed a model to predict the sales of still cameras using 11 different variables:

- Beckerman's standard of living index
- Price of camera goods
- Buying units index (households per adult)
- Temperature
- Rainfall
- Proportion of children in population
- Growth in per capita income per year
- Total population
- Literacy rate
- Proportion of population age 15–64
- Proportion of nonagricultural employment

Data on these variables were collected for 30 countries for the period 1960–1965. A regression model was used to estimate model parameters based on data from 19 of the countries. A multiplicative or 'log–log' model was used to minimize percentage error and give 'unit-free' results. This provided an excellent fit to the data with $R^2$s of over 0.99. The predictive validity of the model was tested by applying the model to the remaining 11 countries and comparing the results with actual trade estimates. The average deviation was in the range of 31%. A backcasting procedure, using the model to predict sales in prior periods (1953–1955), was applied. This led to a reduction in mean absolute percentage error from 30 to 23% compared with backcasts only using trade data. This suggests that the model provides a reasonable fit with the data.

Such models require the availability of historical sales data for a number of countries and assume that similar factors underlie sales in all of these countries. They also assume that extrapolation of these data will enable prediction of future sales. This is likely to be the case only for products that are in the mature or stable phase of the product life cycle. The models also require that there is no change in the relationship between underlying factors and sales. Econometric procedures are only valid to the extent that no new events occur to change the underlying relationship. This presents a problem in international markets where change occurs very rapidly and at different rates in different parts of the world. Consequently, econometric procedures are likely to be subject to substantial error, particularly with the passage of time. In the example of still cameras given above, there has been a dramatic shift to digital cameras. While some of the same factors may be related to the sales of film-based still cameras and digital cameras, any new modeling attempts would have to take into account both products for accurate prediction. Also, disposable film-based cameras were not available at the time of the study and would have to be factored in as well.

## Use of Multiple Methods

In attempting to estimate market demand it is important to use more than one technique. Any given technique has certain biases or shortcomings. Further, the impact of the bias is likely to be nonuniform. A technique is likely to be accurate in some countries, underestimate demand in others and overstate demand in others. By using different methods to estimate demand, the convergence of the different approaches can be assessed. The highest and lowest estimates of demand can be used to establish an upper and lower boundary. One of the key benefits of using multiple methods is that it clearly establishes that there is not just one answer.

In arriving at estimates of market demand, it is equally important to rely on different data sources. If different data sources provide similar information then there is increased confidence in the basic input that is used to arrive at the estimates. However, comparable numbers from different sources may provide a false sense of independence, as many of the sources are based on basic data collected by the UN or World Bank.

The range of estimates of market potential can be quite divergent. Amine and Cavusgil (1986) conducted an actual trade audit of the size of the wallpaper market in Morocco. They looked at local production of wallpaper, then added imports and subtracted exports to arrive at the total size of the market. Employing two different techniques, they came up with estimates that suggested that the market potential was five times and thirteen times greater than the trade audit revealed. This suggests that marketing plans based on the larger estimates would have difficulty in meeting objectives and that investments made in developing the market would not payout.

## Assessing Market Interconnectedness

Up to this point, it has been assumed that country markets are independent and demand can be analyzed and predictions developed on a country-by-country basis. As markets become increasingly interrelated, it becomes important to assess how interrelated different country markets are. Changes in economic and market conditions in interconnected markets or competitor reactions in one market will have repercussions on trends and demand in another market. When a set of markets is highly interconnected, from a planning standpoint they should be treated as a whole and plans and estimates developed for all highly connected markets.

In considering the interconnectedness of markets, two different aspects need to be distinguished: (1) interconnectedness of geographical markets at the macroeconomic, product market or firm-specific level; and (2) interconnectedness across product businesses within a strategic planning unit. The first type of interconnectedness is of primary concern in demand estimation. Product business interconnectedness is relevant primarily in terms of defining the boundaries of the product business or industry for which estimates are to be made. Given the growth of communication and linkages between countries, assessment of geographical interconnectedness becomes increasingly critical. Here again, two aspects need to be considered: the extent to which markets are interlinked and the extent to which they are similar.

Markets are *linked* when they share common customers or competitors, have a high volume of trade with each other, can be reached through common distributors or media networks, or when actions in one market affect operations in another. Markets are *similar* where customers have the same tastes, interests or purchase behavior, and where market environments are similar regarding, for example, product or advertising regulation or media and distribution infrastructure.

Where markets are closely linked, they should be treated as one unit for the purposes of forecasting or demand estimation. Even where management cannot achieve cost efficiencies or synergies by integrating operations or pursuing a common strategy, actions by the firm itself, or by competitors, may affect operations in another market. Where markets are similar, actions in one market will not necessarily affect results in another, but demand estimates for one market, or relevant estimation parameters, may be extrapolated from one market to another.

Geographical markets can be linked in a number of ways. Often markets in close proximity are linked. Firms, including customers, suppliers, distributors and service organizations, may expand into neighboring markets, thereby linking them. Neighboring markets may share common media or have media spillover. Trade flows and other movements of people, or communication, are often high among neighboring countries, and are accentuated by trends toward regional market integration. In some cases, though this does not always occur, customers in proximate countries may exhibit similar behavior patterns.

**Table 4.9** Geographical market linkages

| Macroeconomic | Product market | Firm specific |
|---|---|---|
| Import/exports between countries | Flow of goods | Family branding/corporate name |
| Air traffic | Common distributor/retail organizations | Common production facilities |
| Mail flows | Gray markets and parallel importation | Common suppliers |
| Communication (media links) | Presence of same competition | Shared R&D expenditure |
| Network of service organizations | Presence of same customers | Shared warehouse facilities |
| Tourist flows | | Shared marketing expenditure |
| Geographical proximity | | Common salesforce |
| | | Shared distribution facilities |

*Source*: Douglas and Craig, 1996.

In assessing geographical market interconnectedness, two distinct levels or dimensions need to be distinguished: (1) linkages at the macroeconomic level, which include trade flows, the market infrastructure and regional market integration, reflecting the integration of the context in which a firm does business; and (2) links at the product market level, which include flows of goods or related services, parallel imports, common distributor networks and other factors. Sample indicators for measuring interconnectedness at these two levels as well as at the firm level are shown in Table 4.9.

## Macroeconomic Linkages

These relate to the business environment in which the firm operates. Important macroeconomic indicators include the volume of trade flows between two countries, membership in a regional trade organization and other economic ties. Other indicators include the volume of mail, amount of air traffic (freight and passenger) or the number of tourists from each country. Linkages between the market infrastructure might also be considered, including the rail and road network; a common network of service organizations, banks and other financial institutions; advertising agencies; research agencies; and the existence of common media, for example MTV is owned by Viacom, and

Sky TV in Europe, Star TV in Asia and Direct TV in the US are owned by News Corp. Existence of these linkages facilitates the adoption of a common strategy across markets and integration of the firm's operations. In cases where markets are very closely linked, they may operate as one.

## Product Market Linkages

The second level at which management should consider market interconnectedness is that of the product business. Here important indicators include the flow of goods and materials relating to the specific industry, parallel imports, existence of a common distributor network, and existence of common customers and competitors. In industrial markets, firms may operate in multiple markets and buy centrally for operations in different countries to ensure uniformity of supply or better purchasing terms. Equally, in consumer markets, there are highly mobile customers who travel extensively and look for the same brands and services wherever they are. This includes products such as cigarettes, toothpaste or pain relievers, as well as services such as car hire, hotel chains and telephone service. The existence of common competitors is also an important factor. While in some instances this parallels the existence of common customers, it does not always do so. Existence of common competitors also has an impact on the firm's positioning and ability to adapt strategy to local market conditions.

Most countries actively trade goods and services with other countries. The amount of trade with another country begins to capture one aspect of economic interconnectedness. Mutual trade reflects the degree of interdependence between the two economies. This can be examined at the aggregate level of the economy. Further, it can be refined and examined by specific industry sectors.

Macroeconomic data are very useful for assessing the interconnectedness at the country level. One measure of interconnectedness between any two countries is the exports and imports with another country as a percentage of a country's total exports and imports, or:

$$\text{Country B with country A} = \frac{\text{Exports to A} + \text{Imports from A}}{\text{Total exports of B} + \text{Total imports of B}}$$

To examine the relationship of country A with country B, the process would be reversed. The calculation can be done using total imports and exports or focus more narrowly on certain sectors of the economy.

**Table 4.10** Market interconnectedness for four European and four Asian countries: country import and exports as a percentage of total imports and exports

|  | Germany | France | Italy | UK | Japan | Korea | Thailand | Taiwan |
|---|---|---|---|---|---|---|---|---|
| Germany |  | 11.2[a] | 7.7 | 7.2 | 3.7 | 1.2 | 0.6 | 1.1 |
| France | 17.9[b] |  | 9.7 | 8.6 | 2.7 | 0.7 | 0.5 | 0.7 |
| Italy | 18.9 | 13.4 |  | 6.1 | 2.3 | 0.8 | 0.4 | 0.6 |
| UK | 13.3 | 9.0 | 4.6 |  | 4.2 | 0.9 | 0.6 | 0.8 |
| Japan | 4.4 | 1.6 | 1.3 | 2.7 |  | 6.2 | 1.5 | 5.6 |
| Korea | 4.9 | 1.3 | 1.3 | 2.0 | 19.1 |  | 1.3 | 2.5 |
| Thailand | 4.1 | 2.2 | 1.3 | 2.4 | 23.8 | 2.5 |  | 3.7 |
| Taiwan | 4.9 | 1.7 | 1.2 | 2.0 | 20.1 | 3.0 | 2.2 |  |
| Asia with Europe | 9.9 |  |  |  |  |  |  |  |
| Europe with Asia | 5.7 |  |  |  |  |  |  |  |

[a] Read 11.2% of Germany's exports and imports are with France.
[b] Read 17.9% of France's exports and imports are with Germany.

Since the relative size of the economies is rarely the same, the relationship will not be symmetrical. The calculation reflects the dependence of one country on another for its trade (imports and exports). If there is no dependence, the measure will be zero, and if there is complete dependence, the measure will be one. These numbers can also be interpreted as a simple percentage; that is, what percent of country A's exports and imports are with country B. Mutual interdependence can be assessed by averaging the two measures. In addition to computing this for all pairs of countries, it is also useful to consider groupings of countries. These may be informal groups or more formal trading groups such as NAFTA, the EU or the ASEAN countries.

To illustrate how these data can be used, the degree of interconnectedness was computed for eight different countries (see Table 4.10). The four European countries exhibit a greater degree of interdependence with each other than they do with the four Asian countries. Similarly, the four Asian countries exhibit a greater degree of interconnectedness with each other than they do with the European countries. Also Korea, Thailand and Taiwan are heavily dependent on Japan. As noted earlier, the relationship is not symmetrical, as Japan has a much larger economy than the other three Asian countries. When the countries are aggregated and the calculation of trade dependency run for the two groups, it suggests that the dependence of the Asian countries on the European countries is greater than the European countries on the Asian countries. The four European countries account for 9.9% of the total imports and exports with the four Asian countries. Looked at the other way, the four European countries derive only 5.7% of imports and exports from the four Asian countries.

Given their geographical proximity, it is not surprising that the European countries have a high degree of interconnectedness with each other. The same is true with the four Asian countries. However, there are some exceptions. Only 4.6% of the UK's imports and exports are with Italy. This is similar to the relationship of the four Asian countries to Germany. Thus, even among spatially dispersed countries there may be strong interdependencies, suggesting market opportunities as well as exposure to economic downturns elsewhere in the world.

While macroeconomic data are very useful for providing an overview of interconnectedness, the firm should also look at the interconnectedness of specific product markets. For example, it is useful to determine whether key customers are in multiple markets as well as where major competitors are. Assessing the location of key competitors will apply to both consumer and industrial markets. The location of key customers is more relevant in industrial markets given the dispersion of customers in consumer markets. However, the global expansion of major retailers, such as Wal-Mart, means that consumer markets are becoming more interconnected. Firms are almost forced to offer the same terms and conditions of sale to retailers as well as offer similar merchandise mixes.

In addition to examining interconnectedness of markets, market similarity should be assessed. As in assessing market interconnectedness, market similarity can be examined at two different levels: macroeconomic and product market.

## Macroeconomic Similarity

In assessing the similarity of the macroeconomic context of business, a wide variety of indicators can be used: economic indicators such as GNP or GDP; consumption expenditures per capita, such as steel consumption; energy consumption; demographic indicators, such as age distribution, population growth or urbanization; or sociocultural factors such as similarity of language or religion. The relevant indicators depend on the firm and the industry and need to be determined by management based on company objectives and product positioning. In addition, similarity of the marketing infrastructure, for example the role of organized mass distribution, the number of televisions, print media, transportation, availability of financial institutions or research agencies, needs to be examined, as these factors affect the ability to harmonize market strategy.

# Product Market Similarity

In the same way, various indicators can be used to assess similarity of the product market. These include, for example, product ownership for durables, industry sales volume and growth, stage in the product life cycle, market segmentation and breadth of product lines and product extensions, purchase frequency and amount, desired customer benefits and service requirements. Competitive market structure should also be considered, including number and size of competitors, market share of top three competitors, competitors' market positioning and pricing strategies. Again, relevant indicators would parallel those used in examining product market linkages, but focus on similarity of product market structure and customer and competitor behavior, rather than the linkages.

Market interconnectedness can be looked at in terms of firm-specific operations. However, this applies only in situations where the firm is already involved in those markets. In instances where the firm is considering which markets to enter, this type of information would not be available. The best alternative for assessing market entry would be to examine firms already operating in that market that engage in the same or similar types of businesses. However, in emerging market economies these may not exist.

Market similarity can be assessed on the same two levels as market interconnectedness. The major difference is that with similarity mutual interdependence does not necessarily exist; rather, similarity allows the firm to employ common strategies across multiple markets and enjoy certain scale economies. Most academic literature focusing on market similarity has used macroeconomic data to assess similarity (see Craig *et al.* (1992) for a representative study and brief literature review). One of the basic findings is that proximate countries tend to be more similar.

Similarity measures are relatively easy to capture, using standard multidimensional scaling packages (see Craig *et al.* (1992) for an illustration). However, the interpretation of output can be more problematic. There is often a tenuous leap from the data and their interpretation to the implications for marketing strategy. For this reason, it is more desirable to use product market and firm-specific data. This might include presence or absence of key competitors, stage in the product life cycle, rate of growth, industry rank and presence or absence of key customers. These data can be used to calculate a distance measure for input into multidimensional scaling. Alternatively, they can be used in tabular form, with each aspect rated on a scale from highly similar to highly dissimilar. Weights can also be assigned to distinguish between more and less important aspects.

# Summary

Secondary data can be highly useful in international marketing research. Due to the high cost of gathering primary data and the large number of countries that may be involved, the value of secondary data is greater and its uses more extensive than in domestic marketing research. In this chapter, three major uses of secondary data were identified: determining which countries to enter, developing estimates of demand in these countries, and assessing market interconnectedness.

In evaluating which countries to enter, two major approaches are appropriate. The first is based on clustering or rating countries based on environmental criteria. The second uses a customized approach geared to the specific product market, industry or company. While clustering or rating schemes can provide an initial approximation, adoption of a customized approach is essential before management commits resources. It is vital that the screening techniques used relate to specific corporate objectives and to the realities that management faces.

Demand estimation can be carried out in a variety of ways. Lead–lag analysis and econometric forecasting models both assume that data can be extrapolated over time from one country to another. A more crucial assumption underlying these approaches is that there are no major underlying changes in the factors influencing sales over time. To the extent that this is rarely the case in international markets, use of surrogate indicators or barometric procedures may be more desirable. Surrogate indicators are useful in markets where little data are available, market potential is limited, and relatively crude estimates will suffice. Barometric procedures provide more precise estimates at both the aggregate market level and for specific market segments. Ultimately, the most appropriate technique will depend on the availability of data and the nature of the product market.

Secondary data can be used to assess the extent of market interconnectedness. The extent to which two countries' economies are interrelated can be assessed using macroeconomic trade data and other data concerning flows between countries. Subject to the availability of industry and product market data, interconnectedness can be assessed at that level as well.

Secondary data perform an important function in international research. This is particularly significant in the initial evaluation of marketing opportunities and in identifying key countries or regions for in-depth examination. It provides a useful ongoing contribution in forecasting and identifying new opportunities for growth.

# References

Agarwal, M.K. (2003) Developing Global Segments and Forecasting Market Shares: A Simultaneous Approach Using Survey Data. *Journal of International Marketing*, **11**, 56–80.

Amine, L.S. and Cavusgil, S.T. (1986) Demand Estimation in a Developing Country Environment: Difficulties, Techniques and Examples. *Journal of the Market Research Society*, **28**, 43–65.

Armstrong, J.S. (1970) An Application of Econometric Models to International Marketing. *Journal of Marketing Research*, **7**, 190–198.

Barff, R.A. and Knight, P.L. (1998) Dynamic Shift-share Analysis. *Growth and Change*, **19**(Spring), 1–10.

Bass, F.M. (1969) A New Product Growth Model for Consumer Durables. *Management Science*, **15**, 215–227.

Cavusgil, S.T. (1997) Measuring the Potential of Emerging Markets. *Business Horizons*, **40**, 87–91.

Chow, G.C. (1960) Tests of Equality Between Sets of Coefficients in Two Linear Regressions. *Econometrica*, **28**, 591–605.

Cohen, S. and Neira, L. (2004) Measuring Preferences for Product Benefits across Countries. *Excellence 2004 in International Research*. Amsterdam, ESOMAR, pp. 1–22.

Craig, C.S., Douglas, S.P. and Grein, A. (1992) Patterns of Convergence and Divergence among Industrialized Nations. *Journal of International Business Studies*, Fourth Quarter, 773–787.

Dickensheets, R.J. (1963) Basic and Economical Approaches to International Marketing Research. In *Proceedings of American Marketing Association*. American Marketing Association, Chicago, pp. 359–377.

Douglas, S.P. and Craig, C.S. (1996) Global Portfolio Planning and Market Interconnectedness. *Journal of International Marketing*, **4**, 95–110.

Economist Intelligence Unit (1996) *Global: EIU Market Indexes, 1994.* Economist Intelligence Unit, London.

Eliashberg, J. and Helsen, K. (1994) Modeling Lead/Lag Phenomena in Global Marketing: The Case of VCRs. Working Paper, The Wharton School, Philadelphia, PA, June.

Erickson, L.G. (1963) Analyzing Brazilian Consumer Markets. *Business Topics*, **11**, 7–26.

Green, R.T. and Allaway, A.W. (1985) Identification of Export Opportunities: A Shift-share Approach. *Journal of Marketing*, **49**, 83–88.

Helsen, K., Jedidi, K. and DeSarbo, W.S. (1993) A New Approach to Country Segmentation Utilizing Multinational Diffusion Patterns. *Journal of Marketing*, **57**, 60–71.

Johansson, J.K. and Moinpour, R. (1977) Objective and Perceived Similarity of Pacific Rim Countries. *Columbia Journal of World Business*, **11**, 65–76.

Kogut, B. and Singh, H. (1988) The Effect of National Culture on the Choice of Entry Mode. *Journal of International Business Studies*, **19**, 411–432.

Lattin, J., Carroll, J.D. and Green, P.E. (2003) *Analyzing Multivariate Data.* Thompson Learning, Pacific Grove, CA.

Liander, B. (ed.) (1967) *Comparative Analysis for International Marketing.* Allyn & Bacon, Boston.

Lindberg, B.C. (1982) International Comparison of Growth in Demand for a New Durable Consumer Product. *Journal of Marketing Research*, **19**, 364–371.

Litvak, I.A. and Banting, P.M. (1968) A Conceptual Framework for International Business Arrangement. In King, R.L. (ed.) *Marketing and the New Science of Planning.* American Marketing Association, Chicago, pp. 460–467.

Narayandas, D. and Quelch, J.A. (1997) Orbital Sciences Corporation: ORBCOMM. Harvard Business School, Boston, MA, Case 9–598–027, p. 21.

Rao, V.R. and Steckel, J.H. (1998) *Analysis for Strategic Marketing*. Addison-Wesley, Reading, MA.

Rentz, J.O. and Reynolds, F.D. (1991) Forecasting the Effects of an Aging Population on Product Consumption: An Age-Period-Cohort Framework. *Journal of Marketing Research*, **28**, 355–360.

Rentz, J.O., Reynolds, F.D. and Stout, R.G. (1983) Analyzing Changing Consumption Patterns with Cohort Analysis. *Journal of Marketing Research*, **20**, 12–20.

Samli, C.A. (1977) An Approach for Estimating Market Potential in East Europe. *Journal of International Business Studies*, **8**, 49–53.

Sethi, S.P. (1971) Comparative Cluster Analysis for World Markets. *Journal of Marketing Research*, **8**, 348–354.

Sethi, S.P. and Curry, D. (1973) Variable and Object Clustering of Cross-Cultural Data: Some Implications for Comparative Research and Policy Formulation. In Sethi, S.P. and Sheth, J.N. (eds) *Multinational Business Operations*. Goodyear Publishing Company, Pacific Palisades, CA, 31–61.

Sheth, J. and Lutz, R. (1973) A Multivariate Model of Multinational Business Expansion. In Sethi, S.P. and Sheth, J.N. (eds) *Multinational Business Operations*. Goodyear Publishing Company, Pacific Palisades, CA, pp. 96–103.

Takada, H. and Jain, D. (1991) Cross-national Analysis of Diffusion of Consumer Durable Goods in Pacific Rim Countries. *Journal of Marketing*, **55**, 48–54.

ter Hofstede, F., Steenkamp, J-B.E.M. and Wedel, M. (1999) International Market Segmentation Based on Consumer-product Relations. *Journal of Marketing Research*, **36**, 1–17.

Williamson, R.B. (1980) New Tests of Shift-share Techniques. *Growth and Change*, **11**, 19–25.

Wilson, P. (2000) The Export Competitiveness of Dynamic Asian Economics 1983–95: A Dynamic Shift-share Approach. *Journal of Economic Studies*, **27**(8), November, 541–565.

# Chapter 5

# STRUCTURING PRIMARY DATA COLLECTION

## Introduction

Most research on international markets involves some primary data collection, which can include both qualitative and quantitative data. In undertaking such research, there are a number of design issues that the researcher needs to consider before conducting the research. As a first step, the relevant unit of analysis has to be clearly defined. This helps to minimize the impact of extraneous factors on the issues being studied. This is particularly critical in an international context, given the multiplicity and complexity of environmental and contextual influences that may affect the topic studied. The impact of these various influences needs to be clearly identified and isolated. Otherwise, findings will reflect spurious contextual differences, rather than real differences in the behavior studied.

In the past, the country was typically used as the relevant unit of analysis and comparisons were made between different countries. In essence, this amounts to viewing international or cross-cultural research as quasi-experiments in which countries are viewed as the relevant experimental groups (Campbell and Stanley, 1966) from which data are collected. Observed differences were then attributed to the different groups or contexts. This is, however, subject to a number of limitations as countries are not necessarily comparable or equivalent units and also may not be relevant depending on the nature of the study. Consequently, alternative units, including units both within and across countries, need to be considered.

Once the unit of analysis has been determined, the next step is to establish the overall structure of the research design. This entails determining the number and location of sites at which research will be conducted, as well as whether the impact of external or internal influences on behavior is to be examined. In addition, whether the study is to be conducted at multiple points over time also needs to be decided.

A final issue stems from the involvement of researchers from one cultural environment in conducting research in other sociocultural environments. This can lead to cultural bias. In particular, it is important to avoid problems of cultural bias in identifying and defining the research problem in different sociocultural environments, as well as in the interpretation of data from these environments. Diversity in language and in methods of communication among researchers from different sociocultural environments can give rise to miscommunication between researchers as well as between researchers and respondents from different cultural backgrounds.

# Defining the Unit of Analysis

A first priority in the research design is to define the unit of analysis. This establishes the parameters of the design in terms of the geographical scope, the characteristics of respondents and the situation or context in which data are collected (see Figure 5.1). As noted earlier, this is particularly critical in cross-cultural or cross-national research, since research is conducted in multiple sociocultural environments. Consequently, the equivalence of the unit in each environment needs to be considered. In addition, the unit should be clearly defined so as to be distinct from other units and free of contamination from other entities.

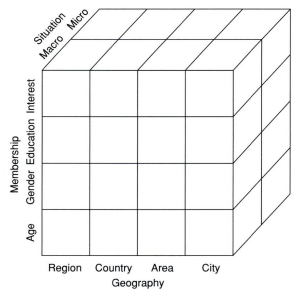

**Figure 5.1**    Defining the unit of analysis

# Issues in Selecting the Unit of Analysis

In many international marketing studies, the country is used as the basic unit of analysis in the research design. The country becomes the spatial unit from which samples are drawn, surveys or experiments designed and inferences made about similarities and differences. The country as a political and organizational entity provides a practical and convenient unit for data collection. Many secondary and industry data are available on a country-by-country basis. In a number of cases, countries also provide linguistic homogeneity and have an official language(s). In addition, as countries are customarily used as the unit of analysis, findings can be related to and interpreted in the light of previous research. However, while use of the country to define the geographical boundaries of the research setting is convenient, it does have unintended consequences.

## Relevance as a unit

First, use of the country assumes that it provides the relevant context or socioeconomic setting for the behavior studied. However, a more appropriate unit may be cities or regions or a specific linguistic grouping. In some instances, it is assumed that a country is synonymous with 'culture' where this is loosely viewed as implying 'national culture' (Hofstede, 2001). Countries may also not be the relevant unit for issues relating to activities that span national boundaries. As markets become increasingly integrated at both the product market and macroenvironmental level, studies may deal with issues such as the impact of global media or the Internet on customer purchase and information-seeking behavior, or the emergence of regional or global lifestyles, or transfer of information or market experience across national boundaries as in studies of patterns of international diffusion. Recent work in spatial segmentation has demonstrated that spatial segments can be identified across national boundaries (ter Hofstede *et al.*, 2002). For such studies, the existence of country boundaries may have little or no relevance, and the relevant spatial unit may be a continent or some other spatial configuration of markets.

## Independence

Use of the country as the unit of analysis also assumes that a country is an isolated or independent unit for the purpose of the behavior studied. As Galton noted in his remarks following E.B. Tylor's presentation of his classic paper on the cross-cultural method at the Royal Statistical Society in 1889, it is typically impossible to obtain cross-cultural sampling units that are independent of each other (Naroll, 1970). Supposedly culturally distinctive traits have often spread between neighboring or historically linked regions through diffusion or migration. This problem, apparent over 100 years ago, is even more significant in today's world where countries are interlinked by the spread of the Internet, e-mail, satellite media, as well as increasing waves of migration coupled with increasing regional economic integration.

Respondents, especially where these are students, are likely to have traveled to other countries or at a minimum have been exposed to ideas and influences emanating from other countries and cultures. Even respondents who have not traveled are exposed to images and information about other countries through television or print media. Consequently, findings relating to differences or similarities between countries, for example in relation to consumption or purchasing patterns, attitudes toward different foreign or global brands, may reflect factors such as consumer mobility and migration, spread of international retailers or the promotional activities of international marketers such as McDonald's, rather than national or country characteristics.

## Comparability of countries

Countries may also not be comparable as units relative to factors that may affect the phenomenon under study (for example size of the internal market, the nature of the market infrastructure, linguistic or cultural heritage, the degree of interconnectedness with other countries and geographical proximity). These factors are key elements of the market context, and as such play an important role in fashioning behavior in the marketplace. Consequently, the comparability of countries with regard to such factors needs to be carefully considered.

In some cases a country is selected as an exemplar of a particular category. When attitudes or behavior are being compared in individualistic vs collectivist societies, the US is often selected as an exemplar of an individualistic Western society, while an Asian society such as Singapore, Hong Kong, Thailand or Taiwan is selected as an exemplar of a collectivist society. Again, comparability needs to be assessed with regard to other confounding factors such as industrialization, political regime or education that may underlie or account for observed differences.

## Heterogeneity within countries

There is also typically substantial variation in attitudes and behavior *within* countries. Various studies have, for example, demonstrated a substantial degree of heterogeneity within countries (ter Hofstede *et al.*, 1999; ter Hofstede, 1999). In some cases, differences within countries may be greater than differences between countries. Even in relation to concepts that are defined in terms of country or national units, for example national culture, there may be considerable heterogeneity within countries. For example, based on Hofstede's measures of national culture, the US rates highly on individualism and low on power distance, and is commonly viewed in cross-cultural psychology and social psychology as exemplifying an individualistic society (Markus and Kitayama, 1991). However, a recent study examining differences in individualism and collectivism within the US, based on a number of sociodemographic measures, found evidence of substantial differences between different states and, in particular, of a greater degree of collectivism in the Deep South. This was hypothesized to be related to its history as an agrarian and slave society (Vandello and Cohen, 1999).

# Refining the Unit of Analysis

The limitations of the country as a unit of analysis have a number of important implications for the choice of units used in international marketing research. In the first place, they suggest the need for a broader definition of the unit of analysis, incorporating not only the geographical scope of the unit but also the nature of the population to be studied or sampled, as well as the time, location or occasion at which it is studied. Once the relevant components of the unit of analysis have been determined, the next step is to select units with regard to factors or characteristics that are relevant to or affect the behavior studied. At the same time, the unit selected should be comparable or equivalent in other respects that may have an impact on the behavior studied. Finally, it is important to ensure that the units are 'pure' and do not reflect other influences that may be a source of contamination and obscure the impact of the specific independent variables under study.

# Geographical Scope

In defining the unit of analysis in international markets, the most important component is its geographical scope. This is relatively straightforward and in essence entails delineating the geographical boundaries of the unit to be studied. As noted earlier, in the past the most commonly used unit has been the country. However, national markets are becoming increasingly integrated and links are established between these markets through political and economic initiatives. Advances in communications and logistics, as well as the increased mobility of people, goods and information across national borders, also serve to link markets. Consequently, use of other types of geographical units is becoming increasingly widespread.

For example, studies of attitudinal and behavioral patterns within regions have been conducted. Within the EU, availability of data on the different regions making up the EU has led to a number of studies examining differences in behavior patterns between regions. Consumer lifestyles, food consumption and washing habits in Western Europe (Audenaert and Steenkamp, 1996; CCA, 1996; van Herk, 2000) have all been studied. These have resulted in observation of significant differences between North and South (van Herk, 2000) and segmentation of markets based on differences between regions (ter Hofstede *et al.*, 2002).

In some instances, the world may be the relevant geographical unit. Studies of consumer lifestyles have been conducted in 71 countries worldwide based on consumer and family expenditure, savings and investment, education, eating and drinking habits, shopping behavior, leisure pursuits, personal care and clothing expenditure, media habits, transportation and tourism (Euromonitor, 2004). Behavior patterns of teenagers and upscale consumers have been studied worldwide. At the same time, the world may be used as the unit of analysis in business-to-business marketing research. This is particularly likely to occur in global industries such as aerospace, shipbuilding and chemicals, which are characterized by a relatively small number of manufacturers.

Research may also focus on units *within* countries, such as cities or urban areas in a region or worldwide. Increasingly, samples are taken from major urban areas within a region or worldwide to examine behavior patterns of urban consumers or urban consumers of a specific sociodemographic background. For example, consumption patterns of young urban professionals in Asian cities have been studied (Worthy, 1990). Particularly in emerging or developing countries, research focuses on urban consumers as they are more affluent and offer more attractive market potential than rural consumers, as well as being more accessible. Equally, differences between affluent urban consumers and rural consumers are becoming more marked in many countries. Ethnographic studies also commonly focus on a community within a region or country in a clearly defined geographical area. In essence, therefore, the geographical boundaries of the unit establish basic parameters for decisions relating to the sampling frame in survey research or where research will be conducted in ethnographic or qualitative research.

## *Membership Criteria*

The second component of the unit of analysis relates to the criteria for membership in the population to be studied. Here, the specific sociodemographic characteristics defining the study population need to be established in order to define the basis for sampling or for selecting respondents to be studied. Here, a distinction needs to be made between research concerned with individual consumers and that concerned with organizations; that is, businesses and nonprofit organizations. While in the case of consumers, membership is determined based on individual sociodemographic, attitudinal or lifestyle characteristics, such as age or gender, traditional or modern consumers, in the case of organizations, the definition is often more complex, entailing several levels or units within the organization. One level may, for example, relate to the industry or size of the organization, while another may relate to a specific type of manager, for instance senior executives or marketing managers within the organization.

Where the research examines a specific consumer population or subgroup in different locations, the unit of analysis may be defined based on demographic characteristics such as age, income, marital status or ethnic identity, and/or on consumption or purchase characteristics such as purchase frequency. For example, a researcher might be interested in comparing interests and consumption patterns of children aged 5–11 in urban middle-class households in Europe and Asia. While identifying the relevant age group is relatively unambiguous, defining middle-class households poses some difficulties. A definition based on household income will result in problems of equivalence due to differences in purchasing power between Europe and Asia, between countries within Europe or within Asia, and even between cities within a country. A definition based on occupation might be more appropriate, but will again give rise to some equivalence issues. Another alternative is to use income percentiles within countries – that is, households in the fourth quintile (upper 60–80%) of the income distribution – though this would need to be adjusted for differences in the skewedness of the distribution.

A study population might also be defined based on values, interests, lifestyles or consumption-related behavior, such as shopping or information seeking. For example, attention might be focused on examining the attitudes and purchase behavior of ecologically concerned consumers worldwide, or on comparing characteristics of innovators in different countries, or examining materialist consumption in different cultures. Again, issues of equivalence need to be considered. Ecological concerns or innovative behavior might not be expressed in the same way in different countries; the concept of materialism may not have the same meaning nor be reflected in the same type of products or consumption behavior in different cultures.

In the case of organizations, the relevant population might be defined based on organizational demographics such as size, industry, national origin, importance of international sales, profit vs nonprofit and so on. In some instances, attention may be focused on attitudinal factors or organizational culture might be used rather than, or in addition to, organizational demographics. For example, research might focus on comparing the performance and prevalence of firms characterized by specific types of organizational cultures across countries (Deshpandé and Farley, 2004).

In some cases, a hierarchical design may be used. First, the characteristics of the organization to be studied are established and then those of relevant respondents or units within the organization. For example, a distinction might be made between organizations based on size. Organizations might first be divided in small, medium and large organizations and then between different types of respondents within each type of organization. At the individual respondent level, a study might focus on a particular respondent class, such as senior marketing executives, brand managers, sales persons or factory workers; or on examining relations between two groups, such as managers or workers, or senior managers and marketing managers; or on comparing their behavior. Alternatively, research might center on different units within a firm or organization, for example retail or service outlets, or managers at corporate headquarters versus country managers or managers of regional sales offices.

# Situational Context

The third component of the unit of analysis is the situational context. This relates to the specific environment, time and place at which the unit of analysis is studied. 'Context' can include various levels of aggregation, ranging from the broad sociocultural setting or macro context in which the unit is embedded, to the micro context – that is, cities, neighborhoods and so on – to the specific situation or occasion on which the research is conducted.

At the *macro* level, if the geographical unit is a country, it is important to identify country characteristics that might affect the behavior studied. For example, differences may exist between countries at different levels of socioeconomic development, or between emerging, newly industrialized nations, transition economies and highly developed economies, which are likely to affect the attitudes or behavior examined. Equally, countries might belong to different linguistic groupings, such as Scandinavian, Spanish-speaking, English-speaking or Chinese-speaking countries, which imply distinct cultural backgrounds. This might underlie differences in the attitudes or behavior studied, especially insofar as language is a key conduit of culture. Consequently, it is important to sample multiple sites within each grouping or type of macro context, to gain some understanding of the impact this might have on research findings.

The situational context might also be specified at the *micro* level, in terms of city units, urban versus rural areas, suburban neighborhoods or outdoor markets, each of which provides a specific environment shaping purchase and consumption patterns. Equally, the climatic context or season might be relevant, insofar as climatic conditions are often important determinants of lifestyle and cultural artifacts. Another relevant factor might be the social setting; that is, whether the study was conducted in a work or business setting, while actually shopping, or in respondents' homes.

In some cases, the specific occasion and time at which research is conducted may need to be specified. For example, when comparing behavior associated with rituals such as weddings or funerals or gift giving across countries or cultures, the relevant occasion will need to be specified, as will the equivalence of different aspects such as the duration or nature of participation in the ritual. Similarly, in the case of business-to-business research, the situation in which behavior is studied may need to be specified. For example, in comparing the negotiating skills of sales people across countries, the type of negotiation and relevant participants will need to be indicated.

# Selecting Units of Analysis

Once the various components of the unit of analysis have been clearly identified, the next step is to select the relevant units to be considered. It is important to ensure that these are clearly defined so as to reflect variation on the key characteristics of interest, as well as comparability with regard to other characteristics. At the same time, it is crucial to design and select units so as to eliminate potential sources of contamination.

## *Purposive Selection*

An important consideration in selecting units of analysis is that they should be purposively selected relevant to the characteristics or variables of interest, and at the same time be comparable relative to other factors. The range of units selected should therefore reflect variation on the factor of interest. If, for example, attention is centered on comparing differences in the impact of intrapersonal influence on purchasing decisions in collectivist and individualistic cultures, a set of cultures scoring high on individualism or selected as prototypes of individualist cultures should be compared with a set of cultures scoring high on collectivism. The importance of personal influence in the two sets of cultures could then be compared, and observed differences attributed to collectivism versus individualism. If, at the same time, the two sets of cultures were balanced so that one or more of the cultures in each set was high on power distance and one or more low on power distance, the impact of power distance and the interaction between individualism/collectivism and power distance on intrapersonal influence could also be examined. It is, however, important to ensure that cultures are equivalent with regard to other factors that might affect the degree of intrapersonal influence, for example the degree of horizontal integration in society, to ensure that such factors do not account for observed differences and thus confound results.

Sociocultural settings may be purposively selected based on some key contextual variables assumed to affect variation in the patterning and/or frequency of the behavior or attitude studied. For example, the frequency with which different types of organizational cultures occur in Western vs Asian countries might be compared. In this case, it might be expected that while all types of organizational cultures occur in both Western and Asian cultures, consensual organizational cultures will occur more frequently in Asian contexts and competitive organizational types in Western or industrialized country settings (Deshpandé *et al.*, 2000). For example, in studying the impact of senior management style on marketing and production management involvement in new product decisions, differences might be observed between consensual and competitive organizational types as well as between Western and Asian organizations.

Similarly, Rose (1999), in comparing consumer socialization and parental style in the US and Japan, hypothesized that differences would exist in the consumer socialization process due to societal differences. In the US, an individualistic self-oriented society, socialization was expected to be characterized by greater emphasis on autonomy compared with Japan, a collectivist interdependent society, where a more patient maturational and protective approach to parenting was anticipated.

## *Independence*

In addition to carefully selecting the unit relative to the purpose of the research, it is also important to ensure that units are independent and free from contamination by other factors that may influence the behavior studied. For example, where a comparison is made between two or more cultures in relation to cultural artifacts, modes of behavior or communication, it is important to control for the degree of cultural intrapenetration in either culture. Cultural intrapenetration can occur in two ways: first, in terms of the extent to which individuals from a country have traveled to other countries and hence are familiar with the mores, artifacts and behavior of other cultures; and second, in terms of the extent to which a society is exposed to other cultures through mass media, the Internet, foreign tourism and other communication links.

Increasingly, individuals are traveling to other countries whether for pleasure, study or business. Foreign exchanges and programs for students and faculty are on the increase as well as foreign tourism, particularly to more distant lesser-known countries, while business is taking business travelers even farther afield. At the same time, communication links between different countries are multiplying at an increasingly rapid rate. With the advent of mobile phones, even remote villages can readily be linked into telecommunication networks. Global media are also reaching an ever-broader audience. As a result, even individuals who do not travel are becoming exposed to events and ways of life in other countries. This makes it important to assess cultural interpenetration based, for example, on measures of the degree to which respondents have been directly or indirectly exposed to other cultures. If, in a survey, those with a high degree of exposure respond differently from those with low exposure, then responses need to be adjusted accordingly. If there is a generally high level of cultural interpenetration in the sample, interpretation of findings should reflect this and their generalizability would be open to some question.

# Structuring the Research Design

Once the unit of analysis has been determined in terms of its geographical scope, the criteria for membership and the situational context, the next step is to determine the structure of the research design. As noted earlier, this is important in international marketing research, insofar as research is conducted in different sociocultural settings and economic contexts. Consequently, the research design has to be structured so that the impact of these multiple influences is clearly identified and possible contamination of findings avoided.

In general, four types of structures can be identified. The first consists of studies conducted at a single site or foreign location. The second and most common type of study involves a static comparison of units located at different geographical sites and different situational or macro contexts. A third involves the impact of exposure to direct or indirect influences from other cultures on attitudes or behavior patterns associated with a given culture or subculture. This type of study can also be longitudinal, though examples are rare. The fourth type of study examines how attitudes, interest and behavior change as a respondent or group moves from one culture to another. While this schema is not intended to be either all-inclusive or definitive, it provides a means of classifying different types of research designs.

# Single-site Studies

The first type of study is one that is conducted in a single country, but where an implicit comparison is made relative to other countries. This may occur where a researcher from one country examines behavior in another country or in commercial research where a study is commissioned by a foreign firm. Academic researchers who conduct ethnographic studies often focus on a single site. While these studies do not deal explicitly with the issues of comparability and equivalence, they do so implicitly. The underlying assumption is that there are real differences between the home country and the foreign country that are not a function of the method employed. With only one site and no explicit comparison, it is not possible to test the validity of this implicit assumption.

Going beyond the implicit assumption, there are also basic issues related to how the research is carried out. Often there is limited involvement on the part of individuals from the home country. A foreign research supplier typically handles all aspects of the research. Alternatively, a research supplier in the home market may act as an intermediary, making all the arrangements with a correspondent supplier in the foreign market to conduct the research and provide a report in the home-country language. However, without attention to the full range of issues necessary to produce comparable results, the findings may be somewhat misleading and biased.

# Multiple-site Studies

Examining units at different geographical sites is the design most frequently used in international research by both academic and commercial researchers. In general, the purpose of the study is to examine variation in attitudes or behavior across geographical settings. Studies have, for example, been conducted comparing the behavior of elite consumers worldwide (Amine, 1993) and comparing lifestyles in 71 countries (Euromonitor, 2004). In some cases, research is explicitly designed to study the impact of the sociocultural setting on the behavior of interest. In this case, sites from different sociocultural settings are selected. For example, the role of mothers in gift giving in Anglo-Celtic, Sino-Vietnamese and Israeli culture has been compared (Hill and Romm, 1996).

In conducting such studies, a key issue is to isolate the influence of the broader sociocultural setting or macro culture on the behavior studied. For example, in examining the attitude, values and consumption behavior of Jewish consumers in different countries, it is important to identify the extent to which these reflect the specific macro culture and situational context to which they belong as well as their Jewish identity. The product symbols and consumption patterns of Jewish New Yorkers are in part a reflection of US culture, as well as the New York context, their level of affluence and country of origin. Similarly, consumption patterns of Jewish consumers in Paris or London are influenced by their European heritage, their urban location, as well as their socioeconomic or occupational status.

In Figure 5.2, Jewish consumers of similar socioeconomic or occupational groupings in Paris, Milan and London (units 1, 2 and 3, respectively) are compared with Jewish consumers of equivalent status in New York and Chicago (units 4 and 5). The Paris/Milan/London comparison helps pinpoint the impact of the Western European Jewish heritage on behavior, through similarities and commonalties observed at all three sites. The Paris/Milan/London versus New York/Chicago comparison helps to isolate differences due to the Western European versus American Jewish heritage. Identifying the national origin of Jewish consumers, and the countries where their families

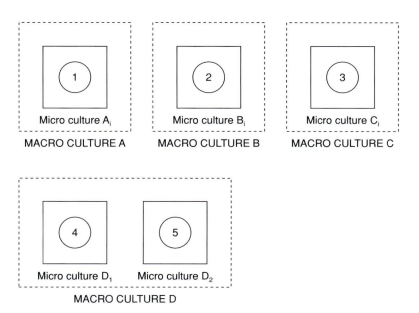

**Figure 5.2**  Multisite cross-cultural studies. Circles indicate a culti-unit
*Source*: Douglas and Craig, 1997.

originated, in order to trace the impact of other heritages such as Russian or Polish may also provide further insights.

In this type of study it is important to identify the confounding effect of situation-specific variables. For example, Jewish teenagers may adopt the values and preferences of global teenagers when purchasing music, or in their choice of leisure activities or clothing, but in relation to food consumption they may exhibit preferences similar to those of their Jewish families. Similarly, on formal occasions such as weddings, Bar Mitzvahs or family dinners, they may conform more closely to the practices of Jewish culture, while with friends they may behave like other teenagers.

The confounding effect of multiple influences implies that in defining the unit of analysis, it is important not only to specify criteria for membership in the study population, but also to identify overlapping membership in other units that might affect their behavior. Consumers often belong to several different groups that might include ethnic, linguistic or religious groups, and they have multiple identities. Thus, a Catholic French Swiss teenager is a member of the French Swiss culture, the Catholic French culture and the European teen culture.

Individuals vary in the strength of their identification with a given cultural group. Some may not identify at all with a specific group to which they belong. Others may identify strongly with multiple groupings. For example, a Muslim Pakistani doctor might identify strongly with his religion as well as his country of origin and the medical profession, or alternatively just one or none of these. It is, therefore, important to identify and isolate the impact of these different influences, and try to determine which identity is operant in a given situation.

## *External Influence Studies*

The third type of study focuses explicitly on examining external contextual influences on behavior. For example, the effect of travel to or living in other cultures on the values, attitudes and product preferences of students might be studied. Such influences can either be direct or indirect. Direct influences arise when an individual travels to or lives for a period of time in another sociocultural setting. Equally, executives working in a foreign country are exposed to the different management styles and negotiating behavior of organizations in another culture and may absorb or adapt to these practices. Indirect influences, on the other hand, arise from passive exposure to mass media, information or other stimuli emanating from other sociocultural settings (Belk, 1988). For example, the impact of exposure to television advertising by Western marketers on product preferences or lifestyle aspirations of Asian teenagers might be studied.

In studying direct influences, use of a longitudinal design may be desirable. For example, in Figure 5.3a attitudes and behavior of members of a specific group or subculture are examined, before and after travel to another macro culture (F). An alternative design is to compare attitudes and behavior of members of a group or subculture who have been exposed to external influences. Two groups could be identified, those traveling to or visiting another culture for a period of time, and members of the same group who have had little or no exposure to external influences. These two groups would then be compared on relevant variables. In this latter type of design it is important to check for self-selection bias; that is, that members exposed to external influences do not differ in some systematic way, for example have higher motivation levels, more active lifestyles or more inquiring minds than those not exposed. In Figure 5.3a this is represented by the shaded area versus

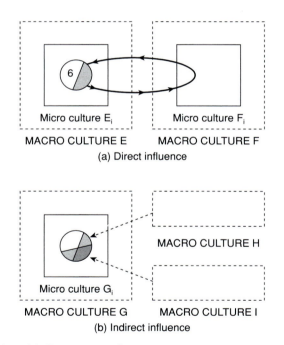

**Figure 5.3**  External cultural influence studies
——, indicates travel to a different macro culture; ----, indicates mass media and communication influence; circles indicate a culti-unit.
*Source*: Douglas and Craig, 1997.

the nonshaded area of culti-unit 6. A culti-unit can be defined in terms of the ethnic, demographic, racial, religious or socioeconomic characteristics of a group. It may also be defined in terms of specific interests or activities, which provide a common bond and similar values. It represents a way to further refine the definition of the unit of analysis for cross-cultural research.

Individuals can be passively exposed to external influences through mass media from other countries, for example by satellite television and foreign magazines. For instance, the impact of exposure to television programming from the West on the brand preferences of consumers in Eastern Europe might be examined. In Figure 5.3b, some individuals belonging to culti-unit 7 in sociocultural setting G are shown being influenced by mass media from culture H, others by media from culture I and some by both (the darkened area).

In examining the impact of external influences, an important issue is that of *cultural interpenetration* (Andreasen, 1990). Waves of migration resulting in increased interaction and communication between different cultural groupings, reinforced by marriage, friendship or other close association, tend to blur cultural boundaries and render demarcation of external influences increasingly difficult. At the same time, immigrants not only assimilate the values and behavior patterns of their host culture, but also introduce ideas and behavior from their culture of origin, which are in turn picked up by members of the host culture. As a result, cultural values, identities and characteristic behavior patterns are evolving over time at both a societal and individual level. Consequently, the task of isolating the impact of external influences on behavior has become increasingly complex and challenging.

## *Transitional Studies*

The fourth type of study deals with transition from one sociocultural group or setting to another, for example through migration to another country (Figure 5.4). Of particular interest in this type of study are the process and speed with which change takes place. For example, interest might be centered on comparing the speed with which immigrant families from Morocco (macro unit J) and Vietnam (macro culture L) become assimilated into the French macro culture (K). Here, the existence of strong and weak links with the macro culture will influence the speed of this process (Granovetter, 1973). For example, individuals or members of the unit may develop links or weak ties to the macro culture such as learning the language, or joining social or professional associations whose members are predominantly from the new culture. As a result, they are likely to absorb values and behavior patterns of that culture more rapidly than those who retain strong ties with

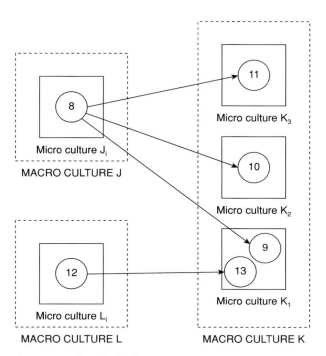

**Figure 5.4**   Transitional cross-cultural studies
——, indicates migration to another macro culture; circles indicate a culti-unit.
*Source*: Douglas and Craig, 1997.

members of their original culture. Similarly, if they establish their own social infrastructure within the macro culture by setting up their own social institutions, schools, banks and retail infrastructure, the process of assimilation is likely to be retarded.

One issue to be considered in transitional studies is that of *maturation*. As an individual moves from one sociocultural setting to another, aging or maturation occurs at the same time as the transition process. This may lead to change in attitudes or behavior. For example, as individuals age they typically become more conservative and tendencies toward ethnocentrism become more pronounced. One way of capturing this effect is through a cross-sectional design comparing the behavior of different age cohorts from the same sociocultural setting. In general, a longitudinal study provides a better means of tracking the effects of maturation and isolating possible confounds, as changes in the behavior of the same respondent can be assessed over time. For example, changes in the attitudes and consumption behavior of young immigrants as they grow up and establish their own households in a new community or culture might be studied over time. Changes in the macro culture as well as in other groups of the community might also be used as a benchmark.

Each of these types of study provides insights into the influence of the sociocultural setting on consumption behavior. Single-site studies help in probing the impact of the sociocultural setting or macro context on attitudes and behavior. Multiple-site studies are the more commonly used and provide insights into the broader cultural setting, which acts as a backdrop against which consumption behavior occurs. In particular, they add to knowledge about variation in attitudes and behavior across different geographical areas and settings. External influence studies shed light on how cultural influences affect behavior and more specifically how the forces underlying cultural change develop and mature over time. Transitional studies provide the richest insights into change as an individual or group is exposed to a new culture and both adapts to it and at the same time introduces a new stimulus that effects internal change.

# Cultural Bias in Research Design, Communication and Interpretation

A final issue to be considered in establishing the research design relates to the composition of the research team undertaking the study. The composition of the team also interacts with the units of analysis being studied. Depending on the units selected, the composition of the team may vary to minimize cultural bias. International marketing research typically involves researchers from one cultural environment conducting research in another cultural environment, or communicating with researchers from another cultural environment. A researcher may not always understand, or correctly interpret, information from another culture (Hall, 1959; Ricks, 1983). Miscommunication among researchers can arise due to differences in styles or modes of communication in different cultures.

In international marketing research, there is always a danger of miscommunication or misinterpretation due to the existence of what has been called the *self-referent cultural* bias (Lee, 1966). In other words, there is always a tendency for a researcher to perceive or interpret phenomena or behavior observed in other countries and cultures in terms of his or her own cultural referents. This means that there is always some risk of bias in research design or interpretation of data collected across different sociocultural settings.

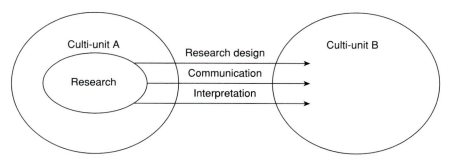

**Figure 5.5**   Cultural bias in multicountry research

Research bias is likely to be particularly acute where a researcher is investigating an unfamiliar sociocultural environment where he or she lacks experience. As, however, the researcher builds up experience and familiarity with different markets, he or she is likely to develop increased sensitivity, which may carry over to other similar markets, in a similar linguistic or cultural group or region. For example, experience in conducting research in Japan might be helpful in South Korea, or experience in Saudi Arabia helpful relative to other Middle Eastern markets.

Cultural bias can affect various aspects of the research process. Figure 5.5 shows research being conducted in culti-units A and B by a researcher in culti-unit A. Cultural bias may start in the design of the research as the researcher designs the research in culti-unit B with reference to the cultural norms and perspective of culti-unit A. It may also manifest itself in the communication between the researcher, the individuals who conduct the research and ultimately with respondents. Finally, cultural bias may enter into the interpretation of results. Even though the research is conducted in two different culti-units, since the research is directed from culti-unit A the biases and perspective of culti-unit A will be imposed on culti-unit B.

# Research Design

Failure to appreciate adequately cultural nuances in other countries, such as differences in the way various attitudes are expressed or what a particular behavior means, can be a major hindrance in the design of effective international marketing research. In particular, it is important to understand the values and cultural behavior patterns underlying consumption and product usage, and how these affect product preferences and market response patterns.

Lack of attention to such factors can lead to designs that do not emphasize sufficiently the need for exploratory research to identify relevant research questions and establish construct equivalence, as well as appropriate operational definitions or measures of these. In particular, there may be a lack of sensitivity to the importance of adapting research instruments to specific sociocultural environments.

# Communication

Communication problems can arise between researchers from two different cultural environments who may perceive the research problem and key issues differently. Their training, experience and frame of reference all contribute to the framing of the research issues and may result in difficulty in communicating how the research should be conducted and interpreting the results once it is completed. If a researcher is using local interviewers, there may be difficulty in communicating how the research should be executed. In other words, it may be difficult for a researcher from one cultural environment to know whether someone from another environment has effectively understood the task or question. At the same time, respondents may have difficulty interpreting the meaning of questions framed by a researcher from another cultural background. Consequently it may be difficult to work out whether a response reflects instrument error or is valid, particularly if the response is not one that has been given before or is not the one expected.

# Interpretation

A researcher lacking familiarity with another cultural environment may misinterpret or misunderstand data relating to that culture. Particularly where the attitudes or behavior expressed differ from those prevalent or expected in the researcher's own culture, he or she may have difficulty in knowing how to interpret them. Suppose, for example, a respondent attaches little value to innovation or expresses conservative opinions about sexual behavior. The question then arises as to how this will affect market response. Does this, for example, imply that the respondent will react negatively to a new product or to appeals to sex?

A number of different solutions to deal with the problem of cultural bias have been proposed. One procedure suggests the following four steps (Lee, 1966):

*Step 1.* Define the business problem or goal in terms of domestic cultural traits, habits or norms.

*Step 2.* Define the business problem or goal in terms of the foreign cultural traits, habits or norms. Make no judgments.

*Step 3.* Isolate the self-referent cultural (SRC) influence in the problem and examine it carefully to see how it complicates the problem.

*Step 4.* Redefine the problem without the SRC influence and solve it for the foreign market situation.

A major limitation of this approach lies in Step 2. This assumes that the researcher *can* define the problem in terms of the foreign environment. However, the problem may lie precisely in the researcher's lack of sensitivity to such cultural nuances.

Another alternative is to collaborate with researchers from other cultural backgrounds, preferably those where the study is being conducted, in the design, collection and interpretation of the research. Here it is important to involve other researchers early in the research design, for example in the definition and formulation of the research problem, as well as in the definition of concepts and design of operational measures. This helps to identify cultural-specific concepts, as well as in decentering concepts and forestalling introduction of a cultural bias in research design.

Frequently, however, collaboration with researchers in other environments begins at the implementation stage, *after* the research has been designed. Often a researcher starts a research project, designs a questionnaire and then enlists the cooperation of researchers in other countries in administering the questionnaire (or in some cases conducting qualitative research). While this helps to minimize bias at the data interpretation stage, there may still be a strong pseudo-etic bias in research design. Involvement of collaborators in the early stages of research design is critical, although this may be somewhat cumbersome and time consuming. It may add to the organizational complexity, as well as giving rise to communication problems. In particular, lengthy discussion may arise with regard to issues such as the need for culture-specific items or use of culture-specific measures.

Malhotra and Bartels (2002) suggest an approach to deal with a specific aspect of CSR that affects survey research. Typically, a researcher looking at product preferences or attitudes begins with a set of attributes that have been successfully used in one country. These attributes are then used in the second country. However, there are considerable differences in the salience of attributes and whether particular attributes are used in making evaluations (Malhotra *et al.*, 1994). Choosing certain attributes and not choosing others interjects an element of bias into the research.

To deal with the problem of pre-specifying attributes, Malhotra and Bartels (2002) propose a nonattribute-based correspondence analysis. The procedure begins by having respondents sort pictures of the various brands of a product category into piles. Each pile represents a grouping based on the respondent's belief concerning the similarity of the brands. If a pair of brands are in the same pile they are considered similar and coded as 1. If they are in different piles they are considered dissimilar and coded 0. The similarity matrices for each individual are aggregated to create a similarity matrix for all brands considered in the study. The overall similarities matrix is used as input into a nonattribute-based correspondence analysis to develop a perceptual map of the different brands. After the output is obtained, the different axes have to be labeled to interpret the dimensions. This presents an intriguing problem, as researchers from different countries may interpret the dimensions differently. In order to label the dimensions more accurately, Malhotra and Bartels propose asking respondents to describe the brands on objective criteria. This helps label the axes and ensures that the labeling is guided by local understanding of the objects.

In essence, cultural bias is probably one of the most difficult and insidious problems to deal with in cross-cultural and cross-national research. Yet, it is also one of the most critical if further progress is to be made in broadening understanding of attitudinal and behavioral phenomena across a wide range of divergent sociocultural settings.

# Summary

In laying the conceptual foundations, a critical issue is the unit of analysis. This establishes the geographical scope of the unit as well as the membership criteria and the situation or context in which data are to be collected. Here, it is important to establish their equivalence in each research context, as well as to select units purposively relative to the characteristics or objectives of the study and to ensure that units are independent and free from contamination by other factors such as cultural intrapenetration, which may influence the behavior studied.

Next, the structure of the research design has to be determined. This involves deciding on the number of sites or research contexts at which data will be collected as well as whether the impact of direct or indirect influences will be examined. A final factor is whether research examines change in behavior patterns over time. Based on these factors, four different types of research design can be identified: single-site, multiple-site, external influence and transitional studies.

Finally, the potential for cultural bias due to the conduct of research in a multicountry environment needs to be assessed. This arises from a researcher interpreting research issues, events or data in other cultures in terms of his or her own culture. Ideally, therefore, research should involve the collaboration of researchers from different national and cultural backgrounds. Comparisons of different perceptions of relevant factors to be examined, appropriate measures of these and interpretation of data collected can prove helpful in identifying possible cultural biases and 'decentering' the effect of a specific country or culture.

# References

Amine, L.S. (1993) Global Marketing to Upscale Consumers. In Hassan, S. and Blackwell, R.D. (eds) *Global Marketing, Perspectives and Cases*. Harcourt Brace, Fort Worth.

Andreasen, A.R. (1990) Cultural Interpretation: A Critical Consumer Research Issue for the 1990s. *Advances in Consumer Research*, **3**, 185–196.

Audenaert, A. and Steenkamp, J-B.E.M. (1996) Qualitative Elicitation, Validation and Cross-cultural Comparison of Means–End Chains for Three Food Products. Working Paper No. 9651, Katholieke Universiteit, Leuven.

Belk, R.W. (1988) Third World Consumer Culture. *Research in Marketing*, Supplement 4, 103–127.

Campbell, D.T. and Stanley, J.C. (1966) *Experimental and Quasi-experimental Designs for Research*. Rand McNally, Chicago.

Cattell, R.B. (1949) The Dimensions of Culture Patterns by Factorization of National Characters. *Journal of Abnormal and Social Psychology*, **44**, 443–469.

CCA (1996) *Les Euro-Styles*. CCA, Paris.

Deshpandé, R., Farley, J.U. and Webster, F.E. Jr. (2000) Triad Lessons: Generalizing Results on High Performance Firms in Five Business-to-Business Markets. *International Journal of Research in Marketing*, **17**, 353–362.

Deshpandé, R. and Farley, J.U. (2004) Organizational Culture, Market Orientation, Innovativeness and Firm Performance: An International Odyssey. *International Journal of Research in Marketing*, **21**, March, 3–22.

Granovetter, M.S. (1973) The Strength of Weak Ties. *American Journal of Sociology*, **78**, 1360–1380.

Hall, E.T. (1959) *The Silent Language*. Doubleday, Garden City, NY.

Hill, C. and Romm, C.T. (1996) The Role of Mothers as Gift Givers: A Comparison across Three Cultures. In Corfman, K.P. and Lynch, J.G. (ed.) *Advances in Consumer Research*, 23. Association for Consumer Research, Provo, UT.

Hofstede, G. (2001) *Culture's Consequences*. 2nd edition, Sage, Thousand Oaks, CA.

Johnson, E.G. and Tomiie, T. (1985) The Development of Color-naming in Four- to Seven-year Old Children: A Cross-cultural Study. *Psychologia – An International Journal of Psychology in the Orient*, **28**, 216–227.

Lee, J.A. (1966) Cultural Analysis of Overseas Operations. *Harvard Business Review*, **44**, 106–114.

Lonner, W.J. and Adamopoulos, J. (1997) Culture as an Antecedent to Behavior. In Berry, J.W., Poortinga, Y.H. and Pandey, J. (eds) *Handbook of Cross-cultural Psychology*, Vol. 2. Allyn & Bacon, Boston.

Mao, L.R. (1994) Beyond Politeness Theory: 'Face' Revisited and Renewed. *Journal of Pragmatics*, **21**, 451–486.

Malhotra, N.K., Ulgado, F., Agarwal, J. and Baalbaki, I. (1994) International Services Marketing: A Comparative Evaluation of the Dimensions of Service Quality between Developed and Developing Countries. *International Marketing Review*, **11**(2), 5–15.

Malhotra, N.K. and Bartels, B.C. (2002) Overcoming the Attribute Prespecification Bias in International Marketing Research by Using Non-attribute-based Correspondence Analysis. *International Marketing Review*, **19**(1), 65–79.

Markus, H.R. and Kitayama, S. (1991) Culture and the Self: Implications for Cognition, Emotion and Motivation. *Psychological Review*, **98**, 224–253.

McNeil, D.G. (1996) This $40 Crank-up Radio Lets Rival Africa Tune In. *New York Times*, 16 February, A1–A4.

Mullen, M. (1995) Diagnosing Measurement Equivalence in Cross-National Research. *Journal of International Business Studies*, Third Quarter, 573–596.

Naroll, R. (1970) The Culture-bearing Unit in Cross-cultural Surveys. In Naroll, R. and Cohen R. (eds) *A Handbook of Method in Cultural Anthropology*, Natural History Press, New York.

Pike, K. (1966) *Language in Relation to a Unified Theory of the Structure of Human Behavior*. Mouton, The Hague.

Ricks, D.A. (1983) *Big Business Blunders*. Dow Jones-Irwin, Homewood, IL.

Rose, G. (1999) Consumer Socialization, Parental Style and Developmental Variables in the United States and Japan. *Journal of Marketing*, **63**, July, 105–119.

ter Hofstede, F. (1999) *Essays in International Market Segmentation*. PhD thesis, Wageningen University. Universal Press, Veenendaal, Netherlands.

ter Hofstede, F., Steenkamp, J-B.E.M. and Wedel, M. (1999) International Market Segmentation Based on Consumer-product Relations. *Journal of Marketing Research*, **36**, February, 1–17.

ter Hofstede, F., Wedel, M. and Steenkamp, J-B.E.M. (2002) Identifying Spatial Segments in International Markets. *Marketing Science*, **21**(2), 160–177.

van Herk, H. (2000) Equivalence in a Cross-national Context: Methodological and Empirical Issues in Marketing Research. H. van Herk, Zeewolde, Netherlands.

Vandello, J.A. and Cohen, D. (1999) Patterns of Individualism and Collectivism across the United States. *Journal of Personality and Social Psychology*, 77(2), 279–292.

Worthy, F.S. (1990) Asia's New Yuppies. *Fortune*, 4 June.

www.euromonitor.com

# Chapter 6

# ESTABLISHING THE COMPARABILITY OF MULTICOUNTRY DATA

## Introduction

Once the unit of analysis has been clearly defined and the basic parameters of the research design determined, the next step is to establish the comparability of the constructs to be studied as well as measures of these constructs. Comparability in this sense is defined as data that have, as far as possible, the same meaning or interpretation and the same level of accuracy, precision of measurement, validity and reliability in all countries and cultures. A number of different types of comparability or equivalence need to be examined. These include the functional, conceptual and category equivalence of constructs, the linguistic and metric equivalence of the measurement instruments, and the equivalence of data collection and survey administration procedures.

Data comparability is important from the standpoint of both researcher and manager. For the manager it is important because strategy is increasingly planned relative to global or regional markets rather than on a country-by-country basis. Decisions such as where and how to expand, whether to launch new products, brands or brand extensions, how to position or reposition products and brands, and which segments to target are made or coordinated across countries. Consequently, it is important to ensure that data and research design are as comparable as possible from one country to another. If not, mistaken inferences may be made about differences or similarities between countries, when in fact these reflect differences in research design, administration procedures and so on.

Even where research is conducted in relation to a single country, such as Japan or Brazil, it is important to bear in mind that research relating to a similar problem may subsequently be conducted in another country. For example, a new product developed in relation to market demand in one country might be test marketed in that country. If it is successful, management may decide to roll it out in other countries. Consequently, it is important that the test market is designed in such a way that findings from test markets in different countries can be compared.

# Establishing Comparability: The Emic/Etic Dilemma

The issue of comparability is one that has traditionally haunted cross-national research in the social sciences. To the extent that each country or cultural context is characterized by a unique pattern of sociocultural behavior patterns and values, attitudinal and behavioral phenomena may be expressed in different ways (Lonner and Adamopoulos, 1997). Consequently, some concepts may be unique to a given country or cultural context. For example, the concept of *giri*, meaning obedience and respect, is unique to the Japanese environment. Other concepts may be common across countries or cultural contexts, but may be expressed in different ways in different contexts. For example, aggressiveness may be salient in different cultures, but in some may be expressed in terms of physical behavior such as fighting, while in others it is expressed in terms of verbal behavior such as shouting. Consequently, the relevant constructs and indicators used to tap the construct will differ across countries and cultures.

An important issue in cross-cultural research is therefore how far to emphasize concepts and constructs that are unique to a given culture or context and how far to emphasize elements that are common across cultures. If concepts and constructs specific to each culture are emphasized, difficulties will arise in making comparisons and deriving generalizations across cultures or contexts. If, on the other hand, commonality between cultures and countries is emphasized, there will be a loss of precision or accuracy in representing phenomena specific to a given country or culture.

## *Emic vs Etic Approaches*

Given this dilemma, two alternative approaches or schools of thought – the 'emic' and the 'etic' – have typically dominated cross-cultural research in the social sciences (Pike, 1966). The emic school holds that attitudes, interests and behavior are unique to a culture and best understood in their own terms. Consequently, emphasis is placed on studying the specific context of each country, and on identifying and understanding its unique facets. Inferences about cross-national differences and similarities are made in qualitative or judgmental terms, since measures are 'culture specific'. The etic school, on the other hand, is primarily concerned with identifying and assessing universal attitudinal and behavioral concepts and developing pan-cultural or 'culture-free' measures (Elder, 1976). The use of such measures facilitates comparison but can give rise to a number of methodological problems. In particular, it frequently results in adoption of a 'pseudo-etic' approach, in which constructs and measures developed in one country are applied without or with minimal adaptation to the specific context in other countries (Triandis, 1972).

These two approaches or schools of thought represent, in essence, two polar extremes on the continuum of cross-national research methodology – the one emphasizing cultural uniqueness, the other pan-culturalism in behavioral patterns and the underlying processes. From the standpoint of the international marketer, an orientation reflecting an etic philosophy is likely to be preferable. The international marketer is primarily interested in identifying similarities across markets, since these offer opportunities for the transfer of products and services and for the integration of strategies across national markets. As a result, in international marketing research, emphasis is typically placed on identifying and developing constructs and measures that are as comparable as possible across countries and cultures.

## The Etic Approach

Different procedures are, however, used to establish this comparability. One common approach is to take clearly identified concepts and measures of these, validated in at least one national context, frequently the US – for example attitudinal scales such as ethnocentrism. These are then translated and administered in another country. Often there is little or no attempt to decenter or adapt the measure to another cultural context. The principal danger with this type of approach is that a 'pseudo-etic' bias is introduced (Triandis, 1972). In other words, an emic construct or measure developed in one country is assumed to be etic or to be appropriate in all cultures and contexts. It is, therefore, important to assess explicitly various aspects of measure validity and to determine whether adaptation to the specific national or cultural context in which the measure is used is needed.

In most cases, the validity of standardized measures and the equivalence of modified measures across countries are examined based on measures of reliability such as Cronbach's alpha. It is typically assumed that the measure (and hence the construct) is equivalent if the internal structure is the same. Where one or more items do not achieve high loadings on the construct (i.e. above 0.5), they are often eliminated. In some cases measures of related concepts are included to establish external validity.

Where a number of items or multiple scales are examined, similarity in patterns of internal variance and interrelation between scales are compared across countries using factor analysis. This approach was used in several of the classic comparative sociological and political studies. Cattell (1949), for example, factor analyzed 72 variables derived from secondary sources and identified 12 main factors of national syntality, including thoughtful industriousness versus emotionality, and fastidiousness versus forcefulness. He held these to be the key dimensions on which Western societies could be meaningfully compared. However, extensive retesting and replication on other samples and the re-emergence of the same constructs within batteries of differing item composition, as well as evidence of similar nomological relationships, is required before these are established as appropriate concepts for cross-national analysis.

A similar approach can be adopted applying a structural equation model. Data for multiple countries or contexts can be analyzed by multiple-group structural equation modeling (Mullen, 1995; Myers *et al.*, 2000). The fit of the model for each group or country is examined as well as for the overall pooled sample. Various tests can be applied – that is, standardized coefficients, unequal reliability rates (Singh, 1995), factor covariance invariance, factor variance invariance and error variance invariance (Baumgartner and Steenkamp, 1996) – to assess the degree of equivalence across groups or countries.

While this approach identifies measures that have equivalent internal validity, the extent to which a measure has construct validity (i.e. actually taps the construct it purports to measure) remains open to question. For example, no allowance is made for explicit identification of culture-specific aspects of the construct. This becomes particularly problematic where some national element or culture specificity is likely to exist.

## The Emic Approach

An alternative approach is to adopt an 'emic' perspective. In this case, the starting point is the local culture or context. A separate study is conducted in each context by local researchers who identify concept and constructs relevant to the specific environmental context. In some cases, an ethnographic approach is adopted, so that generalization across cultures and contexts can only be made in the broadest of terms. Even where concepts and constructs are clearly identified and measured, these may not necessarily be defined in the same terms, again limiting the extent to which generalizations can be made across cultures and contexts. Consequently, while this type of approach provides rich insights into the fabric of society and the culture-specific elements, it is extremely time consuming and permits few generalizations.

The limitations of both approaches as well as their specific advantages suggest the desirability of developing procedures that both assess the validity of existing constructs and measures in a range of different contexts and cultures, as well as allowing for the identification of emic or culture-specific constructs and measures (Wind and Douglas, 1982). Experience gained in assessing constructs and developing appropriate measures of them in specific national contexts can thus be utilized in developing both adapted and pan-cultural measures.

A schema that allows for identifying both emic and etic elements without imposing an etic viewpoint has been proposed by Berry (1989). This is shown in Figure 6.1. Following this approach, the researcher first conducts research in his or her own culture and then applies the construct or instrument developed in that culture to study behavior in another culture (imposed etic). Behavior is

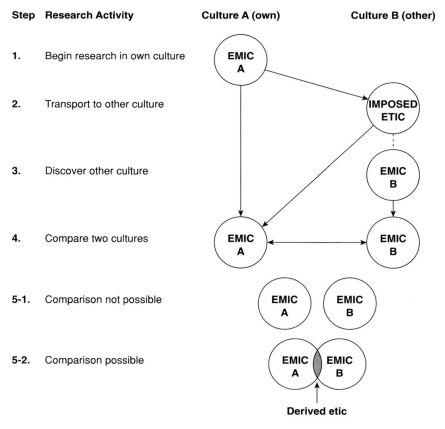

**Figure 6.1**  Steps in operationalizing emics and etics
*Source*: Berry, 1989.

then studied in the second culture from within, in its own terms (i.e. using an emic approach). Next, the results of the emic and imposed etic approach are examined and compared. If no commonality can be identified, no comparison is possible and cultures can only be understood in terms of emic elements. Where some commonality can be identified, a derived etic comparison between cultures is then possible based on the common aspects or features.

While this approach provides a schema for assessing the results of adopting an 'etic' vs an 'emic' approach, it provides limited guidelines with regard to how the two approaches are to be reconciled and how specifically they are operationalized, in particular how common elements are to be identified. It is likely that when the imposed etic model is applied by a researcher from another culture it will be specified in terms and definitions relevant to his or her culture, as the emic model will similarly be specified in terms relevant to the other culture. Consequently, it will be difficult to identify common elements even if the potential for commonality using a broader definition exists.

# A Framework for Cross-Cultural Studies

The above discussion suggests that to harmonize both etic and emic elements, an iterative integrative framework will be needed. This moves progressively toward identifying the key components that are common to all research contexts, while at the same time allowing for identification of elements specific to individual research contexts, so as to ensure some degree of comparability while not neglecting local specificity.

In essence, two alternative iterative approaches can be identified, to arrive at a solution that provides comparability without ignoring emic elements. These differ essentially in terms of the starting or base point. The first, the *adapted etic* approach, starts with a base culture or context, but seeks to adapt the conceptual model developed in the base culture to other contexts, taking explicitly into account differences in the context studied and their implications for the research design. The second, the *linked emic* model, takes as its starting point the local context, but at multiple research sites. Input from each site is then incorporated into building the overall conceptual framework and research design.

## The adapted etic model

The adapted etic model starts with the assumption that the theory or conceptual framework used in the research design is pan-cultural – that is, it applies in all contexts or settings – but that some adaptation to a specific local research context may be necessary. Typically research has been conducted and validated in a single research context or setting and the researcher seeks to examine the extent to which the model and related research findings can be generalized to other research contexts and settings.

An important first step is therefore to explicate the underlying theory and conceptual framework in multiple sociocultural settings. This entails examining whether the assumptions underlying the theory apply and are relevant in other sociocultural settings. For example, the Katz and Lazarsfeld (1955) two-step flow of influence identified was found not to hold in egalitarian Scandinavian societies. This theory postulated that opinion leaders who were better informed would filter information and opinions about events to the population at large, influencing their voting behavior. However, in Scandinavian societies, Cerha (1985) found the flow of influence to be horizontal rather than vertical, as information was exchanged between individuals rather than being filtered through select gatekeepers. Equally, theories and research relating to consumerism or consumer satisfaction may have little relevance in emerging or transitional economies where a consumerist society has not yet emerged and problems relating to the supply or availability of goods are paramount.

Once the relevance of a theory or conceptual framework to a given sociocultural setting has been assessed, the next step is to examine the relevant constructs and hypotheses to determine whether they are equally valid and relevant in all settings. This typically requires obtaining input either directly by conducting research in other settings or indirectly based on experience of other researchers in a given setting. Local researchers with expertise in the area can be asked to adapt constructs to the local research context or identify culture-specific concepts related to the topic studied. For example, Schwartz (1992), in developing his universal values, asked collaborators to examine the source list and identify any other values that might be relevant in their country/culture. The extent to which adaption to the local context will occur depends on the background and training of the local researcher. If the local researcher has been trained in the base country and is familiar with the research con-ducted in that setting, he or she may have a similar etic or pseudo-etic perspective and adaptation may be limited. Where adaptation does occur it may still reflect the influence of concepts identified in the base country. If, on the other hand, the researcher has been locally trained and is sensitive to specific local nuances, a greater degree of adaptation may be incorporated into the research design.

An alternative approach suggested by Triandis is to explicitly build in alternative measures of concepts into the research design. This approach starts with a construct assumed to be etic. Different ways of operationalizing or measuring the construct in different cultures are then developed (Hui and Triandis, 1983). Comparisons based on emic measurements of the etic construct in different contexts are then conducted in order to develop a derived etic construct. This is an iterative, divergent approach, starting with an etic-based conceptual framework and gradually moderating the constructs and relationships in the framework based on successive studies, examining modifications in different contexts. The broader the range of contexts studied, the more likely that modifications will be made in the original conceptual model.

The adapted etic approach is likely to result in emphasis on similarities rather than differences. Even where modifications are made to the original etic construct to fit the specific context, the emphasis is on retaining the essence of that construct and the underlying assumption that it is pan-cultural or universal. The cultural perspective of the base country in which research was first conducted is likely to dominate. Little attention is therefore likely to be paid to identifying emic-specific elements or constructs. This approach is likely to result in emphasis on similarities rather than differences and to facilitate comparison across countries and contexts. Modifications are made for differences in the context or setting, but explicit identification and in-depth examination of emic-specific constructs is less likely. In particular, the perspective of the researcher from the base country is likely to prevail.

## The linked emic model

To incorporate culture-specific elements and effectively build a broader knowledge base, a hybrid or 'linked' emic model is suggested. Emic research starts initially in multiple sites. A group of researchers, including at least one from each of the contexts studied, begin by agreeing on the scope or common parameters of the research and the key research questions. This first step may cause some difficulty insofar as each researcher may view the key research question differently. Particularly problematic may be definitions or understanding of the meaning of terms. In many instances, English is the common language in which the research is discussed and articulated. However, translation and interpretation of the meaning associated with key terms such as leadership, trust and so on in different languages may already give rise to issues of comparability and equivalence, which need to be discussed and resolved.

Once consensus has been reached with regard to the key research questions to be investigated, each researcher draws up a research design. This sets up a conceptual framework for the study taking into consideration characteristics specific to each research context. This should also articulate how each element of the model (i.e. constructs and concepts) is to be operationalized, or more specifically how it is defined and construed in the local context.

At this point, researchers from all contexts discuss differences and similarities in these localized models and the role of contextual factors in accounting for these differences and similarities. This may result in the identification of (1) elements, concepts and relationships that appear to be common across contexts, (2) concepts that are common but are operationalized in different ways in different contexts, (3) relationships between constructs that differ across contexts, and (4) constructs that are unique to a given context. Further discussion is then aimed at moving toward greater harmonization of conceptual models across contexts. This may be achieved by including elements unique to one context in other contexts, or by amalgamating or combining constructs from different contexts so as to develop multifaceted constructs that are then applied to all contexts. Where feasible, a supra model may be developed incorporating all the elements from the local context-specific models and delineating both etic and emic elements. Some theoretical rationale relating to the impact of contextual factors should also be developed to account for the emic components and relationships within the model. For example, in collectivist societies group-related variables may play a more critical role in explaining behavior than in individualistic societies.

In some cases, conceptual models may be developed for different types or groups of contexts, for example similar linguistic or religious contexts, geographical regions, levels of development or affluence and so on. Again, the impact of a specific contextual factor or set of factors on the model constructs and relationships needs to be clearly specified. This may result in a hierarchical type of design, grouped by type of country or other contextual factors.

Research is then conducted in each context or key group of contexts, and findings compared across contexts. This will provide some initial insights with regard to the degree of generality or specificity of model components, concepts, relationships and so on across contexts or groups of contexts. Some additional hypotheses may then be generated relating to the role of contextual factors in explaining model specificity or generality that may in turn generate a further round of research.

This type of emic approach starts with an emphasis on local knowledge and a local perspective. As a result, it tends to emphasize the unique features characterizing each context, rather than pan-cultural or etic aspects or interpreting these elements within the local context. A key issue is how to effectively combine and coordinate activities of researchers at multiple local sites often with different perspectives. This can prove cumbersome if not unwieldy. As a result, progress toward identifying elements or relationships that can be generalized across contexts may be slow.

This approach does, however, avoid potential ethnocentric or pseudo-etic bias insofar as researchers from each local context are responsible for building the research design and interpreting findings from each local context. Coordination at subsequent phases of research may also be facilitated when coordination and integration of findings across research contexts are conducted by a multicultural team of researchers from different backgrounds, each contributing local as well as general knowledge.

# Establishing Data Equivalence

The importance of generating data that are comparable from one country to another suggests that equivalence needs to be carefully monitored at all stages of the research design. In addition to ensuring equivalence in the conceptual model adopted, attention needs to be paid to *construct* equivalence, to ensure that the constructs being studied are equivalent in all contexts and cultural settings, and *measure* equivalence, that operational measures are equivalent in all research settings. In both cases, a number of issues need to be considered. In addition, the equivalence method – that is, data collection procedures – needs to be assessed to ensure that data are comparable and equally reliable in all contexts studied.

# *Construct Equivalence*

Examination of construct equivalence entails examination of three distinct aspects. First, the researcher must assess whether a given concept or behavior serves the same function from country to country; that is, its *functional* equivalence. Second, and most importantly, the researcher must determine whether the same concepts or behaviors occur in different countries, and whether the way in which they are expressed is similar; that is, their *conceptual* equivalence. Finally, where the concept belongs to a specific class of objects or activities, the researcher must examine whether the same classification scheme of objects can be used across countries, or, in other words, whether there is *category* equivalence.

## *Functional Equivalence*

In examining construct equivalence, a first issue to consider is that the concepts, objects or behaviors studied may not necessarily be functionally equivalent; that is, they may not have the same role or function in all countries studied (Berry, 1969). For example, while in the US bicycles are predominantly used for recreation, in the Netherlands, China and other countries they provide a basic mode of transportation. This implies that the relevant competing product set must be defined differently. In the US it will include other recreational products such as tennis rackets and golf equipment, while in the Netherlands or China it will include alternative modes of transportation such as public transportation.

Apparently similar activities may also have different functions. In some countries, regular exercise or participation in sports is considered a key element in staying healthy. In other countries, exercise and sports are primarily viewed as leisure activities. Similarly, in many industrialized nations increasing time pressure means that grocery shopping is a chore to be accomplished as efficiently as possible, resulting in increasing interest in shopping by mail order, catalogues and through the Internet. In other countries grocery shopping plays an important social function. Interaction with local shopkeepers and vendors or with other neighbors and acquaintances in stores or in the marketplace is an integral part of day-to-day living.

Objects may also have different significance in different countries or cultures. In the US, possession of a car is no longer a status symbol (although in certain circles, makes such as Mercedes-Benz or BMW carry prestige). In emerging market countries, ownership or nonownership of a car is still an important indicator of status. In parts of rural Africa, ownership of a radio or bicycle by a young male is an important status symbol, reputed by some sources to ensure that the owner will have little difficulty in finding a wife (McNeil, 1996).

## Conceptual Equivalence

While functional equivalence is concerned with the role of objects and behavior in society at a macrocultural level, conceptual equivalence is concerned with the interpretation that individuals place on objects, stimuli or behavior, and whether these exist or are expressed in similar ways in different countries and cultures (Sears, 1961). The focus is on the measurement of attitudes and behavior at the individual level. It is in this context that some scholars have expressed doubt as to whether truly pan-cultural measures can be developed. While the general concept is the same, the way in which they are expressed is conditioned by their context, which by definition varies from country to country (Schliemann *et al.*, 1997).

Individual values such as materialism or concepts such as 'the self' may not be relevant or not construed in the same way in different countries or cultures (Markus and Kitayama, 1991).

For example, 'saving face' is a concept prevalent in Chinese society and is an important element dominating behavior in relation to others (Mao, 1994). In Western societies, on the other hand, emphasis on the individual means that this is less relevant. Some attitudes or behavior might be unique to a specific country. The concept of *philotimo*, or behaving in the way members of one's in-group expect, for example, is said to be unique to the Greek culture (Triandis and Vassilou, 1972). This involves meeting obligations and sacrificing self to help in-group members, which include family, friends and guests.

Construal of the self and others is strikingly different between Asian and Western societies (Markus and Kitayama, 1991). In Western cultures, the individual or self is viewed as an independent, self-contained entity with a unique set of traits, abilities, motives and values. Behavior is largely directed to maintain independence from others and to express and reinforce one's own unique attributes. In many Asian cultures, on the other hand, emphasis is placed on the fundamental interconnectedness of human beings to each other. Behavior centers around attending to others, fitting in and harmonious interdependence with others.

Rites and social rituals such as weddings, funerals or gift giving may also vary from one country or culture to another. For example, in India funerals tend to be large, public rites, while in many Western societies funerals are more typically private, family affairs. Similarly, high school proms (an end-of-school-year dance for graduating seniors) are an important social function in the US. Their counterpart may not exist in other countries and cultures, where completion of secondary school education may not have the same significance or end at the same stage.

## Category Equivalence

Yet a third type of construct equivalence relates to the category in which objects or other stimuli are placed. Relevant product class definitions may differ from one country to another. In the beverage market, for example, what is considered a soft drink as well as forms of soft drinks such as canned or bottled sodas, mineral waters, fruit juices, iced tea and powdered and liquid fruit concentrates vary significantly from one culture to another. In the Netherlands milk is commonly consumed with meals and viewed as a soft drink, whereas in many other countries it is used primarily as an additive for hot or cold drinks or as a beverage for children.

Careful attention to such factors is an important consideration when defining the relevant product class or category or developing product-related measures. In addition, the characteristics or attributes perceived by customers as relevant in evaluating a product class may differ from one country to another. In France, for example, the hot–cold continuum is a key attribute in characterizing consumers' perceptions of fragrance. In the US and the UK, however, this is not an attribute that is perceived as relevant by consumers.

Differences in sociodemographic classes also have to be considered. In the case of marital status, in various African countries it is not uncommon for a male to have several wives, and in some cases women may have several husbands. Occupational categories do not always have strict equivalents in all countries. The counterpart of the US attorney or the British barrister may be difficult to find. Occupations also differ in status from one country or society to another. In China, for example, a teacher commands considerable respect due to the Buddha's role as a teacher. Similarly, the social prestige attached to government positions varies from society to society.

# Measure Equivalence

Once construct equivalence has been examined, the next step is to consider measure equivalence. Construct and measure equivalence are highly interrelated insofar as the measure is an operational definition of the construct. It is, nonetheless, useful to separate the equivalence of the concept to be measured from that of the actual measurement procedure. Here, equivalence with regard to three aspects has to be considered: (1) the calibration system used in measurement; (2) the translation of the research instrument; and (3) the metric equivalence of the instrument (Mullen, 1995).

## Calibration Equivalence

In developing a research instrument, equivalence has first to be established with regard to the calibration system used in measurement. This includes not only equivalence with regard to monetary units and measures of weight, distance and volume, but also other perceptual cues, such as color, shape or form, which are used to interpret visual stimuli.

The need to establish equivalence with regard to monetary and physical measurement units is clearly apparent. Standard procedures or tables for conversion are readily available. Care needs, however, to be exercised where these fluctuate over time, for example with exchange rates or growth rates, to ensure that these are measured over a comparable time period or relative to the same base rate.

Similarly, comparability with regard to standards such as product grading or product quality may need to be established, since these are often not uniform from one country to another.

More subtle differences in instrument calibration, which are particularly relevant in the case of nonverbal instruments, relate to perceptual cues such as color, pictorial form or shape. Studies in cognitive and cross-cultural psychology suggest that a substantial degree of commonality exists with regard to the manifestations of these in different countries and cultures (Russell *et al.*, 1997). However, the ability to interpret, differentiate among these and develop gradations in these schemata appears to differ. Often this is linked to schooling, language and the physical environment. For example, Japanese children have been found to use fewer color terms than Australian or Greek children (Johnson and Tomiie, 1985).

## Translation Equivalence

A second aspect of measure equivalence concerns translation of the instrument so that it is understood by respondents in different countries and has equivalent meaning in each research context. The need for translation of questionnaires and other verbal stimuli where research is conducted in countries with different languages is readily apparent. The need to translate nonverbal stimuli to ensure that they evoke the desired image and to avoid problems of miscommunication is less widely recognized.

Translation equivalence is a central issue in the establishment of construct equivalence, since this is the stage in the research design at which the construct is defined in operational terms. The translation procedure thus frequently helps to pinpoint problems with regard to whether a concept can be measured by using the same or similar questions in each cultural context, and whether a question has the same meaning in different research contexts. If different questions are used, then issues arise with regard to the minimal level of equivalence necessary for two questions to be considered the same, and what criteria for equivalence can be established.

Translation of nonverbal stimuli requires attention to how perceptual cues are interpreted in each research context. Misunderstanding may arise because the respondent is not familiar with a product or other stimulus, for example with an electrical appliance, or with the way in which it is depicted. As noted above, this may vary with the environmental context or degree of schooling of the respondent. Alternatively, respondents may misinterpret stimuli because the associations evoked by the stimuli differ from one country to another.

Translation of verbal and nonverbal stimuli plays a key role in the establishment of equivalence. Often it provides a focal point both for uncovering equivalence issues and for making pragmatic decisions as to how to resolve them. These issues and various approaches to translation are covered in greater detail in Chapter 8.

## Metric Equivalence

A final concern is metric equivalence. Two aspects have to be considered in determining metric equivalence: the first involves the equivalence of the scale or scoring procedure used to establish the measure; the second, the equivalence of response to a given measure in different countries. The greater the emphasis placed on quantitative measurement in data interpretation, the more important the establishment of metric equivalence becomes. It is an integral part of decisions relating to data analysis, especially where attitudinal scaling or multivariate procedures are used.

Metric equivalence in scale and scoring procedures is of particular relevance as different scales or scoring procedures may be most effective in different countries and cultures. This often depends on what type of scales or scaling procedures are commonly used in schools. While in English-speaking countries use of a five- or seven-point scale is common, in other countries twenty-point or ten-point scales are more common (Douglas and LeMaire, 1974). Similarly, use of nonverbal response procedures requires consideration of their comparability across countries and cultures.

A second aspect of metric equivalence concerns the response to a score obtained on a measure, or scalar equivalence. The question arises as to whether a score obtained in one research context has the same meaning in another context. For example, on an intentions-to-purchase scale, do the top two boxes, commonly used to predict the proportion of likely buyers, indicate a similar likelihood of purchase from one country to another? In many Middle Eastern countries as in Southern Europe, respondents tend to give significantly higher top box ratings than in other countries.

In contrast to other types of equivalence, metric equivalence can only be examined once the data have been collected. Prior experience or examination of similar types of measures in the relevant country or culture may provide some guidelines as to appropriate scales and typical response patterns. This may suggest the types of data analysis and statistical procedures that are most appropriate in view of typical response patterns. Different measures that have different potential biases may be applied, and the results compared to establish equivalence.

# Determining Construct Validity

In addition to examining construct and measure equivalence, another central concern is whether the data collected are a valid measure of the construct. Typically, the measure of a construct is comprised of more than one item. Often this involves a scale or a series of items that are associated with each other. The validity of the construct concerns whether this scale or set of items measures what it is intended to measure. Validity of a construct can be established in three ways: (1) convergent validity, (2) discriminant validity, and (3) nomological validity (Zaltman, Pinson and Angelmar, 1973).

Convergent validity refers to whether the same results are obtained when the construct is measured in two different ways. In international marketing research this also involves measuring the construct two different ways in two or more countries. The agreement, typically the correlation, between the two measures is examined. If the correlation coefficient is not significant, then the convergent validity is suspect. If the correlations obtained in two different countries are significantly different from zero and significantly different from each other, then the degree of convergent validity in the country with the lower correlation is suspect.

Discriminant validity refers to whether a specific concept differs from other concepts. For convergent validity the correlation between two different ways of measuring the same construct should be high. To establish discriminant validity, the correlation between two different concepts should not be significant. In international marketing research, the correlations should not be significant in all the countries in which the constructs are measured.

Nomological validity refers to whether the construct is related to some external criterion. For example, in establishing the nomological validity of the CETSCALE, Shimp and Sharma (1987) assessed the correlation of the scale with attitudes, purchase intentions and ownership of foreign-made products. In multicountry research, one issue that becomes problematic is whether the same external criteria are available in the other country. On a more subtle level is the issue of whether a criterion has the same meaning in both countries.

The discussion above has dealt with the three types of validity from the perspective of simple correlations. More broadly, the issue can be conceptualized in terms of Campbell and Fiske's (1959) multitrait multimethod approach. This is discussed in some detail in Chapter 12. Typically, in marketing research studies researchers use confirmatory factor analysis and structural equation modeling to establish convergent and discriminant validity. These approaches are also discussed in Chapter 12.

# Establishing Construct Reliability

In cross-cultural research there are a number of ways in which reliability can be examined. These include examining whether: (1) the same results are obtained when the measurement is taken on two different occasions; (2) different individuals, especially experts used in initial stages of scale construction, provide comparable input; and (3) the measure or scale is internally consistent. Examination of reliability based on the first two criteria is preferable in cross-cultural research, since internal consistency measures may reflect sampling issues, as well as those arising from the instrument. This does, however, substantially increase costs, as well as increasing the burden of data collection and incurring delays in data processing. Consequently, most attention focuses on internal measures of reliability.

## Consistency over Time

Test–retest reliability is used to assess whether results obtained from administration of a measure on two separate occasions are comparable. Typically, a questionnaire will be administered initially, and then again two to five weeks later. A high correlation between scores obtained on the two occasions suggests that the same underlying element is being measured on both occasions. However, if the time interval is too short, it may only reflect the fact that individuals try to be consistent and repeat the same response as the last time. On the other hand, too lengthy a time interval may result in a real change in an individual's response. For example, the General Perceived Self-Efficacy scale was found to have a retest reliability of .67 after six months in one study. In two other studies it was found to have a retest reliability of .75 and .55 after one year, suggesting some variation in reliability (Schwarzer and Scholz, 2000). As a practical matter, test–retest reliability is not often used in multicountry research as it is sufficiently difficult and time consuming to get an adequate level of response to a single administration of a scale. Procedures for calculating test–retest reliability are shown in Nunnally and Bernstein (1994).

## Consistency across Individuals

Related to test–retest reliability is whether two (or more) independent judges evaluate items or objects in the same way. In the initial stages of scale construction, experts are often used to make judgments about stimuli or questions. When responses to open-ended questions are obtained, judges are used to help identify relevant response categories. In multicountry research, where this procedure is used to develop a scale simultaneously in two or more countries, the consensus categorizations from one country to another can be compared. The Spearman rank correlation coefficient, Kendall's tau and Cohen's kappa can all be used to assess interjudge agreement (Hays, 1994).

Despite its significance, reliability of data in cross-cultural research has received relatively little attention (Davis *et al.*, 1981; Parameswaran and Yaprak, 1987). The studies that have been conducted suggest, however, that the reliability of data varies from country to country and can give rise to problems, especially with regard to attitudinal and lifestyle data.

Internal reliability scores can be influenced by a number of factors. A study conducted by Parameswaran and Yaprak (1987) found that reliability scores were sensitive to the nature of the construct being studied and the nationality of the respondent, as well as country-of-origin effects. They computed a total of 120 reliability scores (Cronbach's alpha), which were then used in an analysis of variance. The reliability scores varied from 0.88 to 0.51. For example, the mean reliability for the US sample was 0.76 and the mean for the Turkish sample was 0.65. Slight, but statistically significant, differences were also found between the reliability coefficients associated with the evaluation of products from different countries (e.g. 0.72 for Germany and 0.68 for Italy). They also found that 'softer' constructs elicited less reliable responses than 'harder' constructs (0.65 versus 0.74).

Another study applied interjudge measures of reliability to demographic, behavioral and lifestyle variables based on responses of couples in five countries (Davis *et al.*, 1981). Data were obtained from husbands and wives in countries from two linguistic groupings: two English-speaking countries (US and UK) and three French-speaking countries (France, Belgium and French Canada). In all, three types of measures were examined: (1) demographic and background characteristics; (2) self-reports of behavior in the form of ratings of involvement in household tasks and decisions; and (3) lifestyle or psychographic variables. Somewhat higher levels of reliability were found for 'hard' variables, for example demographics, than for 'soft' variables, for example lifestyle/attitudinal variables. These spanned the diversity of types of questions and measures commonly employed in consumer surveys.

In the case of the background characteristics and the measures of involvement in household tasks and decisions, husbands' and wives' responses to the same items were cross-tabulated and a measure of agreement between them computed based on Cohen's $k$ coefficient (Cohen, 1960). This measure, $k$, reflects the excess of observed over chance agreement, given the particular marginal distributions observed for the two sets of husbands' and wives' responses. In contrast to measures of association or correlation, the measure focuses on agreement based on the frequency of response in the main diagonal, rather than the overall contingency table.

For the background characteristics, the $k$ values were generally quite high, indicating strong and consistent reliability across variables and samples. This suggests that the reliability of measures such as income or age is not, in general, likely to pose a major problem in cross-cultural surveys. In examining agreement for involvement in household tasks and decisions, the $k$ coefficient showed less agreement than for background characteristics. Thus, while husband and wife agreement in involvement in tasks and decisions exceeded that which might be expected by chance, the degree of agreement was generally moderate. Furthermore, there was some between-sample variation. In the case of the lifestyle variables, an internal consistency measure was used to assess reliability applying the Kuder-Richardson (Formula 20) coefficient. This varied across variables as well as countries, but the measures did appear to possess good discriminant ability.

In situations where longitudinal data are routinely available, test–retest measures of reliability can be made. This is, however, likely to be relatively rare except in the case of panel data or advertising ratings. Data suitable for calculating measures of interjudge reliability are likely to be even rarer, due to the high costs of collecting data from two or more household members or multiple respondents. Consequently, reliance is most likely to be placed on internal consistency of multiple-item measures, as well as split-half reliability measures.

## Internal Consistency of Scales

In multicountry research where multiple measures are used, reliability is typically assessed based on the internal consistency of measures. A commonly used measure is the coefficient alpha (Cronbach, 1951; Nunnally and Bernstein, 1994). Measures of internal consistency are most telling when they indicate a lack of consistency. For example, low Cronbach alphas suggest that the data or scale is unreliable and should not be used. However, high alphas or acceptable levels alone do not indicate measure validity nor the relevance of a given construct in the country or culture being studied. Increasingly, reliance on Cronbach's alpha is being called into question (see Rossiter, 2002).

A typical approach to assessing internal consistency in scale development is to conduct exploratory factor analysis of a large set of variables. Then coefficient alpha is computed for variables that load on a particular factor. Items with a coefficient alpha of < 0.6 are typically dropped from further consideration. This results in a reduced set of variables and a higher coefficient alpha. Correlations can also be compared to assess how highly each item correlates with the total. It is, however, important to note that high internal consistency does not mean that a scale has other desirable properties such as discriminant and nomological validity. The internal consistency of measures can also be assessed using covariance structure modeling (LISREL or EQS), which is discussed in Chapter 12.

When a lengthy scale is used it may be desirable to assess internal consistency using a split-half approach. The scale is split in half, creating two different sets of responses. The most straightforward procedure is to assign the even questions to one half and the odd questions to the other, although more elaborate schemes can be employed. A reliability coefficient is then calculated to determine the extent of agreement between the two halves. As a general rule the scale should have at least 16 to 20 items so that the halves have 8 to 10 items. The procedure also adjusts for the number of items in the scale as a longer scale, in this case the full scale, is more reliable than a shorter one (Green *et al.*, 1988).

In multicountry research it is also possible to treat two countries as halves and compute a reliability coefficient. Alternatively, the odd questions from country A and the even questions from country B can be used to compute a reliability coefficient. The process is then repeated using the even questions from country A and the odd questions from country B. These results are then compared with the split-half reliability calculated for odd/even questions within each country. If the coefficients obtained for the within-country and the across-country calculations are similar, then a higher level of confidence can be put in the results obtained in each country. Procedures for calculating split-half reliability are discussed in Nunnally and Bernstein (1994).

# *Equivalence in Data Collection Techniques*

In addition to considering equivalence in terms of how the research design is developed, how the constructs are defined and how measures of these are designed in different countries and contexts, it is also important to consider comparability in data collection procedures. This includes comparability with regard to the research instrument, the sampling procedures and survey administration techniques.

The first issue is the research instrument. In this context two important considerations are whether the research instrument is self-administered or is administered by an interviewer and whether verbal or pictoral stimuli are used. In well-developed, highly literate cultural contexts, instruments can be self-administered. These may take the form of mail surveys or completion of surveys by email or on the Internet. Increasingly, as more and more households in developed countries have access to the Internet, Internet-based surveys are becoming more popular. They provide a highly flexible method for respondents who can complete them in their own time. In developing countries with low levels of literacy, administration by an interviewer may be necessary to explain questions to the respondent, to ensure that the respondent has clearly understood the questions and to collect other relevant observational data. Another aspect is the use of verbal or pictorial stimuli. Again, in developed countries, verbal stimuli can be used. In different linguistic environments, careful translation will be needed to ensure comparability in meaning. In countries with low literacy levels, on the other hand, use of pictorial stimuli may be needed to ensure comprehension by respondents. This entails developing pictorial stimuli that translate effectively the meaning conveyed in the verbal stimuli. While this may pose little difficulty with objects or physical stimuli, it may constitute more of a challenge with abstract stimuli such as response scales. These issues are covered in more detail in Chapter 8.

The next issue is the comparability of samples drawn from different countries. In sampling households and organizations, the relevant respondent is not necessarily the same from one country to another. For example, in Arab countries husbands often play a more significant role in grocery purchase decisions as compared with Latin American households. With the increasing number of dual-income households in many industrialized nations, both husbands and wives influence brand decisions or participate to a greater extent in day-to-day shopping. Consequently, multiple respondents may need to be interviewed. For example, while in most industrialized countries sampling frames such as electoral lists or telephone directories are readily available, in developing countries no such sampling frames exist, and different procedures such as block sampling may be needed.

In addition, it is important to balance comparability with representativity in samples. Samples that are strictly comparable in composition with regard to characteristics such as age and income may not be representative with regard to the cultural context of such characteristics. Consequently, it may be necessary to draw samples that allow for analysis with regard to representativity as well as comparability.

A final issue is that the suitability of different sampling and survey administration procedures may vary from one country to another. In some countries telephone interviewing may be more reliable, while personal interviewing is more effective in other countries. To the extent that comparability in data accuracy and reliability is required, use of different procedures may therefore be necessary. Similarly, use of self-administered techniques may result in fewer errors as errors due to miscommunication between interviewer and interviewee and interviewer recording error are eliminated. Hence comparability in instruments may also affect comparability in survey administration techniques. In essence, the primary concern should be comparability in results and quality of data collected, rather than in data collection procedures *per se*. This is discussed in more detail in Chapter 9.

In each phase from research design and conceptualization to implementation, issues of comparability need to be considered. While issues with regard to comparability in concepts and measures have been emphasized here, since these are the most troubling and also most frequently neglected, comparability with regard to implementation has also to be assessed. In particular, conduct of research by researchers from different sociocultural backgrounds and research philosophies further compounds these issues.

## Summary

The need to establish comparability in various aspects of research design and implementation gives rise to a number of issues centering on the equivalence of the constructs, appropriate measures of these, and data collection techniques used in each country or culture examined. In the first place, the research approach used to establish comparability needs to be established. Either the research can start with an etic approach and adapt to differences in each research context, or research can be designed first in each research context and differences in design harmonized across multiple contexts.

Construct equivalence has to be assessed first in terms of the *function* performed by the product or activity examined in a particular country or culture. Equivalence in terms of the way in which a *concept* is expressed or perceived by individuals within a culture is also an important consideration. In addition, equivalence in terms of the specific *categories* of stimuli or respondents studied has to be determined.

In the case of measures and measurement procedures, equivalence has to be determined in terms of the units of measurement used, as well as in the translation of verbal and nonverbal instruments to ensure comprehension by respondents in different sociocultural environments. Operationally, this is frequently the most critical stage in the establishment of measure equivalence, since it reveals underlying problems in the operational definitions of the constructs to be examined. It is important to ensure the equivalence of the response obtained given a specific response format. Equivalence in data collection procedures also needs to be considered. Here, achieving comparability in the reliability and validity of the data is more important than strict equivalence of data collection or survey administration procedures. Often, differences in the research infrastructure mean that different procedures will have to be used in order to achieve comparable results.

# References

Baumgartner, H. and Steenkamp, J-B.E.M. (1996) Exploratory Consumer Buying Behavior: Conceptualization and Measurement. *International Journal of Research in Marketing*, **13**, 121–137.

Berry, J.W. (1969) On Cross-cultural Comparability. *International Journal of Psychology*, **4**, 119–28.

Berry, J.W. (1989) Imposed Etics-Emics-Derived Etics: The Operationalization of a Compelling Idea. *International Journal of Psychology*, **24**, 721–735.

Campbell, D.T. and Fiske, D.W. (1959) Convergent and Discriminant Validation by the Multitrait-Multimethod Matrix. *Psychological Bulletin*, **56**, 81–105.

Cattell, R.B. (1949) The Dimensions of Culture Patterns by Factorization of National Character. *Journal of Abnormal and Social Psychology*, **44**, 443–469.

Cerha, J. (1985) The Limits of Influence. *European Research*, **2**, 141–152.

Cohen, J. (1960) A Coefficient of Agreement for Nominal Scales. *Psychological Measurement*, **20**, 37–46.

Cronbach, L.J. (1951) Coefficient Alpha and the Internal Structure of Tests. *Psychometrika*, **16**, 297–334.

Davis, H.L., Douglas, S.P. and Silk, A.J. (1981) Measure Unreliability: A Hidden Threat to Cross-national Marketing Research. *Journal of Marketing*, **45**, 98–109.

Deshpande, R., Farley, J.U. and Webster, F.E. (1997) Factors Affecting Organizational Perform-ance: A Five Country Comparison. MSI Working Paper, 97–108.

Douglas, S.P. and Craig, C.S. (1997) The Changing Dynamic of Consumer Behavior: Implications for Cross-cultural Research. *International Journal of Research in Marketing*, **14**, 379–395.

Douglas, S.P. and LeMaire, P. (1974) Improving the Quality and Efficiency of Life-style Research. In *The Challenges Facing Marketing Research: How Do We Meet Them?* XXV ESOMAR Congress, Hamburg. ESOMAR, pp. 555–570.

Elder, J.W. (1976) Comparative Cross-national Methodology. *Annual Review of Sociology*, **II**, 209–230.

Green, P.E., Tull, D.S. and Albaum, G. (1988) *Research for Marketing Decisions*. 5th edition. Prentice-Hall, Englewood Cliffs, NJ.

Hays, W.L. (1994) *Statistics*, 5th edition. Harcourt Brace, Orlando, FL.

Hui, C.H. and Triandis, H.C. (1983) Multi-strategy Approach to Cross-cultural Research: The Case of Locus of Control. *Journal of Cross-cultural Psychology*, **14**(March), 65–83.

Johnson, E.G. and Tomiie, T. (1985) The Development of Color-naming in Four- to Seven-year Old Children: A Cross-cultural Study. *Psychologia – An International Journal of Psychology in the Orient*, **28**, 216–227.

Katz, E. and Lazarsfeld, P.E. (1955) *Personal Influence*. Free Press, New York.

Lonner, W.J. and Adamopoulos, J. (1997) Culture as an Antecedent to Behavior. In Berry, J.W., Poortinga, Y.H. and Pandey, J. (eds) *Handbook of Cross-cultural Psychology*, Vol. 2. Allyn & Bacon, Boston.

Mao, L.R. (1994) Beyond Politeness Theory: 'Face' Revisited and Renewed. *Journal of Pragmatics*, **21**, 451–486.

Markus, H.R. and Kitayama, S. (1991) Culture and the Self: Implications for Cognition, Emotion and Motivation. *Psychological Review*, **98**, 224–253.

McNeil, D.G. (1996) This $40 Crank-Up Radio Lets Rival Africa Tune In. *New York Times*, 16 February, A1–A4.

Mullen, M. (1995) Diagnosing Measurement Equivalence in Cross-national Research. *Journal of International Business Studies*, Third Quarter, 573–596.

Myers, M.B., Calantone, R.J., Page Jr., T.J. and Taylor, C.R. (2000) An Application of Multiple-group Causal Models in Assessing Cross-cultural Measurement Equivalence. *Journal of International Marketing*, 8(4), 108–121.

Nunnally, J.C. and Bernstein, I.H. (1994) *Psychometric Theory*, 3rd edition. McGraw-Hill, New York.

Parameswaran, R. and Yaprak, A. (1987) A Cross-national Comparison of Consumer Research Measures. *Journal of International Business Studies*, 18, 35–49.

Pike, K. (1966) *Language in Relation to a Unified Theory of the Structure of Human Behavior*. Mouton, The Hague.

Rossiter, J.R. (2002) The C-OAR-SE Procedure for Scale Development in Marketing. *International Journal of Research in Marketing*, 19, 305–355.

Russell, P., Deregowski, J. and Kinnear, P. (1977) Perception and Aesthetics. In Berry, J.W., Poortinga, Y.H. and Pandey, J. (eds) *Handbook of Cross-cultural Psychology*, Vol. 2. Allyn & Bacon, Boston, pp. 109–142.

Schliemann, A., Carraher, D. and Ceci, S.J. (1997) Everyday Cognition. In Berry, J.W., Poortinga, Y.H. and Pandey, J. (eds) *Handbook of Cross-cultural Psychology*, Vol. 2. Allyn & Bacon, Boston, p. 143.

Schwartz, S.H. (1992) Universals in the Content and Structure of Values: Theoretical and Empirical Tests on 20 Countries. In Zane, M. (ed.) *Advances in Experimental Social Psychology*, Vol. 25. Academic Press, New York.

Schwarzer, R. and Scholz, U. (2000) Cross-cultural Assessment of Coping Resources: The General Perceived Self-efficacy Scale. *Asian Conference of Health Psychology 2000. Health Psychology and Culture*. Tokyo, Japan, August 28–29.

Sears, R.R. (1961) Transcultural Variables and Conceptual Equivalence. In Kaplan, B. (ed.) *Studying Personality Cross-culturally*. Row, Peterson, & Co., Evanston, IL, pp. 445–455.

Shimp, T.A. and Sharma, S. (1987) Consumer Ethnocentrism: Construct Validation of the CETSCALE. *Journal of Marketing Research*, **24**, 280–289.

Singh, J. (1995) Measurement Issues in Cross-national Research. *Journal of International Business Studies*, **26**, 597–619.

Steenkamp, J-B.E.M. and Baumgartner, H. (1998) Assessing Measurement Invariance in Cross-national Consumer Research. *Journal of Consumer Research*, **25**, 78–90.

Triandis, H.C. (1972) *The Analysis of Subjective Culture*. John Wiley and Sons Inc., New York.

Triandis, H.C. (1994) *Culture and Social Behavior*. McGraw-Hill, New York.

Triandis, H.C. and Vassilou, V. (1972) A Comparative Analysis of Subjective Culture. In Triandis, H.C. (ed.) *The Analysis of Subjective Culture*. John Wiley and Sons Inc., New York, pp. 299–335.

Wind, Y. and Douglas, S.P. (1982) Comparative Consumer Research: The Next Frontier. *Management Decision*, **4**, 24–35.

Zaltman, G., Pinson, C.R.A. and Angelmar, R. (1973) *Metatheory and Consumer Research*. Holt, Rinehart and Winston, New York.

# Chapter 7

# NONSURVEY DATA COLLECTION TECHNIQUES

## Introduction

The importance of establishing the equivalence and comparability of the concepts, attitudes and behaviors examined in different countries suggests that it is critical to be sensitive to and understand differences in customer behavior patterns and attitudes, as well as the social and cultural context in which they are embedded. Researchers should be wary of interpreting phenomena in terms of their own cultural self-referent, particularly when they lack familiarity with a culture or country or are working in cultures very dissimilar from their own. In these instances, qualitative data collection techniques can be helpful, as they are unstructured in character and facilitate exploring the context in which consumption and purchase decisions are made. Rather than imposing a specific response format, as in a questionnaire, on the respondent, they focus on probing people's underlying cognitive structures, moods and need states, as well as their reactions to specific situations or stimuli.

Qualitative research techniques can be used in a number of different ways in international marketing research. They can be used in exploratory research in order to formulate and define the problem more clearly and to identify language or terms used by consumers, as well as to determine relevant questions and hypotheses to be examined in subsequent research. Here, it is important to cover emotional as well as rational issues in order to ensure as wide a range of coverage as possible. Qualitative research can also be used in pre-testing advertisements, packaging, product concepts and so on, both to generate ideas to be pre-tested and to explore relations with these concepts. Finally, qualitative techniques can be used in exploratory or 'essence' research to probe deeply into attitudes toward product classes, brands, shopping situations and trends in behavior. They help to reduce the psychological distance between the researcher and respondent, especially when the researcher is not familiar with the other country or culture.

Qualitative research techniques help the researcher gain insights into the problems to be studied and into differences as compared with the domestic market. They help to reveal how consumers think and to explore their subconscious feelings and need states that prompt purchasing decisions and lead to the creation of consumer repertoires (Cooper and Patterson, 1996). Qualitative research can also be used to bring to light day-to-day actions and routinized behavior patterns and ingrained habits that do not spring immediately to mind (Branthwaite and Cooper, 2001). Qualitative research can thus generate a better understanding of a given purchase decision or consumption context or underlying values and attitudes present at the time. It helps develop appropriate research questions and hypotheses, as well as to identify and define appropriate concepts and constructs. These can then be tested subsequently where quantification of these concepts is required.

In some cases, qualitative research alone may be adequate. It is used to generate improved understanding of the attitudes and behavior of specific market segments such as teenagers or children, or to understand the patterning of attitudes and cognitions, the meaning of brands and brand associations. It can also provide insights into the role of in-store stimuli, or to generate ideas for new products, advertising or promotional appeals and so on (Barnard, 1997). Here, investigation of relevant issues on a small sample of carefully selected respondents may be adequate. For general references on qualitative research see Banister *et al.* (1994), Denzin and Lincoln (2002) and Mariampolski (2001).

# Different Qualitative Techniques

In general, three major types of qualitative data collection techniques may be identified: (1) observational and quasi-observational techniques; (2) projective techniques and depth interviews; and (3) creative group sessions (synectics). These differ primarily in terms of (1) the degree of structure imposed in data collection; (2) whether data are collected while the respondent is in a real-world or simulated shopping situation; (3) potential reactivity; that is, the extent to which the respondent is aware of being studied and hence may behave differently; (4) the introspectiveness of data; that is, whether the individual respondents talk about themselves and their inner feelings or rationalize their behavior; (5) the subjectivity of the analysis; that is, whether analytic and interpretation procedures and coding schemata are developed prior to data collection, or are established *post hoc* by the researcher based on examination of the data; and (6) the sample size; that is, the number of respondents from which it is feasible to collect data, given typical time and budget constraints. Each of the different data collection techniques is assessed on these criteria in Table 7.1.

*Observational* measures typically do not require the respondent to perform a specific task, but are based on watching how respondents behave, frequently videotaping respondents in specific

**Table 7.1** Characteristics of selected qualitative methods of data collection

| Method | Structure imposed | Actual shopping environment | Potential reactivity | Introspectiveness | Analysis | Sample size |
|---|---|---|---|---|---|---|
| *Observation* | | | | | | |
| Pure observation | None | Yes | Low | No | Subjective or pre-structured | Small |
| Physical trace measures | None | Yes | None | No | Inferential | Moderate to large |
| Archival measures | None | NA | None | No | Inferential | Moderate to large |
| Entrapment measures | Moderate | Yes | Some | No | Inferential | Varies |
| *Protocols* | | | | | | |
| Field | None | Yes | High | Occasional | Subjective | Small |
| Laboratory | Considerable | No | Moderate | No | Pre-structured | Moderate |
| *Projective techniques* | | | | | | |
| Free response | Varies | No | Low | No | Subjective or pre-structured | Small to moderate |
| *Interview* | | | | | | |
| Depth interview | None | No | Low | Yes | Subjective | Small |
| Focus group | Moderate | No | Low | Limited | Subjective | Small |
| Extended creativity groups | Varies | No | Low | Varies | Subjective | Small |

*Source:* adapted from Douglas *et al.,* 1981.

consumption or purchase situations. Generally this is done in a real-world situation, for example while respondents are shopping, doing their laundry or preparing meals. While in classic observation studies respondents are not aware of being observed, videotaping respondents is relatively unobtrusive, especially where small cameras are used and there is little likelihood of reactivity, as the respondent is absorbed by the task in which he or she is engaged. Analysis may be structured where the movements or signs to be observed are specified, or data are analyzed subsequently by the researcher. Sample sizes vary depending on the specific type of observation. In general, observational procedures tend to be labor intensive and time consuming, particularly in the analytic stages.

*Quasi-observational* techniques are becoming increasingly widespread with growing interest in the impact of the consumption or shopping scenario on consumer attitudes and behavior. The ease and relatively low cost of videotaping consumers and widespread availability of instore cameras make use of such techniques highly feasible. Here consumers are typically videotaped in the store or in consumption situations, for example cooking or doing the laundry or using a microwave. They are then shown the videotape and asked to comment on their thoughts or specific actions. Verbalizations can be collected *in situ* but, in general, it is preferable to collect them retrospectively in conjunction with a videotape, since they tend to be highly reactive and give rise to introspection. Analysis of protocols and videotaping is typically subjective and sample sizes are generally small. However, they provide very rich contextual data, especially about the impact of situational and instore stimuli.

*Projective* techniques typically require the respondent to perform a specific task such as word association or sentence completion, or to respond to specific stimuli such as photos or drawings. For example, respondents might be asked which of a set of pictures they felt best expressed their feelings about a brand. Unless a standardized set of stimuli is used, the equivalence in meaning of these stimuli across cultures should be established. This may require some experience on the part of the researcher. With more widespread Internet access, it has become increasingly feasible to administer projective techniques over the Internet, enabling use of a mix of qualitative and quantitative techniques (Pawle and Cooper, 2002). In some cases, respondents may be asked to interpret the actions of others. Here, it is assumed that respondents project their own feelings and reactions in their interpretation. There is little potential for reactivity or introspection among respondents. Analysis can either be subjective or pre-structured, depending on the extent to which the initial task is structured. Generally, small to moderate sample sizes are used, and the procedure is not overly time consuming.

*Depth interviews and focus groups* typically emphasize verbalization of opinions. Both types of interviews are generally conducted in a home or laboratory situation and have low potential for reactivity. Depth interviews can become introspective, though this is less likely to occur with focus groups. The primary limitation of focus groups is that respondents may tend to express socially acceptable views and to avoid opinions or responses that may be controversial. Depth interviews and focus groups typically last two hours or more, though in some cases focus groups can run longer, especially where participants are asked to react to or discuss product samples. The development of appropriate coding and analytic procedures as well as interpretation is complex and requires an experienced researcher. The interviewer/moderator should not only be trained in group interviews, but should also be familiar with the language, culture and patterns of social interaction in the country. Difficulties may also be encountered in comparing results across countries, especially insofar as they reflect the specific cultural environment or context. Research findings should be deduced not only from the verbal content, but also from nonverbal cues such as voice, intonations, gestures and expressions. In addition, sample sizes are small and are not randomly selected. It is advisable to conduct them over a range of geographical areas and with different moderators. If the results begin to converge, then greater confidence can be placed in the findings.

In *creativity groups* respondents are typically required to perform a number of verbal and nonverbal tasks. These may range from being highly unstructured to more structured tasks, but are primarily designed to generate creative new ideas or a fresh perspective on a topic or problem. The effectiveness of these groups is highly dependent on the skills of the moderators. Interpretation of findings is problematic and often generated on site by the moderators as part of the group's task; that is, to obtain a synthesis of the activities and discussion, rather than being undertaken *post hoc* by the moderator.

The appropriate qualitative method depends on the objective of the research and the topic studied. Observational and quasi-observational data are useful where the researcher wishes to gain some idea of the impact of the consumption or purchase scenario, the store or retail environment on behavior, and where respondents are typically not conscious of routinized behavior patterns and hence are likely to have difficulty reporting on them. Projective techniques are used primarily where the respondent may be reluctant or unable to express views or opinions that are subconscious or repressed or would tend to give a biased response if the question were posed directly. This can occur in relation to sensitive topics such as drinking, or where there are strong social norms. Projective techniques can also be used more broadly to stimulate and elicit reactions to stimuli such as brands or packaging that may be unconscious and do not come readily to mind. Focus groups and depth interviews can be instrumental in probing underlying motivations and attitudes concerning a particular topic or product market, or consumption situation. In some cases respondents may be asked to react to stimuli such as product samples, product concepts and packaging, or in some cases perform projective techniques. Use of projective techniques in focus groups and depth interviews can be helpful in understanding cultural and group-level phenomena. Creative groups, on the other hand, are used primarily to generate new ideas about products, packaging or advertising stimuli, or to diagnose future trends in consumer behavior, values and lifestyle.

The different variants of each of these types of qualitative data are next examined in more detail. In each case, some applications of the techniques as well as advantages and limitations are discussed.

# Observational and Quasi-observational Data

Observational and quasi-observational data techniques are commonly used in cross-cultural research in the social sciences. In international marketing research, these methods are well suited to providing an accurate depiction of respondent behavior in purchasing and consumption situations. In some cases, respondents often do not provide truthful verbal responses due to lack of awareness of routinized behavior, social desirability, concern to present a favorable image and other cultural constraints (Bochner, 1986). This is particularly likely to occur in relation to sensitive topics. Observational techniques require the researcher to watch or observe behavior of respondents, for example their daily living patterns and consumption behavior. Observation can take place *in situ* in a real-world situation, such as visits to homes to observe actual consumption behavior and rituals, conduct pantry checks or spend time with families (Cooper *et al.*, 2000). More commonly, however, respondents' behavior is videotaped and the researcher examines and analyzes the videotapes. Videotaping is relatively unobtrusive, as respondents rapidly become absorbed in whatever they are doing and forget they are being observed. This is helpful in cross-cultural research, as it enables researchers to gain insights and understanding into a different and unfamiliar culture without imposing their own cultural frame of reference. Videotaping of respondents means that a visual record is compiled and can be used to illustrate points or findings in a report, thus helping to bring home issues relating to a specific local cultural context. Videotapes of respondents in different cultures can be compared, allowing for identification of similarities and differences across cultures.

Quasi-observational techniques used in the social sciences can be adapted to cross-national research (Webb *et al.*, 1981). These include: (1) *physical trace measures*, which are obtained by collecting traces left by different kinds of behavior, such as fingerprints or empty packages; (2) *archival* records, which consist of historical or public records, sales records or personal documents, photo albums and so on; and (3) *entrapment* measures, where a respondent is induced to respond to an artificially contrived stimulus without being aware of its true purpose, for example actors playing certain roles. In cross-national research, such techniques are primarily useful in researching sensitive topics, or situations where the respondent is not able or willing to respond to direct questioning. They help to uncover attitudes and perceptions or provide insights into situations where there are strong social norms and where 'politically correct' views tend to bias responses. They have the advantage, particularly in countries with low levels of literacy, of not requiring any direct response from respondents. However, they suffer from the same problems as in domestic research, such as contextual effects distorting motivations or the underlying cognitive processes of the behavior observed.

# Pure Observation

A method of data collection extensively used in cultural anthropology and in investigating cross-cultural phenomena in other social sciences is pure observation (Weick, 1985). Here, the researcher observes behavior patterns in the culture under investigation. In some cases, subjects are not aware of being observed, so that the technique is totally nonreactive. In other cases, however, the researcher participates in the life of the culture, playing the role of a 'participant observer'. While initially used to study behavior in specific communities, such as Hopi Indians or Italian-Americans in Boston, this technique has more recently been extended to examine daily life patterns, rituals and consumption behavior of specific cultures and subculture groups, for example Mexican Americans and immigrants (Penaloza, 1994) as well as behavior in situations such as bars and jewelry stores (Spradley and McCurdy, 1972).

In cross-national research, pure or simple observational techniques can be used in a number of different contexts. Consumption behavior can be observed both in and outside the home, and shopping behavior in open-air markets, retail stores or other locations. The researcher can note the length of the bargaining or negotiation process, the amount being purchased, the conditions of sale and so on. Where observation is undertaken in the retail store, the customer's trip through the store and their traffic patterns can be observed and counts made of the number of items examined per product class, their shelf location and time spent looking at product labeling, promotions and so on. Consumers can be videotaped as they move through the stores, and their interaction with others, for example conversations with store personnel or interaction among shoppers, can be studied. The observation can either be made by individuals posted in the store, or by watching instore television monitoring screens, or with hidden cameras in countries where this is legal.

This type of data is useful in providing insights into how people purchase in different shopping environments, and how these environments affect their knowledge and evaluation of products, as well as their actual purchase decisions. It is especially valuable where the shopping environment differs significantly from one country to another, and relative to the researcher's home environment. Comparisons can be made of similar shopping environments in different countries and contexts, such as between supermarkets or small family-owned stores, in order to explore the interaction between a given shopping environment and cultural context.

Consumption behavior can be observed in different environments, for example in the home vs other sites such as restaurants, cafés and bars. For instance, observation of alcohol consumption in style-bar environments in London, Paris and Barcelona helped to provide some important insights into the factors influencing brand choice in these environments (Whiting and Monnier McClure, 2003). In particular, the importance of group dynamics and the interaction between individuals and the bartenders was clearly apparent. Significant differences were observed by gender, with women being more inclined to seek advice from bartenders than were men.

Where it is feasible to enter individual homes and observe behavior, many valuable insights can be gained into how consumers actually use products or perform various tasks. For example, videotaping consumers in their homes as they prepare meals, or observing how consumers do the washing, helps reveal how household tasks are performed in different cultures. As with observations in the purchase environment, such data can provide information not only about actual consumption, but also about interaction among family members. Such information is almost impossible to obtain through survey research, since respondents are rarely able to articulate fully interactions or the influence of others. Furthermore, if the researcher has limited prior knowledge about the culture, he or she may not know what questions to ask. For example, in examining dishwashing behavior, more insights may be gained from actually observing housewives doing the dishes rather than attempting to ask appropriate questions about dishwashing.

Another type of observation is that of expressive behavior, such as facial expressions, body movements, distances kept between individuals in conversations and other forms of social interaction (Hall, 1959). Rules for such behavior often differ significantly from one country to another. Use of voice intonation and inflection, pauses in conversations and verbal expressions vary and have different significance and meaning. Examination of such cues and their meaning in different countries and cultures is often important in understanding the interviewer–interviewee interaction and also that between the customer and sales person. It may be desirable to explore these factors prior to designing a survey in unfamiliar cultures, or where the problem relates to the effectiveness of different sales techniques and, particularly, personal selling.

Observation has several advantages as a methodology in cross-national and cross-cultural research. In addition to providing insights into the role of contextual factors in consumer behavior and response patterns, videotaping provides a wealth of information about visual cues and their role in product evaluation and purchase behavior, which are not easily obtained from other forms of data collection. On the other hand, observation is open to the criticism that its interpretation is highly subjective. The onus is on the researcher to interpret the data collected. This can be problematic where observation is conducted in different cultural contexts by a researcher with little familiarity with these cultures. The researcher may tend to interpret the data in terms of his or her own cultural self-referent. This type of bias can to some degree be minimized, if interpretation of the data is centralized and conducted by several researchers with experience in multiple cultures. Potential bias due to interpretation in terms of local cultural idiosyncrasies is reduced through use of a common analytic framework to interpret data collected locally. Often this results in greater attention to identifying commonalties across cultures that might otherwise be lost if data are interpreted locally.

## Trace Measures

Physical trace measures can also be collected. These differ from pure observation insofar as they are traces of behavior rather than actual behavior. They are primarily useful in tracking the incidence or frequency of different types of behavior where some physical traces can be identified and associated with the behavior. However, some ingenuity is required to devise appropriate measures to track the behavior studied. Examples of physical trace measures used in market research include the number of times a web site has been visited and pantry checks.

In cross-national research, package shapes and designs can be analyzed in different countries to assess those most likely to be the most effective. Similarly, the content of garbage cans can be analyzed to assess the rate of alcohol consumption or use of manufacturer versus private-label brands of canned or bottled items. However, careful attention needs to be paid to the availability and use of different methods of disposal in different countries, such as trash compactors, or prevalence of cans versus returnable bottles, and the importance of in-home versus on-premise consumption, in order to ensure that measures are comparable across countries and cultures. Pantry checks provide another means to check on actual usage of different products or brands where social norms might result in distortion of verbal responses. Again, in cross-national research, careful attention needs to be paid to comparability in the availability of storage space and storage habits.

Artifacts from a particular consumption context or shopping environment can also be collected to provide a reflection of the cultural context. For example, photographs or videotapes can be taken or other materials relating to the environment, for example promotional or point-of-sale materials, may be collected. These can be compared across countries or consumption sites to provide insights into cultural differences in the atmospheric and physical characteristics of the consumption or purchase context.

As with observational measures, physical trace measures avoid the problems of reactivity associated with questionnaires and interviewer-administered surveys. They also eliminate difficulties arising from the interaction between an interviewer and respondent. This is advantageous in cross-national research, due to the potential for miscommunication where research is being conducted in a diversity of cultural environments.

On the other hand, physical trace measures suffer from similar limitations to observational measures. They are open to criticisms of subjectivity in interpretation, especially in terms of inferences made about the link between the indicator or measure used and the behavior studied. The measures selected need to be appropriate and reflective of the specific behavior or context studied. Also, if indicators used are subject to erosion or accretion (that is, of wear or build-up), careful attention needs to be paid to the impact of time factors, such as the rapidity with which erosion takes place or accretion builds up during the period in which measurement takes place.

## *Archival Measures*

Similar types of data are archival records. While not strictly speaking observational data, they are closely related to these measures. Archival records include sources such as official public or government records, mass media, sales records, industrial records and personal documents (Webb *et al.*, 1981). While these can also be classed as secondary data, here they are used as surrogate indicators of the attitudes and behaviors of interest.

A variety of different types of records may be used as surrogate measures of attitudinal and behavioral phenomena. For example, anxiety associated with airplane travel has been assessed based on flight insurance sales and consumption of alcoholic drinks in airports. Violence in a society might be examined in terms of murder or violent crime rates, as well as attendance of violent movies or watching of crime and other violent shows on television. Advertisements provide a record of the ways in which products are used or viewed in a country and can be used to provide insights into different roles in society such as those of women, senior citizens or minorities, by the ways in which they are depicted.

Content analysis of documents and other verbal or visual stimuli may provide indicators of attitudinal and behavioral trends in different countries and cultures. The famous study by McClelland (1961) of achievement motivation in different cultures was, for example, predominantly based on content analysis of different types of stimuli ranging from literature, folk tales and children's stories, to ceramic designs on urns. Content analysis of mass media and of advertisements can be used to identify dominant cultural values and attitudes, for example the degree of materialism or individualism (Belk and Pollay, 1985).

Archival records are useful sources of information in cross-national research because, like observational measures, they are unobtrusive. In addition, they enable examination of phenomena over time while other external or environmental conditions vary. The primary limitation of such measures, as with other observational techniques, consists in the assumptions made about the link between the measure and the specific behavior or attitude studied. Furthermore, the comparability of this link from one country or culture to another has to be considered. In addition, since archival records are collected for a specific purpose other than the one studied, it is important to evaluate how and for whom these records are compiled, and what might be potential sources of error or inaccuracy in the records. Changes in the size or composition of the population for which records are compiled can, for example, give rise to errors in interpretation, especially where cross-national comparisons are to be made.

# Protocols

Another data collection technique that, like observation, is suited to cross-national research is the protocol. In its original form, a protocol is a record of a respondent's verbalized thought processes while problem solving. This is obtained by asking the respondent to 'think out loud' or talk about anything going through his or her head while making a decision. This type of protocol was originally collected either in a laboratory situation while the respondent was making a simulated purchase decision, or in the field while an actual purchase decision was being made. For further discussion of this type of protocol, see Douglas *et al.* (1981).

Protocol methodologies are specifically designed to avoid the imposition of a pre-specified choice model on the respondent, allowing him or her to talk freely in his or her own terms about an actual choice task or decision situation. The researcher does not define or specify the form, or in certain types of protocols the particular stimuli, to which the subject should respond. Hence, the researcher does not impose his or her own cultural frame of reference on the respondent. Rather, each subject identifies, of his or her own accord, the factors of importance to him or her (see Table 7.2 for an example).

Protocols of organizational decision making have been collected while managers are making actual decisions, for example in meetings of buying committees (Montgomery, 1975). Managers have also been asked to recall actual purchase decisions and histories (Farley *et al.*, 1980). Consumer protocols have also been collected both on actual shopping trips and in simulated shopping environments. When protocols are collected on actual shopping trips, it is preferable for the respondent to be accompanied by an interviewer, who then provides an excuse or target for verbalization. These types of protocols tend to be unstructured and the data are often partial in character and difficult to analyze. Alternatively, 'prompted' or retrospective protocols can be collected in a laboratory or other controlled environment. Videotaping of consumers instore has stimulated collection of protocols prompted by the videotape. The consumer is shown the tape and asked to comment on or explain his or her actions (Restall and Auton, 1995).

The absence of a predisposed conceptual framework or verbal stimuli that might generate a culture-specific or pseudo-etic bias makes protocols suitable for use in cross-national research. Protocols can be especially useful in the initial stages of cross-national research in providing insights as to relevant concepts to be examined. They help to identify the terminology used by consumers in relation to products or the store environment. This can be useful when conducting research in different linguistic environments, to identify specific consumer 'speech terms' used in relation to products and usage situations.

While protocol methods offer a number of advantages in cross-national research, they suffer from serious limitations that need to be taken into consideration. In the first place, interpretation of cross-national protocol data is highly subjective. The onus of defining relevant constructs, and determining where there are similarities and differences between countries, is placed on the researcher. This is best resolved by an iterative process using multiple judges, each with different cultural self-referents, to analyze the data and develop relevant coding categories.

| Table 7.2   An excerpt from a protocol collected in France |
|---|
| What are we going to look at next – detergents. Well, detergents, that's a difficult item to buy. I must look at the prices and at the special offers (laughter). Ariel 32.50 francs for 5 kilos. It's always the same weight, it's a good product, is advertised regularly on TV, but I don't think ever has a promotion on these packages. Skip is also good product which washes well, and the promotion is either a jam jar or a freezing tray. Well, I think I'll take the freezing tray, because the weight of the gift is included in the weight of the package, and one certainly gets more detergent with a freezing tray than with a jam jar. |
| *Source*: A Study of Consumer Information Processing at Centre d'Enseignement Superieur des Affaires (1978) Jouy-en-Josas, France. |

Verbalizations also tend to be partial in character, consisting predominantly of 'top of the mind' information. However, if collected in conjunction with other stimuli, for example videotaping of actual shopping trips, store environments and shopping malls, they can be helpful in providing a more complete picture of customer reactions, including visual and verbal data.

In essence, protocols provide a wealth of detail and a breadth of coverage, particularly in relation to the role of situational variables, that is not found in other data collection techniques. Their qualitative character implies that they are best suited for use in conjunction with other types of data collection, rather than to develop precise measures of concepts and behavior.

# Projective Techniques

Projective and elicitation techniques are frequently used in qualitative research, often in conjunction with in-depth interviews, focus groups and extended creativity groups as well as online. The primary purpose of these techniques is to encourage respondents to project their private and unconscious beliefs through unstructured material (projective stimuli), and to express personal and subjective associations in an indirect way using symbols, projected images and signs. Increasingly, the growth of Internet access and ability to use visual stimuli online has meant that projective techniques can be administered over the Internet. They can be used to bring to light aspects of day-to-day life and actions that are routine and hence taken for granted. In a group context, they facilitate the opening up and discussion of personal or emotional issues and unconscious reactions or behavior through the exchange and discussion of images, or response to projective tasks. In this context, projective tasks can, for example, be performed individually and then shared in the group.

According to Cooper (1996) and Branthwaite and Cooper (2001) projective and elicitation techniques aid in:

- indicating emotional as well as rational reactions;
- tapping nonverbal means of communication such as sensations, ambience, visual memories, treasured instances;
- giving permission to express novel and creative ideas;
- encouraging fantasy, idiosyncrasy and imagination;
- reducing social constraints and censorship;
- encouraging group sharing and 'opening up';
- raising awareness of everyday actions commonly taken for granted.

Projective and elicitation tasks are more widely used in Europe than in the US, due to differences in research traditions and philosophy. In the US, focus groups are used to probe specific issues and tend to reflect social interaction as well as the effect of group dynamics. In Europe, focus groups are frequently used to probe unconscious reactions and feelings. Consequently, they rely heavily on projective techniques. Clients are typically more concerned with understanding customers and their cognitions and responses to the world around them, than with focusing on specific problems.

While rooted in Western research traditions, projective and elicitation techniques are used in a range of cultures including the Middle East and Asia, although some adaptation by the moderator may be required (Lindzey, 1961). Even within Europe, adjustments are required. North Europeans, for example, are often more reserved and require deeper probing, while Southern Europeans are more open and verbal. In Asia, respondents are often reluctant to express personal views or to disagree with one another. Projective techniques can be helpful in encouraging expression of these views and opening up freer discussion, although use of tasks requiring confrontation or critical evaluation of relations with others is unlikely to be successful.

An important issue in using projective and elicitation techniques in international marketing research is the extent to which projective techniques and stimuli and their interpretation are standardized across countries or cultures. On the one hand, it can be argued that standardization inhibits creativity and identification or exploration of culture-specific responses, and of understanding how people relate to the world in which they live. On the other hand, consistency and comparability of results are essential if valid comparisons are to be made and genuine similarities and differences identified, rather than variations due to differences in how data are collected and interpreted. Particularly critical in this regard is variation due to interviewer or moderator ability and training. Abilities of local inter-viewers or moderators vary and contribute to differences in results from one country to another.

Any projective or elicitation technique can be used in a culture once interviewers or moderators are appropriately trained and consistent instructions are given to respondents. However, some techniques have been found to be more suitable to address marketing issues, and are easier for moderators to administer as well as more economical. These include collages, picture completion, analogies and metaphors, psycho-drawing and personalization. These are less likely to be subject to cultural bias in, for example, Asian or Muslim countries.

Projective techniques such as bubble drawings, picture completion and personalization can also be administered over the Internet. This has the advantage of allowing respondents to complete the task in their own time without the inhibiting presence of an interviewer. Response to projective stimuli over the Internet has been found to be considerably richer, longer and more revealing. Without the presence of an interviewer or moderator, respondents feel freer to express their inner-most and private feelings, including providing responses that might be censored in a social context (Wilkie, Adams and Girnins, 1999; Taylor, 2000). A major advantage of administering projective techniques over the Internet is that they can be combined with other questions using standardized response formats. The qualitative insights are thus supplemented with quantitative evaluations of similar dimensions of feelings and emotions, or images. This provides a much fuller and richer spectrum of results combining the richness of qualitative data with the precision of quantitative approaches, and telescoping the time normally taken to conduct qualitative followed by quantitative research.

The primary limitation of an Internet-based study is the representativeness of the sample, since Internet penetration varies considerably from country to country, and is quite low in some coun-tries. Equally, interpretation of results may pose some difficulties and require interpretation by local researchers as well as centralized interpretation across countries.

Other techniques are less suited to cross-cultural research. For example, techniques such as role playing or mock selling are less effective in Asian cultures, since they entail social conflict. Tech-niques that are heavily language based or rely on local symbolism, such as telling fables or sorting faces or other local stimuli, are less suitable. Techniques that take time or require high levels of effort on the part of respondents or skill on the part of the moderator, for example, mime, guided dreams and play, are more difficult to use effectively in a number of countries.

**Figure 7.1** Collage constructed by Argentinean teenagers
*Source*: Thiesse, 1996a.

# *Collages*

Collages are increasingly used in cross-national qualitative research, to gain understanding of an individual's lifestyle or to develop perceptions of a brand, product or product class. In collages, respondents are asked to select images and symbols, either from a pre-selected set of stimuli or from magazines and other media of their own choosing, and to assemble them in a collage (Cooper, 1996). This can either be done individually or in groups. For example, part of a study conducted by Research International Qualitatif (Thiesse, 1996a) of teenagers worldwide explored how teenagers viewed their future, and their expected optimism or pessimism about their life as an adult. Since it was difficult for them to verbalize at a rational level, groups of teenagers in each country were asked to develop collages about their feelings with regard to their future life (Thiesse, 1996a). This revealed significant differences between countries. A collage produced by some Argentinean teenagers showed strong signs of pessimism (Figure 7.1), while another constructed by Greek teenagers reflected greater optimism and hedonism (Figure 7.2).

**Figure 7.2**   Collage constructed by Greek teenagers
*Source*: Thiesse, 1996a.

# *Analogies and Metaphors*

Analogies and metaphors can be used to encourage a wider range of expression. Respondents are asked to indicate their associations and make analogies with the subject under discussion, or with products and brands. This technique is helpful when used in a group to open up group discussion and stimulate expression of a wider and richer range of ideas and thoughts.

Another version of this technique is to present the respondent with a set of standardized projective stimuli, for example pictures or icons, and to ask them to select those that best fit the brand or subject examined. Research International has developed a battery of 30 pictures representing symbols such as water, earth, fire and air. These have been validated in 37 countries. For example, one picture showing a bungee jumper gives a positive image full of vitality, energy and strong emotions. Another, showing a mountain lake, conveys feelings of tranquillity, harmony, stability

**Figure 7.3**   Stimulus picture used by Research International

and peace (Figure 7.3). Association of these pictures with products or brands helps to develop a rich picture of the images and emotions evoked by the stimuli.

# Picture Completion

Another technique particularly suited to cross-cultural research is picture completion. Pictures can be designed to fit the specific problem being studied, and respondents asked to indicate associations or attribute words to the figures. Various variants of this technique can be adopted ranging from use of pictures, to stick figures, bubble drawings or other ambiguous stimuli. A standard set of pictures can also be used cross-culturally and differences in associations elicited compared across cultures. Picture completion tasks can also be administered over the Internet using samples drawn from different countries. An important advantage of this approach is that consumers can perform the task in their own time and feel freer to provide a more detailed response than when an interviewer or other persons are present.

# Psycho-drawing

With psycho-drawing, respondents are given papers and crayons and asked to express the brand, product or topic using any color, shape or symbol. This is similar to picture completion except that no specific stimulus is given to respondents. Rather, respondents are allowed full range of expression. This can be particularly helpful in stimulating group discussion. Respondents can, for example, perform the task individually and then discuss their individual drawings in groups. This requires the respondent to verbalize and interpret his or her drawing and may also elicit reaction and interpretation by others. On the other hand, interpretation of psycho-drawings and developing generalizations from them requires some skill. In particular, absence of standardized stimuli and differences in the meaning and associations attached to colors or symbols can make comparisons of results across countries difficult.

# Personalization

Personalization involves asking respondents to treat the brand or product as a person and to articulate associations or images of this person. For example, the brand Ariel is called Mrs Ariel, and respondents are asked to project their images of Mrs Ariel (Cooper, 1996). This helps to bring the brand alive and to understand the personality it has developed through packaging, advertising and so on.

Alternatively, respondents in different countries can be shown a standard set of photos or visuals of a particular type of individual and asked which one best corresponds to a given brand. For example, if a brand is perceived as being typically used by a 'modern woman', different pictures of 'modern women' can be shown and respondents asked to indicate which type best depicts or might be associated with the brand. A brand is viewed as possessing a character and set of associations that can be probed across countries and cultures, although the nature of these characteristics and their value may vary from country to country.

Depending on the specific research problem or type of data required, different techniques may be more useful or appropriate (Cooper, 1996; Branthwaite and Cooper, 2001). Elicitation techniques, together with probing, help to open up group discussion among respondents. Projective techniques, however, are better able to reveal unconscious, cultural images and associations and intuitive feelings. Collages are helpful in understanding the cultural and competitive context. Personalization and picture completion help to probe user imagery, analogies and metaphors of brand images, while core feelings about the brand may best be identified through psycho-drawings or personalization.

These various techniques offer a number of advantages in international or cross-cultural research. They aid in revealing unconscious feelings and images about products, brands and other stimuli. They are useful in starting discussion on topics where there may be social constraints or censoring. On the other hand, data interpretation remains subjective even where standardized stimuli are used, and requires considerable training and skill. Variability in the skill of the moderator can also affect results and the consistency of data collection and comparability of findings across countries or cultures. Development of a validated battery of standardized stimuli and uniform procedures to be adopted across countries can help enhance consistency of results and facilitate comparison across countries.

# In-depth Interviews

In-depth interviews are among the most commonly used methods of data collection in qualitative research and may be used in conjunction with other techniques such as projective techniques, protocols and so on. In-depth interviews can either be conducted on an individual, one-on-one basis or in small groups. In contrast to survey methods, in-depth interviews are unstructured, as the interviewer attempts to probe in-depth attitudes and perceptions about a particular brand, product area or other topic or to stimulate group discussion. The interviewer or moderator plays an important role in eliciting responses, especially where no pre-structured tasks are used.

In cross-national research, in-depth interviews are suited to situations where the interviewer aims to gain understanding of customer attitudes and behavior or feelings and associations about a topic, or the language and terms used in discussion of that topic. The unstructured nature of the interview enables the interviewer to probe and does not require the imposition of a pre-structured format or questions that may reflect a specific cultural background or bias. On the other hand, interpretation of data, especially where researchers come from different research traditions, is subjective and, as with other qualitative techniques, variability in moderator skills can affect consistency of data and comparability across countries.

Training of interviewers to ensure consistency of results is an important issue. Here, different approaches are used. Companies large enough to have their own interviewers, either in local offices or at head or regional offices in the case of telephone interviewers, often have extensive training programs to ensure the quality and consistency of results. Other companies work with local interviewers skilled in the relevant language and provide detailed local briefs on the topic to be probed. In some cases, executives from head office supervise the briefing of local interviewers, and also monitor a number of interviews or focus groups in each country researched. Over time as a research organization gains experience in conducting in-depth interviews in different countries, it will often build up a network of preferred suppliers or interviewers who meet its standards and have a similar research approach or philosophy. Some organizations also centralize data interpretation in order to ensure consistency of findings across countries. Local interviewers or moderators synthesize the results of the interviews and then send these together with the transcripts or videos of the interview to a central location for interpretation and analysis.

## *Individual In-depth Interviews*

Individual in-depth interviews are conducted on a one-to-one basis between the interviewer and respondent. This has the advantage that the interviewer can probe attitudes and pinpoint responses to a specific topic. This may be useful where the purpose of the research is to understand customer attitudes and feelings about a product class or topic area, and to delve in depth into the personal, social and cultural context surrounding purchase or consumption.

Individual interviews were, for example, conducted with young consumers in Latin America to see how they perceived the culture and personality of global brands (Troiano, Costa and Guardado, 2002). Interviews were conducted with 700 male and female consumers aged 15–34 in Brazil, Mexico and Venezuela to examine their images of four global brands: MTV, Coca-Cola, Nike and McDonald's. Visual stimuli were used to study these perceptions, which were highly similar across the three countries.

In-depth individual interviews are useful in business-to-business marketing research where it may be desirable to tailor questions to a company or to a specific respondent's knowledge and background. In addition, in a number of cases, the sample of companies or potential respondents is relatively small and readily identifiable. For example, the research may be designed to elicit response or reactions to a new product concept among potential buyers who are existing clients of the company. Interviews can also be conducted by telephone by bilingual interviewers, cutting down on travel costs and facilitating centralized control, both in terms of the quality and consistency of results.

However, in-depth interviewing requires highly skilled interviewers. Where interviews are conducted locally, this may give rise to a number of problems. In the first place, in industrialized countries, interviewers with experience in conducting in-depth interviews may come from a particular psychology tradition, and hence focus on specific aspects of a topic. For example, interviewers with a psycho-analytical background may emphasize the individual's subconscious relation or involvement with a brand, with less attention to the sociocultural context. It is important to have training and briefing of interviewers in different countries to harmonize their approach and ensure consistent data and results. In addition, in some countries, for example emerging markets, it may be difficult to find trained local interviewers and time and effort will be needed to train them. Use of standardized projective techniques in conjunction with in-depth interviews helps to ensure consistency of results.

Conduct of in-depth interviews by telephone from a centralized location facilitates coordination and comparability of results. As noted earlier, trained bilingual interviewers can be briefed centrally, conduct the interview in multiple countries in the local language, and transcribe the interview into a common language. Discrepancies and problems of interpretation can then be discussed and resolved. While experience suggests that such interviews can successfully be carried out for 45 to 90 minutes, the main drawback is the inability to use visual stimuli or other aids.

# *Focus Groups*

Focus groups are group discussions conducted with individuals who are representative of the target market(s) in an informal setting. The discussion is 'moderated' by an interviewer who plays a key role in stimulating discussion about feelings, attitudes and perceptions relating to the topic being studied, and in centering this interchange on relevant issues. As in the case of other forms of qualitative research, there tend to be differences in approach and emphasis in the conduct of focus groups in different countries, notably between the US and Europe. As discussed earlier, these stem in part from differences in the underlying philosophy of qualitative research, as well as client interest and focus. In the US, groups emphasize direct questioning and specific issues and more direct interpretation. In Europe, groups are more open-ended and make greater use of projective techniques, especially in France and Italy.

Focus groups have been successfully used in all parts of the world, even in countries such as Japan or South Korea, where social norms restrict frank and open discussion of personal or emotional issues or expression of controversial opinions. Typically some adaptation by the moderator to local conventions and sensitivity to social norms will be required.

Focus groups are suited to generating and testing ideas for new products, product concepts and product positioning; studying responses to packaging and advertising themes; and assessing and tracking customer needs and interests and detecting new trends. In particular, they can be used: (1) to explore or probe new themes or areas of interest, and to generate hypotheses to be studied quantitatively in subsequent research; (2) to elicit information helpful in structuring questionnaires, for example about the language terms, key phrases and words used by consumers in relation to a specific product category or brand; (3) to test new product concepts and ideas and brand positioning; (4) to explore relations and associations with specific brands; and (5) to assess and track changes in customer needs and interest relating to a specific product or consumption area.

The primary advantage of group as opposed to individual interviews is that the presence of other group members provides a synergy that stimulates discussion. Comments made by one group member may evoke a response or set off a train of thought or ideas among other group members. The presence and open expression of views by more extroverted group members provides a socially reinforcing situation, which may encourage more timid individuals to verbalize their own attitudes and views. However, sensitivity to cultural norms and social pressures is needed in conducting focus groups in some countries. In Western countries, respondents are willing to talk openly about their own feelings and opinions on various topics. In other countries where 'collectivist' norms prevail, consumers may have difficulty in expressing individual views and particularly in voicing controversial opinions or views contrary to those of other group members. In Japan smaller groups of two or three people are often more successful so that individuals do not take responsibility in front of a large group for their own views.

As in the case of individual in-depth interviews, use of focus groups in multicountry research poses a number of problems, especially with regard to comparability of method and data. In the first place, the role of the moderator is crucial to success. Consequently, trained bilingual moderators, conversant with the appropriate language and also patterns of social interaction in each country or culture, are required. This can pose problems, particularly in emerging countries such as those in Eastern Europe or South East Asia, particularly China, where the research infrastructure is not well established. Consequently the research organization may need to invest in training local interviewers and supervisors.

Secondly, as in the case of other types of qualitative research, interpretation and analysis of focus group data are subjective in character and require considerable skill and experience. In cross-cultural research, understanding not only verbal data but also nonverbal cues such as voice intonation, gestures and expressions used in other countries and cultures is often a key to successful interpretation of findings. The increasing sophistication and quality of videotaping imply, however, that qualitative video reports of groups can also be developed. Thus, in addition to providing transcriptions of the groups translated into the appropriate language, video reports can be used to supplement traditional written reports and to illustrate findings and conclusions (Thiesse, 1996b). The videos themselves can be used as a stimulus. In a study by Tobin *et al.* (1989), child development experts, teachers and parents in three countries were shown videotapes of pre-school classes in three cultures, China, Japan and the US (two plus their own). The most revealing discussions occurred when the actions depicted in the video violated the cultural norms of the observer's culture.

It is also possible to code videotape sessions on each video frame to facilitate subsequent analysis (Greenfield, 1997). Once the frames are coded as to content, the video is digitized and copied to a CD-ROM. This allows direct access to any portion of the video and facilitates aggregation of similarly coded activities. The other advantage of the videotape sessions is that they provide a permanent record of the sessions that can be analyzed by other researchers without having to recreate the conditions.

The extent to which interpretation and reporting are centralized varies according to the research organization. Some centralize transcripts and videotapes of groups and conduct interpretation and analysis centrally. This typically requires availability of bilingual executives at head office, but it helps to 'decenter' interpretation and reduces the extent to which interpretation reflects differences in research traditions rather than 'true' cultural differences and similarities. Others rely on interpretation and analysis by local moderators and then integrate these into a common report.

Increasingly, there is a tendency to adopt a more interactive approach to focus groups, to encourage consumers to participate actively in the discussion and to enlist them as a partner in the discussion and exploration of topics. Conduct of focus groups in a studio environment tends to create a sterile, clinical environment in which consumers will tend to play back images or associations of brands projected by the media. This is particularly likely to occur in emerging country markets such as China, where exposure to the images of Western media, symbols and icons is relatively recent. As a result, increasing efforts are being made to create a more realistic environment and to give the consumer a more active role in the group. This may include conduct of interviews in the home, or conduct of consumer workshops, for example above a bar or café, as well as increased use of projective techniques. Consumers may be asked to bring photographs to the session to discuss, or to go shopping in a different store from the one where they usually shop, or look for a new product. These tasks then form the basis of the discussion. Increasingly, therefore, the distinctions between observation, projective techniques, group interviews and creativity groups are becoming blurred.

## Electronic Focus Groups

Focus groups can also be conducted in different locations in the world using videoconferencing technology, so that participants can interact with each other (Miller, 1991). This does require that participants share a common language, and also that time differences can be accommodated. This leads to an increased administrative burden as two or more focus groups have to be coordinated simultaneously in real time. The high cost means that this approach is most effective in business-to-business studies or for high-end products.

Group support systems can also be conducted in multiple locations using electronic technology. Participants sit at computers and type in responses to questions posed by the facilitator. Contributions to the discussion are processed in parallel so that everyone can 'talk' at once. This avoids the difficulties associated with certain participants dominating the group. Ideas and opinions are anonymous. The facilitator is free to pay full attention to group dynamics without having to control speakers or take notes. This approach can be used to facilitate various types of group processes including brainstorming, discussing and organizing ideas, and evaluating and rating concepts.

The primary limitations in an international context are the need to coordinate time differences across geographical locations. Furthermore, linguistic constraints suggest that the sessions need to be conducted in a common language. Consequently, most global groups are conducted in English, although other language groups such as French or Spanish can also be organized.

Chat rooms on the Internet can also provide a valuable source of ideas for management about new products, product endorsement, promotional campaigns and other marketing activities as well as a conduit for identifying current and future trends. Chat rooms can be started by consumers or marketers and are typically product or interest specific, for example relating to biking, a particular genre of music, gardening or baby products. These can be avatar or more commonly text based (Zanasi, 2003) and can be monitored and content analyzed to obtain information relating to customer interests, needs, complaints and other concerns. Again, language constraints typically limit the scope and type of participant in a chat room, but rooms in different languages can be set up and monitored.

## Extended Creativity Groups

Creativity groups differ from focus groups primarily in terms of the length of time the group meets and the extent to which projective techniques and other tasks are used. Respondents are stimulated to delve into their own feelings and views about a brand or topic or to play out different perspectives on the topic, rather than relying solely on the moderator's skills to encourage discussion (Cooper, 1996). Focus groups typically last between one and a half and two hours, while extended creativity groups can last four hours or longer and in some cases take place over a weekend. The specific tasks performed and the way in which the sessions are organized can vary considerably according to the purpose of the session and the approach of the moderator.

It is considered important to recruit individuals with above-average or high levels of creativity for the groups. Standard screening tasks are administered to select group members. These often have to be adapted appropriately in a given culture or country. For example, a standard question in Western nations is 'How many uses can you think of for a brick?' In Japan and South East Asia, where bricks are rarely used for building, an equivalent question might be 'How many uses can you think of for a single chopstick?'

Extended creativity groups can be used in a number of situations. They are often used to involve respondents in exploring motivations, feelings and points of view and to think creatively about a topic, such as a new positioning for a brand. They can also be used to develop and screen new product ideas and concepts, new advertising ideas or ideas for brand stretching. Creativity groups conducted with children are somewhat shorter than normal due to their shorter attention span, lasting only three to four hours in contrast to the one to two days that is common for those conducted with adults. Creativity groups can also be used to diagnose current attitudinal and consumption trends in a given area, for example food, and to predict future trends as well as those in the society or world at large. In this case, the group is usually conducted over a longer period.

Research International used extended focus groups involving 1500 young urban consumers in 41 countries to probe reactions to global brands. In the discussions a variety of projective techniques were employed to explore consumer feelings and attitudes to over 100 specific global and local brands (Baker, Sterenberg and Taylor, 2004). These revealed that brands had considerable personal meaning and relevance. One Argentine consumer confessed, 'If I could, I would die for a Chanel suit,' while an Italian consumer said, 'If I wear Nike, there is no need to say anything, if I choose another brand it is as though I'm stating something that I have to explain.'

This research identified four different types of global brands: *master* brands like Nike, Sony and Coca-Cola built on a powerful myth or narrative; *prestige* brands such as Chanel and Rolex, with an appeal built on cultural origin or technology; *universal* brands such as Gillette, Pepsi and Shell, defined by the category rather than a myth or narrative; and *glocal* brands such as Dove and Danone, available globally but marketed locally.

Different approaches can be used to conduct creativity groups, depending on the purpose of the study. Where attention is focused on exploring feelings, attitudes and points of view about a brand or developing creative ideas, respondents might, for example, be divided into two or more subgroups to work as separate teams (Restall and Auton, 1995). They might then work on various projective techniques. The subgroups are brought together to represent their viewpoints or present their ideas and discuss these with the other groups. This helps to involve group members to ensure that they 'take responsibility' for their opinions and ideas and justify these to other groups.

Where the purpose of the group is to diagnose trends relating to a specific product market or topic area, the group may be less structured. Greater reliance may be placed on brainstorming or other creativity tasks such as painting masks or psycho-drawing (Cathelat, 1973). Tasks might for example center around the invention of an ideal product at some time in the future. The time span has to be sufficiently close to be realistic, and sufficiently distant to justify the creation of a new product. Scenarios such as journeys into the future, science fiction and so on are often used. The imagery associated with certain brands or other product symbols, desired new products, ideal brands, products and concepts can also be explored.

Creativity groups can also be conducted in a structured sequence over a period of time. This is particularly helpful in generating and screening ideas for new products and studying reactions over time, for example where a product market is changing rapidly or new entrants are coming into the market. As companies are increasingly under pressure to innovate and launch new products rapidly, conducting a structured sequence of creativity groups, provides a means to compress the new product development process and generate new concepts, rapidly and efficiently.

Research International, for example, has developed a set of techniques called the 'Concept Factory' to generate new product concepts and ideas (Thiesse, 1996b). This integrates specialists from R&D, marketing and advertising together with the client into the development process. The approach relies on a series of mini-groups and creativity groups to generate and screen concepts, often in conjunction with video techniques. First, a development taskforce is established consisting of specialists and experts in a range of areas including R&D, marketing and advertising. These taskforce members first conduct interviews with and observe a small number of consumers, probing for problems, needs and expectations. This phase is intended to stimulate idea generation and provide a consumer focus to these ideas. An 'Interactive Innovation' session or workshop is then conducted with the taskforce members to generate innovative ideas quickly, encouraging lateral thinking and exploration of ideas that might not be considered in a more logical or rational process. Next, the ideas generated by the workshop are explored in a series of video clinics of around five consumers in which the consumers react to and free associate with these ideas. From this a series of 'consumer-oriented' concepts is developed. Finally, the concepts are screened through discussion in creativity groups, often using projective techniques. This helps to assess the strengths and weaknesses of the concepts, their associations and relevance to different types of consumers as well as to identify likely target groups for them.

The primary advantage of the creativity group, as opposed to the focus group, is the use of projective techniques and the performance of creative tasks combined with group discussion and interaction. This encourages participants to be more proactive, actively taking responsibility for ideas, representing their own views and opinions and considering different perspectives on the brand or issues at hand, rather than depending exclusively on the skills of the moderator to engage their interest and involvement. The tasks performed and the active participation of respondents reduce the tendency to play back socially acceptable views and opinions or echo those that are projected by the mass media. Positive and negative associations with the topics are evoked and consumers encouraged to go beneath the surface, to express deeper feelings, emotions and thoughts than might otherwise emerge in a group discussion. As a result, creativity groups are particularly valuable in relation to topics or areas such as future trends, where spontaneous expression of thoughts or reactions may pose some difficulties and subjects are often not totally conscious of these.

Creativity groups suffer from some of the same limitations noted earlier in relation to focus groups. The analysis poses even greater problems of subjectivity, since the difficulties associated with qualitative data interpretation are further compounded by those associated with projective techniques. Consequently, the success of a creativity group depends on how it is designed, and the matching of the appropriate technique and approach with the purpose of the study.

# Summary

Nonsurvey data collection techniques play an important role in international marketing research. This role is even more critical than in domestic marketing research, due to the frequent lack of familiarity with cultural mores and behavior in a country. Qualitative data collection procedures can therefore be used to understand and probe the cultural context of attitudes and behavior, as well as consumption and purchase situations, and also to identify what aspects should be studied in subsequent phases of research.

Four major types of qualitative data collection procedures may be identified: observational and quasi-observational data, projective techniques, protocols and in-depth interviews. These differ primarily in terms of the degree of structure imposed on data collection; whether the respondent is aware of being studied and hence alters his or her behavior; and whether the focus is on measuring actual behavior or, rather, attitudes and verbal rationalizations about behavior, as well as the typical sample size and scope of the data collected.

The main advantage of qualitative data collection is that it can be conducted in a relatively short period (including both data collection and analysis phases), in contrast to the somewhat more laborious procedures entailed in organizing and administering a survey. This makes it well suited to the exploratory stages of international marketing research where it provides input into subsequent stages of research and survey design. Analysis and interpretation of qualitative data are, however, frequently open to criticism, due to their subjective nature. In some cases, qualitative data alone are sufficient to respond to management decision problems. More frequently, they provide a source of complementary information to interpret and round out quantitative research.

# References

Arch, D.C., Bettman, J.R. and Kakkar, P. (1978) Subjects' Information Processing in Information Board Studies. In *Advances in Consumer Research, Vol. 5*. Association for Consumer Research, Chicago.

Baker, M., Sterenberg, G. and Taylor, E. (2004) Managing Global Brands to Meet Consumer Expectations. In *Excellence in International Research 2004*. ESOMAR, Amsterdam.

Banister, P., Burman, E., Parker, I., Taylor, M. and Tindall, C. (1994) *Qualitative Methods in Psychology: A Research Guide*. Open University Press, Buckingham.

Barnard, P. (1997) Global Developments and Future Directions in Market Research. MSI Seminar, *Globalization at the Millennium: Opportunities and Imperatives*, Brussels.

Belk R.W., and Pollay, R.W. (1985) Materialism and Status Appeals in Japanese and U.S. Print Advertising. *International Marketing Review*, Winter, 38–47.

Bochner, S. (1986) Observation Methods. In Walter, L. and Berry, J.W. (eds) *Field Methods in Cross-cultural Research*. Sage Publications, Beverley Hills, CA.

Branthwaite, A. and Cooper, P. (2001) A New Role for Projective Techniques. *Proceedings of ESOMAR Qualitative Conference*, Budapest.

Cathelat, B. (1973) Etude Projective Synapse, unpublished document. Centre de Communication Advance, Paris.

Cooper, P. (1996) Internationalization of Qualitative Research. ESOMAR Congress, Monte Carlo.

Cooper, P. and Patterson, S. (1996) The Future of Qualitative Research. ARF Qualitative Workshop, New York, 18 June.

Cooper, P., Pinijarom, P. and Salari, S. (2000) Modern Consumer Everyday Lives: The Power of Observation. ESOMAR Asia Pacific Marketing Research Conference, November.

Denzin, N.K. and Lincoln, Y.S. (eds) (2002) *Handbook of Qualitative Research*. 2nd edition, Sage Publications, Thousand Oaks, CA.

Douglas, S.P., Craig, C.S. and Faivre, J.-P. (1981) Protocols in Consumer Research: Problems, Methods and Uses. In Sheth, J. (ed.) *Research in Marketing, Vol. 5*. JAI Press, Greenwich, CN.

Farley, J.U., Hulbert, J. and Weinstein, D. (1980) Price Setting and Volume Planning by Two European Industrial Companies: A Study and Comparison of Decision Processes. *Journal of Marketing*, 44, 46–54.

Greenfield, P. (1997) Culture as Process: Empirical Methods for Cultural Psychology. In Berry, J.W., Poortinga, Y. and Pandey, J. (eds) *Handbook of Cross-cultural Psychology, Vol. 1. Theory and Method*. Allyn and Bacon, Boston.

Hall, E.T. (1959) *The Silent Language*. Doubleday, Garden City, NY.

Lindzey, G. (1961) *Projective Techniques and Cross-cultural Research*. Appleton Century Crofts, New York.

Mariampolski, H. (2001) *Qualitative Marketing Research*. Sage, Thousand Oaks, CA.

McClelland, D.C. (1961) *The Achieving Society*. Van Nostrand, Princeton, NJ.

Miller, C. (1991) Anybody Ever Hear of Global Focus Groups? *Marketing News*, 27 May, 14.

Montgomery, D.B. (1975) New Product Decisions: An Analysis of Supermarket Buyer Decisions. *Journal of Marketing Research*, 12, 225–264.

Patton, M.Q. (1990) *Qualitative Evaluation and Research Methods*, 2nd edition. Sage, Thousand Oaks, CA.

Pawle, J.S. and Cooper, P. (2002) Using Web Research Technology to Accelerate Innovation. *Excellence in International Research 2002*. ESOMAR, Amsterdam.

Penaloza, L. (1994) Atravesando Fronteras/Border Crossing: A Critical Ethnographic Exploration of the Consumer Acculturation of Mexican Immigrants. *Journal of Consumer Research*, **21**, 32–54.

Restall, C. and Auton, R. (1995) The Future of Qualitative Research – From Passivity to Interaction. Unpublished document. The Research Business Group, London.

Salari, S., Cooper, P. and Pinijarom, J. (2000) Modern Asian Everyday Lives, the Power of Observation. *Proceedings of ESOMAR Asia Pacific Conference on Redefining Business*, November.

Spradley, J.P. and McCurdy, D.W. (1972) *The Cultural Experience*. Science Research Associates, Chicago.

Taylor, H. (2000) Does Internet Research Work? *Journal of Market Research Society*, **42**, 1.

Thiesse, M. (1996a) The Latest Developments in Qualitative Research. Unpublished document. Research International Qualitatif, Paris.

Thiesse, M. (1996b) Facilitating the Innovation Process. Unpublished document. Research International Qualitatif, Paris.

Tobin, J.J., Wu, D.Y.H. and Davidson, D.H. (1989) *Preschool in Three Cultures: Japan, China and the United States*. Yale University Press, New Haven, CN.

Troiano, J., Costa, W. and Guardado, S. (2002) The Sound of Silence. And the Vision that Was Planted in My Brain Still Remains. *Excellence in International Research 2002*. ESOMAR, Amsterdam.

Webb, E.J., Campbell, D.T., Schwartz, R.D., Sechrest, L. and Grove, J.B. (1981) *Non-reactive Measures in the Social Sciences*, 2nd edition. Houghton Mifflin, Boston.

Weick, K.E. (1985) Systematic Observational Methods. In Lindzey, G. and Aronson, E. (eds) *Handbook of Social Psychology, Vol. 1*, 3rd edition. Random House, New York.

Whiting, M. and Monnier-McClure, S. (2003) Qualitative Research – The Glue for Fragmented Brands. *Excellence in International Research 2003*. ESOMAR, Amsterdam.

Wilkie, S., Adams, G. and Girnius T. (1999) Internet Testing – A Landmark Study. ESOMAR Worldwide Internet-Net Effects, Barcelona.

Zanasi, A. (2003) Email, Chat Lines, Newsgroups. A Continuous Opinion Surveys Source Thanks to Text Mining Utilization. *Excellence in International Research 2003*. ESOMAR, Amsterdam.

# Chapter 8

# SURVEY INSTRUMENT DESIGN

## Introduction

While qualitative data collection techniques aid in identifying relevant constructs and concepts to be examined, survey research provides a means of quantifying these concepts and examining relevant relationships in depth. In this context an important consideration is instrument design. In qualitative data collection, it is important to have an instrument that guides data collection. However, instrument design assumes greater significance in survey research where structured data collection techniques and large sample sizes are typically involved. In particular, it is necessary to ensure that the research instrument is adapted to the specific national and cultural environment and that it is not biased in terms of any one country or culture. Such bias may enter into the initial stage when the instrument is being developed. Bias can also result from the way in which it is administered or from the scoring procedures used. The occurrence of bias in the design and development of measures is widely recognized, and in recent years increasing attention has been paid to scoring procedures and to identifying different sources of response bias. An increasing amount of research has also been conducted outside industrialized countries such as Europe, Japan and the US, among illiterate people or those with low levels of education and from widely divergent cultural backgrounds.

Since the instrument used in survey research is typically a questionnaire, whether administered by interviewer or self-administered, questionnaire design and question formulation are first discussed. Procedures for questionnaire translation are then examined, as well as the use of response formats designed to facilitate respondent comprehension and response accuracy. Then potential sources of bias that may arise as a result of the interviewer–respondent interaction, the personal characteristics of the respondent or the cultural context in which the questionnaire is administered are discussed.

Throughout the chapter attention is focused on problems specific to the design of questionnaires in international or multicountry research, such as establishment of equivalence in questions relating to background characteristics or lifestyle, questionnaire translation, and methods of posing questions so as to ensure comprehension by less-educated or illiterate respondents. It is assumed that the reader is already familiar with the basics of questionnaire design, such as question formulation, sequencing, questionnaire layout and so on. These are covered in sources such as Schwarz (2003) and Oppenheim (1992) as well as in standard marketing research texts such as Aaker *et al.* (2003) and Churchill and Iacobucci (2005).

# Questionnaire Design and Question Formulation

The first step in questionnaire design is to determine what information should be obtained, what questions should be asked and how they should be formulated. Information may be required in relation to three types of variables: (1) demographic, background or respondent characteristics; (2) specific questions such as product usage and brand choice and evaluations, purchase intentions and shopping patterns; and (3) category/domain-specific attitudes and behavior and general attitudinal and lifestyle characteristics. Attention needs to be paid to differences in underlying behaviors, decision processes and lifestyles to ensure that the questions asked have equivalent meaning and evoke responses that are comparable across different countries and cultural contexts. Even household size, occupation, income and dwelling unit have to be specified differently across cultures, due to factors such as extended family structures in countries such as China or India. A decision has to be made about whether open-ended or closed questions are used, and whether direct or indirect questions are more likely to provide an accurate response. Furthermore, it is crucial to translate questions so that they are clearly understood and correctly interpreted in different linguistic and cultural contexts. The response formats should be designed so as to encourage accurate and reliable responses and to minimize potential response bias. Each of these issues is now discussed in more detail.

## *Question Formulation*

The issues arising in relation to question formulation differ somewhat, depending on the type of data or content of the question. As might be anticipated, background and demographic characteristics pose somewhat less of a problem than questions relating to product- or brand-related data. Most difficulties are likely to be encountered with attitudinal and lifestyle questions.

## Background and Demographic Characteristics

It is typically easiest to generate comparable data from one country to another for questions relating to background and demographic characteristics. Some categories, such as sex and age, are the same in all countries or cultures, and hence equivalent questions can be posed, though the manner in which they are posed may differ. More difficulty may be encountered with other categories such as income, education and occupation, or the dwelling unit, since these are not always exactly comparable from one culture or country to another.

For example, marital status can present problems, depending on how the question is phrased. The growing number of cohabiting couples as well as same-sex partners creates a particular problem in this regard. An ESOMAR report on the harmonization of sociodemographics in Europe (ESOMAR, 1997) has recommended the use of three major breakdowns to help ensure comparability: (1) married/living together; (2) single; and (3) widowed/divorced/separated. The English expression 'living together' requires slight modification when translated into French (*vivant comme marié*) and German (*leben mit einem Partner zusammen*).

Similarly, how income is defined may vary from one country to another. In many emerging market economies, as well as the former socialist economies, many people have two jobs. Consequently, they may only report income received from their primary job. Farmers may only report cash crops, ignoring produce or livestock that are bartered or produced for family consumption. In some countries employees may be given year-end or other bonuses, which they do not include as monthly income. The range of income may also vary considerably across countries. One method of comparing income levels across countries is to divide incomes within each country into quartiles, thus comparing relative prosperity rather than absolute income.

Similarly, with regard to education, types of schools, colleges or universities are not always comparable from one country to another. For example, in Germany it takes seven years to complete the *Gymnasium* or high school, while a Dutch *gymnasium* takes only six years to complete. Again, this can be resolved by asking the number of years of schooling, based on the assumption that this provides a more comparable measure than the categories of primary, secondary school, college and postgraduate school typically used for research in the UK. Alternatively, the age at which full-time education is terminated can be used, as in the ESOMAR European Social Grade system.

Occupational categories also may not be comparable from one country to another. For example, differences in the legal system or government bureaucracy result in different categories, such as lawyers in the US, solicitors and barristers in the UK and *avocats* in France. In general, the major distinctions or broad categories tend to be similar – that is, farm workers, industrial workers, blue-collar workers, office or white-collar workers, self-employed persons, lower and upper middle management and the professions – but specific categories with these groupings may vary across countries.

In Europe, ESOMAR has established the European Social Grade system to harmonize sociodemographics across the various countries in Europe (ESOMAR, 1997). This consists of eight categories, (A, B, C1, C2, D and E1, E2, E3) based on the occupation and age of terminal education of the main income earner. The economic status of the household, based on the number of consumer durables, is substituted if occupation or age of terminal education is not available. For the purposes of everyday research, these eight categories are aggregated into a four-category classification:

- AB managers and professionals
- C1 well-educated nonmanual and skilled workers
- C2 skilled workers and nonmanual employees
- DE unskilled manual workers and other less well-educated workers and employees

Another category where differences may occur is in the dwelling unit. In most Western societies, dwelling units are primarily apartments or houses, either semi-detached, row houses or freestanding. In African countries dwelling units may be huts, while in some Middle Eastern and Asian countries the dwelling unit may take the form of a sprawling complex, with multiple rooms opening off a central courtyard. Often an extended family lives in the complex. This includes multiple primary units of husband, wife and children, as well as grandparents, other siblings, unmarried aunts, uncles and so on. Consequently, neither the dwelling unit nor the family unit is comparable from one country to another.

## Behavioral and Product Market-related Data

In developing questions relating to purchase, consumption, usage or disposal data, and in relation to specific product markets, two important issues need to be considered. The first is the extent to which such behavior is conditioned by a specific sociocultural or economic environment, and hence will vary from one country or cultural context to another. For example, the retail infrastructure often plays a key role in shaping purchase behavior and shopping patterns. Where retailing is highly concentrated and dominated by mass retailers such as supermarkets or hypermarkets, discount stores or specialty chain stores, consumers may tend to be price conscious, look for bargains and expect to be able to pay for their purchases efficiently and quickly. Where, on the other hand, retailing is highly fragmented and consists predominantly of small mom and pop stores, consumers may shop more frequently, spend more time on shopping and routinely going from store to store to assemble an assortment of goods. As a result, since the depth and breadth of assortment are limited, they spend less time making product and brand comparisons and may rely heavily on the advice of the shop owner. Such factors result not only in significantly different shopping patterns, but also in differences in cognitive structure (i.e. brand awareness) and the salience of product attributes (Van Herk and Verhallen, 1994). Consequently, different questionnaires need to be developed that are tailored to the specific retail environment.

The second issue concerns the extent to which a given product market is defined similarly in all countries and cultural contexts, and hence whether competing and substitute products are the same everywhere. This is becoming increasingly problematic due to differences in the stage of the product life cycle in different countries, as well as the blurring of many product boundaries, as in soft drinks and fruit juices, or toiletries such as soap, moisturizers and creams, deodorants and antiperspirants, body perfumes, body lotions and suncreams.

## Comparability in Purchase, Consumption, Usage and Disposal Behavior

Since purchase, consumption, usage and disposal behavior are an integral part of day-to-day living, they are deeply embedded in the fabric of society and affected by sociocultural norms, cultural conventions and so on. As a result, the sociocultural context in which purchase and consumption take place, as well as the behavioral acts and processes that result in purchase decisions, often vary from one country or culture to another. This leads to significant differences in need states, the purchasing process, purchase occasions and the fit between products or specific product attributes and need states as well as the salience of different product benefits.

Each culture, society or social group has its own particular conventions, rituals and practices relating to behavior on social occasions, such as entertaining family or friends, or behavior on festive occasions, such as marriage, graduation, Christmas or other cultural festivals. Rules relating to the exchange of gifts and products are, for example, governed by local cultural conventions (Levi-Strauss, 1965; Mauss, 1954). Thus, while in some cultures wine may be an appropriate gift for a dinner host, in others flowers are preferred. Japan, for example, has a unique system of gift giving, which plays a key role in maintaining the social structure (Fields, 1989). Gifts are given on two occasions during the year: midsummer (*sheiben*) and in the New Year. Gifts must be carefully matched to the status of the recipient relative to that of the giver, and appropriately wrapped. Consequently, in comparing gift-giving practices, questions relating to gift giving and positioning of products as gifts will need to be tailored to specific practices and behavior patterns.

Similarly, attitudes with regard to the importance of different types of behavior vary from one culture to another. For example, among the middle classes in many industrialized countries cleanliness is considered next to godliness. Considerable importance is attached to activities and products that promote cleanliness, such as household cleaning products that keep the house spick-and-span and smelling fresh, or personal hygiene products. Frequently, advertisements for antiperspirants, deodorants, toothpaste or mouthwash promise the purchaser instant social success, or warn of the dangers of social ostracism without their use. In other countries, less attention may be paid to personal hygiene, clothes may be washed less frequently, and body odors or bad breath may not be considered offensive. The type of questions relating to product benefits and attributes asked in surveys of products such as household cleaning products or personal hygiene will therefore need to be tailored to the specific cultural context.

The way in which purchases are made may also vary from one country or culture to another. In the US, for example, purchasing on credit and the use of debit cards reduces the need to carry cash. In developing countries in Africa and Asia, consumer credit is typically limited and credit cards are rare or nonexistent. In some countries, notably throughout Europe, use of debit cards is widespread and reduces the need to carry substantial amounts of cash. In some countries use of a mobile phone to pay for items such as soft drinks in vending machines has also been introduced. Use of prepaid cards for transportation and telephone systems is also widespread in many industrialized countries. Consequently these factors will need to be taken into consideration in formulating questions relating to different modes of payments, payment systems or services that rely on such forms of payment.

Differences may also exist with regard to product disposal from one country to another due to differences in the strength of the environmental movement and environmental regulation. For example, in the UK bottles and cans are taken to bottle and can banks for recycling, and paper is separated from other garbage. In other countries a deposit is paid to the retailer for glass and plastic bottles, and in some cases aluminum cans. This is refunded on return of the bottle or can. The size of the deposit can vary from 5 cents up, depending on the size of the incentive that regulators wish to establish. Regulation on recycling of other items such as tires and batteries and on littering also varies. Again, these are factors that need to be taken into consideration in formulating questions relating to packaging and so on.

## Comparability in Product Class Boundaries

In addition to such differences in usage, purchase and consumption behavior, competing and substitute products often vary from one country to another. For example, washing machines and other household appliances may be competing with domestic help and professional launderers, as well as with other brands of washing machines. In many Latin American countries in middle-class families domestic help does the washing, although the rising cost of domestic help has encouraged purchase of washing machines by wealthier families. Similarly, in Northern India *dhobis*, men who traditionally did the washing of middle- and upper-class families, have moved to better-paying employment opportunities in hotels, restaurants, office cleaning and so on. Consequently, purchase of small washing machines by the middle classes in India is on the rise.

The range and type of items contained in a product class may also vary. For example, there are significant differences in the type of soft drinks available in different countries, and also in what is considered a soft drink. In the US, soft drinks consist predominantly of different varieties of colas (cherry, diet, caffeine free), lemon-lime sodas, ginger ale, iced teas, mineral waters, alternative beverages (mostly fruit-flavored sodas) and sports and energy drinks. In the Netherlands, milk is frequently consumed as a beverage at lunch and hence is included in the soft drink category. In other countries, fruit juices (apple, orange and grape) are popular as well as concentrates such as blackcurrant, peppermint or anise, which are then diluted. In Asia, freshly squeezed fruit juices, including mango, papaya and pineapple, are also popular soft drinks, and in some South East Asian countries, soybean milk flavored with honey, chocolate or strawberry is widely available. The appropriate definition of the product category and the product variants included will thus vary substantially from one country or region to another.

In addition to the lack of comparability with regard to product class boundaries, competing product set and the type of products included or available within a specific product class, differences may be encountered with regard to brand availability or even the existence of branding. Some product categories tend to be dominated worldwide by large multinational companies such as Coca-Cola and Pepsi in colas, Kellogg's and General Mills in cereal and Gillette and Schick in razors. Generally they compete with local and regional brands, though the strength and significance of these brands may vary from one country or region to another. For example Cott, a Canadian cola company, produces colas for private-label vendors in countries such as the UK, Germany and the Netherlands. In India, a local cola brand 'Thums Up', acquired by Coca-Cola through its acquisition of Parle, a local bottler, is extremely popular. In Iran, a locally produced cola called Zam Zam is popular and has been exported to Saudi Arabia and other Gulf countries as well as Denmark. In the razor market, the degree of local competition varies considerably from one country to another and local brands compete predominantly in the price-sensitive segment of the market. Again, awareness of local brands and relevant product attributes to examine is important in designing an effective questionnaire.

In developing countries and in the former socialist countries, branding of consumer goods has only recently emerged as an important factor. In many former Eastern bloc countries, consumer choice was extremely limited. Consequently, consumers are not accustomed to making finely discriminating comparisons among brands and products. As a result, brands are often broadly categorized as 'Western' or local. Similarly, in developing countries, the market for consumer packaged or pre-processed goods is often limited to more affluent consumers or dual-income households. Such items have to compete with fresh products or food prepared in the home or by local merchants. For example, pasta or noodles may be made in the home, purchased freshly prepared from small merchants or itinerant vendors, or purchased pre-packaged from the store.

Such differences in purchase, consumption and disposal behavior and in the comparability of product categories from one country or culture to another mean that careful attention needs to be paid to such distinctions in designing a questionnaire. Often this implies that some desk and qualitative research is needed to identify relevant factors, especially where management has limited knowledge or experience with attitude and usage behavior in the country. It is also important if the study is designed to assess reactions or purchase intentions relating to a product or service that is new to the country and could potentially stimulate substantial changes in existing consumption and purchase behavior.

## Attitudinal, Psychographic and Lifestyle Data

The most significant problems in drawing up questions in multicountry research are likely to occur in relation to attitudinal, psychographic and lifestyle data. Here, as noted in Chapter 6, it is not always clear whether certain attitudinal or personality constructs – such as aggressiveness, respect for authority and honor – are equally relevant or equivalent in all countries and cultures. Even where similar constructs exist, the same question or attitude statement may not tap them most effectively. There is considerable discussion with regard to this issue and the best way to deal with it. This is examined in more detail in Chapter 10.

Attitudinal, psychographic and lifestyle measures can be examined at two different levels: (1) general constructs, values or long-run orientations that hold across all product categories or areas of life; and (2) domain- or category-specific constructs that apply to specific product domains or life interests, for example food, clothing, sports or leisure activities. In developing measures of both general and domain-specific constructs, the relevant domain of the construct needs first to be specified in each country. General constructs might include personality constructs such as sociability or innovativeness, values such as materialism or self-achievement, lifestyle patterns relating to leisure behavior, attitudes toward work or family life, gender or shopping, and use of credit. Category-specific constructs, on the other hand, might relate to a specific product category such as detergents, automobiles or children's clothing. In each case, the domain of the construct and how it is manifested in each country needs to be specified by examining qualitative data or through focus groups, consumer workshops and so on.

Next, the specific items that best tap the various constructs in each country and culture should be identified. Even where similar constructs are identified in different countries, the specific items making up these constructs may not always be identical. In some cases, the same constructs may be measured by somewhat different items. For example, materialism might be measured in the US by a statement such as: 'The things I own say a lot about how well I'm doing in life'. In France, the following statement might be more appropriate: 'I like a lot of luxury in my life' (Dubois and Laurent, 1993).

Interest in identifying similar lifestyle segments on a regional or worldwide basis has been particularly marked among advertising agencies and market research companies. Euromonitor has, for example, recently profiled consumer lifestyles worldwide based on food and clothing habits, entertainment, education, sports pastimes, shopping habits, media and tourism (Euromonitor, 2004). It is, however, important to establish the link between the lifestyle segment and preferences or purchase behavior relative to a given product category or life interest. Consequently, use of attitudinal or lifestyle characteristics to profile cross-national segments identified on another basis, for example demographics, has been more typical. For instance, the Coca-Cola study of teenagers profiled differences and similarities of teenagers' attitudes, values and lifestyles in different regions throughout the world.

Studies examining domain-specific segments typically collect data relating to domain-specific attitudes and values, usage behavior and purchase criteria and then cluster respondents across countries based on these variables. One study of food cultures in Europe identified 12 different food cultures, seven of which were national, four transnational and one regional (Askegaard and Madsen, 1995). Another study of financial services in Europe (Bijmolt et al., 2004) grouped consumers based on attitudes and usage of financial services and then developed profiles of these segments based on financial service usage patterns.

The degree of commonality may also depend on the specific countries or cultures and on the nature of the topic. There is likely to be more commonality among consumers in relatively similar countries, such as the industrialized Western nations, than between Westernized nations and emerging market countries. Allowance should, however, always be made for the identification of country- or culture-unique concepts, and also idiosyncratic measures of these, as well as pan-cultural concepts and measures, particularly where there are significant economic or cultural differences between countries.

# Type of Question

Another point to be considered is the form in which questions are asked. Questions can be either closed or open-ended. Closed questions require the respondent to reply according to a specific format and select from various alternative responses. Open-ended questions, on the other hand, allow the respondent freedom to provide his or her own response, without constraining the range of options. Similarly, questions may be posed directly, or indirectly so that the purpose of the question is not apparent to the respondent.

## *Open-ended versus Closed Questions*

The most compelling argument in favor of the use of closed questions is that they facilitate analysis. Responses can be pre-coded and entered directly into a computer from the questionnaire. Closed questions also make it easier for interviewers to record responses directly into a laptop, or for respondents to record their response on a computer screen at home or in a shopping mall survey. On the other hand, closed questions mean that the researcher must specify in advance all relevant response categories. This may sometimes be difficult in cross-national research, especially where the researcher lacks extensive experience or familiarity with purchasing behavior or relevant determinants of response in another country or cultural context.

Open-ended questions may be preferable in a number of situations. Since they do not impose any structure or response categories on respondents, they avoid the imposition of cultural bias by the researcher. Particularly where respondents fill in responses on a home computer, they may tend to provide lengthier, more expansive responses. In addition, they do not require the researcher to specify all possible responses. On the other hand, they do entail the somewhat tedious process of establishing coding schemes for responses, and tabulating them once the data have been collected.

The levels of literacy or education of respondents also affect the appropriateness of using open-ended questions as opposed to closed questions. Open-ended questions are often used when a researcher lacks knowledge about factors underlying behavior or attitudes in the country or countries studied. Since a respondent has to respond to open-ended questions in his or her own terms, they require some sophistication and knowledge of the topic on the part of the respondent, otherwise responses will not be meaningful. Consequently, open-ended questions have to be used with care in cross-cultural and cross-national research where respondents have low levels of education.

Open-ended questions are often appropriate in exploratory research, especially where the objective is to identify relevant dimensions, concepts or terminology associated with the problem studied. They might be used to elicit content domains relating to products, attitudes toward products or advertising stimuli, or the associations evoked by various stimuli. For example, in the case of products such as beverages, respondents might be asked to list all the items they perceive as beverages, and the most frequently occurring responses could then be used as the relevant product set. Similarly, in a study of attitudes toward products or advertising stimuli, subjects could be asked to indicate adjectives, words or phrases that best describe or characterize relevant stimuli such as packages or advertisements. This task might then be repeated using different scenarios, such as for family consumption, when entertaining for special occasions and so on.

## Direct versus Indirect Questions

Another consideration is whether direct or indirect questions are utilized. Direct questions avoid any ambiguity concerning question intent and meaning. On the other hand, respondents may be reluctant or unable to answer certain types of questions. In addition, they may tend to provide responses perceived as socially desirable or those that they feel are desired by the interviewer.

Use of indirect questions can help to avoid such biases. In this case, rather than stating the question directly, it is posed in an indirect form. For example, respondents might not be asked their own preferences, but rather the response they anticipate that most respondents, their neighbors or other relevant reference groups would give. This approach may be desirable in certain cultures, for example Japan where there are substantial pressures toward conformity. Alternatively, respondents might be presented with different types of purchase decisions or shopping scenarios, and asked which most closely correspond to their own.

Another approach, especially useful where respondents may have difficulty recalling decisions or behavior, is to ask a series of questions leading up to the purchase decision or behavior. For example, to find out about brand loyalty respondents might be asked first how frequently they shop for groceries, where they typically shop for groceries and what brand they last purchased in particular product categories. This helps the respondent to recall the situation leading up to the actual purchase and increases the likelihood of an accurate response.

Irrespective of the way in which questions are formulated, they need to be adequately pre-tested on an appropriate sample before being administered. While pre-testing is important in domestic research, it is crucial in international markets, due to potential problems of misunderstanding and miscommunication. Successive rounds of testing may be needed in order to ensure that sources of response bias are minimized and that respondents fully understand questions. This is critical if accurate responses and high item response rates are to be obtained.

# Use of Nonverbal Stimuli

Another important consideration in instrument design is whether respondents are shown nonverbal (as opposed to or in addition to verbal) stimuli in order to help them understand and respond accurately. Particularly where research is conducted in countries or cultures with high levels of illiteracy, such as Africa and the Middle East, it is desirable to use nonverbal stimuli. Questionnaires can be administered orally by an interviewer, but respondent comprehension will be facilitated if pictures of products or test packs are provided.

Various types of nonverbal stimuli may be used in conjunction with questionnaires, including photographs, show cards, product samples or pictures. Nonverbal stimuli are also often used in conjunction with other data collection techniques, for example projective techniques, consumer workshops or synectic groups, as discussed in Chapter 7. Here the discussion is focused on the use of nonverbal stimuli in surveys to help respondents understand verbal questions, products and product concepts, or to express feelings.

Show cards such as that in Figure 8.1 can, for example, be used to assist in answering product usage questions. This set was designed to aid consumers in understanding the different types of uses that might be made of a sewing machine. Sketches of products can also be employed to illustrate a questionnaire. In Figure 8.2 the questionnaire used in a study on health in an aboriginal community in Australia (Spark, 1999) was illustrated with sketches of outdoor plumbing, a washing machine and a refrigerator. This not only ensured that respondents clearly understood the question and the particular product covered in the survey, but also attracted their interest.

Illustrations may be useful in rural areas when it is not certain whether the respondent has been exposed to the product and knows what it looks like or what functions it performs. In general, pictures or sketches need to be simple, so that respondents can understand them easily. Product samples can also be shown to respondents. A drawback of this is that respondents tend to become irritated if the samples are removed for the next interview. Consequently, it is advisable to leave a free sample or other reward for each respondent.

Visual stimuli may also be employed to develop rich images and probe consumer associations with products and brands. In international research, they can have the advantage that they are not as directly affected by cultural and linguistic factors as verbal stimuli. In a study of young consumers' attitudes toward global brands in São Paulo, Mexico City and Venezuela, three types of visual stimuli – colors, geometric forms and photos – were used to examine consumer brand associations (Troiano, Costa and Guardado, 2002). Cards with 15 colors grouped into four categories – basic, intense/fashionable, cosmetic and undefined – were shown to consumers as well as 19 cards with geometric forms belonging to four categories – straight lines, regular forms, rhythmic lines and open forms – and 11 photos reflecting different atmospheres, such as lightning, a beach, an art gallery and skiers. The study revealed substantial similarities in the associations across the three cities, reflecting similar underlying values and visual brand identities.

Even where literacy levels are high, use of visual stimuli in conjunction with verbal stimuli helps to provide a check on instrument equivalence and to identify potential biases from questionnaire translation or adaptation of the questionnaire to different linguistic and cultural contexts. The sample can be split, and half the respondents asked questions without the visual stimuli, while the other half are shown the visual stimuli. The results obtained from the two halves can then be compared to see whether there are differences. It is important to recognize that pictorial stimuli are not culture free, as perceptual associations and their interpretation differ from one country or culture to another. However, the types of biases arising from visual stimuli are likely to differ from

**Figure 8.1** Interview show card used in consumer survey in South Africa (assists to answer question 'What is your sewing machine used for?')

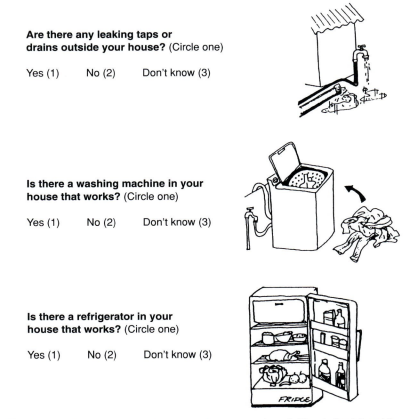

**Are there any leaking taps or drains outside your house?** (Circle one)

Yes (1)     No (2)     Don't know (3)

**Is there a washing machine in your house that works?** (Circle one)

Yes (1)     No (2)     Don't know (3)

**Is there a refrigerator in your house that works?** (Circle one)

Yes (1)     No (2)     Don't know (3)

**Figure 8.2**   Questionnaire with sketches used in a study of Aboriginal health
*Source*: Spark, 1999.

those occurring in a verbal instrument. Consequently, comparison of the two procedures will indicate whether there is a need for further testing and instrument development.

Once the basic form of the questionnaire or research instrument to be used in the survey has been drawn up, the next step is to translate it so as to ensure that it is clearly understood by respondents, and to try to avoid any possible miscommunication. The issues involved in translating verbal and nonverbal instruments, and some standard translation procedures, are next discussed in more detail.

# Instrument Translation

Both verbal and nonverbal instruments need to be translated so that they can be used in different linguistic and cultural contexts. While the need for translation of verbal instruments is widely recognized, and examples of errors arising from mistranslation abound, the need for translation of visual stimuli is generally less well recognized. It is, nonetheless, important to realize that visual stimuli are not necessarily universal or pan-cultural. Consequently, if visual stimuli are developed in relation to a specific cultural context, the same misinterpretation and miscommunication problems can arise as in relation to verbal stimuli. Consequently, attention to how visual stimuli are perceived and interpreted in other contexts is required.

# *Verbal Translation*

In translating a questionnaire or verbal instrument, two principal methods have been identified in the educational and measurement literature: forward translation and back translation (Hambleton, 1993, 1994). In either case, a number of procedures, judgmental and statistical, can be used to evaluate the equivalence and quality of the translations. More recently, the problems arising from back translation, and particularly in detecting errors using this method, have led to advocacy of a committee approach, involving multiple individuals in the translation (Harkness, 2003).

## *Forward Translation*

In the case of forward translation, a single translator or group of translators prepares a translation from the source language into the target language. Several versions can be prepared and then compared. This approach is subject to the risk that the translation may contain errors and not accurately represent the meaning of the original or 'source' questionnaire. Difficulties may be encountered in finding equivalent words or phrases in the target language, resulting in errors.

For example, an item relating to the president or head of state in a country will not have the same meaning in a country with a prime minister. Equally, the Spanish word *paloma* is equivalent to both 'dove' and 'pigeon' in English and *amigo* in Spanish does not always have the same meaning as the English word 'friend'. Similarly, in a survey of health issues among Vietnamese immigrants in Australia (Small *et al.*, 1999), in translating the phrase 'I have been so unhappy I have difficulty in sleeping' into Vietnamese, the term used for 'unhappy' incorporated the concept of irritable, which is not implied in English. However, this was felt more suitable than the word usually used to translate unhappy, as this was not considered strong enough to prevent sleep.

While problems can arise because words do not match up across languages, more fundamental problems can occur when concepts do not match across cultures (Harkness, 2003). One example is differences in grammatical gender. Some languages such as Spanish and French have elaborate systems of grammatical gender. Others such as English have simple systems, and others such as Hungarian have none. English is typically gender neutral, leaving the sex of terms such as doctor, friend or secretary unidentified. In German, however, references to all of these are gender specific, requiring two forms – for example *Freund/Freundin*, *Arzt/Arztin* – to be used when a question may refer to either. Pronouns and adjectives have to agree accordingly. Comparability problems can arise in multilingual studies. For example, the German term for secretary is typically feminine, *eine Sekretarin*. The masculine form *ein Sekretar* either means a desk or a man with a senior executive position, requiring use of a different descriptor.

While attention has been drawn to the need for comparable question wording in different languages, less concern has been exhibited in relation to translation of response scales. Yet this also can pose problems. For example, difficulties may be encountered in translating response categories such as often, sometimes, rarely and never. In Turkish, the equivalents of the terms 'rarely' and 'never' are frequently used interchangeably. Consequently, in one study few respondents picked the term corresponding to rarely, as both terms were understood as 'not at all' or 'never'.

Even where response scales are constructed specifically for a study, attention needs to be paid to comparability across languages. Often the scales traditionally used in each language in which the questionnaire is being developed are adopted, without regard to cross-language comparability. For example in the Eurobarometer, which measures social and political attitudes in the EU on a regular basis, the French and English scales differ in structure and to a lesser extent in semantics. Both use the semantic dimension of agree, but in the French scale the use of *d'accord*, *pas d'accord* suggests a unipolar scale, while the English scale uses a bipolar construction in which the wording is linguistically symmetrical with the endpoints modified by 'strongly'. Equally, the 'don't know' category is 'can't choose' in English compared with *ne sais pas* or 'don't know' in French.

Such issues make it important to ensure that translators are knowledgeable about the subject matter and terms used, or the meaning of the source questionnaire is easily lost in translation. For example, the term 'item pool' was translated into Japanese as 'item ocean'. Such errors are more likely to arise when translating linguistically dissimilar languages such as English to Chinese or Japanese, as compared with English to French or French to Italian.

One means of checking this is to administer the translated questionnaire to respondents and then probe to ask about the meaning of each item and their responses. Respondents are asked how they interpret a given question and to suggest alternative phrasing or wording that might tap the same issue. However, this approach can be somewhat time consuming and cumbersome, and is only feasible where respondents have time available to discuss questions.

## Back Translation

The back translation method has traditionally been widely used in educational testing and psychological measurement (Brislin, 1980; Hambleton, 1993, 1994). It is also extensively used by both academics and marketing research companies. Following this procedure, a questionnaire is translated from the initial or source language by a bilingual translator who is a native speaker of the target language into which the translation is being made. This version is translated back into the original or source language by a bilingual who is a native speaker of that language. The two versions are then compared in the source language to check for errors and the quality of the translation.

This approach is useful in identifying translation errors and the competency of the translator, but is subject to a number of problems (Brislin, 1980). Bilinguals often develop a particular language structure and usage. As a result, they do not always translate into the idioms commonly used by most people and may employ language or terms that are difficult for respondents to understand. Bilinguals tend to have standard rules for translating nonequivalent terms, for example always translating *amigo* as 'friend', which do not always capture the intended meaning. Since they know both languages, they may be able to make sense out of poor translations and do a good job of back translation, so that grammar and syntax errors in the target translation go undetected.

Back translation starts with the assumption of a 'source' language and the evaluation of the adequacy of the translation is made in the source language. Consequently, there is always a question of the extent to which the structure and terms used in that language will dominate the questionnaire. One approach to alleviating this problem is known as 'decentering'. This entails modifying both source and target questionnaire through successive iterations of translation and retranslation to eliminate the dominance of the source language (Triandis, 1972; Werner and Campbell, 1970). At the end of the process, both source and translated questionnaire are modified so that terminology is equally well understood and equivalent in each language context. While this procedure is likely to result in the best translation, it is time consuming and tedious.

A further problem is that few international projects have the resources to effectively 'decenter' questionnaires. Many studies employ materials developed in a source language, which are then back translated by bilinguals, where the survey is to be conducted. The source materials are typically viewed as fixed or providing a base line, and little decentering occurs for fear of deviating too far from this base. Decentering is extremely difficult if not virtually impossible where there are three or more language versions (Bontempo, 1993). As a result, translators typically try to reproduce the source version as faithfully as possible in the target language.

However, a totally faithful or literal translation may not always be desired in marketing research, especially where idiomatic or colloquial phrases are used. Not only are some phrases and terms difficult to render in other languages, but also in some instances it may be desirable to translate into equivalent colloquial phrases. Back translation will not necessarily achieve this. An idiomatic phrase can be faithfully translated and back translated without capturing the accurate meaning in the translated language. For example the phrase *Das Leben in vollen Zugen geneissen* in German might be literally translated into English as 'Enjoy life in full trains' and correctly back translated (Harkness, 2003). This would not, however, result in the English translation with the equivalent colloquial meaning, 'Live life to the full' or 'Live life to the fullest' (American/English).

Similarly, just as errors can occur in forward translation, they can occur in back translation. For example, when 'I have been so unhappy that I have difficulty sleeping' was back translated from Tagalog, the back translation read 'I became so lonely that I find it difficult to sleep', which implies a very different meaning from 'so unhappy' in the original English. Further investigation suggested that the Tagalog might more accurately be rendered as 'I felt so despondent that I had difficulty sleeping', which was in fact very close to the original English. This example illustrates some of the difficulties associated with back translation. While on the surface it is a relatively simple procedure, further examination and discussion are typically required to avoid errors in back translation and ensure an accurate rendering of the term to be translated in the target language.

## Committee Translation

The limitations of back translation suggest the desirability of adopting a committee approach (Harkness, 2003). This can be organized either by parallel translation or split translation. In the case of parallel translation, several translators make independent parallel translations of the same questionnaire. A meeting is then held to review the translations and agree on a final version. An alternative approach, which saves time and effort especially if the questionnaire is long, is split translation. In this case, at least two translators and a reviewer are needed. The translation is then divided up between the translators in an alternating fashion. Each translator translates his or her own section and a meeting is held with the reviewer to examine the translations and agree on a joint version. Here, it is important to ensure that consistency is maintained across the translation and that translation of a similar phrase is harmonized. Once translated, whether by the parallel or split approach, the translation is reviewed by a committee, including the translators, reviewer and an adjucator, and a decision is made whether to accept the revised version. While somewhat time consuming, this approach may be particularly appropriate if questionnaires are complex or different expertise is needed for individual parts, for example different language versions.

In countries that have multiple languages, such as Belgium, India, Canada, Switzerland and South Africa, or where different immigrant groups are to be interviewed, separate versions of the questionnaire or research instrument typically need to be developed. Similarly, if several dialects of a language are used, it may be desirable to treat each as a separate language. Even if the immigrant subgroup can understand the host-country language, translation into the local idiom will enhance willingness to respond and help to provide complete and accurate answers. This is particularly likely to be a factor with older and less well-educated respondents. Similarly, where different versions of the source language are used, adaptation to the appropriate version will be needed. For example, questionnaires originating in the UK or the US will need to be adapted for use in Australia, New Zealand or South Africa. Similarly, questionnaires in Spanish will need to be adapted to the different versions of Spanish spoken in various Latin American countries as well as within the US (Harkness, 2003).

## Assessing Translation Equivalence

Regardless of the specific translation procedure utilized, it is important to verify the quality of the translation and to assess the equivalence of various versions prior to use in the field. Here, two different approaches have been suggested. One is heuristic, based on testing various versions of a questionnaire on monolingual and bilingual subjects. The other applies statistical analysis based on item response theory.

Various procedures for evaluating translation equivalence using both mono- and bilingual subjects have been suggested (Hambleton, 1994). These include: (1) evaluation by monolinguals of the source and target questionnaires based on clarity and comprehension of the items; (2) evaluation by bilinguals of both questionnaires based on possible meaning errors; (3) comparison of results obtained from administering the source and back-translated questionnaires to additional subjects; and (4) comparison of results obtained from administering both original and translated versions to bilingual subjects. The last two procedures are considered the most reliable insofar as the primary objective is to ensure that both the original and translated questionnaires result in the same pattern of response.

## Translation of Nonverbal Stimuli

In addition to translating verbal instruments, it is important to recognize that visual instruments and stimuli will also require translation and testing for miscommunication or misinterpretation in different countries and cultural contexts. This can arise as a result of differences in the interpretation of perceptual cues in different countries and cultural contexts, as well as the associations evoked by visual phenomena and objects. For example, not all African cultures recognize Western conventions using narrowing parallel lines or fainter colors to represent distance. In general, pictorial stimuli, especially where they are not supported by verbal stimuli, tend to generate a broad range of associations. Consequently, care is needed to ensure that the stimuli are interpreted unambiguously.

Once translated, field testing of data collection instruments is necessary in order to identify any final problems and test for appropriate colloquial usage relative to the target respondents and so on. Many examples can be cited where a supposedly good translation of an instrument had to be revised as a result of a field test. This further underscores the importance of care in translation and use of multiple checks to ensure that errors not found in one stage are remedied in another. Where both verbal and visual instruments are used, comparison of results obtained with each method can provide a check on overall results, and problems arising due to miscomprehension be identified.

## Potential Sources of Bias Associated with the Research Instrument

No matter how carefully the instruments have been designed and how well they have been translated to avoid potential problems of miscommunication, some difficulties are likely to arise due to certain sources of bias characteristic of cross-national surveys. The major sources of bias in both international and domestic marketing research are the respondent, the nature of the topic, and the respondent's interaction with the interviewer and with the instrument.

Seven specific types of bias are particularly likely to occur in international research. These are: (1) yea-saying bias or tendency to respond in the affirmative; (2) extreme response bias or a tendency to use the extreme points of a scale; (3) social desirability bias or the desire to provide the socially acceptable response; (4) the nature of the topic being studied; (5) item nonresponse or failure to respond to certain types of questions such as income and education; (6) specific respondent characteristics; and (7) the response format. These are highly interrelated, for example yea-saying bias, extreme response style and respondent characteristics are all closely linked, but each gives rise to specific problems in cross-national research due to differences in the nature and the importance of the effects within and between countries.

In the social sciences emphasis is placed on item nonresponse and social desirability as major sources of bias, while in marketing studies different types of response bias or response styles have received more attention (Baumgartner and Steenkamp, 2001; van Herk, 2003). Examination of five different types of response styles – acquiescent and disacquiescent styles, extreme response styles, midpoint responding and noncontingent responding – on data from 11 EU countries, has, for example, shown these to constitute an important source of bias that can distort correlations between survey items (Baumgartner and Steenkamp, 2001). This effect occurred systematically across all countries. Careful attention to the bias introduced by such response styles is, therefore, needed to assess the extent to which this may contaminate surveys.

## Social Acquiescence or Yea-saying Bias

Social acquiescence or yea-saying bias, i.e. the tendency to provide a positive response or check the highest agreement response categories in rating scales varies from country to country (Skjak and Harkness, 2003). It may stem from positive or optimistic attitudes in some countries and cultures or alternatively from the desire to be socially acquiescent, and provide the response perceived as desired by the interviewer or the sponsor of the study. It is particularly likely to occur on agree/disagree items and ones that offer clear affirm/reject response (Smith, 2003) and also on 5–6- or 7-point Likert scales where the item is not worded in a balanced or neutral way, but reflects a positive or negative attitude.

Yea-saying is common in Asia, where cultural values often lead the respondent to try to avoid distressing, disappointing or offending the interviewer in any way. At the extreme, this can lead to a tendency to agree to any assertion, irrespective of the respondent's actual position. Japanese respondents, for example, always respond in the affirmative, as it would be considered extremely impolite to respond negatively. In addition, affirmative responses may be given where the respondent does not understand the question, but does not want to be impolite or display ignorance by not responding.

In Europe differences occur between countries and regions within countries. Greeks, both men and women, have been consistently found to provide more positive responses (Baumgartner and Steenkamp, 2001; van Herk, 2003). A detailed study of yea-saying bias conducted in relation to both domain-specific and product-specific attitudes on topics such as cooking, washing and shaving as well as in values (using the LOVscale) consistently found Greeks to be most prone to extreme yea-saying bias (van Herk, 2003). Italians and Spanish were the next most prone to yea-saying bias, followed by UK, German and French subjects. At the same time looking at regions within countries in Europe, the further south a region, based on its location and its geographical coordinates, the more likely a respondent was to provide a positive response (van Herk, 2000). This suggests that climate and geographical location affect product-related attitudes (similarly to the way they affect mental health).

In some instances the effects of yea-saying bias can be reduced by concealing sponsorship of the study and by more effective training of interviewers. Careful wording of questions in order to render them more neutral, for example by presenting a choice between two equally strong bipolar opposites rather than using a 5–9-point Likert agree/disagree scale (or making Likert statements more neutral rather than positive or negative), may help to reduce this bias (Smith, 2003). Introduction of balanced Likert scales ensuring that half the response categories agree and half disagree can also be helpful. Translation may cause problems here, as captions for points on the scale may, as noted earlier, translate differently in different languages.

## Extreme Response Bias

Another source of bias is extreme response style. Extreme response bias is the tendency to use the extreme ends of the scale. This again has been found to vary by country (van Herk, 2003). In large-scale surveys of cooking, washing and shaving in six countries in Europe, as in relation to yea-saying bias, Greeks were found to have the most extreme response style. Italians and Spanish had the next most marked extreme response style, followed by the French, the British and lastly the Germans. The Germans were the least prone to extreme response style of any EU subjects, suggesting a more rational, balanced approach to responding to questions. Again, the further south a respondent came from in terms of region within the EU and the global coordinates of each region, the more extreme the response style (van Herk, 2000). This suggests a possible link between climate, hours of sunshine and extreme response style, as no differences were found on the East–West dimension.

## Social Desirability Bias

A source of bias closely related to social acquiescence or yea-saying is social desirability. This is bias relating to the topic studied and has been extensively examined in the social sciences where many topics, for example health education and life satisfaction, may reflect specific social norms and values (Johnson and Van der Vijver, 2003). Social desirability bias may also be triggered by interaction with the interviewer, and varies with the individual and cultural background. Individuals from lower-status backgrounds are likely to defer to the values of higher-status interviewers. Social desirability typically shows less impact with self-completion questions than when face-to-face interviews are used. Similarly, individuals from more affluent societies show low social desirability scores, while social desirability tends to be higher in collectivist societies and particularly among Asians (Johnson and van de Vijver, 2003).

Responses may be intended not only to please the interviewer, but also to reflect behavior perceived as socially acceptable or normal in the respondent's culture. For example, a respondent may say that he or she purchases or uses a product such as toothpaste or deodorant regularly, whether or not this is the case. Equally, questions relating to voting behavior, alcohol consumption or substance abuse are particularly likely to be susceptible to social desirability bias.

Such biases can be reduced by making it easier to provide a socially nonacceptable response. Questions might be prefaced with phrases such as: 'Some people feel this way, some people feel that way. How do you feel?' Questions can also be matched with equally socially desirable responses, and respondents asked to choose the response that they think best describes themselves. Training interviewers to be neutral helps considerably in this regard as well as using interviewers of similar status or background to respondents.

Increased use of observational techniques, videotaping of actual consumption and shopping behavior, and consumer workshops where consumers interact and discuss attitudes and reactions provides another means to identify and also avoid such sources of bias. In these methods, the interviewer is removed from direct interaction with the interviewee and hence the desire to please the interviewer has less impact on interviewee response.

Elimination or rewording of items likely to be subject to social desirability biases can also help to ensure that response styles do not create spurious constructs (Baumgartner and Steenkamp, 2001). Equally, the randomized response approach can be used with sensitive questions (Reinmuth and Geurts, 1975). Alternatively, scale scores can be purified by calculating indices of all the response styles. Respondent scores are then regressed on these indices and analysis conducted on the residualized scores. Corrected covariance and correlation matrices based on purified scale scores can be used as input to structural equation models.

# Topic Bias

Some topics are more socially sensitive in some countries. Willingness to respond to questions such as level of income, or on topics such as sex or alcohol consumption, vary from one country or culture to another. In the Scandinavian countries respondents are considerably more willing to admit to and discuss alcohol consumption or use of contraception than in other countries. In Arab countries anything related to sex tends to be a taboo topic, and even personal hygiene can be sensitive. As a result, researchers need to identify what topics are socially sensitive in each country and cultural context. In addition, use of other research techniques such as collecting observational data, using projective techniques or developing improved interviewer probing techniques also needs to be considered.

# Question Order and Scale Frequency Effects

The order in which questions are placed will also affect response, as well as the recency and frequency of the behavior to which a question relates. Again, differences have been found across cultures both in response to question order and frequency estimation. Since Eastern cultures foster an interdependent perspective of self and emphasize relations with others and fitting in, one may expect Asians to be more knowledgeable about their own and others' behavior. Westerners, on the other hand, view the self as different from others and favor an individualist perspective. Consequently, they are likely to be less attentive to their own and others' behavior. Although publicly observable behavior occurs with similar frequency in both cultures, US students have, for example, been found to report high frequency for public observable behavior (i.e. visiting a library) when provided with high-frequency rather than low-frequency scales, while Chinese students reports were unaffected by the type of scale (Schwarz, 2003). Both US and Chinese students reported higher frequencies for private nonobservable behavior (i.e. having a nightmare) on scales where the response frequencies were higher.

Differences have also been found in contextual effects between Asian and Western respondents that in turn have an impact on question order effects (Schwarz, 2003). East Asian cultures put a premium on maintaining harmony in social relationships and prefer indirect forms of communication that require reading between the lines (Markus and Kitayama, 1991). Asian respondents are, for example, more sensitive to the conversational context of questions, which in turn affects question order. In a study with Chinese and German students about life satisfaction and academic satisfaction, Chinese students were more likely to generalize from general to academic satisfaction questions, when questions were presented in that order rather than the reverse. Germans, on the other hand, were more inclined to generalize from academic to general life satisfaction when academic satisfaction questions were presented first. This suggests that careful attention is needed to the effects of question order and that the order in which questions are presented should be varied in order to minimize such effects.

## Respondent Characteristics

Certain types of respondents are particularly prone to yea-saying, extreme response and social desirability bias. Age, education and to a lesser extent gender are all factors frequently found to be related to response bias (Greenleaf, 1992). The less well-educated, those of lower socioeconomic status and women are all more likely to be prone to response style bias. Consequently, responses are likely to be subject to bias in lower-income countries where respondents also tend to have lower levels of education than in industrialized nations. Item nonresponse has also been found to be related to similar factors, namely gender, age and education, in different countries in Europe (Douglas and Shoemaker, 1981). In Chile, acquiescence biases have been found to be more common among less-educated respondents, suggesting that there may also be a relationship between tendencies toward acquiescence and socioeconomic status.

Examination of the antecedents of yea-saying bias and extreme response style in six European countries – France, Germany, Greece, Italy, Spain and the UK – consistently found yea-saying and extreme response style to be negatively related to education and household income and positively related to age, if over 20 (van Herk, 2003). For gender there were conflicting results, but this may relate to the nature of the studies conducted, since two on cooking and washing were with home-makers and one on shaving was with males only.

These findings imply that the distribution of different national samples on variables such as gender, income and education should be examined, to identify the extent to which such factors are likely to affect results. In some cases, apparent differences between nationally representative samples may reflect the impact of sample characteristics rather than true national or cultural differences. This is further discussed in relation to comparability vs representativity of samples in Chapter 9.

## Item Nonresponse

Item nonresponse is nonresponse that occurs through respondents not answering questions either deliberately or unintentionally. This is an important source of bias in cross-national surveys, as countries differ in rates of item nonresponse. Overall survey rates have been declining internation-ally for some years along with item response rates (Couper and de Leeuw, 2003). The decline has been highest in certain countries such as the Netherlands and the UK and is a cause for significant concern with regard to the quality of survey response.

Cultures vary with regard to their willingness to talk and respond to questions (Lonner and Berry, 1986) and their interest, involvement and information regarding a particular topic. This will affect rates of nonresponse to different questionnaire items. Members of some cultures are more willing to be interviewed and to respond to all types of questions. Others exhibit greater reticence and tend to have high rates of nonresponse to all types of questions (Lonner and Berry, 1986). In Malaysia, the Chinese have been found to be more reticent than Malaysians or Indians in answering questions, giving a higher proportion of 'no' or 'don't know' answers and fewer responses to open-ended questions.

Item nonresponse also varies depending on the mode of data collection, both within and across countries (Skjak and Harkness, 2003). Item nonresponse has been found to be higher in self-completion formats, particularly mail questionnaires, than where the interviewer completes the survey. Respondents may inadvertently skip questions or fail to complete the questionnaire. If a large number of questions are unanswered, it may be preferable to eliminate the respondent from the survey.

Poor design of response formats or inadequate instructions in self-completion questionnaires can also affect item non-response (Skjak and Harkness, 2003). Respondents will make more mistakes if questionnaires are poorly designed. Respondents may, for example, fail to answer questions or overlook items especially where these are filter questions, unless these are very clearly laid out. Inadequate instructions can also result in errors, especially among less-educated respondents. Poor design and poor instruction are especially likely to result in item nonresponse in emerging markets or in cultures where respondents and interviewers are less familiar with answering surveys.

Willingness to respond to certain types of questions, such as questions relating to income or age or that are culturally sensitive, also varies from country to country. In the US there is a lower tendency to fail to respond to questions about personal income than in Europe (Young, 1999). A study of nonresponse to different items in a public opinion survey in eight European countries also found variation (Douglas and Shoemaker, 1981) in nonresponse to questions about income. Nonresponse to political questions was highest in Germany and Italy.

Cultural differences also exist in the confidence with which people know or decide they have the 'right' not to answer (Skjak and Harkness, 2003). If respondents are reluctant to answer questions but are uncertain about the social acceptability of not answering, they may select the 'don't know' category instead. In cultures where they are aware that they cannot respond, they will do so. Similarly respondents who do not want to appear ignorant will not respond rather than ticking 'don't know'. Thus both use of the 'don't know' category and nonresponse can depend on the culture.

Rates of nonresponse are highest in relation to the same types of questions irrespective of country or culture. As might be expected, rates of nonresponse are typically lowest with regard to back-ground characteristics, such as sex or education; moderate with regard to behavioral variables; and highest in relation to complex attitudinal and opinion questions (Douglas and Shoemaker, 1981). This suggests the need for careful attention to wording of questions to ensure that they can be clearly understood by respondents.

The impact of item nonresponse in international marketing research depends largely on the factors underlying nonresponse in different countries or cultures. This can be examined by assessing rates of nonresponse for various items across countries. Characteristics of nonrespondents to these items can then be compared with those of the overall sample, to check for differences. In general, however, the same factors – that is, sex, age and education – appear to be related to nonresponse and hence do not significantly affect comparability of results.

A number of strategies may be used to reduce item nonresponse. First, threatening, monotonous, unclear or ambiguous items should be eliminated or reworded to gain respondent interest. Second, response can be increased by improved formulation of questions in a way that engages or involves the respondent. On the other hand, care is needed to ensure that where closed questions are employed, opinions are not elicited where they do not exist (Mitchell, 1965).

# *Response Format*

In designing questionnaires for use in different environmental and cultural contexts, an important issue concerns the adaptation of response formats to specific countries and cultures. In general, it has been found that adaptation of response format or stimuli to the environmental or cultural context enhances ability to respond or perform a task. This raises the issue of comparability of the instruments.

Verbal rating scales are widely used in international marketing research and appear to be easily understood in many cultures. Even illiterate respondents appear able to express their feelings in words. Verbal rating scales are familiar and easily grasped by all types of respondents. These scales are quick to administer and require little additional explanation. Considerable care needs to be taken in their administration and interpretation. For example, some confusion may arise with interpretation of ends of the scale: '1' may be considered the highest rather than the lowest point on the scale. Equally, Arabs and Israelis read from right to left, rather than left to right.

Consequently, attention needs to be paid to providing clear instructions or, where scales are interviewer administered, providing adequate explanation to avoid misinterpretation. Difficulties can also occur in determining equivalents in different languages and countries of verbal descriptors for scale points (Voss *et al.*, 1996). For example, numerical points can be used to develop measure equivalence scales rather than using verbal descriptors of scale intervals. However, these are not true equal interval scales and also may be context dependent.

Continuous line or graphic rating scales can also cause problems. Respondents with low levels of education often have trouble conceptualizing a continuous scale from an extreme positive to an extreme negative, divided into equal intervals. Consequently, an interviewer may have to spend considerable time explaining the scale. This increases the time required to administer the questionnaire and limits its usefulness.

Such problems suggest that the use of numerical rating scales (for example, pick $x$ points out of 100) might be preferable. However, again, less-educated respondents have difficulty with such scales. In particular, they have difficulty in identifying the midpoint of a scale as well as interpreting distance between points on the scale. Consequently, considerable time is frequently required to explain numerical rating scales to less-educated consumers. This suggests that in countries with low literacy levels, considerable ingenuity will be required in developing mechanisms to record response. Interviewers can pose questions and record categorical responses concerning behavior and background characteristics, but difficulties can arise in obtaining responses to attitudinal questions, especially where indication of position on a scale by the respondent is required.

One approach is to develop pictorial stimuli. Emotional response to a stimulus, for example, can be captured through the Self-Assessment Manikin (SAM). This is a pictorial device (Figure 8.3) that has been used effectively in a cross-cultural study of advertising effectiveness (Morris, 1995). The scale uses three different series of manikins to capture the dimensions of pleasure, arousal and dominance. The graphical portrayal of emotions helps eliminate the problems encountered when using photographs of people in cross-cultural research, where the apparent ethnicity of the models can influence responses. It can also be used among less-literate respondent populations and with children.

Another device is the Funny Faces scale. Some research organizations have used this with illiterate or less-educated respondents in developing countries (Corder, 1978). It consists of five positions, ranging from very happy to very unhappy. Respondents are shown a concept, or read an attitudinal statement, and asked to indicate their degree of agreement or interest by indicating the corresponding position on this scale. For example, strong interest would correspond to being very happy.

Some problems may, however, arise in using this type of rating scale. In particular, it may not be suitable in situations where (1) many attributes have to be rated or (2) a scale that is practical and quick to administer in the field is needed. In addition, the use of Western pictorial conventions in the Funny Faces scale may not be clearly understood. The Funny Faces scale has also been found to arouse negative reactions among better-educated respondents, who considered it childish and insulting to their intelligence.

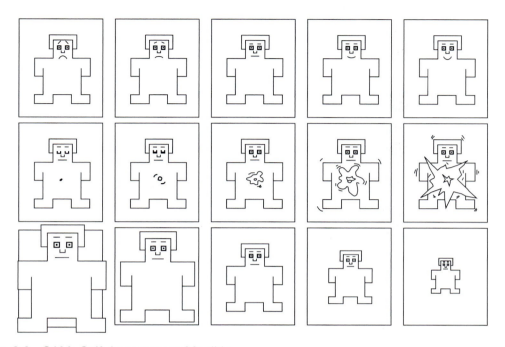

**Figure 8.3** SAM: Self-Assessment Manikin
*Source*: Morris, 1995.

A similar type of scale has been used with aboriginal respondents in Australia (Donovan and Spark, 1997; Spark, 1999). A survey about community health in aboriginal communities used various pictorial scales to assess response to food consumption and health in the community. One response scale consisted of different-sized circles, from 'lots' – strong agreement – to 'not at all' – no agreement (Figure 8.4). Respondents were first given a practice scale to ensure that they understood the meaning of the different circles and then the questionnaire using the scale was administered. Another scale showed people on a hill (Figure 8.5). Those walking up the hill on one side were shown as healthy and strong, while those falling down at the bottom on the other side were 'weak and sick' in body. Respondents were then asked to indicate where they thought most men (women) in their community were. A similar scale was used to indicate whether people were happy or sad in mind.

The most effective approach is to develop a scale that uses concepts familiar to the respondent. Steps of a ladder can be used as a scaling device (Cantril, 1965). Respondents are shown a ladder and asked to indicate their position in response to a given question, with respect to steps in the ladder. In the Middle East, use of an abacus provides an effective means of recording responses. The

**How much does eating TOO MUCH FATTY FOOD like take-away pies, chips and deep fried chicken, cause HEART TROUBLES?** (Tick or circle one dot)

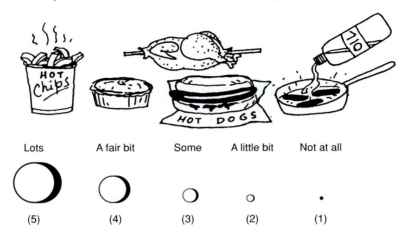

| Lots | A fair bit | Some | A little bit | Not at all |
|------|-----------|------|-------------|-----------|
| (5) | (4) | (3) | (2) | (1) |

**Does eating too much SUGAR cause diabetes?** (Tick one circle or dot)

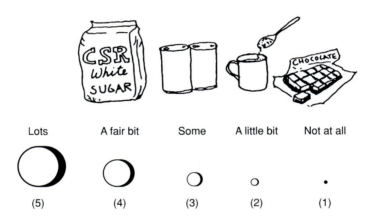

| Lots | A fair bit | Some | A little bit | Not at all |
|------|-----------|------|-------------|-----------|
| (5) | (4) | (3) | (2) | (1) |

**Figure 8.4** Questionnaire used in a study of Aboriginal health
*Source*: Spark, 1999.

interviewer can describe the ends of the abacus as extreme points of a scale, for example agreement or disagreement. The respondent then moves the beads according to his or her degree of agreement or disagreement with the statement.

In designing a response format, it is crucial to devise a format that the respondent can understand and that will enable him or her to respond accurately. As with other aspects of research design, it is

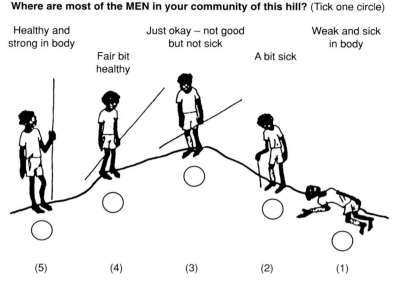

**Where are most of the MEN in your community of this hill?** (Tick one circle)

**Figure 8.5**   Scale used to measure Aboriginal health perception
*Source*: Spark, 1999.

important to consider comparability across different national and cultural contexts, but accuracy is of paramount importance.

# Summary

In designing instruments for use in survey research, the key issue is the development of a question-naire that is clear, easily understandable and easy to administer. Questions need to be formulated so as to obtain the desired information from respondents and to avoid miscommunication between the researcher and the respondent. In multicountry research, one issue is the extent to which questions are formulated in precisely the same terms. This is more likely to be feasible for questions relating to demographic and other background characteristics than for behavioral or product market data. Greatest difficulty is likely to occur in relation to attitudinal and psychographic data. The way in which the question is posed, open-ended versus closed and direct versus indirect formulations, has also to be considered.

Respondent comprehension is likely to be increased considerably by the use of visual stimuli such as show cards, pictures and photos. These can also be used to provide a check on bias arising from miscomprehension of verbal questions. It is, however, important to note that visual stimuli can be misinterpreted as well and need to be translated into the relevant idiom to ensure they are correctly interpreted.

Instruments also need to be designed to minimize potential sources of bias in international surveys. This can arise first as a result of the topics covered in the questionnaire. Second, it can arise from the interaction between the interviewer and the interviewee. Third, it can arise from the characteristics of the respondent, such as his or her response style or socioeconomic and demographic origins.

Finally, the format in which the response is obtained needs to be carefully considered. Here, a key issue is whether scales and response formats need to be adapted to specific countries and cultures. Particularly in developing countries with low levels of literacy, somewhat ingenious devices may need to be used in order to ensure accurate responses. In general, it is preferable to use different formats that generate equal responses, rather than the same format if this results in bias or less accurate responses.

# References

Aaker, D.A., Kumar, V. and Day, G.S. (2003) *Marketing Research*, 8th edition. John Wiley & Sons, New York.

Almond, G. and Verba, S. (1965) *The Civil Culture: Political Attitudes and Democracy in Five Nations*. Princeton University Press, Princeton, NJ.

Askegaard, S. and Madsen, T.K. (1995) Homogeneity and Heterogeneousness in European Food Cultures: An Exploratory Analysis. In *Proceedings of the EMAC Conference*, Cergy-Pontoise.

Baumgartner H. and Steenkamp, J-B.E.M. (2001) Response Styles in Marketing Research: A Cross-national Investigation, *Journal of Marketing Research*, 38(2), 143–156.

Berrien, F.K. (1968) Cross-cultural Equivalence of Personality Measures. *Journal of Social Psychology*, 75, 3–9.

Bijmolt, T.H.A., Paas, L.J. and Vermunt, J.K. (2004) Country and Consumer Segmentation: Multi-level Latent Class Analysis of Financial Product Ownership. Unpublished document. Department of Marketing, Tilburg University.

Bontempo, R. (1993) Translation Fidelity of Psychological Scales. *Journal of Cross-cultural Psychology*, **24**, 149–166.

Brislin, R.W. (1980) Translation and Content Analysis of Oral and Written Material. In Triandis, H.C. and Berry, J.W. (eds) *Handbook of Cross-cultural Psychology*, Vol. 1. Allyn and Bacon, Boston, pp. 389–444.

Cantril, A. (1965) *The Pattern of Human Concerns*. Rutgers University Press, New Brunswick, NJ.

Churchill, G.A., and Iacobucci, D. (2005) *Marketing Research: Methodological Foundations*, 9th edition. SouthWestern Publications, Cincinnati, OH.

Corder, C.K. (1978) Problems and Pitfalls in Conducting Marketing Research in Africa. In Gelb, B. (ed.) *Marketing Expansion in a Shrinking World*. American Marketing Association, Chicago, pp. 867–890.

Couper, M.P. and de Leeuw, E.D. (2003) Nonresponse in Cross-cultural and Cross-national Surveys. In Harkness, J., Van de Vijver, F.J.R. and Mohler, P.Ph., *Cross-cultural Survey Methods*, John Wiley & Sons Inc., New York.

Cowley, E. (2001) Overconfidence in Memory for Brand Information: A Cross-national Study. *Asia Pacific Journal of Marketing and Logistics*, **13**(2), 85–96.

Donovan, R.J. and Spark, R. (1997) Towards Guidelines for Survey Research in Remote Aboriginal Communities. *The Australian and New Zealand Journal of Public Health*, **21**, 89–95.

Douglas, S.P. and Shoemaker, R. (1981) Item Non-response in Cross-national Surveys. *European Research*, **9**, 124–132.

Dragow, F. and Lissak, R.I. (1983) Modified Parallel Analysis. A Procedure for Examining the Latent Dimensionality of Dichotomously Scored Item Responses. *Journal of Applied Psychology*, **68**, 363–373.

Dubois, B. and Laurent, G. (1993) Is There a Euro-consumer for Luxury Goods? In van Raaij, F. and Bamossy, G. (eds) *European Advances in Consumer Research*, Vol. 1. Association for Consumer Research, Provo, UT, pp. 58–69.

ESOMAR (1997) *Harmonization of Socio-demographics: The Development of the ESOMAR European Social Grade*. ESOMAR, Amsterdam.

Fields, G. (1989) *Gucci on the Ginza*. Monitor, New York.

Greenleaf, E.A. (1992) Measuring Extreme Response Style. *Public Opinion Quarterly*, **56**(Fall), 328–351.

Hambleton, R.K. (1993) Translating Achievement Tests for Use in Cross-national Studies. *European Journal of Psychological Assessment*, **9**, 57–68.

Hambleton, R.K. (1994) Guidelines for Adapting Educational and Psychological Tests: A Progress Report. *European Journal of Psychological Assessment (Bulletin of the International Test Commission)*, **10**, 229–244.

Hambleton, R.K. (2005) Issues, Designs and Technical Guidelines for Adapting Tests in Multiple Languages and Cultures. In Hambleton, R.K., Merenda, P.F. and Spielberger, C.D. (eds) *Adapting Educational and Psychological Tests in Cross-cultural Assessment*, Erlbaum, Hillsdale, N.J.

Harkness, J. (2003) Questionnaire Translation. In Harkness, J., Van de Vijver, F.J.R. and Mohler, P.Ph., *Cross-cultural Survey Methods*, John Wiley & Sons Inc., New York.

Hulin, C.L. (1987) Psychometric Theory of Item and Scale Translations: Equivalence Across Languages. *Journal of Cross-cultural Psychology*, **18**, 115–142.

Johnson, T.P. and Van de Vijver, F.J.R. (2003) Social Desirability in Cross-cultural Research. In Harkness, J., Van de Vijver, F.J.R. and Mohler, P.Ph., *Cross-cultural Survey Methods,* John Wiley & Sons Inc., New York.

Keillor, B., Owens, D. and Pettijohn, C. (2001) A Cross-cultural/Cross-national Study of Influencing Factors and Socially Desirable Response Biases. *International Journal of Market Research*, **43**(1), 63–84.

Levi-Strauss, C. (1965) The Principles of Reciprocity. In Coser, L.A. and Rosenberg, B. (eds) *Sociological Theory*. Macmillan, New York.

Lonner, W.J. and Berry, J.W. (eds) (1986) *Field Methods in Cross-cultural Research*. Sage, Beverly Hills, CA.

Malhotra, N.K. (1996) *Marketing Research*, 2nd edition. Prentice Hall, New Jersey.

Markus, H.R. and Kitayama S. (1991) Culture and Self: Implications for Cognition, Emotion and Motivation. *Psychological Review*, **98**, 224–253.

Mauss, M. (1954) *The Gift*. Cohen and West, London.

Mitchell, R.E. (1965) Survey Materials Collected in Developing Countries: Sampling, Measurement and Interviewing: Obstacles to Intra- and Inter-national Comparisons. *International Social Science Journal*, **17**, 4.

Morris, J.D. (1995) SAM: The Self-assessment Manikin: An Effective Cross-cultural Measurement of Emotional Response. *Journal of Advertising Research*, November/December, 63–68.

Oppenheim, A.N. (1992) *Questionnaire Design and Attitude Measurement*. Basic Books, New York.

Reinmuth, J.E. and Geurts, M.D. (1975) The Collection of Sensitive Information Using a Two Stage Randomized Response Model, *Journal of Marketing Research*, **12**, 402–407.

Schwarz, N. (2003) Self-reports in Consumer Research: The Challenge of Comparing Cohorts and Cultures. *Journal of Consumer Research*, **29**(4), 588–594.

Schwarz, N. and Sudman, S. (eds) (1996) *Answering Questions: Methodology for Determining Cognitive and Communicative Processes in Survey Research*. Jossey-Bass, San Francisco, CA.

Skjak, K.K. and Harkness, J. (2003) Data Collection Methods. In Harkness, J., Van de Vijver, F.J.R. and Mohler, P.Ph. *Cross-cultural Survey Methods*, John Wiley & Sons Inc., New York.

Small, R., Yelland, J., Lumley J., Rice P.L. *et al.* (1999) Cross-cultural Research: Trying to Do it Better 2. Enhancing Data Quality. *Australian and New Zealand Journal of Public Health*, **23**(4), 390–395.

Smith, T.W. (2003) Developing Comparable Questions in Cross-national Surveys. In Harkness, J., Van de Vijver, F.J.R. and Mohler, P.Ph., *Cross-cultural Survey Methods*, John Wiley & Sons Inc., New York.

Spark, R. (1999) Developing Health Promotion Methods in Remote Aboriginal Communities. PhD thesis, Curtin University of Technology, Perth.

Steenkamp, J-B.E.M., Avlonitis, G., Grunert, K.G., Trail, B., Vanden Abeele, P., Wedel, M. and Audenaert, A. (1995) Consumer-led Approach to Foods in the EU: Development of Comprehensive Market-oriented Strategies Based on Pan-European Segments. In *Proceedings of EMAC Conference*, Cergy-Pontoise.

Stocking, M.L. and Lord, F.M. (1983) Developing a Common Metric in Item Response Theory. *Applied Psychological Measurement*, 7, 201–210.

Triandis, H.C. (1972) *The Analysis of Subjective Culture*. John Wiley & Sons Inc., New York.

Troiano, J., Costa, W., Guardado, S. (2002) The Sound of Silence. And the Vision that Was Planted in My Brain Still Remains. *Excellence in International Research 2002*. ESOMAR, Amsterdam.

Van Herk, H. and Verhallen, T.M.M. (1994) Methodological Issues in International Segmentation. In *Proceedings of EMAC Conference*, EMAC, Maastricht.

Van Herk, K. (2003) *Equivalence in a Cross-national Context: Methodological and Empirical Issues in Marketing Research*. Tilburg University Press, Tilburg.

Voss, K.E., Stein, D.E., Johnson, L.W. and Arce, C. (1996) An Exploration of the Comparability of Semantic Adjectives in Three Languages. *International Marketing Review*, 13, 214–258.

Werner, O. and Campbell, D. (1970) Translating, Working Through Interpreters and the Problems of Decentering. In Naroll, R. and Cohen, R. (eds) *A Handbook of Method in Cultural Anthropology*. Columbia University Press, New York.

www.euromonitor.com

Young, C.A. (1999) What We Know About 'I Don't Know': An Analysis of the Relationship Between 'Don't Know' and Education. Paper presented to American Association of Public Opinion Research, St Petersburg Beach, FL. May.

# Chapter 9

# SAMPLING AND DATA COLLECTION

## Introduction

Once a research instrument has been designed to collect the required data, the next step is to develop appropriate sampling and survey data collection procedures. Although sampling has to be considered in both survey and nonsurvey research, the main focus in this chapter is on sampling in survey research. Here, it is crucial to develop systematic procedures to ensure that reliable and comparable data are collected. This requires establishing a sampling plan based on the target population, developing a sampling frame or sampling list, and selecting appropriate survey administration procedures. These relationships are shown in Figure 9.1.

In developing a sampling plan for a particular target population, decisions first have to be made with regard to the appropriate sampling frame, for example the world, country groupings, countries or units within countries. Next is the choice of sampling procedures. In the case of global and

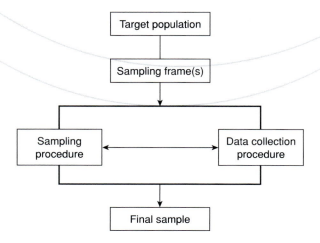

**Figuer 9.1**  Elements involved in developing a sampling plan

regional samples, the main problem is to find procedures that ensure representativeness of the target population. Since few comprehensive global or regional sampling frames are available, judgment or convenience sampling is often more practical and considerably less expensive than random sampling and also more likely to provide reliable and accurate data. This will particularly tend to be the case in business-to-business research, where the absolute population may be relatively small and known. In the case of national sampling units, in addition to finding an appropriate frame, researchers also have to consider whether the use of equivalent procedures for each sampling unit will yield comparable results. Differences in the availability and coverage provided by sampling frames or lists, and in the ease of reaching the target population, suggest that in some cases using different sampling procedures for each unit may provide better representation and be more cost effective (Hader and Gabler, 2003).

A decision then has to be made as to how the survey should be administered. As in domestic research, four major alternatives can be identified, mail, telephone, personal interview or electronic. This latter method is becoming increasingly popular in Europe and the US as e-mail lists become more widely available. It also enables the use of pictorial or photographic stimuli, for example products or advertisements, as well as facilitating use of a combination of qualitative and quantitative techniques.

Whatever the method used, the question of whether equivalent procedures from one country to another will yield comparable results has to be assessed. This, in turn, depends on the availability and adequacy of sampling frames for the target population. Mail surveys require the availability of a mailing list, and telephone surveys a list of telephone numbers although with sufficient density of numbers random digit dialing can be used. Personal interviewing provides greater flexibility, in that where convenience or quota sampling is used, a list of the target population is not required. Use of e-mail or the Internet, on the other hand, requires an adequate base of e-mail or Internet subscribers in the target population.

The final sample, whether global, regional, national or within country, should be as representative as possible of the target population and, in the case of national and within-country sampling units, as comparable as possible across units. Cost considerations and sampling difficulties may limit the feasibility of obtaining representative samples.

This chapter examines the various issues involved in sampling, particularly in obtaining sampling units that are as comparable as possible from one country or region of the world to another. First, the problem of obtaining sampling frames from which to draw the sample is examined. Second, the use of different sampling techniques is discussed. Third, the advantages and disadvantages associated with different survey administration methods in international markets are reviewed. Finally, issues associated with field staff selection and training are discussed.

# Sampling

In designing a sampling plan, the first step is to determine the appropriate geographical unit to be sampled – that is, world, country, region and so on – and to assess whether a sample frame for the target population exists. Appropriate respondents have then to be selected. For example, in a consumer survey of grocery products, the wife may be the relevant respondent; or in a survey of office equipment purchasing, the manager of the buying department. The next step is to determine the sampling procedure and size of the sample.

## *Selecting the Sampling Frame*

Once the target population to be sampled has been identified, the availability of a population list from which the sample may be drawn should be assessed. In international research, this frequently poses difficulties due to the limited amount of information available on industries, businesses or consumer groups in other countries. Even where sampling frames commonly used in Western countries are available, such as electoral or municipal lists, telephone books or listings, they frequently do not provide adequate coverage, particularly in developing countries, and can give rise to frame error.

Lack of sampling frames often leads to use of nonprobability sampling in international marketing research. This can be used effectively in business-to-business marketing, where interviewing of certain key respondents may be more informative than systematic analysis of representative samples.

In international marketing research, sampling may take place in relation to different geographical units. The most aggregate level is that of the world. The next level consists of geographical regions such as Europe or Latin America. Following this is the country level, and geographical units or other subgroups within countries, for example regions, cities, neighborhoods or city blocks.

| Table 9.1 | The levels of the sampling frame | |
|---|---|---|
| Level | Product market examples | Examples of sampling lists |
| World | Financial institutions | D&B's *Principal International Business* |
| | Machine tools | |
| | Power generation | Gale's *Worldwide Business Directory* |
| | Transnational consumer segments | Subscribers to: *Financial Times, Economist, National Geographic* |
| Regions | Airlines | *Latin America 25 000* |
| | Automobiles | *D&B Europe* |
| | Personal computers | Regional trade associations |
| | | *Major Companies of Asia* |
| Countries | Agricultural equipment | National trade associations |
| | Construction supplies | Credit card lists |
| | Consumer durables | Population lists |
| | Consumer package goods | Telephone listings |
| Cities | Upscale consumer goods | Municipal lists |
| | Social services | Church organizations |
| | Specialty foods | Lists of government organizations |
| | | Community organizations |

How the sample is drawn depends to a large extent on the specific product market research objectives and on the availability of lists for each type of unit. Some examples are shown in Table 9.1. The sequencing of research and whether, for example, one region or country is investigated first and then another are related to the availability of information for a given target segment. The issues associated with sampling at each level are next discussed in more detail.

## *The World*

The most aggregate sampling unit is the world. This is likely to be appropriate in business-to-business markets, such as injection molders, medical equipment, machine tools and so on. For these markets, worldwide lists of manufacturers can be obtained from sources such as Dun and Bradstreet's *Principal International Businesses* (PIB), which has an online database listing 500 000 leading businesses in a variety of industries outside the US. CD-ROM versions available include 100 000 companies, 250 000 companies or 500 000 companies worldwide. An abridged print version is also available. Gale's *World Business Directory* (2003) has information on 136 000 businesses worldwide and provides information on sales, net worth and number of employees as well as executive officers' names and titles, e-mail and web addresses. Where a list for a specific country is required, in some cases trade associations are able to provide relevant and detailed information.

Sampling at the world level is likely to be rare in consumer research unless the target population is a small global market segment. For example, subscribers to the *National Geographic* or American Express cardholders might be an appropriate target sample for testing a new foreign travel publication or travel goods, or readers of the *Economist* for business-class travel. Equally, Internet users might provide an appropriate sampling frame for specialized technology-based services. A major restriction on sampling at this level is the lack of information relative to the target population.

## Country Groupings

Samples can be drawn based on country groupings such as the Scandinavian countries. Again, this is most likely to be appropriate in business-to-business markets. Graham and Whiteside publish company directories such as *Major Companies of Europe* in six volumes, which list more than 24 000 of the largest companies in Europe. This also lists the names of 194 000 senior executives, their e-mail and web addresses, as well as a description of business activities, brands and trademarks and financial data for the last two years. More complete information on Graham and Whiteside's directories can be obtained directly from its web site (www.major-co-data.com). Again, trade associations or financial associations also provide lists or directories for a specific industry.

In a few cases, regional sampling of consumer markets may be undertaken. For example, the Europanel, established by a consortium of research agencies throughout Europe (GfK), provides a representative sample of consumers in Europe. In general, such samples are built up from nationally representative samples. Equally, Global Market Insite manages web-based panels in 200 countries on four continents, which can be accessed to develop customized regional or multicountry samples (www.gmi-mr.com).

## Country

Despite the globalization of markets, the country is still the most common level for drawing a sample in international research. In industrialized countries, sample frames such as electoral lists, population censuses and telephone books are commonly used for drawing samples. Such sampling frames are not always available or current in other countries and coverage will vary. In Germany, for example, the publication of household telephone numbers became optional in 1992 and the percentage of households listed dropped from 97% to 72%, substantially reducing the coverage provided by telephone listings. Similarly, in Switzerland when listing became optional in 1998, the proportion of households listed dropped to 88% in 2000 (Hader and Gabler, 2003). Some countries, notably in the Middle East, Africa and parts of Asia, lack any type of population lists. In others, street maps are not available, streets may have no names and houses may not be numbered.

Lack of any commonly used sampling frames means that the researcher will have to construct a sampling list from scratch. In the Middle East, especially in Saudi Arabia, research organizations typically establish a sampling frame based on city blocks in the major cities. This is developed based on accumulated experience in previous surveys. Since different nationalities and socioeconomic groups live in particular areas, these blocks can then be used as a basis for quota or stratified sampling. Random sampling is not feasible, nor likely to be desirable given the stratified nature of the society.

Different biases may be inherent in the use of different sampling frames. Outside industrialized countries, for example, use of telephone lists will provide a relatively skewed sample, consisting primarily of individuals or households of higher socioeconomic status. Similarly, use of city block data may result in underrepresentation of low socioeconomic respondents living in shacks or riverboats.

## Units within Countries

Samples can also be drawn based on subgroups within countries. These might be geographical units such as cities or neighborhoods, or alternatively ethnic, racial, cultural, age or demographic subgroupings such as Asian or Turkish immigrants in Europe or the Middle East, Vietnamese immigrants in Australasia, children or senior citizens in cities of over 500 000 in North America. Similarly, in an organizational context, specific industries or organizations of a certain size – that is, small versus medium-sized businesses – might constitute the relevant population.

The availability of information from which to develop a sample is likely to vary with the specific subgroup. For geographical units, this will pose little problem if maps or local electoral lists can be obtained. Similarly, if ethnic, cultural or socioeconomic groups tend to live in certain neighborhoods, city block frames can be developed as a basis for sampling. Children can be sampled based on school districts and religious or ethnic groups based on church membership, religious or ethnic organizations. Members of such organizations will tend to be those with strong ethnic or cultural affiliation, and are not necessarily typical of all members of a particular cultural or ethnic group, but rather of 'core' members of the group.

# The Choice of Respondent

Once the sampling frame has been identified, the specific respondent to be sampled has to be determined. Here, an important consideration in studying families and organizations is to determine who is the relevant respondent; that is, the wife, husband or other person in a household, or in an organization the buyer, user and so on. In addition, a decision has to be made as to whether a single respondent is used or whether multiple respondents will be required, for example both husbands and wives and children in the family, or several members of a buying committee.

It is important to identify the relevant respondent(s) in each country, since these vary from country to country. In some countries or cultures, for instance Asian and Latin markets, organizational decision making is highly centralized. Consequently, the relevant respondent may be the chairman, CEO or senior management. In other countries, for example Anglo-Saxon cultures, there is a greater tendency to delegate decision making, hence middle management may play a greater role.

Similarly, in households, the relevant respondent(s) and roles of different household members in various purchasing decisions have to be determined. In extended families, for example, one person may be primarily responsible for groceries and other frequently purchased items. In some Middle Eastern countries, the husband may actually purchase groceries, but the wife specifies what items are to be purchased. In other cases, both may go together to purchase items. Husbands also play a major role in wives' clothing decisions. In the case of consumer durables such as automobiles or household appliances, several family members may be involved. Consequently, focus groups to determine the relevant involvement of different family members may be desirable.

The number of respondents to be interviewed from a given household or organizational unit has also to be considered. The cost of collecting data from multiple members is likely to be prohibitively expensive. As a result, especially for frequently purchased consumer goods, a single-family member, often the wife, may be used as a surrogate for other members. Similarly, in the case of organizations, the difficulty and cost of interviewing multiple managers will lead to selection of a single person as representative and as an informant about the decision process.

# Sampling Procedures

The next step is to determine appropriate sampling procedures. First, the researcher has to decide whether research is to be undertaken in all countries and contexts, and whether results and findings are generalizable from one country or context to another.

Ideally, research should be conducted in all countries and contexts where marketing operations are planned. There is a trade-off between the number of countries in which research is undertaken and the depth or quality of research. Consequently, management may decide to use findings in one country as a proxy for another. For example, market response patterns in Scandinavian countries may be sufficiently similar to allow sampling in only one of these countries. Similarly, in the Middle East, strategy may be based on research conducted in Saudi Arabia and then rolled out to other Gulf states. It is important to realize that such a procedure is fraught with danger. Even though previous experience suggests that response patterns are the same or similar, this may change, or not be relevant in relation to the specific product or situation examined.

In selecting sampling procedures, a key decision is whether random or purposive sampling should be used. This is closely linked to the availability of the sampling list and survey administration techniques. If sampling lists of the relevant population are not available, as is often the case in developing countries, probabilistic or random sampling poses some difficulties. Consequently, in much consumer research in international markets quota sampling is more likely to be used, often in conjunction with block sampling or random location sampling points. Similarly, in the case of business-to-business research, convenience or judgment sampling is most likely to be used, since the total population is often relatively small and known.

# Sampling Techniques

The next step is to select an appropriate sampling technique. Here, a major distinction exists between probabilistic and nonprobabilistic sampling. In probabilistic sampling, each respondent in the target population has a known chance of being in the sample. In nonprobabilistic sampling, some criteria are established on the basis of which respondents are selected. For further in-depth discussion of sampling techniques see Aaker *et al.* (2003) or Churchill and Iacobucci (2005).

In industrialized countries, random or probabilistic sampling is generally considered desirable, though the same sampling design does not need to be used in each country (Hader and Gabler, 2003). Different sampling designs may provide equivalent results and representativity due to differences in sampling frames. Comprehensive lists of the target population are frequently available in such countries, though this is not always the case in other countries. Lack of published information about the relevant target population, limited availability of sampling lists and the cost associated with the development of such lists suggest that other methods such as judgment, convenience, snowball or referral sampling may be more cost effective. This may be desirable where personal interviewing is used rather than mail or telephone surveys. The various types of sampling are next discussed in more detail.

## Nonprobabilistic Sampling

*Convenience Sampling*   In some cases, a convenience sample may be used. This implies selecting any respondent who is readily available. In emerging country markets, for example, convenience sampling in the market place provides a low-cost procedure for generating a sample. Given the difficulties and costs of developing sampling frames in such countries and in reaching the rural population, this procedure can be used to generate a sample that, while not strictly representative, may nonetheless be relatively free of any systematic bias.

*Judgment Sampling*   Another procedure is to select respondents based on judgment. Judgment sampling is based on the assumption that certain persons are better informed than others and have expert knowledge in a given field, or are specified in the research brief(s), for example customers of a client company. For instance, in international marketing research, judgment sampling may be used to identify area or industry experts for a given country or region in order to assess trends in the industry or region. In business-to-business research, this often provides a more efficient method of assessing the likelihood of new product acceptance, industry growth, market conditions and so on than use of quota or probabilistic sampling.

The international sales force is also often a valuable source of information, both for identifying respondents and providing customer information, since they know customer needs and interests.

Care should, however, be taken in using them to obtain quantitative estimates, such as of sales potential. Importers or export agents can also be used as 'key informants', though systematic bias may be introduced, reflecting the self-interest of the source.

In emerging markets, questioning of village elders, priests or other local authority figures can be used to obtain information about the number of local inhabitants, their purchase behavior and other issues. In rural areas, or among respondents with high levels of illiteracy, this provides a relatively low-cost and rapid means of obtaining a general indication of relevant information, though not a precise estimate of actual figures.

*Quota Sampling*   A procedure widely used in both industrialized and emerging country markets is quota sampling. Quotas are established by specifying the number of respondents from within a given category, for example by age or socioeconomic group, occupation, nationality, urban versus rural, purchasers versus nonpurchasers and so on. In business-to-business research, quotas may be established by industry or the equivalent of an SIC (Standard Industrial Classification) category, firm size, location and so on. In industrialized countries, as markets become more segmented, quota sampling is increasingly used to ensure coverage of the target population. In emerging markets, quota sampling may also be used where there are known to be significant differences in behavior by nationality, income group, age and so on. For example, in the Gulf states there are significant differences in brand preferences and loyalty for cigarettes by nationality and income group. Consequently, quotas are established by nationality grouping. While this procedure ensures that the sample will be representative based on quota characteristics, there is a danger that these characteristics are systematically associated with other factors that will introduce confounding effects.

*Snowball Sampling*   Snowball or referral sampling is a technique well suited to international marketing research. With snowball sampling, initial respondents are selected randomly or based on judgment, and they are then asked to identify other members of the target population. This procedure continues until a large enough sample is obtained. This technique is helpful where the target population is difficult to identify, for example industrial buyers of a product, financial experts, or users of food stamps. In some cases the initial sample is a random sample, but in others it can be selected by judgment. In either case, the final sample will be nonprobabilistic, since respondents are likely to identify others similar to themselves. In the Middle East, referral sampling is widely used in order to obtain a sample of female respondents. A number of women are first selected, often of different nationalities, for example Arabs from different countries or of different socioeconomic classes. These women are then asked to indicate other women whom they think would be willing to be interviewed. Typically, these will come from the same socioeconomic group and be of the same nationality. This procedure is followed until the desired sample size for each group is obtained.

## Probabilistic Sampling

*Simple Random Sampling*    Random sampling frequently poses a number of problems in international marketing research. In the first place, it requires the availability of a frame or list. Respondents are then picked at random from the list. A simple procedure is to use a random number table to establish a starting point and then select every *n*th name or person on the list until the desired sample size is obtained. These respondents then constitute the sample population. The lack of sampling lists often limits use of this approach, especially in emerging markets.

If the survey is interviewer administered, an alternative procedure is to use the random-walk method. The interviewer then becomes responsible for sampling. He or she is provided with a route and instructed to interview a respondent in every *n*th house. This poses problems in some countries since the interviewer may have difficulty following the route, or determining exactly what is a 'dwelling unit' in villages, shanty towns or where buildings include multiple-family units. Furthermore, if there are no existing maps of an area, a mapping of dwellings in an area will need to be developed. The difficulties and costs associated with random sampling are a key reason why nonprobabilistic sampling is frequently used in international marketing research.

*Stratified Sampling*    In some cases it may be considered important to ensure that samples from different countries are representative on certain characteristics such as income, education, age, nationality, single-family or single-parent households, or business versus consumer users. This is particularly important where similar segments are to be targeted in different countries or regions throughout the world. A random sample is then taken from each group or stratum of interest in the population.

Stratified sampling is either proportionate or disproportionate. In proportionate stratified sampling, the sample should be proportionate to the relative size of that stratum in the total population. In disproportionate sampling, other factors, for example differences in variance in each stratum, determine the size of sample taken from each stratum.

In estimating market size for small power tools, for example, two segments may be of interest: 'do-it-yourselfers' and the professional segment, including craftsmen, repairmen and handymen. Greater variation may be expected in the professional segment in terms of frequency of use, type of user and so on than in the consumer segment. Consequently, it may be desirable to draw a larger sample from the professional segment relative to its size than from the consumer segment.

Quota and stratified sampling are frequently confused. While similar in that the objective is to obtain representativity on certain key characteristics, stratified samples are drawn probabilistically, while in quota sampling respondents are selected on a judgmental basis. In other words, any respondent who meets the specified characteristics may be picked until the desired quota for that subgroup are met. As a result, a quota sample may contain certain biases that are less likely to occur in a stratified sample.

*Cluster Sampling* A related technique is cluster sampling. While in stratified sampling a random sample is selected from each stratum or subgroup, in cluster sampling the target population is first divided into mutually exclusive categories or clusters. A random sample of clusters is then selected, and either one-stage or multistage sampling conducted. In one-stage cluster sampling, all the population elements in each selected cluster are examined. In multistage cluster sampling, a random sample is drawn for each selected cluster.

A common form of cluster sampling is area sampling. In this case, geographical units such as cities, regions, areas or blocks within cities are the clusters. Either one-stage or multistage sampling can then be conducted based on these clusters. This procedure is particularly useful and cost effective where no population lists are available.

Area sampling can be either one-stage or multistage. In one-stage area sampling, the geographical units are selected and all relevant respondents within that unit studied. In multistage area sampling, further sampling within geographical units takes place. Suppose, for example, a manufacturer of detergents was interested in estimating consumption of powdered detergent in urban households in Taiwan. If one-stage area sampling were adopted, he might select four residential areas in three major urban areas, Taipei, Kaioshung and Taichung, and estimate consumption per household of detergent in each of these areas. The average for the four areas in each city could then be used to estimate overall consumption of detergent in the area.

## Multistage Sampling

Multistage sampling can also be used in conjunction with other sampling approaches and often involves a mix of techniques. In business-to-business research, specific industries may be selected for investigation based on judgment and then quota sampled, based on size within each industry. Similarly, in emerging market countries, area sampling may be used to pick major cities and villages to investigate and then stratified sampling employed. Alternatively, block sampling might be applied to select households to be interviewed within the cities, while in the villages judgment sampling of elders is used.

Multistage sampling can help to reduce the costs of international marketing research. Efficiency is increased, since the initial stage(s) is used to pinpoint relevant respondents to be sampled subsequently. It is particularly likely to be appropriate for large-scale surveys and in developing countries, where sampling frames are not readily available. On the other hand, multistage sampling can also result in some loss in precision, since sampling errors accumulate from one stage to another. In addition, more time is likely to be required to identify the initial sample than if sampling were conducted in a single stage. In some cases where the initial stage sampling is based on secondary data sources, for example where the clusters are regions, states, cities or industries, multistage sampling can increase the efficiency and speed of the research process.

A major cross-cultural survey using multistage probability sampling is the Eurobarometer (Hader and Gabler, 2003). The sampling procedure is a multistage random design based on a random selection of primary sampling units (PSU) according to the distribution of the national population by metropolitan, urban and rural areas. In the second stage, a cluster of addresses is selected from each primary unit and addresses to be sampled are chosen systematically using a standard random route procedure. In each household the respondent is selected by a random procedure such as the first birthday method. Up to two recalls are made to obtain an interview with the selected interviewee.

As the preceding example illustrates, multistage random sampling requires extensive resources and is highly laborious. Consequently, it is primarily used by government and other large international organizations. In commercial research, two alternative forms of multistage sampling, double sampling and sequential sampling, are more commonly used.

*Double Sampling*   In double or two-phase sampling, the samples are drawn twice. Once an initial sample has been drawn, data are collected from respondents about characteristics such as purchasing behavior and frequency, demographic variables, location and availability for future interviewing and so on. This information is then used to develop a frame for drawing a second sample, based on respondents in the initial sample. These respondents are interviewed a second time in greater depth.

In evaluating international market potential for web-site construction and management services, for example, an international telephone survey might be conducted to determine which industries and what size of companies are the heaviest purchasers of such services in different countries or regions throughout the world. A preliminary list of companies to contact could be established based on knowledge of heavy-user industries in the domestic market. Based on data collected from this survey, a list could be drawn up of companies and industries that appear to be heavy users and potentially cooperative respondents. A sample could then be drawn from the list, and these companies investigated in greater depth with regard to purchasing behavior, key criteria used for evaluating vendors, importance of service and training, key managers influencing the purchase decision and so on.

*Sequential Sampling*   In the case of sequential sampling, the total sample size is not determined in advance. Respondents are interviewed one after another, and the data analyzed simultaneously or at specific points in time. Depending on the reliability of results, a decision is made about whether more respondents should be interviewed. With the increasing use of laptop computers for interviews and computerized interviewing techniques, this procedure has become increasingly popular. Data are keyed directly into the computer and results updated after each entry. It is also frequently used for Internet-based surveys, where again results can be analyzed instantaneously. The decision when to stop sampling is then based on the stability of results obtained from each successive batch of respondents; that is, the stability of results obtained from the first 100 respondents relative to the second 100 and so on. The cost efficiency of research is increased as the minimum number of respondents to achieve reliable results is interviewed.

# Sample Size

Another decision concerns the appropriate sample size. Assuming a fixed budget, there is a trade-off between the number of countries or contexts sampled and the sample size within each country or region. Use of statistical procedures to determine the appropriate sample size is likely to be rare, as some estimation of population variance is required. Typically, the research budget will determine sample size. Management will decide that samples of 400 or 10 focus groups in each country are adequate, given budget constraints. If a sequential sampling procedure is used, then the sample size will be variable, depending on the stability of successive sample results.

In determining samples within country units, population diversity should also be considered. Differences with regard to key variables or sampling characteristics such as income, age, education, nationality and so on may occur and affect results. For example, different linguistic groups or ethnic or nationality groups may have substantially different behavior and purchase patterns. Equally, there may be wide variation by income or socioeconomic group, as for example in India or Latin America. Consequently, it may be desirable to do quota sampling by these groupings in order to ensure population representativity. This may, however, require larger than normal sample sizes to test for the impact of differences in these variables on cross-national findings. This entails high sampling costs and can pose budgetary difficulties. Use of large sample sizes – that is, of more than 1000 respondents in each country – is rare except in government surveys or those sponsored by international organizations, such as the Eurobarometer.

# Achieving Comparability in Sampling

## *Sample Composition*

A key issue in sampling design in international marketing research is the relative importance attached to representativity, as opposed to the comparability of the samples. If samples are representative of the target population, they are unlikely to be comparable with regard to key characteristics such as income, age and education. This will create a confounding effect if, as is frequently the case, such variables affect the behavior or response patterns studied. For example, income or education might be an important factor underlying interest in tropical fruit in different countries. If national samples are drawn in countries with different income levels, mistaken inferences could be made about national differences or similarities of interest in tropical fruits, when these reflected differences in income rather than 'true' national differences. One might, for example, conclude that there was lack of adequate market potential, when in fact a small, high-income segment constituted a potential spearhead for market entry in a low-income country.

The relative importance attached to representativity vs comparability should depend to a substantial degree on the purpose of the research (Reynolds, Simintras and Diamontopoulos, 2003). In descriptive or contextual studies, where the primary concern is with external validity – that is, generalizing results to the country or cross-national group of interest – attention should be focused on the representativity of the sample. In comparative and theoretical studies, on the other hand, where the primary concern is internal validity and hence the homogeneity of the sample, emphasis should be placed on comparability.

In addition to achieving comparability through a well-thought-out sampling plan, there are statistical procedures such as covariance analysis that can be used to evaluate the impact of different sample compositions on results and to adjust for these. These are discussed in Chapter 11.

# *Sampling Procedures*

Another issue is whether the same sampling procedures should be used across countries, if they vary in reliability from one country to another. In this case, rather than using identical sampling procedures and methods in each country, it may be preferable to employ procedures that have equivalent levels of accuracy or reliability. Suppose, for example, that in one country random sampling is of known validity, and in another country quota sampling. The results will be more comparable in terms of response rate and quality of response if random sampling is used in one country and quota sampling in another, than if the same sampling procedures are blindly applied in each research context (Hader and Gabler, 2003).

Similarly, costs of sampling procedures may differ from country to country. Administrative cost savings achieved from using the same method in many countries may be outweighed by use of the most efficient sampling method in each country. In one country, area sampling may be the most effective, while in another country quota sampling may produce acceptable results at half the cost. Consequently, it may be more appropriate to use the quota method in the latter country, while employing area sampling in other contexts.

Use of different sampling methods can also provide a check on the reliability of results and the potential bias inherent in different methods. For example, in an early study different sampling procedures with different sources of potential bias were used in five different countries (Webster, 1966). With one procedure a consistent bias was found in relation to one of the main variables studied, the percentage of firms in each size category owning the test product. If the same sampling procedure had been utilized in each country, this might not have been detected.

In brief, use of similar sampling procedures will not necessarily ensure comparability of results, since each procedure is subject to different types of bias and these vary from country to country.

Deliberate variation of procedures, on the other hand, if intelligently used, can provide a means of checking the validity of results and detecting biases inherent in different types of procedures.

# Sampling Error

Sampling is also a potential source of error in cross-national surveys. This arises because a sample, rather than a census, is employed to collect data. Sampling error can arise from frame error and from survey nonresponse. Where errors arise due to nonresponse, standard techniques can be used to increase response and to weight results to account for nonresponse. Where frame error occurs, there is little that can be done. As noted earlier, this is particularly likely to give rise to problems in international marketing research, due to the difficulty of obtaining accurate sampling lists, unless the researcher is willing to develop his or her own list or frame.

## Frame Error

The lack of adequate sampling frames or lists in many countries implies that samples may not be strictly comparable from one country to another. Consequently, sampling error may differ from one country or sampling unit to another. For example, the subscription list to the *Economist* provides better coverage of the business population in English-speaking countries than in French- or Spanish-speaking countries. If the limitations of the sampling frame are known, the sample can be weighted to account for these where random sampling procedures are used. If, however, judgment or convenience sampling methods are used, it may be difficult to evaluate the degree of bias arising from sampling error.

## Survey Nonresponse

Nonresponse to surveys is a source of major concern that threatens the validity of results no matter where research is conducted (de Leeuw and de Heer, 2001). As noted earlier (in Chapter 8), response rates in official statistical surveys have been declining internationally for a number of years, though there are differences between countries in the rate of decline as well as in the overall response rate (de Heer, 1999). Responses have for example been found to vary between 60% for the Netherlands and 97% for Germany. A similar trend appears to be occurring in other types of surveys.

Response rates also differ depending on the mode of data collection. A meta-analysis of response rates in mail, telephone and personal interviews found a difference of 10% between response to personal interview and to mail surveys (Hox and de Leeuw, 1994). In personal interviews the most important factors underlying nonresponse are noncontact rates and refusal to participate. Again, differences have been found across countries. In some countries, for example Belgium and Denmark, noncontact rates were the most important, whereas in others, for example the Netherlands and the UK, refusal to participate was more critical.

Nonrespondents appear to have the same profile from country to country and are typically low-income, less-educated consumers. Samples will be underrepresented with regard to the same segments in different countries. This can be corrected by double sampling on high-nonresponse segments. If other factors such as suspiciousness of interviewers or hostility to surveys underlie nonresponse, the relevant determinants and their impact will need to be investigated in each specific case.

Relatively little research has been conducted into ways to increase rates of nonresponse in multicountry surveys, particularly among consumers. Use of monetary incentives, reminder postcards, sponsorship and sponsoring organizations' stationery and personalization have typically been found to increase response in mail surveys, although the increase in response rate varies from country to country (Dawson and Dickinson, 1988; Jobber and Saunders, 1988). Japanese respondents have been found to have higher rates of response and to respond to incentives (Keown, 1985). Follow-up mailings are typically the most effective, particularly in consumer surveys (Nederhof, 1989).

In the case of personal interviews, increasing preparation and effort in fieldwork may be desirable. For example, increasing the number of contact attempts, varying the time at which contact is made and following a prescribed schedule have all been found to reduce the number of noncontacts (Purdon, Campanelli and Sturgis, 1999). The most appropriate time to interview respondents may vary with the culture or country. For example, in the Netherlands it may be more effective to contact respondents early in the evening since the Dutch tend to eat early, while in Spain or Italy a later time may be preferable.

In general, existing evidence suggests that standard procedures such as personalization, sponsorship and follow-ups, successfully used by research organizations in the US and Western Europe, are also effective in other countries and can be used to increase rates of response.

## Nonsampling Error

Surveys have to be examined for bias arising from nonsampling error. This is somewhat insidious in nature. Although the impact of the relevant factors has been extensively studied in the US and

Europe, relatively little is known concerning factors that affect the quality of data provided by respondents in other countries. Few studies have been conducted and these relate primarily to a single country or area.

Nonsampling error can arise as a result of a number of factors: the respondent; the interviewer–respondent interaction; item nonresponse; or recording error. In the case of the respondent, factors such as willingness to respond accurately and completely, response set bias, purposeful misreporting of information, faulty recall or respondent fatigue may all generate error. Item nonresponse is another potential source of error. Respondents may refuse to answer certain questions or state that they have no opinion about certain issues. These have been discussed in relation to instrument design (Chapter 8) and are not covered further here.

The interviewer–respondent interaction, if not handled appropriately, can result in biased responses. Error from this source can be reduced by better research design. For example, questionnaires can be designed that require little or no clarification by the interviewer, and show cards and other stimuli used to assist the respondent. Improved interviewer training in how to administer questionnaires or conjoint tasks, or to create a relaxed interviewing environment so as to obtain better respondent cooperation, can also improve data quality.

Recording error is an important source of error. This may arise either from carelessness or inaccuracy by the respondent where the survey is self-administered, or from lack of care by the interviewer. Recording error is of particular concern in contexts where there is a lack of experienced field staff and interviewer training is required.

Use of computerized techniques can help to reduce some sources of error, particularly those due to interviewer–interviewee interaction, but can give rise to other recording errors and furthermore can only be used in industrialized countries.

# Data Collection Procedures

The next step is to select appropriate data collection or survey administration procedures. Here, a number of factors need to be considered. In domestic marketing research, the relative cost, target population, the length and type of survey and time constraints largely determine the choice of questionnaire administration procedures; that is, mail, telephone, personal interview or electronic.

In international markets, however, other factors, such as the development of the marketing research or communications infrastructure, affect the decision, particularly with regard to telephone, email or web-based surveys.

Levels of literacy, as well as the lack of sampling lists, imply that mail surveys, while potentially a low-cost means of reaching a large target population, are fraught with problems and hence personal interviewing may be preferable. The quality of the mail service and its reliability will further influence the cost effectiveness of mail surveys. Levels of telephone ownership and particularly private telephone ownership also limit use of telephone surveys, except for business-to-business or upscale target populations.

# Mail Surveys

In industrialized countries, mail surveys typically enable coverage of a wide and representative sample, they do not require a field staff, and costs per questionnaire tend to be relatively low. Respondents may be more willing to provide information about certain issues, for example financial matters, and have time to answer questions requiring thought or specific information at their leisure. On the other hand, nonresponse rates may be high, resulting in high costs per returned questionnaire and bias due to nonresponse. Control over questionnaire administration is also lost, and there may be omissions or lack of comprehension of questions. Furthermore, certain types of questions cannot be asked and interviewers cannot probe to obtain further information.

In international marketing research, the absence of mailing lists, poor mail services and high levels of illiteracy limit the use of mail surveys. This does, however, depend on the specific product market and country concerned. Mail surveys can typically be used effectively in international business-to-business research. Mailing lists are often available. The key problem is to identify the relevant respondent within a company, and to personalize the address to ensure that the survey reaches him or her. Prior telephoning to identify the relevant respondent and to obtain his or her cooperation is likely to increase the probability of response. Sending the questionnaire by fax rather than regular mail helps to underscore the urgency of the survey and speeds up response. However, widespread use of fax numbers by direct marketing and sales companies has tended to result in a 'junk fax' phenomenon in many countries. Consequently, it is important to make prior contact regarding the survey in order to substantiate its authenticity and obtain respondent cooperation.

In consumer research, particularly in developing countries, use of mail surveys may give rise to problems. Mailing lists comparable to those in the US and major European markets are often not available, or not sold, for example credit card listings. Lists that are available, for example magazine subscription or membership association lists, are often skewed to certain segments of the population, such as the more affluent. In addition, low levels of literacy and reluctance of respondents to respond to mail surveys limit their effectiveness. Mail surveys are extremely problematic in countries such as Brazil, where it has been reckoned that 30% of the domestic mail is never delivered, or Nicaragua, where all the mail has to be delivered to the post office. In addition, mail surveys are typically slow.

Thus, mail surveys can be effectively used in business-to-business research, especially if administered by fax. In consumer research they are only likely to be effective in industrialized countries and where the goal is to reach specific customer segments, for example when conducting a customer satisfaction survey of patrons. While costs of administering mail surveys may appear low on a per questionnaire mailed out basis, low response rates or poor-quality data may limit the desirability of using them, especially in emerging countries.

## Telephone Interviewing

With the growth of telephone networks, more widespread ownership of telephones and increased ease of international communications through satellite links, use of telephone interviewing in international marketing research has increased considerably, especially in business-to-business research and in industrialized markets. The primary advantage of telephone surveys is that they enable coverage of a broadly distributed sample without requiring a field staff. Telephone interviews provide a quick way of obtaining information and nonresponse is generally low. In addition, control over interviewers and interviewer–interviewee interaction is facilitated. Interviews can be conducted at a central location and bilingual interviewers briefed about the survey. Typically, the interview is computer steered. The interviewer sits in front of a monitor and replies from each respondent are entered directly into the computer, eliminating many sources of interviewer bias and recording error. In addition, as noted earlier, results can be analyzed sequentially and sampling terminated when responses stabilize. Random dialing can also be computer generated, so that each telephone number within a given geographical area has an equal probability of being in the sample. If a respondent is not reached on an initial attempt, he or she can automatically be called back after a specified interval.

Centralizing the administration of international telephone surveys significantly reduces the time and costs associated with negotiating and organizing a research project in each country, establishing quality controls, conducting callbacks, etc. Trained interviewers fluent in the relevant language are required, but with the growth of international research and increased migration of populations, many research organizations now have their own staff of interviewers fluent in key languages. While the additional costs of making international telephone calls are higher, these are typically outweighed by lower administrative costs and accuracy of response. International calls also typically obtain a higher response rate. Results obtained by using this approach have been found to be highly stable, the same results emerging from the first 100 interviews as from the next 200 or 500. Interviewer and client control is much greater. The questionnaire can be modified in the course of the survey and interviewing extended or halted to meet the client's requirements.

In business-to-business research, use of telephone surveys is often quite effective. The majority of businesses except in rural areas are likely to have telephones. It is important as in the case of mail surveys to be able to identify the relevant respondent(s). This can be facilitated by initial probing or prior notification by fax. Willingness to respond may, however, depend on relative time pressures at work and the desired target population. If the target population is upper management, some resistance is likely to be encountered unless substantial interest in the survey can be aroused. For example, suppliers may conduct surveys to identify potential customer needs or to determine customer satisfaction. Again, prior notification and establishment of an appointment to conduct the survey are likely to be helpful.

On the other hand, telephone interviews cannot be too long, though in some cases telephone interviews of 30–90 minutes can be held. Questions have to be short and clear, and certain questions such as similarities or trade-offs cannot be used. Visual aids such as product samples or show cards also cannot be used. In some countries, particularly outside the US and Western Europe, low levels of telephone ownership and poor communication links limit the feasibility of telephone surveys, especially for consumer research. In the poorer countries of South East Asia, telephone mainline connections vary from 99 per 1000 in Thailand to 2 per 1000 in Cambodia and 10 per 1000 in Laos, and cellular phone ownership is equally low, largely precluding use of telephone surveys to reach a broad-based target market. In some countries, ownership of mainline telephones is low but is compensated for by higher levels of cellular phone ownership. For example in Venezuela, ownership of mainline telephones is 109 per 1000 but that of cellular phones is 263 per 1000, while in South Africa the figures are 111 and 242 respectively. Those who own telephones are typically in cities and/or of higher socioeconomic status, so that telephone surveys are only effective in reaching a relatively limited segment of the population. However, in many instances, this may be the relevant segment for other products as well.

In many countries, particularly in Europe, mobile phone usage has increased dramatically in recent years. In the countries shown in Table 9.2, the number of cellular phone subscribers is higher than the number of mainline phones and in some cases more than one per person. This makes it important to consider inclusion of mobile phone users in telephone surveys, though this may depend to some extent on the target population. Mobile phone users, particularly those with no fixed phone, are more likely to be young, single and to move frequently. Consequently, if younger singles are an important component of the target population, it will be important to include mobile phones in a telephone survey. Yet in some countries, even families are becoming important users of mobile

**Table 9.2** Number of phone subscribers and personal computers per 1000 in selected countries (2003)

| | Telephone Mainlines | Cellular Subscribers | Personal Computers |
|---|---|---|---|
| Luxembourg | 797 | 1061 | 594 |
| Israel | 453 | 955 | 243 |
| Hong Kong | 555 | 1057 | 422 |
| Italy | 484 | 1018 | 231 |
| Iceland | 660 | 957 | 451 |
| Sweden | 736 | 889 | 621 |
| Finland | 488 | 901 | 442 |
| Czech Republic | 360 | 947 | 177 |
| Norway | 734 | 909 | 528 |
| Greece | 454 | 780 | 82 |
| UK | 591 | 841 | 406 |
| Slovenia | 407 | 871 | 301 |
| Denmark | 669 | 887 | 577 |
| Portugal | 414 | 904 | 135 |
| Spain | 429 | 916 | 196 |
| Switzerland | 744 | 843 | 709 |

*Source*: ITU, 2004

phones. In Finland, for example, the number of mainline subscribers is declining as more house-holds are giving up fixed-line phones and relying solely on the use of mobile phones (Kuusela and Simpanen, 2003).

Surveying mobile phone users poses its own challenges, not the least of which is identifying mobile phone users. The owner of a mobile phone is often not the user, for example a large number of mobile phones are used by children. Mobile phone users may also be contacted while driving, or in a crowded location with ambient background noise, making interviewing difficult if not impossible. Consequently, it is generally advisable to make an initial phone call to establish a time to call back when the respondent will be in a more suitable location and be available to respond to questions. In many countries surveying mobile phone users adds to costs, as calls to mobile phones, particularly from a fixed phone, are more expensive than those to a fixed phone and roaming costs are added if the mobile phone user is out of the country. Because of these problems, as well as difficulties in obtaining lists of mobile phone users in many countries, mobiles are not usually included in random digit dialing (Jenkins, 2001).

## *Personal Interviewing*

Personal interviewing is the most flexible method of obtaining international research data. The respondent is clearly identified and hence the nature and distribution of the sample can be control-led. Nonresponse is typically low and all types of questions or data collection techniques can be used. On the other hand, personal interviewing does require the availability of a trained local field staff. Control of interviewer cheating is necessary, and procedures are required to administer fieldwork, to back check and to control the quality of fieldwork.

In some cases large international research organizations, notably those with local branch offices, train and develop their own field staff. This provides greater control over the quality of the fieldwork and assures greater cross-country consistency. Research organizations providing coverage in the Middle East establish their field staff by a tiered system of referrals. The local field manager in each country identifies an area manager for each city and for each nationality or ethnic group. These managers, who may be couples or women managers, in turn recruit interviewers for their specific area. In general, interviewers have to be of the same nationality and ethnic group as the people they are interviewing. Both interviewers and interviewees are recruited through personal referrals, requir-ing detailed knowledge and personal contacts for each local neighborhood.

Alternatively, companies may buy fieldwork from a local research organization. In some cases they belong to global networks, such as Global Market Research, and buy from member companies in the organization. In other cases they solicit bids from field organizations in the country and select the supplier based on previous experience with the company, its suitability for the job and so on. Many of these companies belong to international research organizations such as ESOMAR, and conform to their standards and code for conducting fieldwork.

Personal interviewing is commonly used in emerging markets such as India, China, Eastern Europe, the Middle East and South America. Low wage costs imply that personal interviews are not expensive relative to other methods of data collection, as is the case in many industrialized countries. In addition, in some cases it may be the only way of collecting data, due to low levels of telephone ownership, illiteracy and absence of mailing lists.

Personal interviewing provides an effective means of adapting questions to a specific company situation or individual and of probing for answers. In business-to-business research, willingness of management to cooperate and provide desired information will depend to a large extent on the competitiveness of the market environment, and also perceived time pressures. In certain product markets such as pharmaceuticals or electronics, management may be reluctant to provide information for fear this may be leaked to competitors. This may depend on the purpose of the survey. As in the case of telephone or mail surveys, management may be more willing to participate in customer satisfaction or product testing studies than usage surveys.

In consumer research, as noted earlier, personal interviewing is commonly used outside the US and Western Europe. The ease with which the cooperation of respondents can be obtained does, however, vary from one country or culture to another. In Eastern Europe, for example, interviewers are often regarded with considerable suspicion. This is a legacy from the repressive nature of former communist regimes. Similarly, as also noted earlier, referrals are required in order to obtain cooperation of interviewees in the Middle East, and interviews with women have to be conducted in the respondent's home by female interviewers.

Thus, personal interviewing is often the most effective method of questionnaire administration in international marketing research, especially among consumers. In emerging markets in some countries, personal interviewing may be mandatory. Even in other situations, low wage rates coupled with higher rates of response, improved quality of data and representativeness of the target population largely offset higher administrative costs.

# *Electronic Surveys*

The growth of the Internet has also opened up opportunities to use new technologies for primary data collection, particularly in survey research (Worldwide Internet Conference, 1999). Since these technologies require respondents with access to a computer and who are reasonably comfortable with this mode of interaction, they are primarily applicable for consumer surveys in countries with high levels of personal computer ownership (see Table 9.2). They are also commonly used in business-to-business research in developed countries and industries where businesses rely heavily on computerized purchasing and information transfer, for example computer software, banks and other financial services, medical equipment, pharmaceutical products, airlines, hotels and other travel-related products and services.

E-mail or web-based surveys can either be conducted on a one-time or ongoing basis. A key require-ment is the availability of a list of e-mail addresses. Where a topic- or product-specific list is not available, national, regional or global lists can be obtained from commercial sources such as Global Market Insite or Claritas, who maintain panels of Internet subscribers. Global Market Insite, for example, maintains 200 country panels in the Americas, Europe, Asia/Pacific and the Middle East. Data is collected in the local language using a fully integrated, netcentric suite of software. The respondent is pre-notified, and in the case of a web-based survey, provided where necessary with a toll-free number to access the survey online.

E-mail and web-based surveys are generally considerably less expensive than surveys by telephone, mail or personal interview (Harrell, Clayton and Werking, 1999). In comparison to mail surveys, cost of postage, mail processing and editing are eliminated. Equally, interviewer costs associated with phone and personal interview surveys are eliminated as well as telephone charges for pre-notification and prompting. Once initial set-up costs for questionnaire development have been incurred, the sample can be expanded at little extra cost and large samples are feasible. Accuracy is improved as respondents are in direct and immediate communication (Steffensen, 2004). Impossible or unlikely values, irrelevant answers and multiple answers to a question with a single answer can all be eliminated.

Web-based questionnaires are extremely versatile. Structured questionnaires of any form, length or layout can be developed. They have the advantage that product details, pictures of products, brand and shopping environment can be provided as well as links to other sites. Graphics, sound and video can also be integrated, creating a more stimulating and realistic research environment for the respondent. Links can be set up to guide respondents from one part of the questionnaire to another where questions are not applicable to the respondent. In ongoing surveys items can be changed or eliminated without difficulty. Data are more timely and often responses are more reasoned and objective, especially in relation to open-ended questions, since people tend to think more before typing in a response. E-mail and web-based questionnaires are also less intrusive since people can respond in their own time. Equally, as noted earlier, both qualitative and quantitative techniques can be combined in the same questionnaire. The whole process is automated from the posting of the questionnaire to response, thus minimizing recording errors. Responses can also be monitored and readily checked as they are received.

On the other hand, the sample is limited to those with an e-mail address and the response is not always high, especially where the questionnaire is viewed as 'spam' (unsolicited e-mail) by the recipient. Consequently, pre-notification, alerting the respondents and identifying the sponsor is desirable. Where e-mail questionnaires are sent as an attachment, system compatibility may pose some problems, especially in downloading, completing and returning questionnaires. Technical issues may also daunt some respondents, resulting in nonresponse bias. Consequently, use of an incentive and a contact for technical assistance are both desirable.

Valid results will, however, only be achieved if response levels are adequate and there is no nonresponse bias. Response rates are typically quite low, often in the 0.5–2% range (Agrawal, 1999). Consequently, a large number of surveys need to be sent out to obtain a large enough sample to analyze. While lower cost and rapidity of response make this method attractive for use in international research, potential bias problems suggest that such methods should be used with caution.

# Field Staff Organization and Training

A key problem in data collection in international markets is the need for reliable and high-quality local research staff and local research organizations. As noted earlier, large international research organizations have branch offices and in some cases field staff. Other organizations buy or outsource field services from local research organizations. In some cases, there may be limited choice in the number of local field organizations available. This gives rise to issues of coordination and harmonization of fieldwork, as well as issues relating to interviewer training.

# *Organization and Coordination of Fieldwork*

An important issue in conducting international surveys is how to ensure that the same standards of data collection are used, and that the fieldwork is comparable and of the same quality worldwide. ESOMAR has established guidelines for fieldwork in an effort to further professionalize data collection and harmonize fieldwork standards. These relate to interviewer recruitment, interviewer training, survey control, quality control and back checking. These guidelines apply to business-to-business, consumer and retailer research. All member organizations of ESOMAR are required to conform to these standards and to the ICC/ESOMAR International Code of Marketing and Social Research Practice. (See Chapter 14 and the ESOMAR web site, www.esomar.org, for more detail.)

Establishment of these guidelines helps to ensure that local supplier organizations that are ESOMAR members operate according to common, consistent and agreed quality standards. These standards have been developed for personal or face-to-face interviewing and telephone interviewing, as well as for group discussions and in-depth interviews in qualitative research, and retail audits and store checks. They are, however, very general. Consequently, many research organizations, especially where they purchase fieldwork outside the company or from a series of agencies, set up their own checks and controls over the quality of fieldwork. Where the research budget permits, an experienced research manager can visit the country or countries where the fieldwork is being conducted to brief the interviewers, conduct or supervise one or more pilot interviews, and in some cases monitor some field interviews. In addition, independent back checking of 10–20% of the interviews is typically conducted. In some cases where a company is dealing with a new supplier, it may check up to 50% of the interviews.

In the case of firms that have local branch organizations, training programs for field managers are often set up and regular meetings of local research staff held to harmonize procedures and fieldwork standards. This is critical in relation to qualitative research due to the somewhat subjective nature of data interpretation and so on. Research International Qualitatif, for example, holds regular meetings and training programs for staff from its branch offices around the world, to discuss new ideas and uses of different projective techniques, and to compare experiences with various techniques. This not only helps in harmonizing techniques and their interpretation, but also provides a forum for discussing new techniques and improvements in existing techniques, as well as current trends in qualitative research. Where firms do not have local branches and either outsource interviews or employ local interviewers, they typically send an executive to set up the project and brief interviewers. Where feasible, the executive should be fluent in the appropriate language to brief interviewers on the project, be able to monitor a number of interviews, provide feedback and so on. Typically, local interviewers are bilingual. Where there is verbatim response, interviews can be translated and sent to the head office, where interpretation is conducted centrally, to ensure consistency across countries.

# *Training Interviewers*

Another issue relates to the training of field interviewers. This may be problematic in some countries where there is limited experience or history of market research, for example Eastern Europe. Again, ESOMAR has established guidelines for interviewer training in both personal or face-to-face interviewing and telephone interviewing. For face-to-face interviewing a day's training is required, covering issues relating to the ICC/ESOMAR code of conduct, how to approach a respondent, how to cope with refusals, how to conduct an interview and ask certain types of questions. For telephone interviewing only half a day's training is required. The guidelines are somewhat general, but establish a standard for minimum training requirements.

It is important that interviewers should understand the need to establish a good rapport with the respondent and create a good climate for interviewer–respondent interaction. Here, the manner in which the interviewer introduces him- or herself is often a major factor in developing this rapport. Questionnaire administration also needs to be clearly understood, with the application of standard procedures and instructions. Introduction of any type of bias, such as the generation of inferences that a certain type of response might be preferred, needs to be avoided. In essence, the interviewer should be taught to remain as neutral as possible and to avoid interjecting any personal opinions. This is important in developing countries, where respondents are not familiar with surveys and will only respond if they feel comfortable with the interviewer.

In some cases, establishing rapport while remaining neutral requires a delicate balance. A study in South Africa, for example, found that local interviewers tended to help and guide respondents rather than leaving them to follow the instructions in the questionnaire. As a result they influenced the respondent and showed how a task should be undertaken. For example, they might place the Funny Faces in order rather than let respondents do the task alone. Practice interviews can be helpful in order to ensure that interviewers have learned appropriate skills.

Development of a detailed study protocol can be advisable when using interviewers recruited locally for a specific project. Recruiting interviewers locally may be helpful in surveying local ethnic groups and communities, as locals may more easily develop rapport with interviewees than trained interviewers, especially on sensitive topics such as health issues. However, careful attention to selection, training and provision of ongoing support will be needed. For example, a study of the maternity care of recent mothers in Australia from three different ethnic groups, Turkish, Vietnamese and Philippino, recruited interviewers from their local communities to conduct interviews in hospital (Small *et al.*, 1999). Extensive training of the interviewers was provided, including developing skills in recruiting and interviewing, discussing cultural issues relating to the study, help in framing questions, discussing protocols relating to situations that might arise in the interview, and piloting and translating instruments used in the study.

Even in industrialized countries, attention to interviewer training and to briefing and debriefing is essential to ensure maximal response rates and to avoid bias arising from the interviewer–respondent interaction. Particularly where the interview involves open-ended or complex questions and tasks, such as projective techniques or multidimensional scaling, attention to interviewer training is essential. Often this is key to ensuring the quality of the research.

# Summary

In determining appropriate sampling and survey administration procedures, a number of factors have to be taken into consideration. First, the relevant unit or level from which the sample is to be drawn has to be determined. Next is the selection of the technique to be used in drawing the sample. Related to this is the choice of survey administration procedures. In both cases, the impact of such decisions on the comparability and equivalence of the data from one unit to another has to be carefully considered, and weighed against the cost effectiveness of alternative plans and procedures.

In drawing the sample, a number of different levels or units may be considered, including the world, country groupings, countries or groupings within countries. In making this decision, much depends on the purpose of the survey, the specific product or service concerned and the target segment, as well as the availability and adequacy of various sampling frames or lists. Surveys concerned with industrial products or with upscale mobile target segments, such as business people or foreign travelers, are more likely to sample at a global or regional level than surveys concerned with consumer packaged goods aimed at a mass market.

The choice of technique to be used in drawing the sample is closely related to the level at which the sample is drawn. In many countries, especially developing countries, use of systematic random sampling techniques is likely to pose some difficulty. This is due to the lack of sampling lists, street maps and guides, and to sprawling urban developments and scattered rural populations. Consequently, convenience or judgment sampling procedures may have to be used in order to avoid excessive administration costs.

In selecting among survey administration procedures – that is, telephone, mail, personal interview or electronic – careful attention has to be paid to the efficacy of each procedure in reaching the sample population, as well as the potential sources of bias associated with each. In many countries, especially the developing countries, telephone surveys will only tap a relatively limited segment and typically only short questionnaires can be administered by this means. Mail surveys are only effective in countries with high levels of literacy, or where they are in relation to the literate population. Personal interviewing is the most costly and time-consuming method of survey administration in cross-national research. This does require training of competent interviewers in order to minimize bias arising from the interviewer and interviewee interaction. Electronic surveys provide quick results over broad geographical areas. As rates of Internet penetration increase around the world, this method of data collection will become more common in international surveys.

In brief, differences in market characteristics and the research infrastructure from one country to another imply that the development of the sampling plan and survey administration procedures may entail more creative thought and effort than in the case of domestic marketing research. Means may have to be devised to develop and identify appropriate sampling lists and techniques, and to administer surveys without incurring excessive costs in conditions where the available infrastructure is extremely sparse. In addition, attention has to be paid to the issues of comparability from one sampling unit to another, and to minimizing potential sources of sampling error.

# References

Aaker, D.A., Kumar, V. and Day, G.S. (2003) *Marketing Research*, 8th edition. John Wiley & Sons Inc., New York.

Agrawal, D. (1999) Strategy and Market Research on the Internet/Web. Mimeo, Microsoft Corporation, Redmond, WA.

Churchill, G.A. and Iacobucci, D. (2005) *Marketing Research: Methodological Foundations*, 9th edition, South-Western Publishing, Cincinnati, OH.

Dawson, S. and Dickinson, D. (1988) Conducting International Mail Surveys: The Effect of Incentives on Response Rates with an Industry Population. *Journal of International Business Studies*, **19**, 491–496.

De Heer, W. (1999) International Response Trends: Results of an International Study. *Journal of Official Statistics*, **15**, 129–142.

De Leeuw, E.D. and De Heer, W. (2001) Trends in Household Survey Nonresponse: A Longitudinal and International Comparison. In Groves, R.M., Dillman, D.A., Eltinge, J.L. and Little, R.A. (eds) *Survey Nonresponse*. John Wiley & Sons, New York.

Dun and Bradstreet (2003) *Principal International Businesses*. Dun and Bradstreet International, Parsippany, NJ.

Frost, F. (1998) Electronic Surveys – New Methods of Primary Data Collection. In *Proceedings, European Marketing Academy Conference*, Stockholm, pp. 213–232.

*Gale's World Business Directory* (2003) Gale Research, Detroit, MI.

Hader, S. and Gabler, S. (2003) Sampling and Estimation. In Harkness, J.A., Van de Vijver, F.J.R. and Mohler, P.Ph. (2003) *Cross-cultural Survey Methods*. Wiley-InterScience, Hoboken, NJ.

Harkness, J.A., Van de Vijver, F.J.R. and Mohler, P.Ph. (2003) *Cross-cultural Survey Methods*. Wiley-InterScience, Hoboken, NJ.

Harrell, L.J., Clayton, R.L. and Werking, G.S. (1999) TDE and Beyond: Data Collection on the World Wide Web. Bureau of Labor Statistics, Washington, DC.

Hox, J.J. and De Leeuw, E.D. (1994) A Comparison of Nonresponse in Mail, Telephone and Face to Face Surveys, Applying Multilevel Modeling to Meta-analysis, *Quality and Quantity*, **28**, 329–344.

ITU (2004) International Telecommunications Union, www.itu.int/ITU-D/ict/statistics.

Jenkins V. (2001) The Impact of Mobile Phones on Sampling. *The Frame*, September. Survey Sampling (http://www.worldopinion.com/the frame/2001/sept 1.htm).

Jobber, D. and Saunders, J. (1988) An Experimental Investigation into Cross-national Mail Survey Response Rates. *Journal of International Business Studies*, **19**, 483–489.

Keown, C.F. (1985) Foreign Mail Surveys: Response Rates Using Monetary Incentives. *Journal of International Business Studies*, **16**, 151–153.

Kuusela, V. and Simpanen M. (2003) Effects of Mobile Phones on Telephone Survey Practices and Results. Survey Research Unit, Statistics Finland.

*Market: Europe* (1998) Methods for Doing Research on the World Wide Web, May.

Nederhof, A.J. (1989) A Comparison of European and North American Response Patterns in Mail Surveys. *Journal of the Market Research Society*, **27**, 55–63.

Purdon, S., Campanelli. P., Sturgis, P. (1999) Interviewers' Calling Strategies on Face-to Face Interview Surveys. *Journal of Official Statistics*, **15**, 199–216.

Reynolds, N.L., Simintiras, A.C. and Diamantopoulos, A. (2003) Theoretical Justification of Sampling Choices in International Marketing Research: Key Issues and Guidelines for Researchers. *Journal of International Business Studies*, **34**, 80–89.

Schillewaert, N., Langerak, F. and Duhamel, T. (1998) Non-probability Sampling for WWW Surveys: A Comparison of Methods. In *Proceedings, European Marketing Academy Conference*, Stockholm, pp. 201–212.

Small, R., Yelland, J., Lumley, J. and Rice, P.L. (1999) Cross-cultural Research: Trying to Do It Better: Issues in Study Design. *Australian and New Zealand Journal of Public Health*, **23**(4), 385–389.

Steffensen, J.B. (2004) WWW Data Collection: Analysis of Methodological Aspects and Presentation of Principles behind Web Question: A Tool for Design and Analysis of WWW Surveys (http://www2.db.dk/jbs/wwwcoll/art/html/wwwcoll1.htm).

Webster, L. (1966) Comparability in Multi-country Surveys. *Journal of Advertising Research*, **6**, 14–18.

Worldwide Internet Conference (1999) *Net Effects. Book Number 227*. ESOMAR, Amsterdam.

www.esomar.org

# Chapter 10

# MULTICOUNTRY SCALES

## Introduction

At the core of much multicountry research is the development of operational measures of a construct to be examined in more than one country. Often a researcher is interested in testing whether a construct developed in one country holds in another country, or in examining similarities and differences in constructs across countries or geographical areas. Typically, an operational measure of the construct has already been developed in the base country and the task facing the researcher is to see whether the construct can be meaningfully measured in the same way in another country.

Many of the conceptual issues and difficulties in establishing construct equivalence were examined in Chapter 5. However, operational measurement of the construct presents its own set of issues and difficulties. Constructs are often complex and multifaceted phenomena and require a multiple-item scale for adequate measurement. In addition, as noted earlier, constructs are not necessarily expressed in the same way in different countries. To complicate matters further, methods of measurement and measurement instruments are subject to different types of bias in different countries.

Procedures for developing a scale to measure an underlying construct in a single country are relatively straightforward and well understood (Churchill, 1979). Developing a scale in a multicountry environment is considerably more complex and challenging and presents the researcher with two intertwined issues. The first and most fundamental question is whether the same construct exists in different countries. A particular construct identified in one country may not exist in another country or may not be expressed in the same terms. Consequently, attempts to assess the universality of a construct need to allow for the possibility that it may not take the same form or have different elements in other countries. Given this difficulty, some external criteria are needed to assess validity, rather than relying simply on internal criteria, such as reliability and convergent and discriminant validity. Once the underlying validity of the measure has been established, the second issue is to assess how individuals in a given country fall on the construct. Individuals in one country may score much higher, lower or the same as individuals in another country. Here, a key problem is whether this score reflects real differences in response or some form of metric bias. However, the issues only become relevant once the validity of the construct has been established.

This chapter examines the various issues in developing scales to be used in multicountry research. A number of issues, such as types of data, assessing whether different scale items function in the same way and whether measures are reliable, pertain to all approaches to scale development and are covered first. To illustrate the different approaches to scale development, examples of how scales have been applied cross-culturally are discussed in detail. Finally, an approach to developing 'decentered' cross-cultural scales is suggested.

# General Issues in Scale Development

## Types of Measures

A critical first step in developing a measure to be used in international marketing research is to select the type of response scale. The construct is an abstract concept that exists in the individuals' minds. The first stage is to devise an instrument that allows respondents to express that construct verbally, or on paper, or directly in electronic form. The challenge is to develop an instrument that accurately captures the construct, expressing salient elements in a simple, familiar fashion.

Responses can be collected in a variety of ways, but ultimately they reduce to the type of items used. These vary in terms of task difficulty and, hence, ease of use and reliability in multicountry research. Based on their underlying properties, three alternative types of items can be used in data collection: (1) nominal; (2) ordinal; and (3) interval. There is also a fourth type, ratio, but this is rarely applicable when collecting data from individual respondents.

### Nominal Measures

Nominal or categorical measures are often the easiest and seemingly most unambiguous means of collecting information in multicountry research. The respondent or interviewer simply indicates the presence or absence of a characteristic. For example, information about gender, occupation, ethnicity and type of dwelling unit are all collected using nominal measures. These can be used to categorize individuals or groups and may be useful in order to split the sample into groups and compare responses of different groups. Nominal measures can also be used to develop scales of economic development or standard of living using a Guttman scaling procedure (Manfield, 1971). The Guttman scale requires use of nominal data and is based on presence or absence of a number of objects. If the construct is standard of living, then ownership or nonownership of appliances such as radios, televisions, washing machines, refrigerators and so on would be the input to the scaling routine.

Nominal measures are the simplest type of measure and place the least burden on the respondent. They are appropriate for illiterate respondents or those with low levels of education. The respondent simply has to decide whether or not the characteristic or category applies. Such measures do, however, require that the definition of a category is unambiguous and familiar to the respondent. Also, as discussed in Chapter 8, pictures or illustrations may be used with less-literate respondents. The major limiting factor of using nominal data is that, with rare exceptions, categorical data do not lend themselves to scale development. It is difficult to aggregate nominal data as the categories or objects, even within a country, are not comparable.

## Ordinal Measures

While nominal measures provide information on category membership, ordinal measures indicate whether an object is greater than, less than or equal to some other object. The most direct way to collect ordinal data is to ask respondents to rank order objects in relation to some attribute. Respondents could be asked to rank order a set of brands or rank order five different leisure-time activities from most preferred to least preferred. For respondents in most developed countries this is a relatively simple and straightforward task. However, when the research is conducted among less-literate populations, physical stimuli may be needed. As discussed in Chapter 7, such stimuli should be familiar to the respondent to ensure meaningful responses. Less-literate respondents will have difficulty reading the instructions or recognizing the written words for the different stimulus objects. Consequently, questions will need to be interviewer administered and physical stimuli used rather than words.

Ordinal measures are relatively easy to collect. Even respondents with low education levels typically have little difficulty ranking objects, or expressing preferences in terms of rank ordering. Such data can be used as inputs in multidimensional scaling. However, unless the same set of objects is ranked in each country, rankings have limited use for comparative purposes. Ranking of one set of objects cannot be readily combined with that of another set to form a combined scale. Also, rankings between countries can only be compared if the same set of objects exists in both countries. When the same set of objects, activities or statements can be ranked in more than one country, rank order correlations can be computed to assess the degree of agreement in rankings between countries. However, as with ordinal data, there are limited instances where ordinal data can be used to construct a scale.

When only two objects are rank ordered at a time, the procedure is referred to as paired comparison. Respondents are asked to indicate a preference or similarity judgment for two objects at a time. Data collected in this fashion can be used as input for multidimensional scaling routines. Ordinal or paired comparison data can also be used to create a unidimensional interval scale using Thurstone's Case V Scaling model (Thurstone, 1959). An interval scale is created based on the extent to which certain stimuli dominate others. For example, if A is preferred to B 51% of the time, there is little perceived difference between the two stimuli. However, if A is preferred to B 90% of the time, there is a much greater perceived difference between the two stimuli. These relationships are used across all stimuli to create an interval scale that reflects the perceived difference between objects.

## Interval Measures

Most data collected in multicountry research is based on interval measures, or data assumed to be interval scaled. Technically, interval measures allow direct comparison of different positions on a scale. A frequently given example is that of temperature. For example, the temperature on an August day might be 97°F in New Delhi and 91°F in Beijing. Based on this, one can conclude that the temperature in New Delhi was 6°F warmer than in Beijing. The same data can be converted to °C and the same conclusion would be reached, although the absolute difference would be smaller.

In addition, measurements of temperature from other cities in other countries at different times or seasons would be directly comparable to the data already obtained. For example, the temperature in Moscow might be 71°F, the temperature in Santiago, Chile 55°F, and the temperature in Singapore 88°F. Someone planning a trip to any of these cities would only have to compare their home climate with the city they were visiting to select appropriate clothing. In this example, an instrument used to measure the temperature in one city could be used in another city and would provide the same result. Thus, any measurement of temperature would be comparable.

However, this is typically not the case when the same measurement instrument is used to collect questionnaire data in different countries. In multicountry research, responses to 5-point (or $n$-point) scales are often treated as interval data. Mean values are computed, comparisons made between countries and sophisticated analyses performed on the data. However, it is important to recognize that the underlying data do not possess the same properties as true interval data, as the distance between points may not have the same meaning in different countries. Consequently, comparability across countries is open to some question. A mean response of 4.3 on a 5-point scale in one country may or may not be equivalent to a mean response of 4.3 on the same question in another country.

Also, the task presented to the respondent is more difficult and more abstract than for nominal or ordinal data. Collection of interval data requires a greater degree of sophistication and literacy among respondents. Also, providing meaningful responses to a 5-point scale that ranges from 'strongly agree' to 'strongly disagree' requires some familiarity with conventions used to collect these types of data. However, as the examples in Chapter 8 illustrate, with a little creativity in stimulus development these types of data can be collected among less-literate populations (see Donovan and Spark, 1997).

# Differential Item Functioning

The building blocks of any scale are individual items that together measure an underlying construct. The critical issue in international marketing research is whether the individual items function in the same way from one country to another. Unless the individual scale items measure the construct in the same way in each country, the sum of the scale items will not properly reflect the construct. For example, consider a scale that measures consumer 'innovativeness' in the US. It might employ 16 different items that are measured with a 5-point Likert scale. Each item taps a different aspect of innovativeness. However, these items may not necessarily function in the same way in other countries or cultures. The problem becomes that of arriving at a set of items that accurately and adequately measure the construct in multiple settings. An important aspect of this approach is that the researcher assumes that the same construct exists and can be measured in a similar but not identical fashion.

Three approaches can be used to deal with differential item functioning or item bias: analysis of variance, the Mantel-Haenszel statistic and item response theory. The first approach involves applying the standard analysis of variance model. Respondents are divided into groups that have the same scores on the overall scale. With the scale for innovativeness the total score could range from 16 to 80 (sixteen items scaled one to five). Respondents with the extreme scores, 16 and 80, would not be included since individuals giving those responses would have responded the same in all cultures. Groupings of respondents would be formed using the remaining scores. Based on the response to the scale on innovativeness, respondents could be grouped into seven mutually exclusive categories. When the responses of the individuals from one country are plotted against the mean of another country, it is relatively easy to see whether there is any item bias present. Figure 10.1

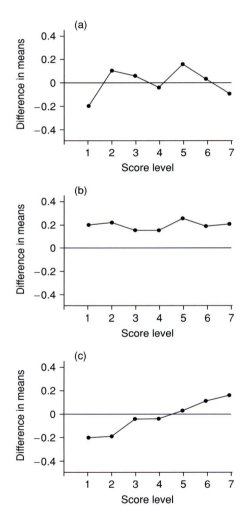

**Figure 10.1**    Hypothetical examples of (a) an unbiased item; (b) an item with uniform bias; and (c) an item with nonuniform bias

*Source*: Van de Vijver and Leung, 1997.

illustrates situations where the plot reveals no bias (a), uniform bias (b) and nonuniform bias (c). Uniform bias (b) is the easiest to interpret in that respondents in one country consistently score higher or lower on a construct, in this case innovativeness, than individuals in another country. Nonuniform bias (c) is more difficult to interpret in that over part of the range some respondents score higher, and over part of the range they score lower than others.

Analysis of variance can be used to arrive at an analytical solution to differential item functioning. Country would be one factor in the analysis of variance and the score groupings, or level, the other factor. Significant differences in the score grouping are to be expected since each grouping is based on score differences and hence ignored. A significant country main effect would indicate the presence of a uniform bias. A significant country by level interaction would indicate a nonuniform bias. Depending on the extent and degree of bias, the researcher may decide to eliminate certain items, resulting in a reduced set of items. If too many items are eliminated it is also possible to address the problem in an iterative fashion, eliminating one variable at a time, starting with the most statistically significant first and proceeding until none is significant (Van de Vijver and Leung, 1997).

The Mantel-Haenszel statistic uses as input dichotomous data and allows for pair-wise comparisons only. This is particularly problematic when a large number of countries are studied, as the number of pair-wise comparisons needed increases rapidly. Item response theory (IRT) is also typically applied to dichotomous variables. As a starting point, IRT assumes that a scale is unidimensional. If the scale is multidimensional, then each component needs to be examined separately.

Item response theory identifies three parameters that need to be satisfied to determine whether an item is unbiased across countries. The three parameters are: (a) item discrimination; (b) item difficulty; and (c) the lower asymptote. The three parameters are illustrated in Figure 10.2 as they relate to item characteristic curves. Item discrimination refers to the ability of the item to discriminate between individuals who score differently on the underlying latent trait, for example an attitude, value or belief. Differences in the discriminant ability of an item across two countries indicate nonuniform bias (Figure 10.2a). Item difficulty, which is a major concern in assessing educational test scores, relates to the ability of an individual to respond correctly to an item. In other words, whether individuals who have high scores on a latent trait underlying the test, either an ability measure or an attitudinal measure, have high scores on a particular item. Differences in the item difficulty parameter suggest uniform bias (Figure 10.2b). The third parameter, lower asymptote, relates to the probability of guessing a correct response and pertains to ability tests.

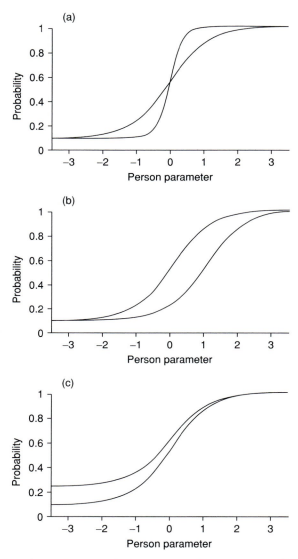

**Figure 10.2** Hypothetical item characteristic curves of items that differ only in (a) the item discrimination parameter; (b) the item difficulty parameter; and (c) the lower asymptote

*Source*: Van de Vijver and Leung, 1997.

In applying item response theory to multicountry attitudinal and belief data, a two-parameter model consisting of item discrimination and item difficulty is most appropriate. The third parameter, lower asymptote, is not meaningful in this context, since guessing *per se* is not an issue. The model is estimated for each country to identify biased items. These are identified through the use of item characteristic curves and a chi square test (Lord, 1980). Items that are biased are deleted from the scale before comparisons are made between countries. For more detail on the procedures for detecting and eliminating item bias, see Van de Vijver and Leung (1997, pp. 62–88).

Differential item functioning and item bias are closely related to measurement equivalence. In general, bias will tend to lower or may even preclude equivalence. Bias at the construct level – that is, the construct measured is not the same across countries or groups – precludes equivalence at any other level. Equally, bias at the method level precludes equivalence at the item level, while bias at the item level means that items will be nonequivalent.

Eliminating items that function differently between two countries does not necessarily lead to elimination of differences in the average scores between groups (Poortinga and Van der Flier, 1988). However, taking out biased items does ensure that the score differences between two or more countries are free from item bias. The differences that remain suggest actual differences between countries. As noted earlier, when a large number of items have to be removed from the scale, this raises the more general question of whether the scale can be applied in more than one country.

The application of item bias detection by researchers has revealed some interesting problems. First, it is often difficult to explain why a particular item is biased. Second, use of different statistical techniques suggests different results. Third, item bias statistics are not stable in test–retest studies or in cross-validations. Most problematic for those developing multicountry scales are low levels of agreement between expert judgment of biased items and statistical methods (Van de Vijver and Leung, 1997, pp. 84–88). Often researchers developing or modifying a scale for use in another country will use panels of experts to select or modify scale items. The lack of agreement between statistical approaches and judgmental approaches suggests that reliance on experts may not provide a scale that is unbiased in another country. This conclusion should, however, be tempered by the observation that different statistical techniques do not necessarily agree with one another, and that they show limited consistency when repeated a second time.

# Reliability Issues in Scale Development

Scales used to measure constructs should be reliable across all countries in which they are administered. Reliability, as it relates to construct measurement, was discussed in Chapter 6. These issues are particularly important in countries or contexts where little research has been conducted, or with which the researcher has little prior experience. In these cases, the reliability of different types of data or measures may not be well documented and, particularly in the case of attitudinal data, will need to be verified and established. There is a requirement to understand the limitations and possible errors associated with different types of measures. Furthermore, reliability does not exist in isolation, as the nature of the instrument and the method of data collection can influence the reliability of results.

Linguistic and conceptual nonequivalence in measurement instruments used in cross-cultural surveys can produce differences in measure reliability. This poses a threat to the validity of conclusions reached. Examination of reliability, while costly and time consuming, is nonetheless critical and attention should be paid to include reliability checks as standard procedure in multicountry research.

When examining reliability – in contrast to measure validity or equivalence – attention is centered on whether the same result is obtained when a measure is repeated in a different context, fashion or time. Despite efforts to design an instrument that is adapted to all countries and cultures, it may not be equally reliable in all contexts. Different types of measures, such as attitudinal, lifestyle and other measures, also vary in their level of reliability. The stability of data over time may also vary. It is thus important to compare the reliability of data obtained in different countries or contexts, since this may attenuate the precision of estimation and reduce the power of statistical tests.

# Scale Dimensionality

When a scale developed in one country is used in another country, an issue is whether the scale has the same number of dimensions in both countries. Differences in the number of dimensions begin to suggest a lack of comparability in the construct between countries. For example, if a scale is initially developed in one country to measure a construct and the construct is unidimensional, subsequent use of the scale in other countries should also reveal one dimension. If more dimensions were found, one would conclude that there is a lack of comparability between the two countries. The CETSCALE (for more details see later) has generally been found to be unidimensional (Netemeyer *et al.*, 1991;

Druvasal *et al.*, 1993). However, Douglas and Nijssen (2003), using principal components analysis with varimax rotation, found two distinct dimensions in the CETSCALE in the Netherlands. The first factor explained 47.5% of the variance, contained all but two of the questions and corresponded to the core elements of consumer ethnocentrism. The second factor explained 11.1% of the variance and captured an element that may be unique to the Netherlands or a smaller market with relatively few domestic manufacturers of consumer durables. The two questions that loaded on the second factor were: 'Only those products that are unavailable in the Netherlands should be imported' and 'We should buy from foreign countries only those products that we cannot obtain within our own country.'

The stability of dimensionality of the Maslach Burnout Inventory (MBI) was examined in a review of 35 studies that used it cross-culturally (Hwang *et al.*, 2003). The original scale (Maslach and Jackson, 1986) had three dimensions and was designed to measure the burnout of individuals in various occupations. There are 22 items that are used to form the three scales: (1) emotional exhaustion; (2) depersonalization; and (3) personal accomplishment. Almost all the studies (91.8%) in the other countries identified a similar three-factor structure. However, only one study replicated the three factors with a similar pattern of strong loadings on the three primary factors. In addition, four studies identified four factors and three studies identified only two factors. This suggests that while dramatically different results will not be obtained when using scales in different countries, one must be prepared for differences that need to be explained. Further, a different dimensionality suggests that the construct is in fact different in the other countries.

Another scale that has been widely used in the US as a measure of psychological wellbeing is Bradburn's (1969) Affect Balance Scale (ABS). Macintosh (1998, p. 83) asserts, 'If cross national research is to be meaningful, the validity of measuring devices must be demonstrated. Specifically, it must be shown that measuring devices developed primarily in the United States are consistently applicable in other cultures and regions.' He undertook a cross-cultural assessment of the ABS and found that the full model did not fit, based on four different goodness-of-fit measures, in any of the 38 countries examined. Further, attempts to develop alternative models did not find any models that fit across the countries studied. The lack of fit was consistent with concerns that had been raised about the ABS over the past 20 years (see Macintosh, 1998).

Some recent applications of the NATID scale further illustrate the difficulty of achieving the same factor structure with the same scale across multiple countries and time periods. Huntington (1993) identified four components of national identity: religion, history, customs and social institutions.

These components guided development of the NATID scale by Keillor *et al.* (1996). Starting with 70 items, the 17-item CETSCALE and 53 new items, they used confirmatory factor analysis to reduce it to 17 items, including five from the CETSCALE. This was then applied in the US, Japan and Sweden (Column 1 of Table 10.1). Cui and Adams (2002) applied the NATID in Yemen. They added four emic items and used exploratory factor analysis and confirmatory factor analysis to evaluate and refine the scale. They tested two models, the original items (columns 2) and the expanded scale (column 3). To achieve the best fit they had to drop five items and restructure the four dimensions. Thelen and Honeycutt (2004) examined the NATID scale in Russia and also found four dimensions, but had to reassign one variable and relabeled two of the dimensions. Across the four uses of the NATID scale shown in Table 10.1 there were always four dimensions, but not necessarily the same four. The number of items in the scale varied from 12 to 17 and only four of the items were consistent across all four analyses. The construct of national identity clearly exists, but how it is measured appears to vary considerably from country to country.

In a study of the Generalized Perceived Self-efficacy scale in 22 countries, Schwarzer and Scholz (2000) found that the unidimensionality of the scale held across all countries. There were differences in scores on the scale between countries and also by gender, with men typically scoring higher. An earlier study by Schwarzer and Born (1997) also found that the scale's unidimensionality held across 13 different cultures. The scale was initially developed in German and subsequently translated into 26 different languages. More information on the scale and the different language versions is available at www.RalfSchwarzer.de.

The dimensionality of a scale, and by implication the underlying construct it is measuring, is relatively straightforward and fairly unambiguous in its interpretation. Less evident is why the difference was observed and precisely how to interpret it. If the dimensionality is the same, greater confidence can be placed in the use of the scale in another country. Analytic approaches for looking at the comparability of scales are covered in the next two chapters. In the remainder of this chapter, examples of scale use in multiple countries are covered as well as suggestions for developing scales.

# Using Multi-item Scales in Cross-cultural Research

When using multi-item scales in multi-country research, a common procedure is to take a scale that has been developed in one country or context, translate it and then administer it in a number of countries, with relatively limited consideration of its validity or equivalence in other countries or

**Table 10.1** Comparison of models, included items and dimensions

| Item | Keillor et al. 1996 | Cui and Adams 2002, Model 1 | Cui and Adams 2002, Model 2 | Thelen and Honeycutt 2004 |
|---|---|---|---|---|
| N1. Important people from the country's past are admired by people today. | NH | CR | CR | NH |
| N2. One of country X's strengths is that it emphasizes events of historical importance. | NH | BT | — | NH |
| N3. The country X has a strong historical heritage. | NH | — | — | — |
| C1. A country X person possesses certain cultural attributes that other people do not possess. | CH | CH | — | NO |
| C2. Country X citizens in general feel that they come from a common background. | CH | CH | CH | NO |
| C3. Country X citizens are proud of their nationality. | CH | BT | CH | NH |
| C4. People frequently engage in activities that identify them as country X citizens. | CH | CR | CR | NO |
| C5. Country X citizens are proud of their [ethnic] and [religious] roots. | — | — | CH | — |
| C6. One of the things that distinguish country X citizens from other countries is its traditions and customs. | — | — | BT | — |
| B1. A specific religious philosophy is what makes a person uniquely a country X citizen. | BT | BT | CH | BT |
| B2. It is impossible for an individual to be truly a country X citizen without taking part in some form of religious activity. | BT | — | — | BT |

**Table 10.1** (continued)

| Item | Keillor et al. 1996 | Cui and Adams 2002, Model 1 | Cui and Adams 2002, Model 2 | Thelen and Honeycutt 2004 |
|------|------|------|------|------|
| B3. Religious education is essential to preserve the cohesiveness of the country X society. | BT | BT | BT | BT |
| B4. A specific religious philosophy is not an important part of being an American. (reverse-coded) | BT | — | — | — |
| B5. A true country X person would never reject his or her religious beliefs. | BT | BT | BT | BT |
| E1. We should purchase products manufactured in country X instead of letting other countries get rich off of us. | CE | CE | CE | — |
| E2. It is always best to purchase country X products. (Russian products, first, last and foremost) | CE | — | — | CE |
| E3. Country X's citizens should not buy foreign products, because it hurts the country's business and causes unemployment. | CE | CE | CE | CE |
| E4. It may cost me in the long run but I prefer to support country X products. | CE | CE | CE | CE |
| E5. Only those products that are unavailable in country X should be imported. | CE | — | — | CE |

Notes: NH = national heritage, CH = cultural homogeneity, BT = belief tradition, CE = consumer ethnocentrism, CR = cultural heritage, NO = national homogeneity.

*Source:* Thelen and Honeycutt, 2004.

contexts. This approach is based on the assumption that the underlying construct is both relevant and present in other countries. An additional assumption is that it can be measured using the same instrument. In some cases the internal consistency is examined using Cronbach's alpha. Where high alphas are obtained, the scale is considered appropriate and applicable in that context. Increasingly, nomological or structural validity is also examined; that is, the relation of the measure to measures of other related constructs. Development of context-specific measures of constructs and examination of how and whether a construct is manifested in the same terms in other countries or contexts is rare.

In this section alternative approaches to applying a scale developed in one cultural context to another are examined.* These include assessment of single or context-specific constructs, single-context scale development, and cross-cultural assessment of single-context scales as well as approaches to developing shorter versions of the original scale. In addition, 'decentered' scale development in multiple cultural contexts is examined to illustrate a more culturally balanced design, in which no one country or context dominates scale or measure development.

# Single-context Scale Development

A scale that has been widely used in multicountry and in country-of-origin studies is the CETSCALE. It was developed by Shimp and Sharma (1987) to apply the construct of ethnocentrism to marketing and consumer behavior. More specifically, it represented an attempt by the researchers to measure consumers' orientation toward the purchase of foreign products. Consumer ethnocentrism is rooted in the original construct of ethnocentrism, or the attitude that one's own group (race or people) is superior, first discussed by Summers (1906) almost 100 years ago. A scale to measure the construct of ethnocentrism, the California Ethnocentrism scale, was developed by Adorno *et al.* (1950) and is closely related to patriotism and political-economic conservatism. The construct had also been measured among different populations such as black college students (Chang and Ritter, 1976) and in the UK (Warr *et al.*, 1967).

The first step in the development of the CETSCALE was to take the construct of ethnocentrism and apply it to consumers' thoughts about foreign-made products. More than 800 US consumers were

---

* Hambleton (1994) summarizes 22 guidelines formulated by an international committee for the translation and adaptation of psychological and educational instruments. The guidelines cover: (1) the context; (2) instrument development, translation and adaptation; (3) administration; and (4) documentation and score interpretation.

asked to 'describe your views of whether it is appropriate for American consumers to purchase products that are manufactured in foreign countries' (Shimp and Sharma, 1987, p. 281). Content analysis of the statements led to the identification of seven different aspects of consumers' orientation toward foreign products, one of which was identified as consumer ethnocentric tendencies. These seven dimensions led to the generation of 225 statements, which were later reduced to 180. Six judges then evaluated all 180 statements and classified them into the different dimensions. Only those statements that were categorized in the same way by at least five of the six judges and were not redundant were retained. This resulted in 100 statements.

A questionnaire consisting of 117 Likert-type statements (the 100 plus 17 items from Adorno *et al.*'s original scale) was then mailed to 850 households. A factor analysis of the responses resulted in 54 items loading 0.5 or better on the relevant dimensions. These 54 items formed a new questionnaire of 7-point Likert statements that was mailed to almost 4000 households in four different areas of the US. Confirmatory factor analysis was then used to examine the five-factor structure identified in the early stages and to eliminate items that were not considered reliable. One of the five dimensions was rejected and only one of the remaining conceptual dimensions was strongly supported. Of the original 43 non-Adorno items, only 18 were retained as reliable and related to the four constructs. Twelve of these items loaded on the consumer ethnocentrism dimension and two variables loaded on each of the remaining dimensions. However, these remaining six variables were also highly correlated with the 12-item scale.

Scale development proceeded with the 25 items that were reliable, but focused only on one dimension, consumer ethnocentrism. Confirmatory factor analysis was performed on the pooled data (all four geographical areas combined) and for each of the four areas separately. The 17 items that loaded 0.5 or greater were retained and formed the CETSCALE (Table 10.2).

The reliability of the scale was first assessed using Cronbach's alpha. This ranged from 0.94 to 0.96 over the four surveys. In an additional two-phase study the test–retest reliability was assessed. The correlation between the two administrations of the scale separated by five weeks was 0.77. It was possible to assess convergent validity for one of the samples since respondents had answered a question two years earlier concerning purchase of foreign products. The correlation between this response and the CETSCALE was 0.54. Discriminant validity was examined by correlating the CETSCALE score with the related constructs of patriotism, politico-economic conservatism and dogmatism. While these constructs were correlated with the CETSCALE (range 0.39 to 0.65), the authors believe that there is discriminant validity. Finally, nomological validity was established by

**Table 10.2** 17-item CETSCALE[a]

| | Item | Reliability[b] |
|---|---|---|
| 1. | American people should always buy American-made products instead of imports. | 0.65 |
| 2. | Only those products that are unavailable in the US should be imported. | 0.63 |
| 3. | Buy American-made products. Keep America working. | 0.51 |
| 4. | American products, first, last, and foremost. | 0.65 |
| 5. | Purchasing foreign-made products is un-American. | 0.64 |
| 6. | It is not right to purchase foreign products, because it puts Americans out of jobs. | 0.72 |
| 7. | A real American should always buy American-made products. | 0.70 |
| 8. | We should purchase products manufactured in America instead of letting other countries get rich off us. | 0.67 |
| 9. | It is always best to purchase American products. | 0.59 |
| 10. | There should be very little trading or purchasing of goods from other countries unless out of necessity. | 0.53 |
| 11. | Americans should not buy foreign products, because this hurts American business and causes unemployment. | 0.67 |
| 12. | Curbs should be put on all imports. | 0.52 |
| 13. | It may cost me in the long run but I prefer to support American products. | 0.55 |
| 14. | Foreigners should not be allowed to put their products on our markets. | 0.52 |
| 15. | Foreign products should be taxed heavily to reduce their entry into the US. | 0.58 |
| 16. | We should buy from foreign countries only those products that we cannot obtain within our own country. | 0.60 |
| 17. | American consumers who purchase products made in other countries are responsible for putting their fellow Americans out of work. | 0.65 |

[a] Response format is 7-point Likert-type scale (strongly agree = 7, strongly disagree = 1). Range of scores is from 17 to 119.

[b] Calculated from confirmatory factor analysis of data from four-areas study.

*Source*: Shimp and Sharma, 1987.

looking at how the CETSCALE correlated with attitudes, purchase intentions and ownership of foreign-made products.

# Cross-cultural Assessment of Single-context Scales

The development of the CETSCALE described in the above section illustrates a systematic approach to measuring a construct in one country. However, a central issue is whether the same instrument can be used in other countries or cultures. In making this assessment, the typical approach is to take the scale, translate it, administer it in a number of countries and then assess its reliability and validity. This approach bypasses a number of important steps in scale development. For example, the development of the CETSCALE started with over 800 US consumers providing responses to an open-ended question that probed their attitudes toward buying foreign-made products. This step generally is not included in the typical cross-cultural assessment. Further, all the purification and refinement steps used to arrive at the final 17 items were performed on US data. This allows the very real possibility that if another country had been the base, a different scale would have evolved.

Examining the fit of a scale developed in one country in another country should be understood in terms of the types of inherent biases interjected. Comparing results obtained in country B using a scale developed in country A interjects a pseudo-etic bias (Triandis, 1972) and skews results toward commonality. It is also unlikely to lead to the same findings when the same procedures are followed to develop a scale to measure the construct in country B and then the results of the two scales (country A with country B) are compared. In particular, if the construct is not the same it is unlikely that any comparison is feasible or meaningful.

The reliability and validity of the CETSCALE were examined in four countries by Netemeyer *et al.* (1991). In addition to the US, the CETSCALE was administered to students in France, Japan and West Germany. The sample sizes in the four countries ranged from 70 to 76. The English-language version of the questionnaire was first translated in the other three languages. The translated version was back translated and pretested on a small sample of US students as well as small samples of students from the three countries who were studying in the US. In addition to the 17-item CETSCALE, questions relating to attitudes toward purchasing foreign products, beliefs about the quality of certain products from foreign countries and preferences for products in general from those countries as well as cars and television sets were also administered.

The results of a confirmatory factor analysis showed that the scale had a unidimensional factor structure across all four countries. Factor structure invariance was examined using two methods, multigroup analysis and the coefficient of congruence. Both approaches showed that the factor loadings were invariant across countries. The reliability of the scale was assessed in three different ways. First, composite reliability coefficients (Fornell and Larker, 1981) showed a high degree of reliability (0.91 or higher) in the same range as those obtained when the scale was originally developed in the US. Variance extracted estimates, which measure the amount of variance due to a construct's measurement relative to random measurement error, were also calculated. Consistency was found across the four countries, although the levels in the French and Japanese sample were lower. Finally, corrected item-to-total correlations were calculated. These were higher for the US sample, but the ranges were similar for the other three countries. Collectively, the three measures suggest that the CETSCALE is reliable, not only in the US but in the other three countries studied.

Discriminant validity, or the extent to which the CETSCALE is distinct from another construct, attitude toward home country, was assessed by three different methods. One-factor and two-factor models were estimated. In the one-factor model a unity correlation is assumed and in the two-factor model the correlation between the two scales is freely estimated. The fit of the two-factor model was better, suggesting discriminant validity. Second, the variance extracted estimates were greater than the squared parameter estimate (phi squared). Finally, the correlation between the two constructs was significantly $< 1$.

Nomological validity was assessed by examining the correlation between the CETSCALE and the importance of buying foreign products, attitudes toward buying domestic products in general, attitudes toward buying foreign products in general, as well as attitudes toward buying specific products. While the overall pattern supports the nomological validity of the CETSCALE, the relationships were strongest for the US and weaker for the other three countries, with the least support in the former West Germany.

More recently, the sensitivity of the CETSCALE to the context in which it is administered has been examined (Douglas and Nijssen, 2003). Earlier studies examine the CETSCALE in industrialized countries with large domestic industries and relatively strong feelings of national identity and patriotism. This study examined the CETSCALE in the Netherlands, a relatively small country with no or few domestic brands in many consumer durable product categories. As noted earlier in this chapter, their study revealed a two-dimensional factor structure rather than the single dimension found elsewhere. The first dimension captured core elements of consumer ethnocentrism, while the second dimension related to a distinction between products that were not available from domestic firms. In addition to finding a two-dimensional factor structure, the intensity of consumer ethnocentrism was lower in the Netherlands than was observed in studies in other countries.

The study also compared two different translations of the CETSCALE into Dutch. The first, a literal translation, followed typical translation protocols of back translation. Based on in-depth interviews dealing with the construct of consumer ethnocentrism, its meaning to Dutch consumers, as well as the meaning of different phrases and items, a second version of the questionnaire was created. This modified version was found to provide a better fit of the data as well as a lower correlation between the two dimensions of the CETSCALE found in the Netherlands.

This study suggests that attention needs to be paid to contextual factors that may influence observed results. If there is a high degree of contextual similarity, then greater confidence can be placed on results that show similarity in responses. If there are differences in responses, it may reflect true differences, or differences brought about by differences in contextual factors. Further, the study suggests the importance of using qualitative research first to more fully understand the construct and the instrument used to measure it initially.

## Examining Related and Context-specific Constructs

The above description of the cross-cultural assessment of the reliability and validity of the CETSCALE provides a good illustration of the approach typically adopted by researchers. As indicated at the outset, it answers the specific question of whether a scale developed in one country exhibits the same properties when it is used in another. Assessment of the reliability provides reassurance that respondents are answering the questions in a consistent manner. Discriminant validity answers the question whether the scale is distinct from other constructs in the other countries. Nomological validity looks more broadly at the question of whether the scale measures the construct in the other countries. However, the approach to assessing discriminant and nomological validity does not address the more fundamental issue of whether a scale developed *de novo* in the foreign country would be the same as the one being tested.

The complexity of establishing equivalence of constructs in multicountry research can be seen by examining the relation between the CETSCALE and an Animosity scale in the People's Republic of China (Klein *et al.*, 1998). The context for the study was Nanjing, China, a city that suffered during

Japanese occupation from 1931 to 1945. This provided a respondent population that was likely to have residual feeling of animosity toward the Japanese.

While the CETSCALE captures beliefs about buying foreign products in general, the Animosity scale is designed to measure attitudes toward a specific country. The Animosity scale has two major dimensions, Economic Animosity and War Animosity, both of which were administered relative to the Japanese (Figure 10.3). As expected, the Animosity scale and the CETSCALE were correlated (path coefficient 0.50). Interestingly, while both scales influenced willingness to buy, only the CETSCALE was related to product judgments.

The Animosity scale and CETSCALE were also used to examine Dutch consumers' attitudes toward Germans and German products (Nijssen and Douglas, 2004). One variation was to study two product categories, televisions, where there was a Dutch manufacturer, and cars, where there was none. The Netherlands provides a very different context from China in that it is a relatively small market with an open society. The findings were similar to Klein *et al.* (1998) with some differences in the product evaluations. In particular, German cars were evaluated more favorably than German televisions.

These studies suggest that while a scale developed in one country (i.e. the CETSCALE) may be useful in another country, there may also be unique facets or constructs operating in the other country. Thus, it may be desirable to develop context-specific scales that are capable of measuring the indigenous constructs that affect the behavior of interest.

## Developing Shorter Scales

Scales originally developed to measure a construct are often quite long. In some cases it is desirable to shorten them to focus on core elements. Further, unlike initial efforts to develop a scale, in multicountry research a scale is typically part of a larger series of questions where a scale is used as a predictor or explanatory variable. In order to arrive at a more manageable questionnaire length, a shorter but psychometrically equivalent form of the scale is often used. For example, the Change Seeker Index (CSI) developed by Garlington and Shimote (1964) consists of 95 items that assess variety seeking. This is quite lengthy in its full form and would add considerably to the length of any instrument. An important consideration in reducing its length is whether a shortened version has equivalent psychometric properties. Steenkamp and Baumgartner (1995) have developed a seven-item version of the CSI that actually has better psychometric properties than the original scale.

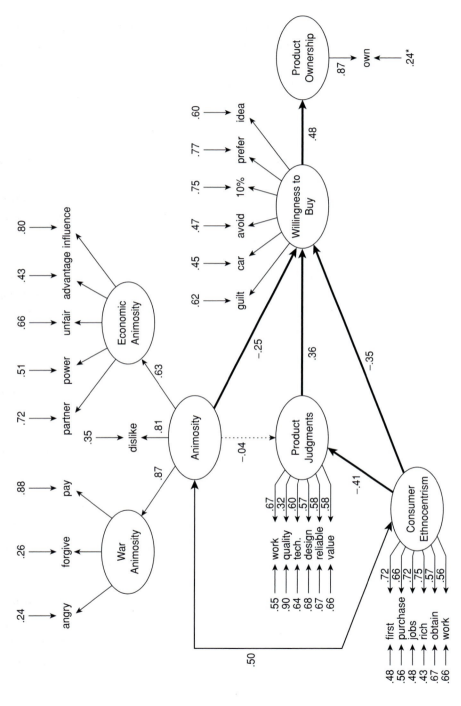

**Figure 10.3** Structural equation model results

* the variance was constrained.

All coefficients are standardized. All solid line path coefficients are significant at P < 0.001. The dotted line coefficient is nonsignificant.

*Source:* Klein *et al.*, 1998.

The full 95-item scale was first administered to a group of US subjects. Item-total correlations were run and the 67 items with correlations below 0.40 were dropped. The remaining 28 items were factor analyzed (principal components) and 13 items with a factor loading of below 0.50 on the first factor were dropped. The remaining 15 items were analyzed using LISREL. Two different models were evaluated: (1) all 15 items; and (2) the 7 items with a factor loading exceeding 0.7. While both models provided an acceptable fit, the fit for the 7-item scale was superior. The 7-item scale was then administered to another US sample as well as Dutch and Belgian samples to cross-validate and assess its nomological validity. These tests supported the superior qualities of the shortened scale. These results suggest that reducing scales to their core elements may enhance both their power and predictive efficiency.

## Generalizability across Countries

The emic/etic dilemma was discussed in Chapter 6. In the context of scales, it relates to whether a scale can be generalized across countries. A scale that consists exclusively of etic items can be generalized across countries, while a scale that consists of emic items cannot. Typically, a scale will end up containing both types of items. The earlier discussion of differential item functioning in this chapter begins to address this issue at the individual item level and helps to identify emic items.

There are two different approaches that can be used to assess the generalizability of the entire scale across countries, confirmatory factor analysis (CFA) and generalizability theory (G theory). Sharma and Weathers (2003) examined both techniques to see whether the CETSCALE could be used to make valid comparison across countries. To conduct the comparison they used the data from the Netemeyer *et al.* (1991) study discussed earlier in this chapter.

In using CFA, Sharma and Weathers followed Steenkamp and Baumgartner's (1995) approach to testing equality of metric, factor and error variance, although they were unable to test for equality of covariance matrices because the number of parameters to be estimated was greater than the sample sizes. There was support for metric and factor variance equivalence, but not for error variance equivalence. They concluded that their analysis supports the notion that the CETSCALE is invariant across the four countries. To provide a comparison they analyzed the same data using G theory. The first step is to compute a generalizability coefficient that can be done for either random or fixed effects. The coefficient captures the variance due to countries, subjects and items as well as the interactions. Values of the coefficient greater than .90 suggest that a scale can be generalized across items (Shavelson and Webb, 1991). Sharma and Weathers obtained a generalizability coefficient of .936 and concluded that the CETSCALE can be generalized across items and, by implication, across countries. One of the main advantages of generalizability theory is that it can help determine the number of items and the number of subjects required to obtain a coefficient of at least .90. This is based on the initial study and can be used to guide the number of respondents and items for future studies. While CFA and G theory should be viewed as complementary approaches to assessing scales used in multiple countries, CFA is more useful in refining scales and identifying items that are problematic.

## Multiple-context Scale Development

The preceding approaches for assessing scales cross-culturally focus on examining the 'fit' of a scale developed in one country in another country or cultural context, and whether it exhibits high levels of reliability and internal consistency (or absence of item bias) in that context. While this provides evidence of reliability of the measurement instrument and equivalence of psychometric properties, it does not address the issue of whether the specific instrument provides an adequate measure of the construct being studied. The construct may, for example, be expressed in different terms, requiring an emic-specific instrument. Equally, it may consist of different components or dimensions. In either case, prior investigation of the construct in each country or context is needed before developing an instrument adapted to that country or context.

A time-consuming but more theoretically sound approach is to develop a new scale for a given construct in each country studied to see whether the same dimensions are uncovered. Aaker (1997) developed a scale to measure brand personality in the US. Her scale revealed five different dimensions of brand personality: (1) sincerity; (2) excitement; (3) competence; (4) sophistication; and (5) ruggedness. The next issue was to determine whether the same dimensions existed outside the US. To examine this issue she adopted an emic approach and developed a scale for Japan following the same procedures used initially to develop the scale in the US (Aaker, 1998). The Japanese brand personality scale also yielded five factors.

To determine how unique the set of five dimensions was, the two scales were administered to two additional samples, a group of US subjects and a group of Japanese subjects. From the set of 40 brands used in the initial studies, a subset of 10 brands that were highly familiar and for which there were no cultural differences in familiarity and liking was identified. Further, the brands represent the range of brand categories: symbolic, utilitarian and symbolic/utilitarian. The 10 brands were rated on 70 traits (42 English traits, 36 Japanese traits, minus the 8 overlapping traits). The two groups were factor analyzed separately to arrive at two sets of five brand personality dimensions. The first four dimensions were highly correlated (> 0.80) with each other (sincerity, excitement, competence, sophistication). However, a Japanese dimension labeled dependence and a US dimension of ruggedness were not strongly related to each other, suggesting that both were unique to their respective countries.

Developing the scales separately in each country ensures an emic-centered measurement instrument and avoids the pitfalls of an etic approach. Since scales are developed independently of each other, they each provide insights into the unique components of brand personality in the US and Japan. There are still issues related to why the differences occur, but at a minimum, this approach avoids imposing a structure that is biased toward finding similarities.

# Developing Cross-cultural Scales

One of the greatest challenges facing cross-cultural researchers is the development of scales that measure a construct in multiple countries. In addition to all the issues related to achieving comparability and equivalence in the instrument, sampling frame, survey administration procedures and analysis, there is the underlying issue discussed in Chapter 6 of whether the construct exists and can be measured using the same or similar instruments in more than one context. Approaches based on existing scales are first examined. Much of this discussion relates to assessing the application of single-context scales in additional contexts. Then an alternative approach is covered based on 'decentering' measure development, which can be used to arrive at cross-cultural scales with fewer confounds.

## *Approaches Based on an Existing Scale*

Most published research dealing with cross-cultural scales report the results where a scale that has been developed in one country, typically the US, is applied in one or more additional countries. Few, if any, modifications are made to the original scale, with the exception of dropping items that do not exhibit high levels of reliability. In taking this approach, the researchers are assuming that a construct found in one country is manifested in the same form in another. Researchers may also adapt the scale by adding items to enhance their ability to identify culture-specific constructs.

## Assumed Etic Approach

The most common approach is the 'assumed etic' approach. This is similar to Berry's (1969) notion of 'imposed etic' and Triandis's (1972) notion of 'pseudo etic'. The choice of the term 'assumed' is meant to draw attention to the implicit assumptions being made by the researcher. The impact of these implicit assumptions on the soundness of the conclusions depends on how the scale is being used. In some cases, the researcher is primarily concerned with establishing the universality of the construct. The researcher assumes that the construct identified in country A exists in country B and can be measured in the same way in country B. Scale items are translated into the local language, the scale administered and results analyzed. In other cases, the scale is used as an independent variable to see whether it can predict some behavior or outcome in another country. Here, the emphasis shifts to focus on the predictive ability of the scale, rather than the universality of the construct.

In both cases, minor adjustments will be made to the scale based on internal reliability. For example, items that do not contribute to improved levels of reliability based on Cronbach's alpha are dropped. In all other respects, the scale is assumed to apply to the other countries. The criteria for item elimination are reliability and whether the item is correlated with other items that are supposed to measure the same construct, or more simply whether the item 'fits' with the other items. A related approach is to take a scale that has been developed in country A, administer it in country B and eliminate items that are biased. The biased items are dropped from the scale, so that the new scale has a reduced total number of items. Items are eliminated if they are found to be biased based on item response curves. This is a more rigorous criterion and can be done in an iterative fashion.

The prevalence of the assumed etic approach is explained in part by the widespread availability of scales that have been developed to measure constructs in a single country, typically the US. Researchers become intrigued by the scale and attempt to apply it elsewhere. Underlying this process is the explicit belief that concepts are universal and that a properly modified scale can measure them. An implicit belief is that the concept is expressed in the same way in different contexts. A fundamental problem is that the starting point of the research is a scale anchored in one context and that elimination of items will reduce its length and improve its reliability, but not shift it to encompass another culture.

## Adding Emic Components

Another approach is to add new items to a scale developed in one country in order to capture elements that are unique to the second country or context. Here, it is assumed that the core construct is etic or universal, but may be expressed in somewhat different terms in other contexts. Consequently, the measurement instrument may require some modification or the addition of culture-specific items. For example, Schwartz (1992), in developing his value survey to measure universal value types, identified values drawn from the world's major religions and previous research on values, as well as inviting collaborators in many countries to add values. A total of 56 values were selected for the survey to represent value types. These were subsequently reduced to 45 based on an examination of the intercorrelations among the values (smallest space analyses [SSA]; Guttman, 1968).

Adding emic elements results in a new scale for country B consisting of the items that measured the construct in country A, together with some items that are unique to country B. This approach provides a much richer set of scales, but at the same time creates a scale that is different from the original. It is also more complicated to analyze, as there are both common elements and elements that are unique to each country. The analysis becomes highly complex as more countries are added to the research. In this case, the procedure is repeated for each country studied, resulting in a common core across all countries and emic elements in each country.

# Developing Decentered Scales

An alternative and more desirable approach is to adopt a 'decentered' approach to scale development. Collaborators in other countries with culturally diverse backgrounds are asked to participate in defining emic or culture-specific dimensions of the phenomenon studied and provide input into instrument design and development of items relating to their specific country or culture. This item pool can then be analyzed to develop an appropriate scale identifying both common and culture-specific elements. This approach helps to eliminate the dominance of a specific country or cultural context in the operationalization of the construct and design of research instruments and procedures.

## Item Development

Development of a decentered scale must start with a clear initial definition of the construct that is to be examined. After the construct has been defined, the team of researchers should be broadened to include researchers from each of the countries to be studied. The domain of the construct should be refined and a determination made of whether or not the construct is operative in each of the different cultural contexts. At this point the initial construct definition may be redefined to encompass different manifestations.

Once the construct is defined, the next step is to generate an item pool in each country or context studied. Suppose that a multicountry study is conducted to develop a scale of xenophilia or 'love for things foreign'. This would be hypothesized to be positively related to the purchase or a willingness to buy foreign-made products and a tendency to rate these as superior or of better quality than domestic products. The construct might also be hypothesized to be negatively correlated with consumer ethnocentrism. Collaborators in the different countries would conduct studies to identify relevant dimensions of xenophilia in their own countries. Part of this process would be to identify context-specific factors that could affect feelings of xenophilia. For example, macroeconomic factors such as per capita GDP, the availability of locally made substitutes and regulations limiting imports would all affect the results.

In addition, surveys of consumers in each country might be conducted. Consumers might be asked to describe their attitudes and behavior toward foreign items or to mention the first words that come to mind in relation to foreign products. Further probing might relate to images as well as words associated with foreign things. Projective techniques might also be employed. For example, respondents might be asked to describe a person who typically purchases foreign products. These country-specific studies could then be content analyzed to identify relevant dimensions of xenophilia in each country or research context.

The next step is for a team of multicultural judges to determine which dimensions are common across countries (or regions) and which are emic or culture specific. If no common dimensions are identified, then it may be determined that the construct is best measured in different ways in each context, and no direct (or statistical) comparison is feasible. This is an important step that precedes actual data analysis. This step also adds to the understanding of the construct. In either case, a pool of items to tap the various dimensions needs to be identified.

## Analyzing and Comparing Decentered Scales

Data analysis presents its own unique challenges. For the sake of simplicity of exposition, the discussion will focus on the situation where the construct of xenophilia is being examined in only two countries, A and B. Adding more countries typically means that an iterative process will need to be followed. The researcher can either successively compare each unique pair or, when a large number of countries are being studied, one country can be treated as the target and each additional country can be compared to the target. If a construct is truly universal, changing the target should produce similar results.

To start the analysis process, the combined item pool is administered in all countries studied. The items are analyzed first within each country to purify the scale and eliminate items showing item bias or low levels of reliability in each country. Next, within-country analysis is performed to identify emic or country-specific items. Factor analysis can be performed within each country on respondents' standardized scores to identify factors common across countries and those specific to each country. Items with low alpha levels within a given country are dropped and the remaining items from each country used to determine emic-specific and etic components of the scale. To test whether the factor structures are similar, a Procrustes or target rotation can be performed. With two countries, either can be selected as the target. With more than two countries, the target should be rotated to see if the factor congruence coefficients hold for all unique pairs. This procedure is discussed in Chapter 12.

In addition to items designed to measure xenophilia, some additional scales should be included so that discriminant and convergent validity can be established as well. Given that xenophilia is a love for things foreign, the researchers might want to include other scales such as a cosmopolitanism scale or the CETSCALE. The EAP scale mentioned earlier might also be included, to determine whether xenophilia is distinct from the desire to try new products in general. In attempting to establish convergent and discriminant validity, there is also the issue of whether the additional scales have etic properties. Ideally, the researcher would find scales that had already been developed or validated in each of the countries being studied. However, this is unlikely to be the case and will present the researcher with an additional set of validation problems.

At this point, confirmatory factor analysis should be applied to the data. As part of this analysis it is desirable to have sufficiently large samples to be able to split the within-country samples into two samples for cross-validation purposes. Since confirmatory factor analysis is best with samples of 200–300, a sample of approximately 500 is desirable in each country. One subsample is used to estimate the model and the other is used to validate it. The confirmatory factor analysis will provide the best indication of whether the same model holds across both countries. If it does hold, the researchers can conclude that xenophilia is an etic construct. Alternatively, certain factors that are identified may be common and certain may be unique, suggesting emic components.

So far the analysis procedures have established the reliability of the xenophilia scale and convergent and discriminant validity. Nomological validity would also have to be established. Information on the purchase, purchase intention, willingness to buy and ownership of foreign-made products should also be collected. The extent to which the xenophilia scale predicts these variables would establish its nomological validity. Differences between countries might suggest that the construct is not as etic as believed, does not bear the same relationship to purchase behavior, or that certain macro-context variables, such as availability or cost of foreign products, inhibit individuals' ability to act on their xenophilia.

The above discussion suggests some approaches to developing a decentered scale to measure a construct, in this case xenophilia. There are, however, different approaches that will allow the researcher to derive a decentered scale. The critical aspect is not to let one culture or perspective dominate the identification of the construct and the development of items to measure it. Thus, the most critical steps are the ones that precede the analysis; that is, construct definition and item identification. If the construct and the items are heavily influenced by one perspective, then examination in another context will simply mirror, albeit imperfectly, the original. Further, it will help perpetuate the belief in the universality of a construct that is more limited in its applicability.

# Summary

Developing scales to measure constructs that exist in multiple countries is one of the greatest challenges facing researchers engaged in cross-cultural research. Issues of nonequivalence that perplex researchers dealing with single items are magnified as single items are combined to form multiple-item scales that measure complex constructs. In this chapter approaches to developing better cross-cultural scales were covered.

Critical issues in multicountry scale development are the types of measurement techniques used to gather the data as well as the underlying reliability of the data. As scale construction begins, the researcher must assess whether individual scale items function in the same way in each context or culture. Further, an assessment must be made as to whether the measures are in fact equivalent.

Typically, in multicountry research a scale developed in one country is applied and evaluated in another country. While this is a common practice, it gives rise to a range of problems. The researcher needs to be cognizant of these, particularly if the original scale was developed in a single context. More theoretically correct approaches involve developing the scale with input from multiple contexts at the outset, thus decentering the perspective adopted in scale development and developing a culturally unbiased scale.

# References

Aaker, J.L. (1997) Dimensions of Brand Personality. *Journal of Marketing Research*, **34**, 347–356.

Aaker, J.L. (1998) Brand Personality in Japan: Examining the Cross-cultural Meaning of Brand Personality Dimensions. Working Paper No. 324, John E. Anderson Graduate School of Management, Los Angeles.

Adorno, T.W., Frenkel-Brunswik, E., Levinson, D.J. and Sanford, R.N. (1950) *The Authoritarian Personality*. Harper & Row, New York.

Baumgartner, H. and Steenkamp, J-B.E.M. (1996) Exploratory Consumer Buying Behavior: Conceptualization and Measurement. *International Journal of Research in Marketing*, **13**, 121–137.

Berry, J.W. (1969) On Cross-cultural Comparability. *International Journal of Psychology*, **4**, 119–128.

Bradburn, N. (1969) *The Structure of Psychological Well-being*. Aldine, Chicago.

Cavusgil, S.T. and Zou, S. (1994) Marketing Strategy–Performance Relationship: An Investigation of the Empirical Link in Export Market Ventures. *Journal of Marketing*, **58**, 1–21.

Chang, E.C. and Ritter, E.H. (1976) Ethnocentrism in Black College Students. *Journal of Social Psychology*, **100**, 89–98.

Churchill, G.A. Jr (1979) A Paradigm for Developing Better Measures of Marketing Constructs. *Journal of Marketing Research*, **16**, 64–73.

Cohen, J. (1960) A Coefficient of Agreement for Nominal Scales. *Psychological Measurement*, **20**, 37–46.

Cronbach, L.J. (1951) Coefficient Alpha and the Internal Structure of Tests. *Psychometrika*, **16**, 297–334.

Cui, C.C. and Adams, E.I. (2002) National Identity and NATID: An Assessment in Yemen. *International Marketing Review*, **19**, 637–663.

Davis, H.L., Douglas, S.P. and Silk, A.J. (1981) Measure Unreliability: A Hidden Threat to Cross-national Marketing Research. *Journal of Marketing*, **45**, 98–109.

Donovan, R.J. and Spark, R. (1997) Towards Guidelines for Survey Research in Remote Aboriginal Communities. *The Australian and New Zealand Journal of Public Health*, **21**, 89–95.

Douglas, S.P. and Nijssen, E.J. (2003) On the Use of 'Borrowed' Scales in Cross-national Research: A Cautionary Note. *International Marketing Review*, **30**, 621–642.

Fornell, C. and Larker, D.F. (1981) Evaluating Structural Equation Models with Unobservable Variables and Measurement Error. *Journal of Marketing Research*, **18**, 39–50.

Garlington, W.K. and Shimote, H.E. (1964) The Change Seeker Index: A Measure of the Need for Variable Stimulus Input. *Psychological Reports*, **14**, 919–924.

Green, P.E., Tull, D.S. and Albaum, G. (1988) *Research for Marketing Decisions*. 5th edition. Prentice-Hall, Englewood Cliffs, NJ.

Guttman, L. (1968) A General Nonmetric Technique for Finding the Smallest Coordinate Space for a Configuration of Points. *Psychometrika*, **33**, 469–506.

Hambleton, R.K. (1994) Guidelines for Adapting Educational and Psychological Tests: A Progress Report. *European Journal of Psychological Assessment*, **10**, 229–244.

Hays, W.L. (1994) *Statistics*, 5th edition. Harcourt Brace, Orlando, FL.

Hofstede, G. (1980) *Culture's Consequences: International Differences in Work-related Values*. Sage, Beverly Hills, CA.

Huntington, S.P. (1993) The Clash of Civilizations. *Foreign Affairs*, **72**, 22–49.

Hwang, C.E., Scherer, R.F. and Ainina M.F. (2003) Utilizing the Maslach Burnout Inventory in Cross-cultural Research, *International Journal of Management*, **20**, 3–10.

Keillor, B.D., Hult, G.T.M., Erffmeyer, R.C. and Babkus, E. (1996) NATID: The Development and Application of National Identity Measures for Use in International Marketing. *Journal of International Marketing*, **4**, 57–73.

Klein, J.G., Ettenson, R. and Morris, M.D. (1998) The Animosity Model of Foreign Product Purchase: An Empirical Test in the People's Republic of China. *Journal of Marketing*, **62**, 89–100.

Lord, F.M. (1980) *Applications of Item Response Theory to Practical Testing Problems*. Erlbaum, Hillsdale, NJ.

Macintosh, R. (1998) A Confirmatory Factor Analysis of the Affect Balance Scale in 38 Nations: A Research Note. *Social Psychology Quarterly*, **61**, 83–95.

Manfield, M.N. (1971) The Guttman Scale. In Albaum, G. and Vankatesan, M. (eds) *Scientific Marketing Research*. Free Press, New York, pp. 167–178.

Netemeyer, R., Durvasula, S. and Lichtenstein, D.R. (1991) A Cross-national Assessment of the Reliability and Validity of the CETSCALE. *Journal of Marketing Research*, **28**, 320–327.

Nijessen, E.J. and Douglas, S.P. (2004) Examining the Animosity Scale in a Country with a High Level of Foreign Trade. *International Journal of Research in Marketing*, **21**, 23–38.

Nunnally, J.C. and Bernstein, I.H. (1994) *Psychometric Theory*, 3rd edition. McGraw-Hill, New York.

Parameswaran, R. and Yaprak, A. (1987) A Cross-national Comparison of Consumer Research Measures. *Journal of International Business Studies*, **18**, 35–49.

Poortinga, Y.H. (1989) Equivalence of Cross-cultural Data: An Overview of Basic Issues. *International Journal of Psychology*, **24**, 737–756.

Poortinga, Y.H. and Van der Flier, H. (1988) The Meaning of Item Bias in Ability Tests. In Irvine, S.H. and Berry, J.W. (eds) *Human Abilities in a Cultural Context*. Cambridge University Press, Cambridge, pp. 166–183.

Schwartz, S.H. (1992) Universals in the Content and Structure of Values: Theoretical Advances and Empirical Tests in 20 Countries. In Zana, M. (ed.) *Advances in Experimental Social Psychology*, Vol. 25. Academic Press, Orlando, FL, pp. 1–65.

Schwarzer, R. and Born, A. (1997) Optimistic Self-Beliefs: Assessment of General Perceived Self-Efficacy in Thirteen Countries. *World Psychology*, 3, 177–190.

Schwarzer, R. and Scholz, U. (2000) Cross-cultural Assessment of Coping Resources: The General Perceived Self-efficacy Scale. *Asian Conference of Health Psychology 2000. Health Psychology and Culture*. Tokyo, Japan, August 28–29.

Sharma, S. and Weathers, D. (2003) Assessing Generalizability of Scales Used in Cross-national Research. *International Journal of Research in Marketing*, 20, 287–295.

Shavelson, R.J. and Webb, N.M. (1991) *Generalizability Theory: A Primer*. Sage, Newbury Park, CA.

Shimp, T.A. and Sharma, S. (1987) Consumer Ethnocentrism: Construct Validation of the CETSCALE. *Journal of Marketing Research*, 24, 280–289.

Steenkamp, J-B.E.M. and Baumgartner, H. (1995) Development and Cross-cultural Validation of a Short Form of CSI as a Measure of Optimal Stimulation Level. *International Journal of Research Marketing*, 12, 97–104.

Steenkamp, J-B.E.M. and Van Trijp, H.C.M. (1996) To Buy or Not to Buy? Modeling Purchase of New Products Using Marketing Mix Variables and Consumer Characteristics. *Marketing Science Conference*, Gainesville, FL.

Steenkamp, J-B.E.M., ter Hofstede, F. and Wedel, M. (1999) A Cross-national Investigation into the Individual and Cultural Antecedents of Consumer Innovativeness. *Journal of Marketing*, 63, 55–69.

Styles, C. (1998) Export Performance Measures in Australia and the United Kingdom. *Journal of International Marketing*, **6**, 12–36.

Summers, G.A. (1906) *Folkways*. Ginn Custom Publishing, New York.

Thelen, S.T. and Honeycutt, E.D. Jr. (2004) Assessing National Identity in Russia Between Generations Using the National Identity Scale. *Journal of International Marketing*, **12**, 58–81.

Thurstone, L.L. (1959) *The Measurement of Values*. University of Chicago Press, Chicago.

Triandis, H.C. (1972) *The Analysis of Subjective Culture*. John Wiley & Sons, New York.

Van de Vijver, F. and Leung, K. (1997) *Methods and Data Analysis for Cross-cultural Research*. Sage, Thousand Oaks, CA.

Warr, P.B., Faust, J. and Harrison, G. (1967) A British Ethnocentrism Scale. *British Journal of Social Clinical Psychology*, **13**, 145–155.

Zou, S., Taylor, C.R. and Osland, G.E. (1998) The EXPERF Scale: A Cross-national Generalized Export Performance Measure. *Journal of International Marketing*, **6**, 37–58.

# Chapter 11

# ANALYSIS OF MULTICOUNTRY DATA

## Introduction

Once procedures for collecting data have been determined using either survey or nonsurvey methods, the next step is the choice of appropriate methods and procedures for data analysis. These two steps are interrelated as certain types of analysis, for example multidimensional scaling, require collection of specific types of data. There are a number of issues to be considered in relation to how data analysis is conducted and organized. For nonsurvey research data analysis is typically qualitative. Survey research requires some type of quantitative analysis or, at a bare minimum, tabulation of the responses. When research is conducted in a single country, these issues are the same as in domestic research. In multicountry research, the issues become more complex due to the existence of multiple units of analysis. The analysis is often conducted in different phases, starting with a within-country analysis and progressing to an across-country analysis. To ensure that the appropriate data are collected, a data analysis plan has to be established beforehand.

The complexity of multicountry data analysis is due to the multitier character of the research design, entailing analysis not only at the country level but also across regions and eventually at a global level. In domestic marketing research, decision problems and analysis typically relate to a single national sample. In multicountry research, management is concerned not only with developing marketing strategy or tactics relative to a single national market, but also with assessing the extent to which such strategies or tactics can be standardized across different geographical areas. Consequently, analysis needs to be conducted within countries and across countries. This poses a number of issues with regard to the level of aggregation and procedures used to analyze data.

In this chapter the problems associated with both within- and across-country phases of data analysis are examined, as well as procedures for minimizing difficulties. The discussion focuses primarily on the analysis of quantitative data. It is assumed that the reader is already familiar with standard marketing research texts (Churchill and Iacobucci, 2005; Kumar *et al.*, 2002; Lehmann *et al.*, 1998) and with the procedures commonly used to edit, code and analyze data. Methods of analyzing cross-national data that focus on the differences in the level of variables are examined, including use of both univariate and multivariate techniques. Here, knowledge of statistical methods commonly applied to analyze domestic marketing data is assumed, and emphasis is placed on how analytical procedures and methods are used to test for similarities and differences between data from different countries. Standard texts on multivariate analysis can be consulted for more background on data analysis techniques (Lattin *et al.*, 2003; Hair *et al.*, 1998; Johnson and Wichern, 1998).

# Multicountry Data Analysis

## *Analysis of Data at Different Levels of Aggregation*

A first concern is the specific level at which the analysis should be conducted. This issue needs to be considered before data are actually collected, as the ability to conduct analysis for more than one unit depends on how the data are collected and the size of the sample for each unit. Given adequate pre-planning and sufficient sample size, there are three basic levels at which multicountry data can be analyzed: intra-, inter- and pan-country.

### *Intracountry*

Intracountry analysis is the most direct and straightforward. Data are analyzed within a country and inferences made about the nature of the relationship between variables within the country. The approach is identical to marketing research carried out in a domestic market where the unit of analysis is the individual. To the extent that intracountry analysis is carried out in multiple countries, comparisons can be made about the relationships in each of the countries. However, any comparisons across countries are made with the knowledge that there may be elements that are not comparable across countries. Observed differences may reflect real differences between countries or simply be a function of differences in sampling, measurement or background factors.

### *Intercountry*

Intercountry analysis shifts the focus away from relationships within a country to examination of relationships between countries. Analysis is at the country level and the observations are the means of variables from each country. The most critical assumption for this type of analysis is that the individuals sampled are representative of the country. Since the country is now the unit of analysis, it is desirable to have as many countries as possible. However, even if all possible countries are included in the analysis, the maximum sample size would be in the neighborhood of 210. Realistically, the number of observations would be far less due to both the time and cost of obtaining additional data and the high degree of heterogeneity across a wide range of countries. Even within the 20 original OECD countries, there are not only sizable differences but also considerable heterogeneity. A critical issue in this type of analysis is that the variables chosen for the analysis should be representative of the country.

## Pan-country

With pan-country analysis all respondents are grouped together and analyzed without regard to their geographical location. The focus shifts back to analysis at the individual level and inferences are made about the entire sample without regard to the country. If no relationship is found, there still remains the possibility that there is a relationship within specific countries. Further, if a significant relationship is found, it does not necessarily hold for all countries represented in the sample.

Each of the three approaches to analyzing the data allows for different inferences and is appropriate for different circumstances. Intracountry analyses are most suited to situations where the firm needs to develop strategies on a country-by-country basis and there is minimal concern for achieving standardization across countries. Intercountry analysis is appropriate when the researcher wants to make inferences about countries and is less concerned about the individuals that make up the country. If there is a high degree of homogeneity in the composition of the country samples, then it may also be possible to make observations about individuals in that country. Finally, the pan-country analysis is useful to see whether a relationship can be found that holds across all individuals and countries. However, the results will tend toward the mean and conceal important variations that exist in different countries or within different segments.

# Approaches to Data Analysis

The different units of analysis suggest that multicountry data analysis can focus on making inferences *within* a country or *across* multiple countries. Analysis can also examine whether or not variables differ in terms of *level*, typically differences in mean values. This can be done within a

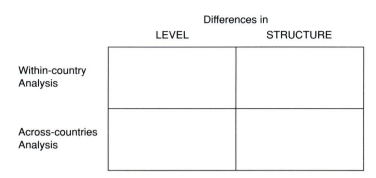

**Figure 11.1**  Multicountry data analysis

country, looking at different groups (within countries) or across countries. Analysis may also be conducted to examine the *structure*, or relationships, of variables. This can be done either within or across countries (Figure 11.1).

## *Analysis within and across Countries*

In analyzing cross-national data, the existence of multicountry, or other data units, implies the desirability of adopting a two-stage or sequential approach to analysis. In the first stage, data are analyzed *within* countries or other relevant organization units. In the second stage, the comparability of findings *across* different countries or organizational units is investigated, and the significance of observed differences and similarities examined.

In the first, *within*-country phase of analysis, relationships are examined among the independent variables, for example among different attitudinal or socioeconomic variables; or among various dependent variables, such as purchases of different brands or preferences for different product benefits. This enables identification or verification of relevant constructs to be examined in subsequent stages of analysis. In the case of lifestyle variables, it may be desirable to reduce the number of variables examined; or in the case of preference or purchase data, to identify relevant bundles of benefits or purchases. Then the association between the dependent and independent variables can be studied using standard statistical techniques.

In the second, *cross-national* phase of the analysis, the comparability of findings from one country to another is investigated. An important consideration is whether the comparison is made on an implicit, judgmental basis, or whether differences and similarities are explicitly analyzed. In the first case, the interpretation of the significance of observed variation across countries is based on subjective judgment incorporating previous management or researcher experience. In the second case, analytical techniques are applied to test the magnitude of differences and similarities between countries or units of analysis. Various different procedures may be used. Subsequent discussion focuses on the advantages and limitations of these techniques in multicountry analysis.

## Differences in the Level and Structure of Variables

When making cross-country comparisons, the analysis can focus on either the differences in the *level* of variables or the *structure* of variables (Van de Vijver and Leung, 1997). The majority of analyses focus on answering the question: is there a significant difference in variable X between country A and country B? This type of analysis is generally straightforward and employs techniques that are easy to use and interpret, although more complex multivariate techniques can also be employed. Typically, if no difference is found, the researcher concludes that they are the same. If a difference is found, then the researcher seeks to find out why a difference exists.

When addressing structure issues the researcher asks a more complex research question: is there a difference in the relation of variables X and Y between country A and country B? Answering questions relating to structure requires the use of more sophisticated statistical techniques and is often more difficult to interpret. The structure of variables often represents complex patterns of relationships and interactions. Some of this complexity is simply the result of the number of variables being considered and some is due to the inherent complexity of multicountry relationships.

The discussion so far has implicitly assumed that the country is the relevant unit of analysis. This may be the case when a company is organized on a country-by-country basis and plans strategy accordingly. However, in many instances it may be desirable to aggregate the data along other than country lines. Countries may be aggregated to form regional groupings that are relevant to the firm's operation. Alternatively, subgroups within a country may also serve as the relevant level of aggregation. It may be desirable to aggregate consumers living in geographical sections of a country. Within Canada, it makes sense to aggregate consumers from different provinces, particularly since Quebec is different in many respects from other parts of Canada.

To deal with these inconsistencies, the plan of analysis should start with a clear definition of the appropriate unit of analysis (Douglas and Craig, 1997). In some instances, the country is the appropriate unit. More typically, there are smaller units within a country that form the appropriate unit of analysis. With the units defined, the analysis can be structured accordingly and, more importantly, inferences made at the appropriate level of aggregation.

# Assessing the Differences in the Level of Variables between Countries

The remainder of this chapter is devoted to a discussion of statistical techniques used to assess differences in the level of variables between countries. Examples are used to illustrate the use of the techniques in multicountry research. In Chapter 12, techniques that are used to examine the structure of variables between countries are examined. A number of the techniques, for example multiple regression, can be used to consider differences in structure as well as level. The different ways to use each technique are illustrated.

The discussion assumes that the reader is already familiar with the underlying statistical formulas and computational procedures, and merely illustrates use of these formulas and procedures in international marketing research, based on examples drawn from available published sources. Readers not familiar with these techniques are referred to standard sources, such as Hays (1994), Winer (1991) and Siegel and Castellani (1988).

## *Cross-tabulation*

One of the most common approaches to data analysis in marketing research is the cross-tabulation of data. Typically, two variables are cross-tabulated with each other to see whether there are differences. If the researcher were interested in the relationship between income and age of respondents, the first step would be to code income and age into mutually exclusive discrete categories. The two variables would then be cross-tabulated to see if income differed by age category. The responses to questionnaire data can also be split into mutually exclusive groups, such as users versus nonusers, male versus female consumers, and consumers living in one country versus those living in another. A chi-square statistic can be computed to see whether there are significant differences in the distribution of responses between the two groupings. This is a technique for determining the probability that differences between the expected and observed number of cases in each cell are significant. Where results are cross-tabulated by national sample or by different subgroups within a country, chi-square can be used to test for independence between national

**Table 11.1** Comparison of characteristics of commercials in which men and women appear in the US, Mexico and Australia

| Ad characteristics | US (%) Women | US (%) Men | Mexico (%) Women | Mexico (%) Men | Australia (%) Women | Australia (%) Men |
|---|---|---|---|---|---|---|
| **Product user** | | | | | | |
| Female | 13.0 | 2.3 | 25.0 | 4.0 | 7.7 | 4.1 |
| Male | 0.6 | 3.0 | 6.8 | 11.9 | 0.0 | 4.1 |
| Either | 86.4 | 94.7 | 69.2 | 84.2 | 92.3 | 91.8 |
| | $\chi^2 = 13.52$* | | $\chi^2 = 19.73$* | | n.s. | |
| **Setting** | | | | | | |
| Home | 33.5 | 22.7 | 25.9 | 20.2 | 28.8 | 16.3 |
| Store | 9.0 | 6.8 | 15.5 | 14.1 | 5.8 | 14.3 |
| Occupational | 3.6 | 15.2 | 0.9 | 3.0 | 0.0 | 4.1 |
| Outdoors | 11.4 | 7.6 | 12.1 | 18.2 | 5.8 | 14.2 |
| Other | 42.5 | 47.7 | 45.7 | 44.4 | 59.6 | 51.0 |
| | $\chi^2 = 16.30$** | | n.s. | | n.s. | |
| **Voice-over** | | | | | | |
| Female | 12.4 | | 11.5 | | 10.9 | |
| Male | 67.2 | | 66.5 | | 76.9 | |
| Chorus | 9.5 | | 13.5 | | 9.4 | |
| None | 10.9 | | 8.5 | | 2.9 | |

* $P \leq 0.001$, ** $P \leq 0.01$.
*Source*: Gilly, 1988.

samples or subgroups. The researcher might want to determine whether the income distribution varied between two countries. The chi-square statistic would indicate whether the differences were significant.

Table 11.1 contains data on characteristics of commercials in three countries, the US, Mexico and Australia, in which both men and women appear (Gilly, 1988). The table shows at whom the products were targeted (columns) and the characteristics of the ads (rows). In the US there were differences between the product user and the portrayal and gender in commercials, with women appearing in commercials for women or for either gender, but infrequently in commercials for men's products. There were also gender differences in the setting, with women more likely to be portrayed in the home and men more likely to be shown in occupational settings. For Mexico there were also differences, as indicated by a significant chi-square, in gender portrayal based on the product user. Women were more likely to appear in commercials aimed at women and men in commercials targeted toward men. There was no significant difference in setting in Mexico. In Australia, none of the differences was significant. While the chi-square statistic indicates that there is a significant difference, it does not provide an explanation. One can conclude that there is a greater equality in sex roles in Australian ads. However, the reasons behind the differences observed in the US and the lack of differences in Australia are open to a broader interpretation and would require more extensive data collection to answer.

Chi-square analysis is a test of independence and as such provides no indication of the degree of association between two variables. Additional statistics, such as the contingency coefficient, phi, tau or gamma, can be computed to provide an indication of the association between variables. Most importantly, the variables used for the cross-tabulation must be ordinal so that an interpretation of the measure of association is meaningful. If one variable is nominal or both are, then interpretation becomes problematic (see Siegel and Castellani, 1988, for computational procedures and limitations).

The example illustrates two-way cross-tabulations. In analyzing cross-national data, the researcher may want to use three-way or $n$-way cross-tabulations. For example, gender, purchase rate of a particular product and country can be cross-tabulated. The computed chi-square statistic provides an indication of the overall degree of independence. Partial gammas can then be computed to provide a measure of the relationship between two variables, controlling for a third (or more) variable. In the above example, this would allow determination of whether the relationship between gender and purchase of a particular product is affected by the country.

## *t-tests*

Often the researcher is interested in whether the mean values of a variable are different between countries. The t-test provides a relatively simple way of testing for differences in means obtained from national samples. A t-test is a statistic that provides a measure of the significance of differences between means drawn from two sample populations. It thus indicates whether there is a statistically significant difference between values on a given variable for two samples. In international marketing research, t-tests can be used to test whether mean scores on a given variable are significantly different between countries. Alternatively, they can be used to test whether different subgroups or segments within countries exhibit significant differences in behavior, attitudes and so on, and the level of significance in each country can then be compared. When using t-tests, or for that matter any time a comparative statistic is used when variables are not comparable, there are a number of cautions. For example, if a survey were conducted in China and the Lebanon examining the relationship of purchasing behavior to income, there would be a significant difference between the two countries on income. In 2002 the per capita GNP in the Lebanon was over four times greater than the per capita GNP of China (Lebanon US$3990 and China US$960). However, if the income levels are adjusted to account for purchasing power parity (PPP), then the differences largely disappear. The PPP adjusted GNPs for the two countries are virtually identical (Lebanon $4660 and China $4520). Thus, the reported mean incomes may be statistically different, but the 'real' incomes of the respondents do not differ.

The same type of problem can exist when attitudinal or purchase intention data are collected, particularly in one-time cross-sectional research. For example, Germans tend to understate purchase intentions for new products relative to Italians (Bhalla and Lin, 1987). With a single study conducted in both countries, one is likely to conclude that a new product launch in Italy would be more successful than in Germany. In situations where a company has conducted multiple studies over time, it is possible to norm the purchase intentions against past responses to assess how the purchase intentions compare to previous studies. Thus, the higher mean purchase intention in Italy and the lower purchase intention score for Germany may both predict the same level of sales.

A potentially more serious problem in using t-tests in international marketing research is the issue of multiple t-tests. Often there are a number of variables that the researcher is interested in comparing between countries. Typically, in international marketing research whenever there is a large set of variables, there will be differences between some variables. The traditional approach is to set a significance level, typically $P < 0.05$, and test whether differences are significant between all pairs of means. In many instances this is an acceptable procedure, particularly where the variables being tested do not represent a logical grouping of variables and can be construed as being independent observations. However, in situations where the variables cover a range of interrelated variables, the use of multiple t-tests with an alpha level of 0.05 will artificially inflate the likelihood of getting significant results. These variables are not independent of each other but represent a *family* of variables.

To provide an adequate protection level from type I errors requires establishment of the *familywise error rate*. To control for the familywise error rate, Bonferroni-adjusted tests can be conducted

(Hays, 1994). The procedure adjusts the alpha level for the number of t-tests being performed. The critical value of alpha used in all the tests is alpha divided by the number of tests being performed. For example, if the alpha level were set initially at $P < 0.05$ and there were five t-tests, then the adjusted alpha would be 0.01 and this value would be used for all five t-tests. This procedure controls for the overall *type I error rate* or the probability of rejecting the null hypothesis that there is no difference between means. Other procedures devised for multiple comparisons, such as Tukey's procedure or the Scheffe method, can also be used (Winer, 1991).

Not adjusting for the number of t-tests being performed increases the likelihood of obtaining significant differences between some of the means. This is magnified by the fact that researchers are typically looking for differences between countries and consequently are not surprised when they find some. The extent of the upward bias is fairly severe. For example, when there are 10 sets of variables and 10 t-tests are performed with an alpha level of 0.05, the probability of obtaining a significant difference increases to 0.5. When there are 20 sets of variables and the alpha level is not adjusted, the probability of finding at least one significant difference increases to 1.

## *Analysis of Variance*

Analysis of variance is a very useful technique in international marketing research as country differences can be included as a factor in the design. It can be used to test for the significance of differences within a national sample or between different national samples. One-way analysis of variance tests whether the means of several additional samples are significantly different for a single variable. Two-way analysis of variance extends this logic to the situation where there are two influencing variables. Two-way analysis of variance thus tests for the effect of two variables, as well as interactions between those two variables. (See Winer, 1991, for detailed discussion of procedures and limitations.)

The use of two-way analysis of variance in international marketing research is illustrated by a study conducted by Pieters and Baumgartner (1993). In their study, they compared attitudes toward advertising of three groups (practitioners, homemakers and students) in two countries (the Netherlands and Belgium). The results of their study indicate a significant effect of group, country and a country-by-group interaction. Additional analysis in the same study compared the mean scores on 20 attitudinal variables toward advertising (Table 11.2). Since all variables reflect

**Table 11.2**  Mean scores of groups in countries on the attitude toward advertising items

| Label | Advertising | Effects[b] | The Netherlands | | | Belgium | | |
|---|---|---|---|---|---|---|---|---|
| | | | 1 | 2 | 3 | 1 | 2 | 3 |
| CHE: | Makes society cheerful | C,G,I | 3.3 | 4.0 | 2.9 | 4.1 | 4.5 | 2.9 |
| INF: | Information about new products | C,G,I | 4.2 | 2.7 | 3.9 | 4.9 | 3.7 | 3.8 |
| NOT: | Makes buy things not needed | C,G,I | 2.3 | 3.9 | 3.5 | 4.1 | 3.6 | 4.1 |
| PRO: | Is progressive | C,G | 3.2 | 3.1 | 2.6 | 3.6 | 4.2 | 2.9 |
| FAL: | False and misleading info | C,G | 1.6 | 3.5 | 3.0 | 4.1 | 2.2 | 3.2 |
| FOS: | Fosters the need for products | C,I | 3.4 | 3.8 | 4.0 | 4.4 | 4.4 | 4.2 |
| IRR: | Irritates | C | 3.4 | 3.6 | 2.9 | 2.8 | 2.5 | 2.6 |
| AWA: | Can influence without awareness | C | 4.0 | 3.9 | 4.2 | 4.5 | 4.5 | 4.4 |
| AMU: | Amuses | C | 3.9 | 3.6 | 4.1 | 4.1 | 4.3 | 4.1 |
| ART: | Is art | C | 2.6 | 3.3 | 3.5 | 3.3 | 3.7 | 3.8 |
| PRE: | Confirms all kinds of prejudices | G,I | 2.9 | 3.0 | 3.6 | 3.4 | 2.1 | 3.5 |
| LOW: | Plays on lower needs of people | G | 2.4 | 2.9 | 2.7 | 3.0 | 2.7 | 2.7 |
| CUL: | Positive influence on culture | G | 3.5 | 3.0 | 3.0 | 3.1 | 4.1 | 2.9 |
| EXA: | Exaggerates advantages | G | 3.7 | 2.6 | 2.6 | 2.5 | 4.0 | 2.3 |
| DIS: | Makes people dissatisfied | G | 2.2 | 3.1 | 2.9 | 3.3 | 1.9 | 3.2 |
| BET: | Helps to make better decisions | G | 3.7 | 2.6 | 2.5 | 2.0 | 4.0 | 2.3 |
| KNO: | Stimulates self-knowledge | G | 2.7 | 2.5 | 2.2 | 2.3 | 2.7 | 1.7 |
| DUM: | Keeps people dumb | G | 1.8 | 2.6 | 2.4 | 2.3 | 1.2 | 2.3 |
| EXP: | Makes products expensive | G | 1.9 | 3.3 | 2.8 | 3.7 | 1.8 | 3.0 |
| OFF: | Is offensive to certain people | — | 2.5 | 3.0 | 2.9 | 2.5 | 2.1 | 2.8 |

[a]  Groups: 1, Practitioners; 2, Homemakers; 3, Students. Responses: 1, completely disagree; 5, completely agree; 3, don't know/no opinion. $n$ per group = 60.

[b]  Letters indicate statistically significant effects in the univariate ANOVAs: C, country effect is significant; G, group effect is significant; I, interaction effect is significant. All effects are significant at $p < 0.05$, Bonferroni adjusted (original $P/20$).

*Source*: Pieters and Baumgartner, 1993.

attitudes toward advertising, the significance levels were Bonferroni adjusted. This procedure insures that the alpha level of $P < 0.05$ is adjusted for all the comparisons being made and that conclusions about statistical significance accurately reflect the number of comparisons being made.

# Analysis of Covariance

Analysis of variance is a powerful method of analyzing data from multiple countries. It allows the researcher to examine mean differences between countries and treatments and make inferences about significant differences as well as adjusting for variables that may affect results. In multicountry research there is often the need to account for dramatic differences that exist between countries in contextual factors on sample characteristics that may have an impact on results. There may be concerns that subjects' responses are influenced by their income levels, age, educational attainment or other factors. Often, it may be these factors that account for the observed differences, rather than the more fundamental differences between countries. There are two ways to deal with this problem. The simplest and most direct is to match the samples from different countries so that they are the same on the relevant background variables. This ensures that the samples are matched on the variables of interest, for example income, but at the same time it may cause one of the samples to be nonrepresentative of the country from which it is drawn. Consider a situation where subjects in the US and Thailand are being compared. The per capita income in the US is more than 17 times that of Thailand (US $35 400; Thailand $2000, per capita GNI; *World Development Indicators*, 2004). If a research project is being conducted in Thailand and the US, one option would be to select Thai subjects that match the income of the US subjects. Taking this approach will result in a group of Thai subjects who are at the upper end of the Thai income distribution. So in controlling for income level by matching, the researcher has lost the ability to generalize to one of the populations from which subjects were drawn.

It should be noted that the per capita gross national income numbers used above are not adjusted for purchasing power parity. The US and Thai income figures adjusted for PPP are $36 110 and $6890, resulting in the US per capita income being only five times greater than that of Thailand. While the income disparity between the two countries is not as great as the unadjusted numbers suggest, it is important to remember that income figures that respondents provide to a survey question do not reflect any adjustments. One procedure to deal with this issue is to express income data relative to the strata into which respondents fall within their country.

The other approach involves analysis of covariance, which allows for the effect of a particular variable to be accounted for directly in the analysis. In the example above, the experiment would be carried out using two groups of subjects, one from the US and one from Thailand. In addition to collecting data on the dependent variable, information would also be collected on the subject's income. The analysis of covariance model provides for statistical control and allows adjustment of the influence of income. The most critical assumptions of the analysis of covariance are that the relationship between the covariate and the dependent variable is linear and that the degree of relationship does not depend on the experimental variable (Hays, 1994).

In applying covariance analysis, each national sample is treated as an experimental group. Although this implies nonrandom assignment to treatment groups, this has been found not to generate biased estimates (Overall and Woodward, 1977). The relevant socioeconomic and demographic or other sample characteristics likely to affect treatment response (that is, the dependent variable) are then used as covariates. Next, the group response means and associated F statistics from the analysis of variance are compared with the corresponding means and F statistics in the covariance analysis (that is, after adjustment for the background characteristics). This indicates the extent to which the results are affected by sampling characteristics. National or group response means are adjusted for variance in the covariates, and the impact of such variables is accounted for. The magnitude of this adjustment can also be examined to gauge its overall impact. Caution should be exercised in the interpretation of results where there is the possibility of an association or common factor underlying the treatment means and the covariates.

The significance of the F statistics associated with each of the covariates can also be examined to identify which specific sampling characteristics, such as age or income, are most strongly related to the dependent variable. Here again, caution in interpretation needs to be exercised, due to the likelihood of multicollinearity among sample characteristics such as age and income. Also, these are often discrete variables that violate the linearity assumptions of the underlying model. Some preliminary analysis and data reduction procedures, for example factor analysis or a step-down MANOVA procedure, may be desirable (Homans and Messner, 1976).

Univariate analysis of covariance was applied in a study examining the impact of administrative heritage on acquisitions of British and French firms made by either British or French firms (Lubatkin et al., 1998). Six covariates were used: relatedness of the merger, growth prospects of the acquired firm, firm's relative size, local resources used, age of the merger (years) and the merger type (domestic or cross-national). The authors first examined the relationship between the six covariates and the

**Table 11.3**  Analysis of covariance: Administrative heritage in domestic and cross-national mergers

Part 1: Within-cells Regressions (Covariate Model)[a]

| Dependent Variables | Univariate F | $R^2$ |
|---|---|---|
| Managerial Transfer | 2.21* | 0.17 |
| Structural Control | 6.60*** | 0.38 |
| Resource Control | 5.14*** | 0.32 |
| Strategic Control | 6.62*** | 0.38 |
| Socialization | 1.93† | 0.15 |
| Wilk's Lambda | 0.31 | |
| Multivariate F | 2.84*** | |

Part 2: Main Effect (French/British Buyers), Adjusted for Covariates

| Dependent Variables | Univariate F | French Mean (SD) | British Mean (SD) |
|---|---|---|---|
| Managerial Transfer | 4.17* | 0.64 (0.49) | 0.40 (0.50) |
| Structural Control | 0.13 | 0.23 (0.43) | 0.18 (0.39) |
| Resource Control | 0.00 | 2.88 (0.91) | 2.90 (1.00) |
| Strategic Control | 11.62*** | 3.20 (1.00) | 2.65 (1.02) |
| Socialization | 0.53 | 3.17 (0.98) | 3.38 (0.85) |
| Wilk's Lambda | 0.79 | | |
| Multivariate F | 3.27** | | |

† $p < 0.10$, * $p < 0.05$, ** $p < 0.01$, *** $p < 0.001$

[a] The covariate model consists of Merger Relatedness, Growth, Relative Size, Local Resources, Age, and 0/1 variable signifying whether the merger is domestic or cross-national.

*Source*: Lubatkin *et al.*, 1998.

five dependent variables used in the study (see Table 11.3, part 1). A significant relationship was found between the two sets of variables, suggesting that overall the British and French firms appear to establish different headquarters–subsidiary control linkages.

The main effect of the firm's nationality was examined for each of the five dependent variables (managerial transfer, structural control, strategic control, resource control and socialization) while controlling for the six covariates (see Table 11.3, part 2). There were significant differences between French and British firms for two of the dependent variables, managerial transfer and strategic control. The study did not report the results for a test of differences without adjusting for the covariates. Once the authors established that the covariates had a significant effect on the dependent variables, that step would not have generated meaningful results.

As a general rule, whenever countries are one of the factors in an experimental design, it is advisable to conduct an analysis of covariance in addition to an analysis of variance. Additional data should always be collected on variables that vary between countries and that might have some impact on the dependent variable. For example, consider a hypothetical analysis of variance where there is a significant main effect for an intention-to-purchase measure for a consumer durable between the US and Thailand. One would conclude that there is a significant difference between Thai and US subjects in terms of their intention to purchase the durable. However, when an analysis of covariance with income as a covariate was run, the main effect was not significant, although the covariate was. The latter analysis portrays a more accurate picture of the phenomenon and allows for more valid inferences about the relationships being investigated. In this type of application, there is the assumption that the regression lines within each cultural group are parallel (Lord, 1967). If the regression lines are parallel, then the relationship between the variables is the same in both countries, although the intercept may vary. This indicates that the nature of the relationship is the same, but the level of the variable, for example strength of intention to purchase, differs.

Hsieh *et al.* (2004) examined the effect of brand image perception on automobile brand purchase behavior across 20 different countries. To deal with concerns about country differences, they used three covariates. Brand awareness and the brand's market share in each market were used to control for level of familiarity and the popularity of the brand. Whether the brand was foreign or local was also used as a dichotomous covariate. Market share and local origin were significant, but brand awareness was not.

# Multivariate Analysis of Covariance

Multivariate analysis of covariance is a generalization of the analysis of the covariance model to the case involving more than one dependent variable (Winer, 1991). It explicitly takes into account intercorrelations among dependent variables. Thus, differences significant in a univariate analysis may disappear in an overall multivariate analysis and, conversely, differences that do not appear in a univariate analysis may emerge in a multivariate analysis.

In cross-national research, multivariate analysis of covariance can be used when analyzing within-country data to control for the effect of sampling characteristics on the interaction between other variables; for example, different measures of response to advertising commercials for brand users and nonbrand users. Results for different countries can then be compared. As in univariate analysis of variance, multivariate analysis of covariance can also be applied to data pooled across countries, to take out the effects of sampling characteristics or other variables such as attitudinal characteristics when making comparisons between countries.

The technique is particularly suited to a more elaborate experimental design with multiple dependent variables. It allows for the impact of experimental factors to be assessed on more than one dependent variable simultaneously. Gibson (1995) conducted a study to examine the emphasis that female and male managers place on leadership behaviors and styles across four countries (Norway, Sweden, Australia and the US). Five leadership behaviors and six leadership styles were examined in the study. The analysis consisted of a 2 × 4 MANOVA (gender by country) with 11 dependent variables. The results of the analysis are shown in Table 11.4. Overall significance was tested using F-test approximations. Country and gender were significant, but the interaction was not. After finding significance for the main effects, univariate F-tests for each covariate were conducted to determine the specific factors accounting for the differences.

To see whether company size influenced the outcome, Gibson then conducted an analysis of covariance with goal setting as the dependent variable, gender as the independent variable and company size as the covariate. Even after accounting for the effect of company size, gender still had a significant effect on goal setting. A multivariate analysis of covariance was then performed with three dependent variables (goal setting, benevolent autocratic style and laissez-faire style), country as the independent variable, and industry and company size as covariates. Even after adjusting for the covariates, there was still a country main effect.

## Multiple Regression

Regression analysis is a robust statistical technique that has a variety of uses in multicountry research. In simple regression, the dependent variable is assumed to depend on a single independent variable.

**Table 11.4**  Results of multivariate analysis of variance: Wilks' $\Lambda$, $F$-test approximations, degrees of freedom (df) and multivariate $\eta^2$ for country, gender and country $\times$ gender

| Effect | Wilks' $\Lambda$ | $F(\Lambda)$ | df($\Lambda$) | $\eta^2(\Lambda)$ | Univariate $F$-tests |
|---|---|---|---|---|---|
| Country | 0.75 | 1.19** | 30 | 0.25 | |
| Goal setting | | | | | 0.59 |
| Interaction facilitation | | | | | 6.53*** |
| Work facilitation | | | | | 1.32 |
| Support behavior | | | | | 0.75 |
| Personnel development | | | | | 0.14 |
| Autocratic style | | | | | 1.07 |
| Benevolent autocratic style | | | | | 2.96* |
| Consultative style | | | | | 1.39 |
| Participative style | | | | | 2.30 |
| Consensus style | | | | | 0.72 |
| Laissez-faire style | | | | | 3.83* |
| Gender | 0.91 | 1.89* | 10 | 0.09 | |
| Goal setting | | | | | 4.43* |
| Interaction facilitation | | | | | 6.33* |
| Work facilitation | | | | | 0.70 |
| Support behavior | | | | | 0.01 |
| Personnel development | | | | | 2.41 |
| Autocratic style | | | | | 0.72 |
| Benevolent autocratic style | | | | | 0.21 |
| Consultative style | | | | | 0.07 |
| Participative style | | | | | 0.39 |
| Consensus style | | | | | 0.02 |
| Laissez-faire style | | | | | 3.24 |
| Country $\times$ Gender | 0.83 | 1.26 | 30 | 0.17 | |

* $P < 0.05$. ** $P < 0.01$. *** $P < 0.001$.

[a] df, 3 for country; df, 1 for gender.

*Source*: Gibson, 1995.

In the example in Chapter 4, sugar consumption was the dependent variable and GNP the independent variable. Overall there was a good fit, particularly when the high-income and low-income countries were examined separately. In multiple regression, a number of independent variables are assumed to underlie variance in the dependent variable. In multicountry research, multiple regression can be used to examine the extent to which certain variables account for variation in one variable within countries, and the results compared from one country to another, either qualitatively or by explicit statistical testing. Data from different countries can also be pooled and countries entered as dummy variables in the regression. For further discussion of regression techniques, see Greene (2003).

## Regression Coefficients

One of the issues in using multiple regression in international research is whether to use standardized or unstandardized coefficients. According to Singh (1995) the choice depends on the specific situation facing the researchers. In situations where the researcher has established construct equivalence and the task is that of comparing regression coefficients across two or more groups, the unstandardized coefficients should be used. In situations where equivalence has not been established and the objective is to make within-group comparisons, then standardized coefficients should be used.

Using standardized coefficients often makes it easier to interpret the results, since all the coefficients are on a common metric and not influenced by the actual scale used to measure the variable. Further, standardized coefficients make possible emic comparisons, since the individual regression coefficients have been adjusted to account for within-sample variability. It is important to point out that this is a within-sample adjustment and uses the same metric within a sample, but not across samples.

Use of unstandardized regression coefficients allows for etic comparisons, if construct equivalence has been established. Further, the unstandardized coefficient can provide a more comparable measure across samples since they have not been adjusted for within-group variability. Also, unstandardized coefficients are more likely to be structurally invariant; that is, they are more likely to be the same from sample to sample within a country and hence provide a better basis for comparison. For a more complete discussion of the issues and an example see Singh (1995).

Another option that can be useful in multicountry research is to conduct the regression so that the resulting coefficients are elasticities. Elasticities can be computed by expressing the dependent and independent variables as percent change. Alternatively, as the example in Chapter 4 from Rao and Steckel (1998) illustrates, the variables can be transformed into logarithms. Using the logarithms of the variables will also result in estimates of elasticities. The regression coefficients are then interpreted as the percentage change in the dependent variable that would result from a 1% change in an independent variable. For example, regressions could be run in two or more different countries on the relationship between sales and advertising expenditures. The regression coefficients for advertising expenditures, computed as an elasticity, would provide an indication of the likely effect of increasing or decreasing advertising spending on sales in each of the countries. A 1% increase in advertising might result in a predicted sales increase of 0.4%, while a 1% increase in another country might result in a 1.6% increase in sales. With limited funds, the manager would be inclined to allocate more money for advertising in the second country.

## Using Regression in Multicountry Research

When regression analysis is used in international marketing research, it can be employed to address issues related to the differences in the level of variables between countries or issues related to structure or interrelation of variables. When used to look at level issues, hypotheses are tested by examining whether the intercept of a regression equation is the same across different countries. Regression can also be used to examine structure issues as well. In evaluating structure issues, a pan-country regression should be run first using data from all countries. As a second step, a dummy variable is added to the regression for each country. The second regression includes the country dummies, as well as an interaction term for the dummy variable interacting with the independent variable. If the intercept and the regression weights are similar across all countries, then it can be concluded that the relationship holds not only within a country, but also across countries (Van de Vijver and Leung, 1997).

In a study that examined the performance of US films in eight foreign markets (Argentina, Austria, Australia, Chile, Germany, Mexico, Spain and the UK) multiple regression analysis was used (Craig *et al.*, 2005). Foreign box-office revenues were predicted based on a country's cultural distance from the US, the number of McDonald's outlets per capita, the language spoken locally (English vs a language other than English) and the film's genre (13 categories coded as dummy variables). Per capita income was used as a control variable. Cultural distance had a significant effect on the performance of films (see Table 11.5). The coefficient was negative (−0.157) and highly significant. Films released in countries that were culturally closer to the US were more likely to perform well. Conversely, films released in countries that were farther from the US in terms of cultural distance did not perform as well. The coefficient for the number of McDonald's per capita was also significant (0.0399). Countries that exhibit greater acceptance of McDonald's also tend to place a greater value on American

**Table 11.5** Estimated regressions for log per capita box office, all countries and by language group (estimated standard errors in parentheses)[a]

|  | All | All | English | German | Spanish |
|---|---|---|---|---|---|
|  | Nonrandom Parameters | | | | |
| Drama | −0.0933 | −0.0832 | −0.269 | −0.260 | −0.154 |
|  | (0.0919) | (0.0933) | (0.085)** | (0.060)** | (0.176) |
| Romance | 0.177 | 0.171 | 0.362 | 0.770 | −0.118 |
|  | (0.129) | (0.132) | (0.124)** | (0.088)** | (0.229) |
| Comedy | −0.0942 | −0.0927 | 0.0208 | 0.0362 | −0.395 |
|  | (0.0901) | (0.092) | (0.084) | (0.058) | (0.171)** |
| Action | 0.179 | 0.185 | 0.132 | 0.303 | 0.0531 |
|  | (0.089)** | (0.092)** | (0.084) | (0.058)** | (0.171) |
| Fantasy | 0.557 | 0.558 | 0.462 | 0.816 | 0.252 |
|  | (0.133)** | (0.136)** | (0.124)** | (0.085)** | (0.252) |
| Adventure | 0.197 | 0.204 | 0.0896 | 0.0356 | 0.139 |
|  | (0.107)* | (0.109)* | (0.101) | (0.0682) | (0.205) |
| Family | −0.287 | −0.189 | −0.027 | 0.0216 | −0.764 |
|  | (0.101)** | (0.103)** | (0.099) | (0.0701) | (0.189)** |
| Animated | 0.281 | 0.284 | 0.168 | −0.351 | 0.450 |
|  | (0.108)** | (0.110)** | (0.101)* | (0.069)** | (0.208)** |
| Thriller | 0.0827 | 0.081 | −0.132 | −0.202 | 0.172 |
|  | (0.113) | (0.115) | (0.107) | (0.075)** | (0.209) |
| Mystery | 0.685 | 0.679 | 0.256 | 1.176 | 0.803 |
|  | (0.201)** | (0.207)** | (0.185) | (0.145)** | (0.375)** |
| Science Fiction | 0.162 | 0.166 | 0.207 | 0.251 | −0.0478 |
|  | (0.117) | (0.119) | (0.111) | (0.076)** | (0.228) |
| Horror | 0.279 | 0.294 | 0.132 | 0.251 | 0.276 |
|  | (0.108)** | (0.111)** | (0.100) | (0.026)** | (0.206) |

**Table 11.5**    (continued)

|  | All | All | English | German | Spanish |
|---|---|---|---|---|---|
| Macs Per Cap. | 0.0399 (0.0033)** | 0.070 (0.001)** | 0.0274 (0.002)** | 0.0329 (0.0031)** | 0.238 (0.017)** |
| Cultural Distance | −0.157 (0.012)** | | | | |
| English Speaking | 0.140 (0.0593)** | | | | |
| | | Random Parameters | | | |
| | | Constant Term = $\alpha_0 + \alpha_1 \log\text{Income} + \sigma_\alpha w_\alpha$ | | | |
| Intercept $\alpha_0$ | 1.611 (1.366) | 0.845 (1.402) | −2.252 (3.022) | −1.715 (0.419)** | −1.211 (0.761) |
| Income $\alpha_1$ | −0.386 (0.169)** | −0.392 (0.174)** | 0.181 (0.419) | 0.0291 (0.0521) | −0.249 (0.093)** |
| Std. Dev. $\sigma_\alpha$ | 0.172 (0.013)** | 0.158 (0.014)** | 0.035 (0.013)** | 0.509 (0.011)** | 0.121 (0.026)** |
| | | Coefficient on PCUSBox = $\beta_0 + \beta_1 \log\text{Income} + \sigma_\beta w_\beta$ | | | |
| Intercept $\beta_0$ | 4.226 (0.967)** | 4.054 (0.995)** | 3.328 (1.890) | 3.497 (0.301)** | 1.439 (0.526) |
| Income $\beta_1$ | −0.384 (0.121)** | −0.363 (0.124)** | −0.286 (0.263) | −0.279 (0.037)** | −0.047 (0.066) |
| Std. Dev. $\sigma_\beta$ | 0.406 (0.011)** | 0.403 (0.011)** | 0.445 (0.009)** | 0.653 (0.009)** | 0.368 (0.019)** |
| | | Regression Disturbance Standard Deviation | | | |
| Std. Dev. $\sigma$ | 0.940 (0.0075)** | 0.967 (0.008)** | 0.454 (0.008)** | 0.319 (0.006)** | 1.178 (0.012)** |
| Log L | −3042.035 | −3094.537 | −526.765 | −510.2834 | −1680.854 |
| Sample | 2198 | 2198 | 597 | 559 | 1042 |

[a] * (**) Indicates significant at 95% (99%) significance level.

*Source*: Craig *et al.*, 2005.

films. In this case it was important to control for a country's per capita income so that a greater number of McDonald's restaurants did not simply indicate a higher level of economic development. The genre of the film also had an impact on its performance, with action, fantasy, adventure, animated and horror doing better and family films doing worse. Overall the variables used in the regression explained 58% of the variance in performance of US films in foreign markets.

Multiple regression can also be conducted on data pooled across countries. Each country is then entered as a dummy variable (0,1). If the effect of gender and age on soft drink consumption were to be compared across four countries, a single multiple regression could be run. Soft drink consumption data in the four countries would be the dependent variable; the data on gender and age in each country the independent variables; and the four countries represented by three dummy variables. This would enable examination of whether there were differences between countries; that is, whether the dummy variables were significant. Alternatively, separate models can be estimated for each country and the different equations compared (see Grein *et al.* (2001) for an example).

## Hierarchical Linear Modeling

Hierarchical linear modeling (HLM) is a relatively new technique that is ideally suited to handling the type of multilevel data encountered in international marketing research (Bryk and Raudenbush, 1992). The principal advantage of the technique is that it allows for the simultaneous estimation of the relationships of variables at multiple levels. In doing so it allows for the testing of hypotheses on variables measured at the country level and an assessment of how these variables affect relations at the individual or within-country level. More importantly, the use of HLM helps resolve some of the problems inherent in using both country-level and individual-level variables in the same study.

Use of HLM deals with the problems of dependency, random effects, hierarchical nesting and cross-level interactions (Hox and Kreft, 1994). The problem of dependency discussed earlier in this chapter with respect to multiple t-test and familywise error rates can be dealt with through HLM, as well as other multivariate techniques. HLM allows specification of a multilevel analysis model that incorporates random effects. An important feature is that it can handle unequal sample sizes as well as different time periods for repeated measures. Also, HLM allows for the effect of cross-level interactions to be estimated directly. This is particularly important where there are hypotheses about how country-level variables interact with individual-level variables.

HLM was applied in a multicountry setting by Steenkamp *et al.* (1999). Data for the study were collected from over 3000 consumers in 11 different European countries. In addition to individual-level data on variables such as attitude toward the past, consumer ethnocentrism and self-enhancement, the researchers used three measures of national culture (individualism, uncertainty avoidance and masculinity). In the analysis they assessed the impact of four individual-level variables and the three national culture-level variables on consumer innovativeness. The analysis also incorporated three interaction terms as well as three covariates (Table 11.6). Both individual-level variables and national culture-level variables were found to be significant, indicating that variables at both levels influence the degree of consumer innovativeness. The individual-level variables explained 12% of the variance while the country-level variables explained 56% of the variance. Further, the interaction between two of the national culture variables with the individual variables was significant.

Fu *et al.* (2004) used HLM to assess the impact of societal and individual beliefs on the effectiveness of different managerial influence strategies in 12 different countries. The four individual beliefs – social cynicism, reward for application, religiosity and fate control – predicted respondents' perceived effectiveness of the three different influence strategies (persuasive, assertive or relationship based). The measures of national culture were found to moderate the strength of the relationship between individual beliefs and the perceived effectiveness of the influence strategies.

# Multiple Discriminant Analysis

Discriminant analysis is similar in principle to regression except that the dependent variable is categorical rather than continuous. Discriminant analysis attempts to predict group membership based on a number of independent variables. It also indicates which variables are significant in discriminating between groups. It might, for example, be used to predict the purchase of private versus manufacturer brands, based on variables such as age, income, price sensitivity or purchase volume. The reader is referred to Hair *et al.* (1998) and Lattin *et al.* (2003) for more detailed discussion of the underlying assumptions and statistical formulation.

In international marketing research, discriminant analysis can be used to identify which variables are significantly different between two or more national samples. Each national sample is thus treated as a categorical variable or group, and differences in relevant independent variables examined. Similarly, it can be applied to test for differences between subgroups or segments within a

**Table 11.6** Effects on consumer innovativeness

| Independent variables | Unstandardized coefficient | Relative effect size |
|---|---|---|
| Intercept ($\gamma_{00}$) | 2.6975* | |
| | | |
| Main effects: individual level | | |
| Resultant conservation ($\gamma_{10}$) | −0.838[a] | 0.114 |
| Resultant self-enhancement ($\gamma_{20}$) | −0.0100 | 0.031 |
| Consumer ethnocentrism ($\gamma_{30}$) | −0.1789[a] | 0.122 |
| Attitude toward the past ($\gamma_{40}$) | −0.1210[a] | 0.114 |
| | | |
| Main effects: national culture level | | |
| Individualism ($\gamma_{01}$) | 0.0073[a] | 0.100 |
| Uncertainty avoidance ($\gamma_{02}$) | −0.0074[a] | 0.101 |
| Masculinity ($\gamma_{03}$) | 0.0067[b] | 0.075 |
| | | |
| Cross-level interactions | | |
| Uncertainty avoidance × Res. conservation ($\gamma_{11}$) | −0.0013[b] | 0.069 |
| Masculinity × Res. self-enhancement ($\gamma_{21}$) | 0.0009 | 0.042 |
| Individualism × Consumer ethnocentrism ($\gamma_{31}$) | 0.0022[b] | 0.068 |
| | | |
| Covariates | | |
| Income (×100 ECU) ($\gamma_{50}$) | −0.0011 | 0.028 |
| Age ($\gamma_{60}$) | −0.0060[a] | 0.116 |
| Level of education ($\gamma_{70}$) | −0.0094 | 0.020 |
| | | |
| Explained variance (%) | | |
| Individual-level | 12.3 | |
| Country-level | 56.2 | |

*Note*: Test of significance is based on one-tailed test.
[a] $P < 0.01$. [b] $P < 0.05$.
*Source*: Steenkamp *et al.*, 1999.

country, and the results compared across countries. Husted *et al.* (1996) used discriminant analysis to test whether Mexican, Spanish and US MBAs differed in their moral reasoning, as indicated by responses to the Inventory of Questionable Practice and the Defining Issues Test (DIT). Discriminant analysis was used to determine whether the responses differed between pairs of countries. Only the MBAs from the US and Mexico were found to be different and only the DIT test discriminated between the two groups.

# Conjoint Analysis

Conjoint analysis is a technique that allows the researcher to determine how individuals value different components of a product or service offering. It assumes that an individual's overall evaluation or judgment of an object or product can be broken down into part-worth judgments about different product or object attributes. The analysis provides estimates of the value or utility of different attributes and the different levels of an attribute. Collection of data for conjoint analysis involves obtaining a number of overall evaluations of different combinations of levels on the different attributes. In a single-country study, consumers would be presented with a number of multi-attribute profiles and asked to evaluate each profile. Depending on the number of profiles, they would be asked either to rank order or to rate each of the profiles. These evaluations are then decomposed to assess the utilities assigned to different levels of attributes. This is discussed in detail in Green and Wind (1973). (See also Green and Wind, 1975; Green and Srinivasan, 1978, 1990.)

In multicountry research, conjoint analysis can be used to examine buyers' preferences for, and evaluations of, products or other objects with regard to certain product attributes in different countries. These preferences can then be compared across countries to assess differences and similarities. The following example will help to illustrate the use of conjoint analysis in multicountry research. Consider the situation facing a Japanese manufacturer of medical imaging equipment. The company is developing the next generation of medical imaging equipment intended for use in hospitals throughout the world. To determine the best design features for the new device, a conjoint analysis study was planned for the US that would subsequently be modified for other countries. The study focused on determining the 'optimal level' of five product attributes: (1) *image quality*, six times better than industry standard, three times better than industry standard and equivalent to industry standard; (2) *length of time required to produce an image*, 1 s, 5 s and 10 s; (3) *color image versus black-and-white image*; (4) *cost*, $100 000, $300 000 and $500 000; and (5) *manufacturer*,

GE, Siemens and Toshiba. The levels of each attribute would be combined into the appropriate number of full profiles. For example, profile 1 might be: image quality, three times better than industry standard; length of time to produce an image, 5 s; color image; cost, $300 000; and manufacturer, Siemens. The last attribute is not a product design element, but provides some indication of whether there are differences in the perceptions of different manufacturers. The different medical specialties that use medical imaging equipment might value different attributes differently and there are at least two different constituencies for the study, physicians and hospital administrators. Not surprisingly, one would expect hospital administrators to be more concerned about the cost of the equipment than would physicians.

In applying the basic study beyond the US, one would first have to express the cost in local currency units. One would also have to calibrate the quality of image attribute in terms of the prevailing industry standard in that country. This would be less of a problem in Western Europe but more of a problem in some of the developing countries where the current standard is very low. Alternatively, it might be possible to express the image quality in terms of dots per square inch or pixels per square centimeter. However, the researcher would have to make certain that the more technical expression of image quality is understood by everyone who is filling out the questionnaire.

In each country that the study was conducted, the company would have two sets of utilities for the five different design features, one for physicians and one for administrators. If the study were conducted in 20 different countries, this would result in 40 different sets. The company is then faced with sorting through all 40 to find groups of countries that value similar design elements. This is used as input into the final design of the imaging device to make it appeal to the broadest possible audiences.

Conjoint analysis was used in a study conducted in Nigeria to examine the effect of where a product was manufactured on consumers' perceptions of the product and their likelihood of purchase (Okechuku and Onyemah, 1999). The central thrust of the study was to determine the effect that 'Made in Nigeria' had on respondents' perception of a product. Two product categories (cars and televisions) and four different countries (Nigeria, South Korea, Japan and either Germany (cars) or the Netherlands (televisions)) were used in the study. Sixteen conjoint profiles were developed for each product based on five different attributes. A main-effects only orthogonal design was created from the $4 \times 4 \times 3 \times 2 \times 2$ overall full factorial design. Data were gathered from respondents in nine major Nigerian cities. Rural populations were not included as they have much lower incomes and would be unlikely to purchase either televisions or cars. The final sample of 1721 had an average income of almost twice the Nigerian average, which was appropriate as these individuals were much more likely to purchase the products being studied. The key variable, country of manufacture (COM), was found to be more important than price, brand name, reliability, safety (cars) and picture quality (televisions). Figure 11.2 shows the part-worth utilities obtained from the conjoint analysis. For both cars and televisions, respondents exhibited significantly lower preferences for products identified as being manufactured in Nigeria.

In an early study, conjoint analysis was used to assess buyers' perceived needs and preferences for car models in Britain, France, Germany and Sweden (Colvin *et al.*, 1980). A sample of consumers in each country was asked first to evaluate a set of 27 product attributes. This was done pair-wise and enabled identification of a reduced set of alternatives. Respondents were then required to rate a new car model on these attributes at two levels: a 'low' awareness level, where respondents were only shown photographs of the exterior of the car; and a 'high' awareness level, where respondents were

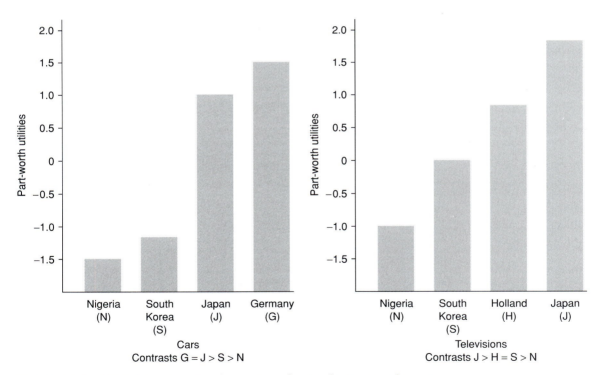

**Figure 11.2**   Nigerian consumers' country of manufacture preference
*Source*: Based on data in Okechuku and Onyemah, 1999.

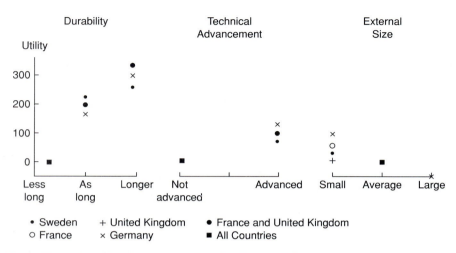

**Figure 11.3** Utility values for four countries for three attributes
Source: Colvin et al., 1980.

given a full photographic and verbal briefing on the interior and exterior appearance, features, performance and so on. Both current and new models were evaluated in this way. From this, utility values for the various attributes in each country were obtained. These showed significant differences between countries in technical advancement and external size, as indicated in Figure 11.3. The utilities obtained for each individual in the conjoint analysis were then used to predict purchase intentions for different model types.

There are a number of commercially available conjoint design and analysis programs that can be used to conduct studies. Packages are available from Sawtooth (www.sawtoothsoftware.com). It offers PC-based ACA (Adaptive Conjoint Analysis) as well as additional software that allows for multimedia presentation of the stimuli. The software allows conjoint data to be collected efficiently and analyzed easily.

# Summary

In multicountry research, as in domestic marketing research, data analysis needs to be carefully planned in advance. The existence of multiple countries in the research greatly complicates the data collection as well as the analysis. In addition to deciding what types of data are necessary for the specific analytical technique, the researcher has to decide on the appropriate unit of analysis.

Since management is often concerned with determining whether strategy can be developed that transcends a single country, it is important to have an analysis plan that can incorporate different levels of aggregation. A robust analysis plan should allow for data analysis within a country as well as across countries. Further, it should allow for analysis of smaller units within a particular country. Coupled with this is the choice of whether the *level* of variables or the *structure* of variables will be compared between two or more countries.

In this chapter, techniques that are commonly used to examine the differences in the level of variables were examined. In commercial research, data are typically cross-tabulated and a chi-square statistic computed. The t-test is also frequently used to determine whether the difference between two country means is significant. Analysis of variance can be used in situations where there is an experimental design or theory to suggest the impact of multiple factors on a dependent variable. Analysis of covariance can be used to control for the effect of some contextual variable on the dependent measure. This can be extended to multivariate analysis of covariance.

Multiple regression is used to examine differences in the level of variables, but it can also be used to assess differences in the structure of variables. A particularly powerful technique is hierarchical linear modeling, which allows country-level variables to be combined with individual-level variables in the same analysis. Multiple discriminant analysis can be used to determine what variables differentiate between countries. Finally, conjoint analysis is particularly well suited to designing products or services that have the potential to meet the needs of buyers in multiple countries.

# References

Bhalla, G. and Lin, L.Y.S. (1987) Cross-cultural Marketing Research: A Discussion of Equivalence Issues and Measurement Strategies. *Psychology and Marketing*, **4**, 275–285.

Bryk, A.S. and Raudenbush, S.W. (1992) *Hierarchical Linear Models: Applications and Data Analysis Methods*. Sage, Thousand Oaks, CA.

Chow, G.C. (1960) Tests of Equality Between Sets of Coefficients in Two Linear Regressions. *Econometrica*, **28**, 591–605.

Churchill, G.A. and Iacobucci, D. (2005) *Marketing Research: Methodological Foundations*, 9th edition. South-Western, Cincinnati, OH.

Cohen, J. and Cohen, P. (1983) *Applied Multiple Regression/Correlation Analysis for the Behavioral Sciences*, 2nd edition. Erlbaum Associates, Hillsdale, NJ.

Colvin, M., Heeler, R. and Thorpe, J. (1980) Developing International Advertising Strategy. *Journal of Marketing*, **44**, 73–79.

Craig, C.S., Greene, W.H. and Douglas, S.P. (2005) Culture Matters: Consumer Acceptance of US Films in Foreign Markets. Stern School of Business, working paper.

Davis, H.L. (1976) Decision Making with the Household. *Journal of Consumer Research*, **2**, 241–260.

Dinardo, J., Johnston, J. and Johnston, J. (1996) *Econometric Methods*, 4th edition. McGraw-Hill, New York.

Douglas, S.P. (1980) Examining the Impact of Sampling Characteristics in Multi-country Survey Research. *Proceedings of 9th Annual Meeting of European Academy for Advanced Research in Marketing*, Edinburgh.

Douglas, S.P. and Craig, C.S. (1983) Examining Performance of US Multinationals in Foreign Markets. *Journal of International Business Studies*, Winter, 51–62.

Douglas, S.P. and Craig, C.S. (1997) The Changing Dynamic of Consumer Behavior: Implications for Cross-cultural Research. *International Journal of Research Marketing*, **14**, 379–395.

Fisher, F.M. (1970) Tests of Equality between Sets of Coefficients in Two Linear Regressions: An Expository Note. *Econometrica*, **38**, 361–366.

Fu, P.P. *et al.* (2004) The Impact of Societal Cultural Values and Individual Social Beliefs on the Perceptual Effectiveness of Managerial Influence Strategies: A Meso Approach. *Journal of International Business Studies*, **35**, 284–305.

Gibson, C.B. (1995) An Investigation of Gender Differences in Leadership across Four Countries. *Journal of International Business Studies*, **26**, 255–279.

Gilly, M.C. (1988) Sex Roles in Advertising: A Comparison of Television Advertisements in Australia, Mexico, and the United States. *Journal of Marketing*, 52, 75–85.

Green, P.E. and Srinivasan, V. (1978) Conjoint Analysis in Consumer Research: Issues and Outlook. *Journal of Consumer Research*, 5, 102–123.

Green, P.E. and Srinivasan, V. (1990) Conjoint Analysis in Marketing: New Developments with Implications for Research and Practice. *Journal of Marketing*, 54, 3–19.

Green, P.E. and Wind, Y. (1973) *Multiattribute Decisions in Marketing: A Measurement Approach*. Dryden Press, Hinsdale, IL.

Green, P.E. and Wind, Y. (1975) New Way to Measure Consumers' Judgments. *Harvard Business Review*, 53, 107–117.

Green, P.E., Tull, D.S. and Albaum, G. (1988) *Research for Marketing Decisions*, 5th edition. Prentice-Hall, Englewood Cliffs, NJ.

Greene, W.H. (2003) *Econometric Analysis*, 5th edition. Prentice Hall, Upper Saddle River, NJ.

Grein, A.F., Craig, C.S. and Takada H. (2001) Integration and Responsiveness: Marketing Strategies of Japanese and European Automobile Manufacturers. *Journal of International Marketing*, 9, 19–50.

Hair, J.F. Jr, Anderson, R.E., Tatham, R.L. and Black, W.C. (1998) *Multivariate Data Analysis*, 5th edition. Prentice Hall, Upper Saddle River, NJ.

Hays, W.L. (1994) *Statistics*, 5th edition. Harcourt Brace, Orlando, FL.

Homans, R.E. and Messner, D.J. (1976) On the Use of Multi-variate Analysis of Variance and Covariance in the Analysis of Marketing Experiments. *Proceedings of the American Marketing Association*. American Marketing Association, Chicago.

Hox, J.J. and Kreft, I.G. (1994) Multilevel Analysis Methods. *Sociological Methods and Research*, 22, 283–299.

Hsieh, M.H., Pan, S.L. and Setiono, R. (2004) Product-, Corporate-, and Country-image Dimensions and Purchase Behavior: A Multicountry Analysis. *Journal of the Academy of Marketing Science*, 32, 251–270.

Husted, B.W., Dozier, J.B., McMahon, J.T. and Kattan, M.W. (1996) The Impact of Cross-national Carriers of Business Ethics or Attitudes about Questionable Practices and Form of Moral Reasoning. *Journal of International Business Studies*, 27, 391–411.

Johnson, R.A. and Wichern, D.W. (1998) *Applied Multivariate Statistical Analysis*, 4th edition. Prentice-Hall, Upper Saddle River, NJ.

Kumar, V., Aaker, D.A. and Day, G.S. (2002) *Essentials of Marketing Research*, 2nd Edition. John Wiley & Sons, New York.

Lattin, J., Carroll, J.D. and Green, P.E. (2003) *Analyzing Multivariate Data*. Thompson Learning, Pacific Grove, CA.

Lehmann, D.R., Gupta, S. and Steckel, J.H. (1998) *Marketing Research*. Addison-Wesley Longman, Boston.

Lord, F.M. (1967) A Paradox in the Interpretation of Group Comparisons. *Psychological Bulletin*, 68, 304–305.

Lubatkin, M., Calori, R., Very, P. and Veiga, J.F. (1998) Managing Mergers across Borders: A Two-nation Exploration of a Nationally Bound Administrative Heritage. *Organizational Science*, 9, 670–684.

Morrison, D.F. (1990) *Multivariate Statistical Methods*, 3rd edition. McGraw-Hill, New York.

Okechuku, C. and Onyemah, V. (1999) Nigerian Consumer Attitudes toward Foreign and Domestic Products. *Journal of International Business Studies*, 30, 611–622.

Overall, J.E. and Woodward, J.A. (1977) Common Misconceptions Concerning the Analysis of Covariance. *Multivariate Behavioral Research*, 12, 171–185.

Pieters, R. and Baumgartner, H. (1993) Attitudes toward Advertising of Advertising Practitioners, Homemakers and Students in the Netherlands and Belgium. In Van Raaij, W.F. and Bamossy, G.J. (eds) *European Advances in Consumer Research*, Vol. 1, Association for Consumer Research, Provo, UT, pp. 39–45.

Rao, V.R. and Steckel, J.H. (1998) *Analysis for Strategic Marketing*. Addison-Wesley, Reading, MA.

Siegel, S. and Castellani, N.J. Jr (1988) *Nonparametric Statistics for the Behavioral Sciences*, 2nd edition. McGraw-Hill, New York.

Singh, J. (1995) Measurement Issues in Cross-national Research. *Journal of International Business Studies*, **26**, 597–619.

Snedcore, G.W. and Cochran, W.G. (1989) *Statistical Methods*, 8th edition. Iowa State University Press, Ames, IA.

Steenkamp, J-B.E.M., ter Hofstede, F. and Wedel, M. (1999) A Cross-national Investigation into the Individual and National-cultural Antecedents of Consumer Innovativeness. *Journal of Marketing*, **63**, 55–69.

Tatsuoka, M.M. (1970) *Discriminant Analysis: The Study of Group Differences*. Institute for Personality and Ability Testing, Champaign, IL.

Van de Vijver, F. and Leung, K. (1997) Methods and Data Analysis of Comparative Research. In Berry, J.W., Poortinga, Y.H. and Pandey, J. (eds) *Handbook of Cross-cultural Psychology*, 2nd edition. Allyn and Bacon, Boston.

Winer, B.J. (1991) *Statistical Principles in Experimental Design*, 3rd edition. McGraw-Hill, New York.

# Chapter 12

# ASSESSING DIFFERENCES IN THE STRUCTURE OF VARIABLES

## Introduction

The techniques described in Chapter 11 provide insight into the differences in the level of variables between countries. They allow inferences to be made about whether the value of a particular variable is greater in one country than in another. Certain techniques such as regression analysis also allow inferences to be made about the strength of the relationship and whether it differs between countries. However, the cross-national researcher is often interested in comparing the nature of the relationship among a set of variables across countries. These questions are frequently the most interesting, but also the most complex. Answering these questions allows inferences to be made about the underlying structure of the relationships and whether it is the same between countries.

When only two variables are involved, the simplest way to examine structural issues is to compute the correlation between two variables. However, typically more than two variables are examined at once. This requires the use of multivariate techniques such as cluster analysis, multidimensional scaling, factor analysis, confirmatory factor analysis and structural equation modeling. Also, given the number of variables that are examined at once, it is often difficult to draw a simple inference about differences and similarities and the nature of the overall structure.

In this chapter, the various techniques that can be used to examine structural relationships between countries are discussed. Correlational analysis is covered first, as it establishes the foundation by considering the association between two variables. The multivariate techniques rely on measures of association or similarity and examine a range of variables simultaneously. This has the effect of examining relationships while controlling for the effect of the other variables.

# Correlation Analysis

Sometimes in multicountry research the researcher is interested in the association between two variables and whether this association holds across a number of countries. The researcher might be interested in the correlation between teenage girls' age and expenditures on clothing. The correlation could be positive, suggesting that as girls got older they spent more. Alternatively it could be negative, suggesting that they spent less as they grew older; or not significantly different from zero, indicating that expenditures do not vary as a function of age. Once this relationship is established in each country, it can be compared across countries.

As a first step in analyzing a set of data, the correlation coefficient provides some indication of the strength of association. An advisable first step in any multicountry research study is to calculate an intracountry correlation matrix of all variables to get some idea of the strength of associations within each country. This analysis suggests what variables are redundant or unique. This also helps identify potential problems arising from multicollinearity among variables, if regression analysis is to be conducted subsequently. It is possible to test directly whether two correlation matrices are significantly different from each other using the asymptotic chi-square test (Jennrich, 1970). With more than two countries this approach for testing differences becomes cumbersome. It is also useful to run a pan-country correlation analysis, as this provides an initial indication of the correlations for the combined sample. If there are a sufficient number of countries, then an intercountry analysis can be conducted where the observations are the country means.

Correlation analysis can be used to test hypotheses concerning the strength of associations as well as to examine the pattern of associations. In applying and interpreting correlation coefficients there are some important things to remember. First, a significant correlation between two variables does not mean that there is a causal relation between them. Second, if two variables are correlated, there is still the question of interpreting meaning and directionality. If there is a strong correlation between advertising expenditure and sales one might conclude that advertising was responsible for the sales. Alternatively, if one looks more closely at the way the firm sets advertising expenditures and finds that the spending levels were based on forecasted sales, then in reality the anticipated sales drove the advertising expenditure. The third issue is that another underlying variable(s) may be responsible for the observed relationship. These cautions apply to any use of the correlation coefficient, but can be even more troubling in the international environment. In situations where the researcher is unfamiliar with the research context, there is a tendency to rely on the numbers as a representation of what is actually occurring, rather than to probe more deeply for alternative explanations.

When using correlation analysis it is important to conduct both intracountry analysis and pan-country analysis. Each type of analysis provides a different kind of insight. A good example of the use of correlation analysis in multicountry research is provided by Glick *et al.* (2004). In a major research project, they examined attitudes toward men and gender inequality in 16 countries. They used two different scales, AMI (Ambivalence toward Men Inventory) and the ASI (Ambivalence toward Sexism Inventory). While they examine a number of different variables, only two of the variables from the AMI will be used for illustration, HM (Hostility toward Men) and BM (Benevolence toward Men). When they examined the correlation between HM and BM for the 16 countries, the coefficients were all significant except for one. Correlation coefficients ranged from 0.81 to 0.15 for the male respondents and 0.70 to 0.19 for the female respondents. Interestingly, the mean correlation coefficient was identical, 0.46, for both groups. However, only two of the 32 coefficients were exactly 0.46 and less than a third (nine) fell within ± 0.04 of the average. When correlation coefficients were computed for HM and BM for males and females across the entire sample a different picture emerged. For males the correlation between HM and BM was 0.85 and for female respondents it was 0.75. Both of the correlation coefficients were much higher than the means that were computed based on the within-country correlations.

The type of context can also influence the nature of the relationship between two variables. Suh *et al.* (1998) looked at whether the correlation between life satisfaction and affect was greater for different types of societies. Life satisfaction was operationalized as a 'global cognitive judgment of one's life' while affect balance captured 'relative preponderance of pleasant compared with unpleasant emotional experiences'. Overall, the correlation was 0.46 between life satisfaction and affect, with the range being 0.07 to 0.74. For collectivist societies the correlations ranged around 0.30 or lower, while for many of the individualistic societies they were around 0.60. Based on this, the researchers concluded that individuals' emotional experiences in individualistic societies are more strongly related to life satisfaction than they are in collectivist societies.

One of the problems in applying the correlation coefficient to multicountry research is that differences exist between correlations obtained at the individual level and at the country level. Country-level correlations can be equal to, stronger than or weaker than those obtained at the individual level. Ostroff (1993, p. 569) asserts that the 'failure to consider random error and measurement error can result in erroneous interpretations about the strength of relationships among variables at different levels of the analysis'. She maintains that the issue is not so much whether to aggregate data or treat it at the individual level, but the need to understand the consequences of either. Further, when correlations are calculated at the individual level, they should be used to make inferences about individuals. When correlations are made at country level, inferences should be at the country level. To do otherwise can result in the *ecological fallacy*; that is, incorrectly ascribing country-level characteristics to individuals (Robinson, 1950).

The process of aggregating individuals into larger units can increase the size of the correlation coefficient (Hannan, 1971). As smaller groups such as countries are combined into larger groups such as regions, there is increased heterogeneity. This causes the correlation within the larger aggregate to increase. For example, consider a situation where individuals in one country are asked among other things how much they spent to purchase their automobile. In a country such as Sweden, incomes are relatively similar and car choices are as well, where many of the inhabitants purchase either Volvos or Saabs. Thus, there would be a very weak but positive correlation between income and amount spent to purchase an automobile. If this same study were conducted in four additional European countries (Germany, France, Spain and Italy), there would continue to be positive correlations of various magnitudes. If all the countries were aggregated, this would increase the heterogeneity in income as well as the amount paid for automobiles. This would result in a stronger correlation at the aggregate level than was observed at the individual country level.

Correlation coefficients can provide a useful first look at the data and provide some idea of bivariate relationships. However, relationships are typically much more complex and influenced by many different variables. For that reason it is often desirable to calculate a partial correlation coefficient. This measures the association between two variables after controlling for the effect of one or more variables. In the example of income and amount spent on an automobile, it might be desirable to control for the age of the respondent. Thus, the partial correlation coefficient would represent the association between income and the amount spent on an automobile, while removing the effect of age.

In regression analysis where there is more than one independent variable, the standardized coefficients represent the partial correlation coefficient. In the case of bivariate regression (a dependent variable and one independent variable), the standardized regression coefficient is the same as the correlation coefficient. This is true for the Pearson correlation coefficient, which is the most generally used. Depending on the type of data, a form of the correlation coefficient other than the Pearson correlation may be appropriate. When one of the variables takes on only two values, the point-biserial correlation should be used. When both variables are arranged into dichotomous classes, the tetrachoric correlation should be used, or the polychoric for categorical data with more than two categories. Finally, if one is dealing with ordinal data, then the Spearman rank correlation coefficient is appropriate. For more detail on correlation see Hays (1994) or any other basic statistics book. There are also measures of association that were mentioned in Chapter 11 that can be used when data are cross-tabulated, such as the phi coefficient.

# Means–End Hierarchies

A technique with considerable potential in cross-national research is means–end hierarchies. The technique has been applied primarily in single-country research, but has received some application in multicountry research. The technique focuses on the links between the *means*, which are typically product attributes, and *ends*, which are the consequences and values associated with the attributes. For example, for perfume, attributes might be fragrance, price and image. Specific consequences of using a particular perfume might be prestige, fantasy or comfort. The values connected with the attributes might include romanticism, sense of beauty and self-satisfaction. Typically these relationships are looked at in the context of a single country. When more than one country is examined, the means–end links can be similar or different. The divergence begins to suggest how these relationships vary across countries.

## *Collection of Means–End Data*

Means–end analysis involves a number of different techniques. First, there is the issue of how to collect the data. The basic technique is referred to as *laddering* and is used to elicit the links between attributes, consequences and values. A thorough but time-consuming way to collect means–end data from consumers is through in-depth interviews. A series of questions and in-depth probes are used to determine the links and associations. This method of data collection is, however, extremely cumbersome, as well as onerous to analyze. Consequently, a number of more structured approaches to data collection have been developed that also simplify data analysis. A simpler approach, proposed by Valette-Florence and Rapacchi (1991), is to use card sorting. Subjects are presented with cards that contain product attributes and asked to sort them into three piles, most important, average and not important. From the most important pile, subjects are then asked to select the most important attributes. This process is repeated at both the consequence level and the value level. To allow for the fact that some attributes, values or consequences were not captured in the original list, subjects can write in their own response and include it in the sorting task.

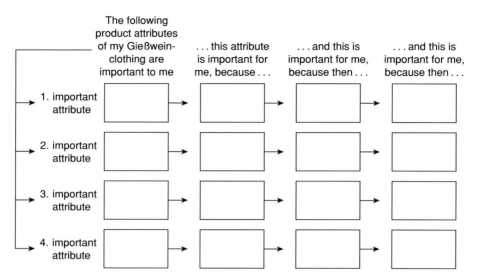

**Figure 12.1**   Paper and pencil version of laddering interview
*Source*: Botschen and Hemetsberger, 1998.

Both these techniques are time consuming and involve one-on-one interaction with respondents. To increase the efficiency of the data collection procedure a pencil and paper approach can be used (Botschen and Hemetsberger, 1998). This greatly reduces the amount of time required to collect laddering data from each respondent and facilitates collection of multicountry data. Respondents are presented with a series of boxes connected by arrows that facilitate the collection of the laddering data (Figure 12.1). They are asked to list up to four attributes that are important and then indicate why a specific attribute is important to them. Up to three reasons can be given for each attribute.

Another pencil and paper approach to measuring means–end chains is the associative pattern technique (APT; ter Hofstede *et al.*, 1998). Respondents are presented with two matrices and instructed to indicate when the intersection of a row and column is relevant. There is an attribute–consequence matrix (AC matrix) that portrays consequences and attributes as the rows and columns, as well as a consequences–value matrix (CV matrix) that has the consequences and values as the rows and columns. For the AC matrix, respondents indicate what consequences an attribute leads to. Similarly, for the CV matrix, respondents indicate the values that result from the consequences. The data collection technique is highly structured and leads to straightforward analysis. A good example of the use of the APT approach is found in ter Hofstede *et al.* (1999), where it was used to collect data from 3000 consumers in 11 EU countries.

A pencil and paper approach is efficient and convenient. Since the respondents are responding freely, it is more driven by their own cognitive structure rather than the researchers' and avoids interviewer bias (Grunert and Grunert, 1995). Further, respondents can stop the laddering process at any time and do not feel any pressure to complete all levels. This can also be a disadvantage, as there is no opportunity to probe more deeply. There is also a problem of how representative the responses to a pencil and paper instrument are when faced with low response rates. With one-on-one depth interviews, if the sample that is recruited is representative of the population, then the means–end hierarchies will reflect those of the overall population. When using a mail survey, there is always the nonresponse problem. For example, Botschen and Hemetsberger (1998) sent out 10 000 questionnaires and received 1081 completed questionnaires back. The relatively low response rate raises the possibility that those who responded are somehow systematically different from those who did not.

## Analysis of Means–End Data

A variety of approaches can be adopted to analyze the laddering data. The first step is to have independent judges content analyze the responses for meaning. In the Botschen and Hemetsberger (1998) study the judges identified 33 meaning categories for a brand of clothing manufactured in Austria. The responses for each of the three countries were constructed into $33 \times 33$ asymmetric implication matrices (Reynolds and Gutman, 1988). Indices of abstractness and centrality were calculated and appropriate cut-off levels determined. The next step was to draw hierarchical value maps for each of the three countries. Figure 12.2 shows the hierarchical value map for Austrian customers. The maps for Italy and Germany were similar in many respects. The product attributes 'natural materials,' 'warmth' and 'appearance' were associated in all three countries. 'Quality' was an association in all three countries. In Austria 'Austrian product' and 'national pride' were also associated with 'quality', while in the other two countries 'quality', was associated with 'durability' and did not have the additional associations.

Another approach is suggested by Valette-Florence *et al.* (1997). They used a card sort approach to collect data in France and Denmark on fish consumption. Responses were pre-coded and the ladders were converted into a sequence of numbers. Data were initially analyzed using nonlinear generalized canonical analysis. This attempts to find the best representation of the original variables. The authors liken it to a categorical discriminant analysis. The results in Figure 12.3 show the various attributes as well as the position of the two countries in the same space.

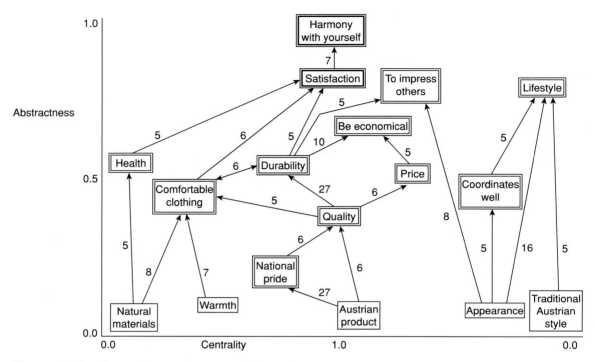

**Figure 12.2** Hierarchical value map of Austrian customers
*Source*: Botschen and Hemetsberger, 1998.

Once the stimuli coordinates are obtained a cluster analysis can be performed to determine the number of groups of means–end solutions. The analysis revealed seven predominant chains of attributes, consequences and values. Three chains applied to over 80% of the respondents, taste (30.4%), variety seeking (26.5%) and lack of experience/health (23.2%). Some of the chains were quite complex with as many as five attributes and four consequences. The freshness/nature chain represented 1.1% of respondents and was relatively straightforward. It had two attributes, 'is fresh' and 'the fish has lived a free, natural life', one consequence, 'enjoy family meal', and one value, 'inner harmony'. The differences between countries were quite interesting. The dominant solution for Denmark, 'taste', fit 52.9% of the respondents, but was appropriate for only 10.4% of the French respondents. The dominant solution for French respondents, 'lack of experience/health' (43.8%), did not show up for the Danish respondents.

Means–end analysis is only beginning to be applied in cross-national research. It has considerable potential to provide insights into the different cognitive structures in different countries. As such, it

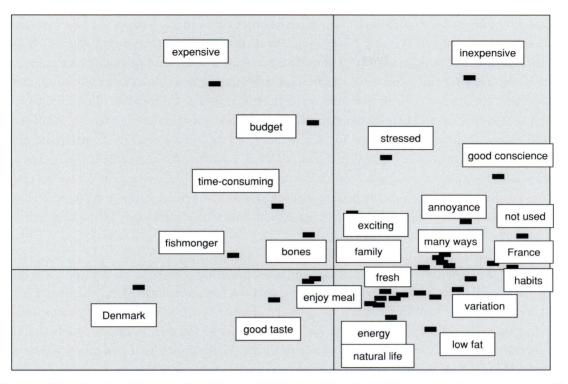

**Figure 12.3**    Nonlinear generalized canonical analysis results: projected centroids (plane 1–2)
*Source*: Valette-Florence *et al.*, 1997, The Haworth Press.

can suggest how a product 'fits' into a particular culture and whether a firm can pursue the same positioning strategy in different countries. It can also suggest segmentation strategies as well as providing insights into marketing mix development. For more detail on means–end analysis, a special issue of the *International Journal of Research in Marketing* on means–end chains is a particularly helpful source, particularly the article by Grunert and Grunert (1995).

# Cluster Analysis

One of the more fundamental issues in examining the structure of variables concerns the similarity and differences between objects or constructs. In international marketing research, clustering proced-ures are most often applied to countries in an attempt to determine those that are similar to each other. Cluster analysis actually refers to a family of related techniques that can be used to group variables, objects or individuals into clusters based on commonalities. Two major types of cluster analysis can be identified: (1) hierarchical; and (2) centroid. Hierarchical clustering starts by linking together the two most similar objects or variables, based on a measure of distance or similarity, the next two most similar and so on, until all variables or objects are in a single cluster (Johnson, 1967). In centroid clustering, objects or variables are divided first into two groups or clusters, such that, overall, a member of a cluster is more similar to a typical group member than to members of another group. Objects and variables are then divided into three, four or as many groupings as are desired, based on the same principle. Cluster analysis can be used in multicountry research to identify different subgroups within countries, and to assess whether these are similar across countries. It can also be and is commonly used to identify groups of countries that appear to be similar in terms of some relevant factors. For a more complete discussion of cluster analysis, see Everitt (1993) and Aldenderfer and Bashfield (1984).

The most critical decision the researcher faces in applying cluster analysis is what variables to select as the basis for the clustering technique. While this decision is often influenced by what variables are available, even within that set there are choices to be made. If clusters of countries are formed based primarily on macroeconomic data such as GDP, exports and so on, then countries with high standards of living such as the US, Japan and many of the Western European countries will cluster together. If the variables chosen reflect population and the land area of countries, then another set of clusters will emerge, with China, India, Russia and the US being grouped together. In both cases the US appears in clusters with 'similar' countries. However, depending on the variables used in these cases, the clustering technique places the US in two dissimilar clusters where the other members of one share little in common with the members of the other.

In addition to selecting the variables on which to base the clustering, there is also the issue of how to express the variables. Consider a situation where one is interested in clustering countries based on GDP. If total GDP is used, then large poor countries will end up being grouped with small rich countries. In this instance it would be better to express GDP on a per capita basis. When only one variable is used, it seems obvious that such an adjustment is desirable. However, when a larger number of variables are used to cluster objects, this may be less evident. A related issue is whether to use the numerical values or to standardize the values. If there is a variable, such as life expectancy, which does not have a very wide range across industrialized countries, then standardizing it will tend to exaggerate the minimal differences between countries. On the other hand, with a variable such as per capita GDP, which varies widely, standardizing it will tend to minimize the differences. In making these decisions about whether to standardize a variable, the important issue is to understand what the implications are and how they affect the conclusions.

One approach to dealing with the measurement issue is to use the correlation between two objects as a measure of similarity. If per capita GDPs of two countries are highly correlated, then the two are considered similar. This expresses everything in common units and is not influenced by the relative magnitudes. A series of correlations would be used as input to capture the range of similarities between the different objects.

Cluster analysis can also be used to group countries into clusters that are similar in terms of a set of characteristics. Typically, these clusters are based on macroeconomic data such as GDP per capita, degree of urbanization, population, imports and exports, percentage of the population in agriculture, level of literacy, energy consumption and so on. This assumes that these factors imply similar marketing environments and, hence, lead to meaningful groupings for planning international marketing strategies.

Countries can also be clustered based on behavioral and preference data. Cluster analysis has, for example, been used to group regions based on food habits and patterns (Askegaard and Madsen, 1995). In a pan-European lifestyle survey of 20 000 respondents in 16 European countries, respondents were asked 138 questions relating to food preferences and behavior, such as preferences for types of flavors or consistencies, and general ways of cooking, grilled, fried and so on. A factor analysis was used to reduce these questions to 41 latent or underlying factors reflecting general food behavior/attitudes, product-related behavior such as nibbling and drinking habits, and health-related habits. Rather than treat the countries as the units of analysis, the researchers divided the countries into 79 regions. These regions were then clustered based on these 41 factors. This resulted in the identification of 12 clusters. Seven of the clusters were nation states, Denmark, Norway, Sweden, Portugal, Spain, Italy and Greece, and five were transnational clusters, including a Germanic cluster consisting of Germany, Austria and Switzerland, the British Isles, the Netherlands and Flanders, France and French-speaking Switzerland, and Brussels, Wallonia and Luxembourg (Figure 12.4).

One of the difficulties in using cluster analysis is the interpretation of the clusters. Typically, once clusters are formed the researcher has to examine the clusters and construct a rationale for the observed clusters. There is also the dilemma of how many clusters to include in the final solution. Often objects will move around as an additional cluster is added to or deleted from the solution.

The example used in Chapter 4 to illustrate demand estimation is also a good example of a sophisticated use of cluster analysis (Helsen *et al.*, 1993). First, the researchers factor analyzed 23 country trait variables, mainly macro-level data such as GDP, telephones, air cargo, life expectancy,

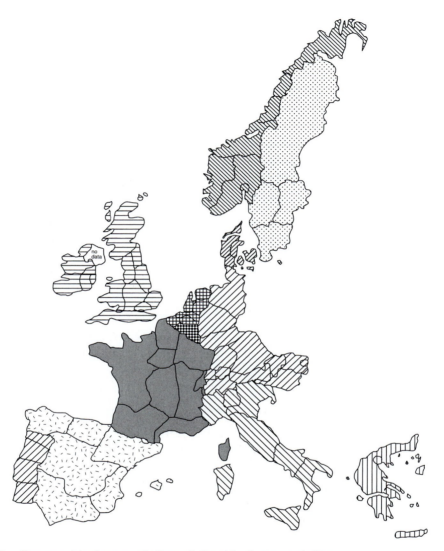

**Figure 12.4** Geographical presentation of the 12-cluster solution
*Source*: Askegaard and Madsen, 1995.

hospitals and so on, for 10 European countries, the US and Japan. Five factors explained 88% of the variance (Table 12.1). The researchers then calculated factor scores for the 12 countries on each factor. The five factors reflected: (1) MOBIL, overall mobility; (2) HEALTH, the country's health situation; (3) TRADE, foreign trade activity; (4) LIFE, standard of living; and (5) COSMO,

**Table 12.1**    Factor loadings of macro-level country characteristics (after Varimax Rotation)

| Item | Factor 1 (MOBIL) | Factor 2 (HEALTH) | Factor 3 (TRADE) | Factor 4 (LIFE) | Factor 5 (COSMO) | Factor 6 |
|---|---|---|---|---|---|---|
| Passengers | .969 | .050 | −.139 | .060 | −.104 | .115 |
| Air Cargo | .943 | .133 | −.192 | −.062 | −.167 | .121 |
| Newspapers | .975 | .025 | −.104 | .113 | −.071 | .036 |
| Population | .880 | .225 | −.330 | −.099 | −.214 | .041 |
| GDP | .187 | .149 | −.142 | .841 | .180 | −.050 |
| Cars | .784 | −.172 | .196 | .355 | .150 | .360 |
| Gas | .904 | −.029 | −.048 | .337 | .035 | .193 |
| Circulation | −.121 | .510 | −.593 | −.118 | −.240 | .059 |
| Phones | .175 | .071 | −.036 | .839 | −.009 | .275 |
| Imports | −.349 | −.014 | .902 | −.160 | .087 | −.031 |
| Exports | −.379 | −.033 | .897 | −.127 | −.045 | −.106 |
| CPI | −.166 | −.655 | −.236 | .258 | −.433 | .424 |
| Life Exp. | −.268 | .716 | −.247 | .287 | −.070 | −.207 |
| Visitors | −.110 | .046 | −.013 | −.028 | .982 | .087 |
| Tourist Exp. | −.401 | −.072 | .330 | .470 | .607 | −.142 |
| Tourist Rec. | −.161 | −.032 | .050 | .011 | .969 | .018 |
| Pol. Stab. | .261 | .888 | .070 | −.066 | −.001 | .193 |
| High Educ. | .910 | −.325 | .058 | .114 | −.060 | −.197 |
| Hospitals | .623 | −.128 | −.147 | −.314 | −.032 | .598 |
| Physicians | −.133 | .677 | −.566 | −.025 | −.028 | .169 |
| Elec. Cons. | .048 | −.347 | −.057 | .761 | −.181 | −.250 |
| Elec. Prod. | .957 | .091 | −.209 | .048 | −.143 | .054 |
| Educ. Gvt. | −.399 | −.415 | .341 | −.164 | −.197 | −.666 |
| Variance Explained | 39.9 | 16.4 | 13.3 | 11.1 | 7.0 | 4.6 |
| Cronbach $\alpha$ | .979 | .752 | .993 | .783 | .899 | |

Source: Helsen et al., 1993.

cosmopolitanism. The factor scores were then used in a standard K-means clustering algorithm (PROC FASTCLUS in SAS). Table 4.2 (p. 114) shows the results of the two- and three-segment solutions. In the two-segment solution, the first consists of most of the European countries, while Japan, Sweden and the US form the second cluster. In the three-segment solution, the US by itself forms segment 3 and Japan and Sweden form a segment with the Netherlands and the UK. Looking at the centroids of each segment, it appears that MOBIL is driving the solution, with HEALTH and COSMO playing a lesser role.

Using factor scores deals with the problem of selecting the appropriate units for the variables. Also, as the authors point out, the use of different variables would result in a different clustering. Specifically, they obtained a different result when they used only macroeconomic variables as opposed to all 23 variables. In this and most applications of clustering techniques, there is the implicit assumption that all the variables have equal weight. More advanced clustering algorithms such as SYNCLUS (DeSarbo *et al.*, 1984) or CONCLUS (Helsen and Green, 1991) allow the assignment of different weights to different variables.

# Multidimensional Scaling

In some instances the researcher is concerned with examining the relationship between objects, based on either perceptions or objective characteristics. Multidimensional scaling allows the researcher to develop a mapping of objects. When used with individuals it assumes that they evaluate objects, such as product concepts or other stimuli, relative to each other, rather than independently. A measure of similarity between each pair of objects examined is developed, based on perceptual or preference data. This measure is then used to generate a mapping, indicating the relative proximity of the various objects or stimuli to each other. The mapping may be two-, three- or *n*-dimensional in character, depending on the number of dimensions that appear to underlie similarity judgments. This is evaluated based on a measure of closeness of fit to the original data each time an additional dimension is added (see Kruskal and Wish, 1978, for a more complete discussion).

When perceptual data are used, respondents are asked to make similarity judgments about objects or other stimuli. In a multicountry setting, perceptions of the same objects will often differ dramatically. This may indicate lack of equivalence between objects or fundamental differences in the way in which things are perceived. In addition to relying on perceptions, respondents also can be asked to indicate their preferences. Preference data can consist of ratings or rankings of objects or stimuli on different attributes, such as price or taste. Judgments can also be made under different scenarios, as for example, 'suitable for the family' or 'when entertaining guests'.

Preference data can then be combined with perceptual data to develop joint-space maps. The perceptual data determine the initial configuration of objects, and the preference data are super-imposed on the mapping. If, for example, PREFMAP is used, the data are shown as vectors from the origin, each representing a specific attribute or scenario. The proximity of an object to a vector (as measured by a line drawn horizontally to the vector) thus indicates its rating on that attribute or scenario. The ideal points of individual subjects or of groups can also be projected on the mapping, indicating the position of the subject's or group's ideal object.

In international marketing research, multidimensional scaling can be used in a variety of ways. As in the case of other multivariate techniques, it can be used to analyze national data or assess similarit-ies and differences across countries. For example, product positioning or concept evaluation studies can be conducted in a number of countries. Consumers in different countries might, for example, be asked to indicate the similarity of different vegetable- or fruit-flavored crisps relative to other snack products such as regular potato chips, fruit, dried fruit mixes, cookies or salty crackers. They might also be asked to rate these on the basis of different attributes such as fattening, nutritious, expensive or liked by the entire family. Joint-space maps of both perception and preferences can be generated for each national sample. Similarities of mappings can then be compared across countries.

Alternatively, analysis can be conducted across countries. The initial perceptual configuration of stimuli is based on data pooled across national samples. This indicates the overall positioning of the products or other stimuli. Preference data are then grouped by country and can be shown as ideal points for each national sample or vector ratings on attributes for each national sample. In the preceding example, an overall perceptual configuration of snack products is developed. Preference ratings for attributes could also be collected for each sample and projected on this mapping. For example, there would be a vector for 'fattening' for French consumers, another for 'fattening' for German consumers and so on.

Multidimensional scaling can also be applied to the types of secondary international data discussed in Chapter 3. In this case mappings of countries can be developed based on similarities in macroeconomic characteristics such as political, economic or sociocultural factors rather than using perceptual data. In studying changes in 16 European countries, Japan and the US over a 28-year period, Craig *et al.* (1992) used multidimensional scaling to examine changes in patterns of

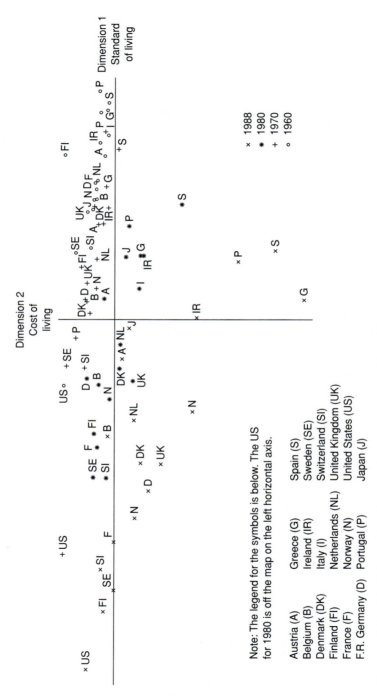

**Figure 12.5** Multidimensional map of European countries, US and Japan

*Source*: adapted from Craig *et al.*, 1992.

similarity among countries over time. Data on 15 variables such as infant mortality, cost of living, per capita income, electricity production, aviation passengers and telephones in use were used to construct a dissimilarities matrix for the 18 countries at four time periods (1960, 1970, 1980, 1988). The dissimilarities matrix was used as input to the ALSCAL multidimensional scaling routine. This analysis resulted in a three-dimensional solution suggesting that the countries are becoming less similar over time, in spite of increased communication and consumer mobility. Figure 12.5 shows the 18 countries for the four time periods on the first two dimensions, standard of living and cost of living. In 1960 and 1970, the countries were relatively close together and in the upper right quadrant. By 1980 and 1988, the pattern had become much more dispersed. The increased dissimilarity evident in the mapping was also confirmed by greater mean dissimilarity across countries over time.

In international research, multidimensional scaling is useful in suggesting how perceptions of products, brands, activities and so on differ between countries. Mappings can be constructed for each country and the results compared. One of the main issues is naming the different dimensions across the different countries and determining whether these are similar. Since the naming process is judgmental, there is often a tendency to 'anchor' on one country and interpret subsequent countries in light of this country. A way to deal with the 'anchoring' problem is to have equally knowledgeable members of the research team label the various dimensions independently. Different maps and solutions can then be compared and the differences interpreted and reconciled. With a limited number of countries, it is feasible to construct combined maps using all the perceptual data, and then construct individual maps for each country. This approach has the advantage of providing a common starting point for the comparison. An added value of multidimensional scaling is that it provides graphical portrayals of objects (for example brands) that can easily be communicated to managers.

# Factor Analysis

Factor analysis is particularly useful in multicountry research in that it allows examination of interrelationships among a set of variables. Essentially, factor analysis groups together variables into factors consisting of intercorrelated variables. While cluster analysis relies on a measure of distance to group objects, factor analysis uses the intercorrelation among variables to develop the factor structure. There are, however, applications of factor analysis that provide results similar to those obtained with cluster analysis. Q-factor analysis shifts the focus from variables to objects and provides groupings of objects, rather than variables.

Exploratory or principal components factor analysis can be used for two basic purposes. It can be used to reduce the number of variables to be analyzed and to ensure that there is no multicollinearity between variables. Alternatively, it can be used to identify underlying relationships or structures within the data. (See Harman (1976) or Gorsuch (1983) for a complete reference on factor analysis.) Various types of factor analysis can be identified. Principal components analysis is the most commonly used form. This identifies factors based on the correlation matrix of variables and forms a number of 'factors' that effectively summarize the interrelationships among the variables. A reduced number of variables, those that load most heavily on the salient factors, is obtained that can be used in subsequent stages of the analysis. In Q-type factor analysis, on the other hand, rather than grouping variables, the original data matrix is transposed and objects are grouped based on variables.

Given a set of data, it is important to determine whether they are appropriate for factor analysis. As a first step the correlation matrix can be subjectively examined to identify groupings of variables that are highly correlated. This begins to suggest that the variables can be grouped into more homogeneous subsets that constitute unique factors. More formally, the Kaiser–Meyer–Olin (KMO; Kaiser, 1970) measure can be used to examine the homogeneity of the variables to be factor analyzed. Kaiser and Rice (1974) suggest that the overall KMO should exceed 0.80, with a value of 0.60 being acceptable. This indicates that the data are suitable for factor analysis.

Often the researcher is interested in comparing the results of a factor analysis of a set of variables in one country with a factor analysis of the same set in another country. There are three ways to determine whether the factor structures are similar: (1) visual and judgmental inspection; (2) target rotation; and (3) confirmatory factor analysis. Visual inspection is the weakest approach and can only begin to suggest whether there is any similarity in the factor structure. Typically, an attempt will be made to see whether the same variables load on the same factors. Unless the factor structures are highly similar in all respects, this will be extremely difficult to determine and different researchers may interpret the same structures differently. A researcher looking for similarity will tend to interpret a complex and ambiguous pattern as being more similar than different. This may involve reaching conclusions on the overall similarity, or focusing on the factors that are most similar and disregarding those that are least similar.

An analytical approach to assessing factor structure similarity suggested by McDonald (1985) is known as target rotation. Given factor analyses in two countries, one country is selected as the 'target' and the other country's factor analysis is rotated to maximize the agreement between the two. Once the rotation has optimized the relationship between the two factor structures, the similarity can be assessed, factor by factor, using Tucker's coefficient of agreement (Van de Vijver and Leung, 1997). The coefficient is similar to a correlation coefficient. Alternatively, the identity coefficient can be used (Zegers and Ten Berge, 1985). Identity coefficient values higher than 0.95 indicate similarity of the factor matrices, while values below 0.90 suggest lack of agreement (Van de Vijver and Leung, 1997). While target rotation is superior to visual inspection, neither is as strong an approach as confirmatory factor analysis. This is discussed in the next section of this chapter.

In the study cited earlier of food preferences and behavior in Europe, factor analysis was used to reduce the number of variables included in subsequent phases of analysis. It can also be used to identify underlying latent factors. For example, in a cross-cultural study of consumer values, the LOV (List of Values) instrument consisting of nine personal value items was administered to students and their parents in five countries, the US, Japan, France, Denmark and Germany (Grunert *et al.*, 1994). The data for both students and parents were pooled across countries and principal components analyses with oblique rotations performed to identify underlying dimensions. Both two- and three-factor solutions were interpretable for the student samples, and a three-factor solution for the parent sample. However, it is important to note that when the authors used confirmatory factor analysis it showed poor goodness of fit in terms of similarity of mean values, variance–covariance, factor loadings and factor structure across countries, suggesting no cultural comparability.

There are three major limitations in the use of exploratory factor analysis in multicountry research. First, by its very nature it is exploratory. There are no *a priori* hypotheses that can be tested and no way to test them if one wanted to. Typically, the researcher begins with a set of variables related to the topic being investigated and uses factor analysis to reduce their number based on the interrelations of variables. The final set of variables arrived at is totally dependent on the nature of the initial larger set. Theoretical constructs may guide formulation and selection of the initial set of variables, but this does not provide a way of 'testing' the theory. Second, while orthogonal rotation of factors is the commonly accepted method of rotation, some researchers apply nonorthogonal methods. A nonorthogonal rotation will tend to provide a unique factor structure that may be difficult to reproduce. The final limitation relates to the difficulty of comparing factor structures between countries, as revealed in the Grunert *et al.* (1994) study. As indicated above, target rotation can be used, but it is subject to some criticism in the literature (Bijnen *et al.*, 1986; Van de Vijver and Poortinga, 1994). The most serious limitation of factor analysis is, however, its atheoretical nature, which makes it unsuitable for theory testing.

# Confirmatory Factor Analysis

In many instances the researcher has sufficient theory to specify relationships and test theory related to differences and similarities across countries. Confirmatory factor analysis is a particularly useful method to test and refine conceptual models across countries. It allows both a test of the overall model and of very specific relationships among variables to be specified and tested. The researcher begins by specifying a theoretically based model that captures the relationships between constructs. Typically, the theory that guides the specification is one that was initially developed in one country. Thus, in most applications confirmatory factor analysis is implicitly used to determine whether relationships are universal. For example, the researcher may be interested in how the construct of 'involvement' influences certain types of purchases in more than one country and how similar this relationship is from one country to another. The constructs used in the research may be single variables or groupings of variables that form a particular construct. The relationships between the various constructs are then expressed as a series of causal relationships that portray the hypo-thesized links between variables.

The focus of confirmatory factor analysis is on the measurement model; that is, developing accurate and reliable measures of constructs. Typical applications include determining the dimensionality of a construct in multiple countries (Netemeyer *et al.*, 1991; Hsieh, 2002); the relationship of one set of constructs to another set in multiple countries (Abe *et al.*, 1996); whether a particular consumer behavior model holds in more than one country (Durvasula *et al.*, 1993); the reliability and validity of constructs across different countries (Keillor *et al.*, 2004); and whether a construct is manifested in the same way in a different country or context (Nijssen and Douglas, 2004). It can also be used to examine measure invariance in cross-national consumer research (see Steenkamp and Baumgartner, 1998).

As indicated earlier, with exploratory factor analysis the researcher relies on the intercorrelation among variables to find groupings of related variables. These groupings of variables are referred to as factors. The analysis is heavily data driven and may suggest how constructs are defined or operationalized, but it cannot be used to test a theory. Confirmatory factor analysis allows the researcher to specify relationships *a priori* and to test them explicitly. Confirmatory factor analysis uses either correlation or covariance matrices as input. The appropriate input data depends on the specific application. When the researcher is interested in the pattern of relationships between constructs, the correlation matrix should be used. The variance–covariance matrix should be used when the constructs' total variance is of interest. The chi-square test and other goodness-of-fit indicators are used to determine whether the same factor solution is appropriate for different samples. Confirmatory factor analysis also allows the researcher to specify a model and test the invariance of different parameters (Marsh and Hocevar, 1985). Once the initial model has been tested, alternative models can be examined to see whether the overall goodness-of-fit measures improve. The technique is also sample-size sensitive. A sample of 150 to 200 is desirable. With much larger samples, relatively small between-group differences become statistically significant. To deal with this problem, Bollen and Long (1993) have developed goodness-of-fit measures that are less sample-size dependent. More information on the technique can be found in Long (1983a), Hair *et al.* (1998) and Lattin *et al.* (2003).

In multicountry research, confirmatory factor analysis typically involves testing the covariance matrix of measures for all countries to see whether they are the same (Van de Vijver and Leung, 1997). If there are differences, then a set of hierarchically nested models are tested while successively increasing the number of equality constraints across countries. LISREL (Jöreskog and Sörbom, 1993) and EQS (Bentler, 1995) are the most commonly used computer packages for confirmatory factor analysis. Hair *et al.* (1998) provide a clear discussion of how to apply confirmatory factor analysis and relate it to LISREL.

# Applications of Confirmatory Factor Analysis

Confirmatory factor analysis has been used in multicountry research to assess whether attitudinal and behavioral models hold across countries. Durvasula *et al.* (1993) examined the cross-national applicability of a model of attitude toward advertising based on data from five countries (New Zealand, Denmark, Greece, the US and India). The purpose was to see whether the relationships among the constructs affecting attitudes toward advertising in general were applicable across countries, or were culturally bound. The model initially conceptualized in the US postulated two indirect and two direct antecedents of attitude toward advertising. Four different models of the relationships between the constructs were tested: (1) the null model, where relationships among observable constructs are set to zero (this also serves as the baseline against which the other models are tested); (2) the original model (Figure 12.6); (3) an alternative model (Figure 12.6), which added paths from both indirect antecedents to the direct antecedents; and (4) a full model, which added paths from net function thoughts and net practice thoughts to attitudes toward advertising in general. The alternative model was found to provide the best fit.

Durvasula *et al.* (1993) followed a number of steps in their analysis of multicountry data. First, the equivalence of the measures and the relationships among the constructs were examined at three

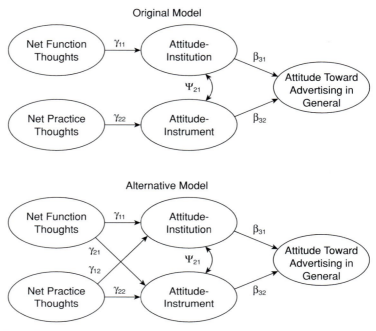

Note: For the purpose of clarity, only the latent constructs are shown here. Three items were used to measure attitude-institution, four items were used to measure attitude-instrument, and three items were used to measure attitude toward advertising in general. Net function and net practice thoughts were measured with single indicators, in which their measurement loadings were fixed to one. The $\Psi_{21}$ curved arrow represents the covariance between attitude-institution and attitude-instrument.

**Figure 12.6**    Models of attitude toward advertising in general

*Source*: Durvasula *et al.*, 1993.

different levels, a national level, a multigroup level and a pooled data level. Analysis at the *national level* examines measures and relationships in each country separately. The next step is *multigroup analysis*, which examines whether patterns of measurement and construct relationships are invariant across countries. Finally, *pooled analysis* is performed. An important element of this analysis is to 'deculture' the data first by standardizing responses within each country before examining whether a common core of relationships exists across countries (Bond, 1988). In general, the pattern of these relationships was found to be invariant across cultures, though some differences were observed in their strength.

Confirmatory factor analysis can also be used to examine theoretical constructs between countries. Abe *et al.* (1996) looked at the self-concept in the context of an interdependent culture (Japan) and an independent culture (US). Three separate scales were administered to Japanese and US subjects: (1) a 23-item self-consciousness scale that measured private and public self-consciousness as well as social anxiety (Fenigstein *et al.*, 1975); (2) a 13-item attention to social comparison information scale (Lennox and Wolfe, 1984); and (3) a 20-item action control scale (Kuhl, 1985). Confirmatory factor analysis was used to examine the reliability, the convergent validity and the uniqueness of each of the components. In addition, the researchers tested 12 hypotheses concerning differences and similarities about how the constructs would operate in the two cultures. For example, the researchers found that Japanese experienced higher levels of social anxiety than Americans, but lower levels of private self-consciousness. In both samples, attention to social comparison information was positively correlated with public self-consciousness and social anxiety.

These applications suggest that confirmatory factor analysis can be a very powerful tool for examining multicountry data, ideally suited for dealing with the complexity of the data. It allows the researcher to specify within-country relationships and at the same time allows assessment of between-country differences. More fundamentally, confirmatory factor analysis can contribute to the development of theoretically sound constructs that enhance understanding of phenomena occurring in more than one country.

## Multitrait Multimethod

Confirmatory factor analysis can also be used to examine multitrait multimethod matrices to determine whether there is convergent and discriminant validity. The multitrait multimethod approach was proposed by Campbell and Fiske (1959). They suggest four criteria for evaluating a matrix that has the correlations of different traits measured by different methods. First, correlations of the same trait measured by different methods should be statistically significant and of sufficient magnitude to warrant further use. This suggests convergent validity. Second, these (convergent) correlations should be greater than those obtained between different traits measured by different methods. Third, the convergent correlations should be greater than the correlation between different traits measured by the same method. Finally, a similar pattern of intercorrelations should be found for the heterotrait–monomethod and the heterotrait–heteromethod components of the matrix.

However, Jackson (1969) has suggested that there are difficulties in applying these criteria in practice. He suggests that there are some practical issues such as the sheer number of correlation coefficients and the fact that it is often difficult to get an unequivocal answer to issues of convergent

**Table 12.2** Goodness of fit statistics to hypothesized trait/method models (after Watkins and Hattie, 1981)

| Models | $x^2$ | df | $x^2$/df |
|---|---|---|---|
| I (2-method factors) | 391.11 | 20 | 19.55 |
| II (1 general, 2-method factors) | 133.36 | 12 | 11.11 |
| III (4 correlated trait factors) | 63.82 | 6 | 10.64 |
| IV (1 general, 4 correlated trait factors) | 20.13 | 2 | 10.06 |
| V (2 method, 4 uncorrelated trait factors) | 166.44 | 12 | 13.87 |
| VI (2 uncorrelated method, 4 correlated trait factors) | 16.23 | 6 | 2.71 |

*Source*: Watkins, 1989.

and discriminant validity. He also points out four much more methodological issues, such as the fact that 'Correlations will fluctuate as a function of the sampling error, as well as of error of measurement and of the respective reliabilities of the variables' (Jackson, 1969, p. 32). As a solution, cross-cultural researchers have suggested applying confirmatory factor analysis to multitrait multimethod matrices to assess method bias (Van de Vijver and Leung, 1997). Watkins (1989) provides an example of the application of confirmatory factor analysis to assess four different traits (self-esteem, extroversion, anxiety and flexibility) measured by two different methods (questionnaire and rating scale). Six different models were tested and the results are shown in Table 12.2. The sixth model treated the two methods as uncorrelated and the four trait factors as correlated. It was the only model that had an acceptable fit level (chi-square/df < 5.00).

While the data used in this study were from a single country, the technique can be easily extended to a multicountry situation. The analysis is first done within country and then across countries. The extent to which both measures and traits vary across countries can then be examined. Using a confirmatory factor approach to multitrait multimethod analysis requires that careful thought be given to how the data are collected. The added level of complexity is that not only may the traits being measured vary between countries, but also the methods used to collect data across countries may not be comparable.

Cadogan *et al.* (1999) used the multitrait multimethod approach to examine the convergent and discriminant validity for a scale that measures export market orientation. They collected data from a sample of US executives and a sample of Dutch executives. Their results, shown in Table 12.3, indicate both convergent and discriminant validity as well as consistency between the two samples.

**Table 12.3** Multitrait-multimethod Matrix

| (a) U.K. Sample | | | | | | | |
|---|---|---|---|---|---|---|---|
| | 1. | 2. | 3. | 4. | 5. | 6. | 7. |
| 1. EMI Gen (V) | | | | | | | |
| 2. EMI Diss (V) | 0.398 | | | | | | |
| 3. EM Resp (V) | 0.365 | 0.443 | | | | | |
| 4. CM (V) | 0.356 | 0.346 | 0.314 | | | | |
| 5. EMI Gen (S) | (0.743) | 0.459 | 0.437 | 0.408 | | | |
| 6. EMI Diss (S) | 0.474 | (0.741) | 0.506 | 0.463 | 0.584 | | |
| 7. EM Resp (S) | 0.554 | 0.559 | (0.726) | 0.415 | 0.683 | 0.685 | |
| 8. CM (S) | 0.412 | 0.494 | 0.447 | (0.705) | 0.477 | 0.589 | 0.615 |

| (b) Dutch Sample | | | | | | | |
|---|---|---|---|---|---|---|---|
| | 1. | 2. | 3. | 4. | 5. | 6. | 7. |
| 1. EMI Gen (V) | | | | | | | |
| 2. EMI Diss (V) | 0.426 | | | | | | |
| 3. EM Resp (V) | 0.342 | 0.278 | | | | | |
| 4. CM (V) | 0.173 | 0.137 | −0.091 | | | | |
| 5. EMI Gen (S) | (0.572) | 0.479 | 0.421 | 0.045 | | | |
| 6. EMI Diss (S) | 0.505 | (0.707) | 0.306 | 0.087 | 0.635 | | |
| 7. EM Resp (S) | 0.336 | 0.436 | (0.631) | 0.437 | 0.621 | 0.585 | |
| 8. CM (S) | 0.376 | 0.530 | 0.447 | (0.717) | 0.491 | 0.581 | 0.599 |

Key:

EMI Gen (V): Validation item – Export market intelligence generation
EMI Diss (V): Validation item – Export market intelligence dissemination
EM Resp (V): Validation item – Export market responsiveness
CM (V)    : Validation item – Coordinating mechanism
EMI Gen (S): Scale measure – Export market intelligence generation
EMI Diss (S): Scale measure – Export market intelligence dissemination
EM Resp (S): Scale measure – Export market responsiveness
CM (S)    : Scale measure – Coordinating mechanism

*Source*: Cadogan *et al.*, 1999.

# Covariance Structure Models

Structural equation modeling provides the cross-national researcher with a means to test conceptual models and refine theories. As such, it represents a powerful tool that can help explain relationships between unobserved variables specified by a theory and observed variables measured by the researcher. It has been used extensively by academic marketing researchers and, due to its power and flexibility, it is being used increasingly to analyze multicountry data. As with confirmatory factor analysis, the most common approach to structural equation modeling is to use LISREL (Jöreskog and Sörbom, 1993) or EQS (Bentler, 1995) to estimate and test the model. For more background on these techniques see Long's (1983b) monograph on the subject, Hair *et al.* (1998) and Lattin *et al.* (2003).

Structural equation models and confirmatory models share a number of elements and use the same statistical packages for estimation. It may be easiest to think of confirmatory factor analysis in terms of traditional factor analytical models where there is an attempt to understand the constructs, their underlying dimensionality and the relationship between constructs. Structural equation models, on the other hand, are used in a manner analogous to path models to examine predictive relationships. While this distinction is somewhat arbitrary, as the two purposes may overlap, it is a useful way to distinguish between the two approaches. The Durvasula *et al.* (1993) and Abe *et al.* (1996) examples mentioned earlier illustrate the use of LISREL for confirmatory factor analysis. The examples discussed here show how LISREL can be used to establish causal paths and estimate dependencies.

Structural equation modeling starts with a theoretically based model. In multicountry research the theory that drives the initial model formulation has frequently been developed in one country and the researcher seeks to answer the question of whether the theory holds in additional countries. The next step is to express the theory in terms of a path diagram that portrays the causal relationships suggested by the theory. The path diagram is then formally structured as a measurement model and a structural model, which incorporate the interdependencies and the dependencies between constructs. The overall goodness of fit of the model is assessed using measures such as the likelihood ratio chi-square, the goodness of fit (GFI) and the root mean square residual (RMSR). Changes in model fit can be assessed by using incremental measures such as the adjusted goodness of fit (AGFI) or the Tucker-Lewis index. Once the fit of the model is deemed acceptable, the researcher is in a position to estimate coefficients and test the fit of competing models. In multicountry research, the challenge is to see whether the same model provides equally good fit across all countries.

# *Use of Covariance Structure Models*

Calantone *et al.* (1996) used confirmatory factor analysis and structural equation modeling to examine factors related to new product success in China and the US with the goal of identifying managerially controllable factors. They gathered data on 142 new product development projects in the US and 470 in China. Baseline data were obtained from an earlier new product development study conducted in Canada on 195 new products (Cooper, 1979). Confirmatory factor analysis was used to refine the number of items in each construct and to ensure the unidimensionality of each construct. Two-group confirmatory factor analysis was then used to assess the measurement models' equivalence across the US and Chinese samples. The model fit well in both countries with nine of the ten hypothesized relationships being significant. In the US model, the path coefficient for product quality was not significantly related to new product success and in the Chinese sample the path coefficient for technical proficiency was not related to product quality. Figure 12.7 shows the path coefficients for the six variables that are related to new product success for the US and China. Only one of the path coefficients was not significantly related to new product success (product quality for the US sample). In the US sample proficiency of technical activities was most important, while in the Chinese sample competitive and market intelligence was the most important.

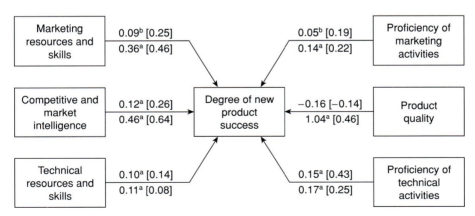

Notes: The top number represents the US sample, the bottom number represents the Chinese sample. Number in brackets is standardized effect, number without brackets is unstandardized effect. [a]$p < 0.01$; [b]$p < 0.05$.

**Figure 12.7**    Total effects on new product successes

*Source*: Calantone, *et al.*, 1996.

Broderick *et al.* (1998) used both confirmatory factor analysis and structural equation modeling to examine how involvement in food purchases affects purchase behavior across the five largest European countries (UK, France, Spain, Germany and Italy). The initial step was to factor analyze a 12-item scale measuring respondents' food involvement. Four factors were identified: (1) normative involvement; (2) situational involvement; (3) enduring involvement; and (4) risk involvement. These four factors were used in a confirmatory factor analysis, first for the pooled sample and then for each national sample. The goodness-of-fit measures suggested that the fit for all six models was acceptable and similar across the six samples. While the factors were the same, the level of involvement with food purchases varied across all five countries, suggesting differences in the level of the variables.

A second step in the research was the construction of a structural equation model to examine the mediating effect of involvement on purchase behavior (Figure 12.8). The four types of involvement

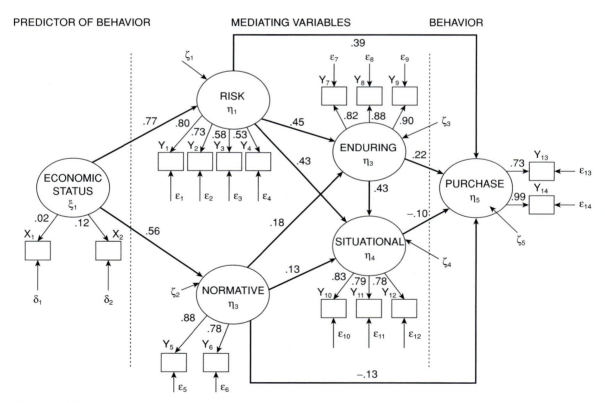

**Figure 12.8** Structural coefficients of path model
*Source:* Broderick *et al.*, 1998.

were shown to mediate the effect of economic status on purchase behavior. Risk involvement had the greatest effect on purchase as well as influence on both enduring and situational involvement. The $R^2$ for the overall impact of the five factors on purchase was 0.66. Further, the findings supported the convergent and discriminant validity of the model and alternative forms of the model did not improve the fit.

The virtue of structural equation modeling is that it allows the researcher to find the best model to explain differences. The initial model should be specified based on theory and testing of the theory can proceed while controlling for other factors. When a 'revised' model provides a better fit, it is necessary to find additional theory that might explain the new relationship or suggest a revision to the theory. As with confirmatory factor analysis, covariance structure modeling is a technique that is ideally suited to multicountry research.

# Advances in Data Analysis

Substantial strides are being made in how data are analyzed. The techniques and examples in this chapter illustrate how multicountry data can be effectively analyzed. In addition, substantial progress is being made along two fronts that are likely to result in even greater understanding and insights into multicountry phenomena. First, more powerful statistical packages have become more accessible and user friendly. Second, new statistical techniques are being applied (or developed) that are well suited to the analysis of multicountry data. These advances mean that once data are collected, there is a greater likelihood that more sophisticated analysis adapted to the complex hierarchical character of multicountry data can be conducted.

Extremely powerful versions of SPSS and SAS are available for the PC. This allows data to be uploaded at remote locations and analyzed on a notebook computer. Results and data files can be transferred via the Internet to a central location for integration with data from other countries. In addition to the standard statistical packages, more sophisticated packages such as Mathematica and Gauss are available. Along with the increases in the statistical power and sophistication that are available on the computer, the ease with which the programs can be used has improved as well.

In addition, there are a number of relatively new statistical techniques that are beginning to be applied to multicountry data. Hierarchical linear modeling, discussed in Chapter 11, has seen limited use in international marketing research. Its chief virtue is that it allows both individual- and country-level variables to be included in the same analysis. Covariance structure modeling has been and will continue to be used in multicountry data analysis. Its main virtue in multicountry research is that it allows for both within-country and between-country effects to be assessed in the same model.

Data warehousing and data mining are two related approaches that have tremendous potential for international marketing research. Data warehousing is a term that refers to the practice of consolidating all relevant data into a unified database that can be used to support decision making (see Banquin and Edelstein, 1996, for more detail). The data acquisition and refinement processes were covered in Chapter 3. The data analysis aspect is referred to as data mining. This covers a variety of techniques that are used to identify patterns in the data. Its use in international markets has been somewhat limited to date, but the potential is enormous. With vast amounts of data on the firm's marketing activities and performance in multiple countries, data mining techniques can identify common patterns across countries. Many of the analytical techniques that can be used in the data mining stage were discussed in Chapters 11 and this chapter. In addition, there are techniques such as CHAID (Chi Square Interaction Detector) and CART (Classification and Regression Trees). Both techniques sequentially partition a set of data so as to maximize the differences on the dependent variable. The analysis can be run once using country as a variable and once without country as a splitting variable to see which solution provides the best fit.

Another data analysis technique that is strongly associated with data mining is neural networks (see Bigus (1996) and Hertz (1991) for more detail). The neural networks approach to data analysis is capable of sifting through large data sets and finding patterns. The most unique feature of neural networks is that they are adaptive. They are able to learn from the initial stages of the analysis and incorporate that learning into the final model. Once a model is arrived at, it can be assessed by how well it predicts or classifies the data. Veiga et al. (2000) used neural network analysis to examine the impact of perceived cultural compatibility on postmerger performance in the UK and France. They were able to predict postmerger performance with 88% accuracy for each sample. Of the 16 items used to make the predictions, five were unique to the French sample, one was unique to the British sample and ten were common. The value of neural network analysis is suggested by the fact that an index constructed from the 16 items was more highly correlated with postmerger performance than one comprised of the 23 original items (0.31 versus 0.23). The potential applications of neural networks in multicountry data analysis are extremely promising. With vast amounts of data being accumulated daily, there is a need for analysis and more importantly incorporation of the results in a decision support system.

# Summary

Assessing the differences in the structural relationship of variables between countries is the most complex type of analysis the researcher can undertake. There are a variety of techniques that are well suited to examining whether the structures are similar between countries. Correlation analysis allows the researcher to determine whether the relationship between two variables is of the same strength and in the same direction in two or more countries. Even in more complex analyses, it is often useful to begin with correlational analysis in order to understand the basic patterns.

Means–end hierarchies provide an approach to structuring data collection as well as using several related techniques to analyze the data. At the core of the method is a desire to understand how means, typically product attributes, relate to ends, typically the consequences and values associated with the attributes.

When the researcher's objective is to group objects or variables, there are three techniques that can be used: (1) cluster analysis; (2) multidimensional scaling; and (3) factor analysis. Cluster analysis can be used to group objects into clusters based on their similarity. Multidimensional scaling is a very effective way to show the interrelationship of different objects along two or more dimensions. The mapping is graphical in nature and effectively conveys how different objects, such as brands or type of products, relate to each other. Factor analysis can be used to group variables together to help identify composite factors comprised of multiple variables. These groupings may suggest constructs that are common or different across countries. Factor analysis can also be used to reduce a large set of variables to a smaller, more manageable set of variables.

One of the limitations of the various clustering techniques is that they cannot be used to test hypotheses. Confirmatory factor analysis is a powerful technique that enables the researcher to explicitly test multicountry hypotheses across countries or contexts. It can also be used to implement multitrait multimethod procedures in multicountry research. A related technique is covariance structure modeling. This examines relationships among variables, with country as one of the explicit factors in the equation. Both techniques make use of LISREL or EQS statistical packages and are quite sophisticated and complex to use. However, both offer considerable potential for providing insights into the complex problems facing international marketing researchers.

# References

Aaker, J.L. (1997) Dimensions of Brand Personality. *Journal of Marketing Research*, **34**, 347–356.

Abe, S., Bagozzi, R.P. and Sadarangani, P. (1996) An Investigation of Construct Validity and Generalizability of the Self Concept: Self Consciousness in Japan and the United States. *Journal of International Consumer Marketing*, **8**, 97–123.

Aldenderfer, M.S. and Bashfield, R.K. (1984) *Cluster Analysis*. Sage, Thousand Oaks, CA.

Askegaard, S. and Madsen, T.K. (1995) Homogeneity and Heterogeneousness in European Food Culture: An Exploratory Analysis, EMAC Conference, pp. 25–46.

Banquin, R. and Edelstein, H. (eds) (1996) *Planning and Designing the Data Warehouse*. Prentice Hall, Upper Saddle River, NJ.

Bentler, P.M. (1995) *EQS Structural Equation Program Manual*. Multivariate Software, Englewood Cliffs, NJ.

Bigus, J. (1996) *Data Mining with Neural Networks: Solving Business Problems – From Application Development to Decision Support*. McGraw-Hill, New York.

Bijnen, E.J., Van der Net, T.Z. and Poortinga, Y. (1986) On Cross-cultural Comparative Studies with the Eysenck Personality Questionnaire. *Journal of Cross-cultural Psychology*, **17**, 3–16.

Bollen, K.J. and Long, J.S. (eds) (1993) *Testing Structural Equation Models*. Sage, Newbury Park, CA.

Bond, M.H. (1988) Finding Universal Dimensions of Individual Variation in Multicultural Studies of Values: The Rokeach and Chinese Value Surveys. *Journal of Personality and Social Psychology*, **55**, 1009–1015.

Botschen, G. and Hemetsberger, A. (1998) Diagnosing Means–End Structures to Determine the Degree of Potential Marketing Program Standardization. *Journal of Business Research*, **42**, 151–159.

Broderick, A.J., Greenley, G. and Mueller, R.D. (1998) Utilising Consumer Involvement for International Decision-making in the Food Retail Market. In Andersson, P. (ed.) *Proceedings of the 27th EMAC Conference, Track 2 International Marketing*, Stockholm, May, pp. 481–500.

Cadogan, J.W., Diamantopoulos, A. and Pahud de Mortanges, C. (1999) A Measure of Export Market Orientation: Scale Development and Cross-cultural Validation. *Journal of International Business Studies*, 30(4), 689–707.

Calantone, R.J., Schmidt, J.B. and Song, X.M. (1996) Controllable Factors of New Product Success: A Cross-national Comparison. *Marketing Science*, 15, 341–358.

Campbell, D.T. and Fiske, D.W. (1959) Convergent and Discriminant Validation by the Multitrait-Multimethod Matrix. *Psychological Bulletin*, 56, 81–105.

Cooper, R.G. (1979) Identifying Industrial New Product Success, Project NewProd. *Industrial Marketing Management*, 8(2), 124–135.

Craig, C.S., Douglas, S.P. and Grein, A. (1992) Patterns of Convergence and Divergence Among Industrialized Nations: 1960–1988. *Journal of International Business Studies*, 23, 773–787.

DeSarbo, W.S., Carroll, J.D., Clark, L. and Green, P.E. (1984) Synthesized Clustering: A Method for Amalgamating Alternative Clustering Bases with Differential Weighting of Variables. *Psychometrica*, 49, 59–78.

Durvasula, S., Andrews, J.C., Lysonski, S. and Netemeyer, R. (1993) Assessing the Cross-national Applicability of Consumer Behavior Models: A Model of Attitude Toward Advertising in General. *Journal of Consumer Research*, 19, 626–636.

Everitt, B.S. (1993) *Cluster Analysis*, 3rd edition. John Wiley & Sons Inc., New York.

Fenigstein, A., Scheier, M.F. and Buss, A.H. (1975) Public and Private Self-consciousness: Assessment and Theory. *Journal of Consulting and Clinical Psychology*, 43, 522–527.

Glick, P., Fiske, S.T., Masser, B. *et al.* (2004) Bad but Bold: Ambivalent Attitudes Toward Men Predict Gender Inequality in 16 Nations. *Journal of Personality and Social Psychology*, 86(5), 713–728.

Gorsuch, R.L. (1983) *Factor Analysis*, 2nd edition. Erlbaum, Hillsdale, NJ.

Green, P.E. (1978) *Analyzing Multivariate Data*. Dryden Press, Hinsdale, IL.

Grunert, K.G. and Grunert, S.C. (1995) Measuring Subjective Meaning Structures by the Laddering Method: Theoretical Considerations and Methodological Problems. *International Journal of Research in Marketing*, **12**, 205–225.

Grunert, S.C., Grunert, K.G. and Kristensen, K. (1994) On a Method for Estimating the Cross-cultural Validity of Measurement Instruments: The Case of Measuring Consumer Values by the List of Values LOV. Working Papers in Marketing, No. 2 July, Odense Universitet.

Hair, J.F. Jr, Anderson, R.E., Tatham, R.L. and Black, W.C. (1998) *Multivariate Data Analysis*, 5th edition. Prentice Hall, Upper Saddle River, NJ.

Hannan, M.T. (1971) *Aggregation and Disaggregation in Sociology*. Lexington Books, Lexington, MA.

Harman, H.H. (1976) *Modern Factor Analysis*, 3rd edition. University of Chicago Press, Chicago.

Hays, W.L. (1994) *Statistics*, 5th edition. Harcourt Brace, Orlando, FL.

Helsen, K. and Green, P.E. (1991) A Computational Study of Replicated Clustering with Application in Market Segmentation. *Decision Science*, **22**, 1124–1141.

Helsen, K., Jedidi, K. and DeSarbo, W.S. (1993) A New Approach to Country Segmentation Utilizing Multinational Diffusion Patterns. *Journal of Marketing*, **57**, 60–71.

Hertz, J. (1991) *Introduction to the Theory of Neural Computing*. Addison-Wesley, Reading, MA.

Hsieh, M.H. (2002) Identifying Brand Image Dimensionality and Measuring the Degree of Brand Globalization: A Cross-national Study. *Journal of International Marketing*, **10**, 46–67.

Jackson, D.N. (1969) Multimethod Factor Analysis in the Evaluation of Convergent and Discriminant Validity. *Psychological Bulletin*, **72**, 30–49.

Jennrich, R.I. (1970) An Asymptotic Chi-square Test for the Equality of Two Correlation Matrices. *Journal of the American Statistical Association*, **65**, 904–912.

Johnson, S.C. (1967) Hierarchical Clustering Schemes. *Psychometrika*, **32**, 241–254.

Jöreskog, K.G. and Sörbom, D. (1993) *LISREL 8*. Scientific Software International, Chicago.

Kaiser, H.F. (1970) A Second Generation Little Jiffy. *Psychometrika*, **35**, 401–415.

Kaiser, H.F. and Rice, J. (1974) Little Jiffy Mark IV. *Education and Psychological Measurement*, **34**, 111–117.

Keillor, B.D., Hult, T.M. and Kandemir, D. (2004) A Study of the Service Encounter in Eight Countries. *Journal of International Marketing*, **12**, 9–35.

Kruskal, J.B. and Wish, M. (1978) *Multidimensional Scaling*. Sage, Beverly Hills, CA.

Kuhl, J. (1985) Volitional Mediators of Cognition–Behavior Consistency: Self-regulatory Processes and Action Versus State Orientation. In Kuhl, J. and Beckmann, J. (eds) *Action Control: From Cognition to Behavior*. Springer, New York, pp. 101–128.

Lattin, J., Carroll, J.D. and Green, P.E. (2003) *Analyzing Multivariate Data*. Thompson Learning, Pacific Grove, CA.

Lennox, R.D. and Wolfe, R.N. (1984) Revision of the Self-monitoring Scale. *Journal of Personality and Social Psychology*, **46**, 1349–1369.

Long, J.S. (1983a) *Confirmatory Factor Analysis*. Sage, Beverly Hills, CA.

Long, J.S. (1983b) *Covariance Structure Models: An Introduction to LISREL*. Sage, Beverly Hills, CA.

Marsh, H.W. and Hocevar, D. (1985) Application of Confirmatory Factor Analysis to the Study of Self-concept: First- and Higher Order Factor Models and Their Invariance across Groups. *Psychological Bulletin*, **97**, 562–582.

McDonald, R.P. (1985) *Factor Analysis and Related Methods.* Erlbaum, Hillsdale, NJ.

Netemeyer, R., Durvasula, S. and Lichenstein, D.R. (1991) A Cross-national Assessment of the Reliability and Validity of the CETSCALE. *Journal of Marketing Research*, **28**, 320–327.

Nijssen, E.J. and Douglas, S.P. (2004) Examining the Animosity Model in a Country with a High Level of Foreign Trade. *International Journal of Research in Marketing*, **21**, 23–38.

Ostroff, C. (1993) Comparing Correlations Based on Individual-level and Aggregated Data. *Journal of Applied Psychology*, **78**, 569–582.

Reynolds, T.J. and Gutman, J. (1988) Laddering Theory, Method, Analysis, and Interpretation. *Journal of Advertising Research*, **28**, 11–31.

Robinson, W.S. (1950) Ecological Correlations and the Behavior of Individuals. *American Sociological Review*, **15**, 351–357.

Steenkamp, J-B.E.M. and Baumgartner, H. (1998) Assessing Measurement Invariance in Cross-national Consumer Research. *Journal of Consumer Research*, **25**, 78–90.

Suh, E., Diener, E., Oishi, S. and Triandis, H.C. (1998) The Shifting Basis of Life Satisfaction Judgments across Cultures: Emotions Versus Norms. *Journal of Personality and Social Psychology*, **74**, 482–493.

ter Hofstede, F., Audenaert, A., Steenkamp, J-B.E.M. and Wedel, M. (1998) An Investigation into the Association Pattern Technique as a Qualitative Technique to Measuring Means–End Chains. *International Journal of Research in Marketing*, **15**, 37–50.

ter Hofstede, F., Steenkamp, J-B.E.M. and Wedel, M. (1999) International Market Segmentation Based on Consumer-product Relations. *Journal of Marketing Research*, **36**, 1–17.

Valette-Florence, P. and Rapacchi, B. (1991) A Cross-cultural Means–End Chain Analysis of Perfume Purchases. *Proceedings of the Third Symposium on Cross-cultural Consumer and Business Studies*, pp. 161–173. The Haworth Press, Binghamton, NY.

Valette-Florence, P., Sirieix, L., Grunert, K. and Nielsen, N. (1997) A Comparison of Fish Consumption in Denmark and France: A Means–End Perspective. In Smith, S.M. (ed.) *Sixth Symposium on Cross-cultural Consumer and Business Studies*, 10–13 December, Honolulu, Hawaii, pp. 1–6.

Van de Vijver, F. and Leung, K. (1997) Methods and Data Analysis of Comparative Research. In Berry, J.W., Poortinga, Y.H. and Pandey, J. (eds) *Handbook of Cross-cultural Psychology*, 2nd edition. Allyn and Bacon, Boston, pp. 257–300.

Van de Vijver, F.J.R. and Poortinga, Y.H. (1994) Methodological Issues in Cross-cultural Studies on Parental Rearing Behavior and Psychopathology. In Perris, C., Arrindell, W.A. and Eisemann, M. (eds) *Parental Rearing and Psychopathology*. John Wiley & Sons Ltd., Chichester, pp. 173–197.

Veiga, J.F., Lubatkin, M., Calori, R., Very, P. and Tung, Y.A. (2000) Using Neural Network Analysis to Uncover the Trace Effect of National Culture. *Journal of International Business Studies*, **31**, 223–238.

Watkins, D. (1989) The Role of Confirmatory Factor Analysis in Cross-cultural Research. *International Journal of Psychology*, **24**, 685–702.

Watkins, D. and Hattie, J. (1981) An Investigation of the Construct Validity of Three Recently Developed Personality Instruments: An Application of Confirmatory Multimethod Factor Analysis. *Australian Journal of Psychology*, **33**, 277–284.

Zegers, F.E. and Ten Berge, J.M.F. (1985) A Family of Association Coefficients for Metric Scales. *Psychometrika*, **50**, 17–24.

# Chapter 13

# THE INTERNATIONAL MARKETING INFORMATION SYSTEM

## Introduction

Once research has been conducted, the data collected and analyzed, the next step is to incorporate this information into management decision making. For research to be useful, it must be in a form that is easily understood by managers and accessible to all who could benefit from the findings. This in many respects is one of the most crucial aspects of the research process. All too frequently, research is conducted and a number of conclusions or implications for marketing strategy and tactics drawn, and yet these are not acted on. Management's inaction can be due to many reasons, including alternative interpretations of the results, ambiguity of the findings, internal political considerations or external competitive factors. These are legitimate reasons and there is often not a clear and consistent way to get management to act on the information. In some cases, however, the reason is that the information does not reach the relevant decision makers or is not readily accessible. Typically, when the research is initially conducted this presents less of a problem, as those who commissioned and paid for the research are interested in the results. However, there may be other managers working in different countries who could use the findings. In addition, there may be research studies conducted in the recent past that are relevant to problems currently facing a manager. The solution is to develop an international information system to facilitate dissemination and use of the data.

The Internet is the main force behind dramatic changes in determining who has access to information and how rapidly it can be disseminated within an organization. Firms establish intranets, internal company information systems, which make available required information to decision makers at all levels of the organization and at different locations scattered throughout the world. They provide both internal information linking operations in different parts of the world and also access to external information sources. In addition, elaborate security features are established so that only authorized individuals have access to the information. Even within the organization, information access is restricted to those who 'need to know'.

The growth of company intranets and groupware has radically changed the organizational structure of many large multinationals. The most profound effect is a flattening of organizational structures, a shift toward outsourcing of various functions and networking between organizations. In addition, these developments have increased the firm's capacity to reach and service customers worldwide. Firms can now easily and rapidly identify opportunities and assess customer needs in different parts of the world and supply products and services tailored to those needs. The expansion of 'born global' firms targeting niche markets worldwide has largely been facilitated by the growth of international information systems (Knight and Cavusgil, 2004).

Global information systems make possible improved communication and control, better coordination of operations, and integration of operations on a global scale (Kim and Oh, 2000). The rapid development of the Internet has accelerated the speed with which information can be disseminated throughout the organization, and facilitated the integration of different types of information systems, for example financial, production, sourcing and inbound logistics, distribution and outbound logistics, as well as marketing. The primary focus of this chapter is on the marketing-related portion of the international information system, particularly that related to strategic and international tactical decisions, rather than operational decisions. These latter decisions require an interface and integration with financial and logistical information.

In building international marketing information systems, data from a number of different sources need to be integrated into the system. In the first place, external data from both secondary and primary sources need to be included. As discussed in Chapter 3, secondary data provide information relating to the macro environment in different countries and regions of the world, for example country risk, market size and growth, industry and product market data and in some cases competitor data. As noted earlier, this often provides an important input for strategic decisions relating to market entry and expansion, industry and product market trends, and changes in economic, political and technological factors affecting market conditions. Data from specific research projects, for example attitude and usage studies, new product tests and advertising effectiveness, also need to be included. These types of data are typically collected prior to making tactical marketing decisions, relating, for example, to product extension and positioning, standardization of advertising campaigns, transferability of promotional ideas and other aspects of the marketing mix. Experience with regard to successful new product launches and promotional ideas can also be fed into the system and transmitted from one country or geographical area to another. In addition, data from internal company sources relating to performance in specific countries and product markets will need to be integrated into the system. This provides input on how effective different strategic and marketing decisions have been and how well they have been implemented.

The sheer volume and scope of information available from different countries, product markets and organizational units throughout the world implies that it is critical to structure the international information system, to avoid overload and to make sure that the right information is accessible to managers at different levels. This ranges all the way from information required for making strategic decisions such as whether to enter new markets, or expand within existing markets, to operational decisions relating to production scheduling and sourcing, distribution logistics and so on.

The system should take into consideration that marketing managers are typically under severe time pressures and need integrated, easily accessible and predigested information (Heede *et al.*, 1995). This is particularly important in the context of international information systems, given the volume and range of information available, as well as the uncertainty that characterizes these markets and the rapidity with which they are changing. The design of the system must also take into account how the organization is structured, primarily in terms of the degree of centralization and the extent of dispersion of activities (Gwynne, 2001).

Access to secondary databases and web sites at world, regional, country and product level allows monitoring of emerging market opportunities and potential risks and detection of changes in the environment or events that may have short- or long-run implications for different regions or product markets. Electronic news services may signal events with dramatic impact on specific markets or markets worldwide. Experience developed with product innovation and positioning, and with testing advertising campaigns or promotional tactics in different countries and market environments and in relation to different market segments, needs to be assimilated and transferred from one market to another in order to develop and disseminate 'best practices'. Sales and performance data complement this information and provide specific measures of the effectiveness of different marketing strategies and tactics.

A key role of the information system is to integrate these different types of information and to provide information spanning different geographical markets. It can then be used to aid not only in tactical decisions relating to specific product markets in different countries, but also in strategic decisions relating to allocation of resources across countries and regions of the world. More specifically, the international information system can be used to:

1.  Scan the global environment in order to monitor emerging and changing environmental trends, and to pinpoint developments in one area of the world that may have implications for product markets in other parts of the world, or cataclysmic events that may have a watershed effect on economies worldwide.

2.  Assess how to reallocate resources and effort across different countries, product markets and target markets, in the light of changing market trends and opportunities so as to maximize long-run profitability.

3.  Monitor performance in different countries and product markets, to benchmark performance relative to regional or other comparable markets, and to pinpoint emerging problems and opportunities for future growth.

4.  Transfer experience, ideas, knowledge and know-how from one area of the world and product market to another so as to identify and disseminate best practices worldwide.

In developing an international marketing information system, the first step is to assess management information requirements for strategic planning and decision making. Management's needs in turn guide determination of the relevant components of the system. Next, procedures need to be developed to collect, access and feed data into the system as well as to update information and ensure access to relevant databases. Software to access and analyze information and to enable managers to communicate with each other will also be required. Finally, specific applications and ways in which this information can be utilized in management decision making at different levels of the organization need to be considered in order to ensure its effectiveness. Figure 13.1 provides an overview of the components of the international information system.

# Information Components of the International Marketing System

In building the marketing component of the international information system, information necessary for both strategic and tactical decisions is required. Attention focuses on information likely to be useful primarily in relation to strategic decision making, for example in coordinating information in relation to different countries, making decisions relative to market entry and expansion, and resource allocation across countries. The information is helpful in controlling and evaluating performance in different countries and product markets. In addition, it is important to integrate experience gained from primary research and from new product launches, promotional initiatives and pricing decisions in different countries, since this can aid in short-term tactical decisions within

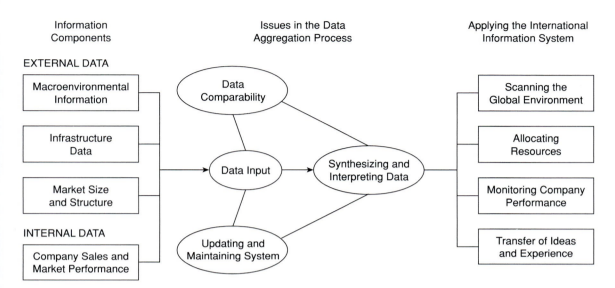

**Figure 13.1**    The international information system

the same market as well as long-run strategic decisions. Information systems can also be established to help guide executives who are exporting to different international markets (see Leonidon and Theodosion, 2004).

The need for both long- and short-term perspectives suggests that information at different levels of aggregation is required. The first consists of data and databases relating to macroeconomic factors or the business environment, for example GDP and population as well as lifestyle trends and attitudes. The next level concerns data relating to specific product and supplier markets, their size, rate of growth and per capita consumption. And the third relates to company sales and performance in specific product markets and geographical areas. Each of these levels can be structured by geographical area; that is, the world, region, country or city, as shown in Figure 13.2.

# External Data

## Macroeconomic Data

The types of macroeconomic data that are of potential use in international marketing decisions have already been discussed in Chapter 3 and hence are not discussed in detail here. It should be noted

| | | GEOGRAPHICAL SCOPE | | | | |
| --- | --- | --- | --- | --- | --- | --- |
| | | City | Intracountry | Country | Region | World |
| LEVEL | Macroeconomic Data | | | | | |
| | Product Market Data | | | | | |
| | Company-specific Data | | | | | |

**Figure 13.2**   Information system structure

that the specific factors included depend to a large extent on the company and the product markets in which it is involved. In order to be relevant for management purposes, the information systems should be tailored to meet specific corporate needs.

In general, it is likely to include access to key international databases discussed earlier, for example UN or World Bank databases, as well as others that may be of particular interest to the company given the product markets in which it is involved. Background information relating to specific countries in which the firm is involved might also be included, for example OECD Economic Indicators. Companies involved in the Scandinavian countries might have access to Nordic statistics, or those in Europe to databases such as Eurostat or Kompass Europe.

## Infrastructure Data

The next type of information that should be included relates to the market infrastructure of different countries or regions of the world in which the company is involved. This might, for example, include data relating to the media infrastructure, the costs and reach of different media – television, print, radio, outdoor and so on. Again, this might be structured by geographical coverage or area, for example global, regional, national, urban or local. Data relating to the retail distribution infrastructure might also be included for consumer goods, such as the organization and structure of the retail system, the sales volume and turnover or sales per square foot of different types of retailers, the strength of international, regional or national players. In the case of pharmaceutical companies, information relating to the health system in a country, the number and size of hospitals, clinics, doctors, as well as pharmacies and so on might also be included. In each case, the specific information and database will need to be tailored to the company's product market.

## Market Size and Structure

The next level consists of data relating to specific product businesses and markets in which the company is involved. This may include databases relating to the company's product markets as well as related product markets such as complementary and substitute products. As noted in Chapter 3, it is important to have a broad definition of the product market to encompass the full range of competitive products and the extent to which trends in a given product market may be affected by those in other, related markets. This is the case in product markets such as soft drinks or detergents where the product market may include different product lines, variants or brands.

In some instances this may include portions of macroeconomic databases. For example, an auto-mobile manufacturer might include information on auto sales and ownership from the Eurostat database, or information from the EIU database relating to different geographical markets such as the US or Japan. This part of the information system should include any relevant database relating to different aspects of the product market.

Where such databases do not exist, data will be needed relating to production, sales or consumption of specific products and product types within a market, including ownership for durables. Where feasible, this might be obtained in units and dollars or other monetary units. For example, personal toiletries might be broken down by shampoos and conditioners, antiperspirants, soaps and so on. Then, within the shampoo market, data might be broken down by hair type, frequency of washing, combination shampoo/conditioner, size and so on. Where feasible, detailed breakdown by geographical area or user type might also be included. In larger markets, Nielsen or IRI data are available, providing data relating to movement of goods and sales by time period, geographical area, type of outlet and so on. Information at the brand or product level provides input on competition, market share and market coverage.

In some industries information on supply factors, such as availability of raw materials and labor as well as prices and price fluctuations, provides important indicators of operating costs in different countries. In the case of the labor market for example, the availability of labor of different skills, or average hourly and weekly rates by industry, helps to provide insights on costs in different countries and regions of the world. Again, international databases such as UN sources are helpful in this regard.

# *Internal Data*

## *Company Sales and Market Performance*

Internal company data are also an important component of the information system. The same types of information as those necessary in domestic marketing decisions are likely to be required, but in this case relating to each country or geographical area and organizational unit. The exact form that this information takes is likely to vary from company to company, depending on the nature and organization of existing operations. Differences are likely to exist between business-to-business and consumer goods companies, due to differences in distribution, promotion and so on. Regardless of interfirm variation, certain data will be common to all companies. These include, for example, ROI, market share as a percent of total industry sales, market share relative to top three or leading competitors, expenditure relative to sales, sales growth by product line, brand and so on.

Parallel to the product market data, these data should also be broken down by geographical area, distribution channel and so on to reflect geographical measures of performance. For example, market share estimates might be available worldwide, by region, country or geographical area within country, similarly for sales expenditure relative to sales ratio and so on. Equally, sales and marketing expenses might be broken down by type of distribution channel, for example direct or indirect or types of outlets or user segments.

In addition to aggregate or overall performance measures, more specific measures relating to individual marketing tools might be included, such as salesforce or advertising, distribution channels and logistics, or sales by outlet. These will, however, vary depending on the type of company. Business-to-business companies may, for example, collect more detailed information relating to performance by sales person or sales by outlet or distribution channel.

Such data will only be available in relation to the specific geographical market or product markets in which a company is already involved. Under certain circumstances it may be feasible to extrapolate from one country to another based on similarity in market conditions in order to forecast sales or establish benchmarks for performance. In each case, however, comparability with regard to performance standards and measures would need to be carefully assessed.

## Results of Marketing Research Studies

In large organizations marketing research studies are continually being conducted. Some are commissioned centrally, while others are commissioned locally by country managers or brand managers. The centrally commissioned studies tend to be more strategic in nature, while the local studies either examine strategic issues in a particular country or simply provide information that helps managers make tactical decisions. The value of the firm's international information system can be greatly enhanced if the results of these studies are included in the database. Managers in different countries facing similar problems can access the information and determine whether the study results apply to his or her current problem. This will help to eliminate redundant marketing research studies. More importantly, as more studies are added to the database, meta-analyses (Farley and Lehmann, 2001) can be conducted to discover general rules that apply across a wide range of countries.

As with other proprietary information, care must be taken to limit who has access to the data. Much of the database will be comprised of country macroeconomic data or data that are obtained from syndicated sources. These types of data can be shared throughout the company with little fear of confidential information falling into the wrong hands. However, tiers of access need to be established for sensitive financial data and the results of marketing research studies. While search engines can find different types of data, topics and variables, the greatest value from the data is obtained if there is human indexing at the input stage as well. This makes it much easier to retrieve certain types of studies by topic, country, year and so on.

# Other Sources of Information

In addition to information from databases and data sources that can be directly tied into the system, two other sources of information are also important in making international marketing decisions. These are human sources of information and observation of physical stimuli. These sources are particularly useful insofar as they aid in interpreting and understanding documentary information and in the case of human sources provide a means of transferring ideas, experience and know-how across organizational units and different areas of the world.

*Human* sources of information include all forms of intrapersonal communication, including conversations, meetings, e-mail messages, teleconferencing or groupware. These contacts may be either *internal* – that is, between managers or employees within a company – or *external* – that is, with government or trade officials, managers in other countries, advertising agencies or distributors.

*Internal* intrapersonal communications are integral to the successful functioning of any organization. In international marketing, the establishment of an effective system of intrapersonal communications is crucial due to the far-flung character of operations. Consequently, mechanisms for facilitating communication between managers in different parts of the world are essential in order to coordinate operations and to ensure effective transmission of information and exchange of ideas and experience from one geographical location to another. A variety of different mechanisms can be utilized for internal communication within the company (Konsynski and Karimi, 1993). These range from traditional methods such as visits by corporate or regional staff to local country operations or vice versa, regular meetings of managers within a given geographical area, at the national, regional or world level, to teleconferencing, e-mail, faxing or use of groupware to write or communicate reports. While technological advances such as e-mail have considerably facilitated and accelerated international communications, they have not eliminated the need for face-to-face communication and discussion, but rather enhanced the firm's ability to manage operations and transmit information across long distances.

Use of *external* sources of information is also an important consideration, and can provide a highly valuable input into management decision making. Government and trade officials can, for example, provide much information concerning government economic and social policy and regulation, and their impact on various product markets, possible support and assistance in marketing products such as nutritional supplements, contraceptives and farming or medical equipment, or current trends in different industries. This is helpful not only in determining whether to enter a particular country or region, but also in determining the mode of operation and the extent to which marketing strategy needs to be adapted to local market conditions.

Similarly, conversations with or information collected from advertising agency personnel or distributors can frequently be helpful in developing marketing mix tactics. Opinions may be solicited with regard to the value of different measures of advertising copy effectiveness, or the advisability of a given media plan. Distributors might, for example, provide information relating to instore promotions and issues relating to physical distribution and logistics as well as at point of sale.

The importance of intrapersonal communication in international markets may be attributed in part to lack of familiarity with or difficulty in understanding the market context and environment in other countries. The dynamics of personal interaction may also provide certain types of information that cannot be communicated otherwise, influencing the perceived value of such information.

Face-to-face communication often has a greater impact than written sources, and in many respects provides a more efficient method of communication.

Lack of familiarity with the market environment in other countries also makes observation of physical stimuli and visits to local country markets critical. Management may, for example, only become aware of the size of a country and its physical terrain through actually traveling there. Similarly, observation of different conditions in other countries or parts of the world, for example consumer shopping habits, climatic conditions, the distribution network, how products are displayed instore or the type of advertising and other promotional stimuli, may be the best way to appreciate their significance. The latter type of information is particularly crucial due to differences in environmental conditions from one country to another.

Information from personal sources and direct observation thus plays an important role in international information systems. Lack of familiarity with conditions in other countries and parts of the world and the absence of an intuitive basis on which to select and interpret relevant documentary information results in greater reliance on and a need for more selective sources of information. These help to interpret and understand other types of information. In addition, use of e-mail and other internal communication systems facilitates communication within the system. Reports and other formalized types of communication can be sent via e-mail to relevant managers. Equally, local country managers can post or document their experience with specific products, brands, test markets or marketing programs, which can then be readily accessed by managers in other countries. Alternatively, such communications can be screened centrally to identify 'best practices', which are then disseminated worldwide.

Once the specific types of data to be contained in the information system have been determined, the next step is to establish procedures for the collection and processing of these data, in order to provide an appropriate and comprehensive basis for management decision making.

# Data Collection and Processing for the International Marketing Information System

In developing an international marketing information system, a number of issues are likely to arise with regard to technical aspects such as data quality, data inputting and data accessing. First, problems can arise with regard to comparability of data from different countries or parts of the world due to differences in relevant definitions and data collection procedures, as well as accounting practices from one country to another. Second, procedures are needed for inputting data and software to access and analyze it are required. Third, procedures are needed for updating and maintaining the system on an ongoing basis.

# Data Comparability

The issues with regard to the comparability of macroeconomic and product market data have already been discussed elsewhere and hence are not repeated here. Some more specific considerations arise, however, in relation to internal company data. Incorporation of data from operations in different parts of the world into an international databank initially appears relatively straightforward. However, data comparability from one country to another presents a major obstacle. It is important to realize that the value of a number supplied by a subsidiary in one country is not necessarily identical to the supposedly comparable figure supplied by a subsidiary in another country. Consequently, values or figures need to be adjusted into equivalent units so they can serve as a meaningful input for marketing decisions.

Sales volume measures, for example, may be expressed in real or monetary units. Real units, while accurately reflecting the number sold, may be misleading as noted in Chapter 5, in that the nature of the product can vary from country to country corresponding to different market requirements. Automobile and pharmaceutical products frequently require modification to conform to specific national regulations, thus entailing different costs.

Monetary units may be doubly misleading. The price of the product may not only reflect design differences, but in addition differences in pricing policy, transfer pricing practices and local taxation rules, for example VAT (value added tax). In addition, monetary units require conversion by an appropriate exchange rate. This gives rise to further difficulties in that exchange rates are subject to fluctuations and hence this needs to be taken into consideration when comparing annual figures. The creation of the euro as the currency unit for the EU has begun to deal with this problem for much of Europe.

These difficulties are further compounded by variation in accounting procedures and standards in different countries. Although there is a movement toward the standardization of accounting procedures across countries, there are still important differences, especially in emerging markets.

Costs may not be estimated in the same way or may include different expense items. Rules for depreciation or how the book value of assets or the value of brand equity is estimated may vary from one country to another (Pagell and Halperin, 1998). Methods of compensation also vary from country to country. Companies in countries with high rates of taxation, for example, often provide substantial fringe benefits, rather than salary increases, to compensate management. Countries have different rates of social security payments and methods for allocating and billing them. Some adjustment has, therefore, to be made in comparing, for example, salesforce costs as a percentage of total sales.

Even seemingly unambiguous measures of performance such as market share may be misleading. As discussed in Chapter 6, the definition of the relevant product market may vary from country to country, for example in the case of soft drinks or pharmaceuticals, resulting in market share measures that are not comparable from one country to another. Certain types of distribution channels used in one country may not exist in another, and hence margins and distribution costs may not be comparable. Advertising to sales ratios may be affected by the availability of various media and their reach. Media mixes – that is, of television, print or outdoor advertising – vary considerably, rendering strict comparison of advertising to sales ratios difficult.

## *Procedures for Inputting Data*

Lack of comparability in data from different national contexts and different sources suggests that a number of issues are likely to arise in inputting data into the international information system. In the first place, wherever possible, similar formats and data definitions need to be used across countries. The more specific the data, the more problematic this is likely to become. Second, procedures for inputting data need to be established. For electronic secondary databases, this requires establishing links with these data or integrating them into the information system. In the case of internal data, companies need to establish procedures at each level of data in order to ensure that the data are systematically incorporated into the information system. Rules for transforming data so that they are comparable from one context to another have to be devised, and procedures for implementing and checking the viability of these translation rules need to be established.

In the case of external data sources and databases, attention to the comparability of data across countries is an important issue. In the case of global macroeconomic databases, for example the World Bank or UN data, comparability of data across countries has already been covered in

Chapter 3 and hence is not discussed in more detail here. Issues of comparability across data sources and databases need to be considered, for example, in terms of aggregate production or consumption data, or even national income. Comparability issues are likely to become even more problematic where regional or country databases are to be included in the information system. Considerable time and effort may be needed to make such data comparable. In addition, data from different sources or databases need to be entered in a standard format or a common language so that it can easily be combined and integrated in a common document or used in analysis.

As noted earlier, comparability becomes even more critical at the product market level due to differences in the definition of the product market. Syndicated data sources such as Nielsen have attempted to harmonize product market classes across countries. However, substantial difficulties in doing so remain. Again, significant problems are likely to be encountered due to differences in product classifications in different databases. A company may therefore need to try to harmonize these data for internal use by establishing its own definition or following industry standards, where available, or those used in a syndicated database, such as Nielsen or IRI for consumer packaged goods.

In the case of internal data, a company will need to establish its own classification system and rules for translating data from one country or context to another. Guidelines for translation rules and a reporting format are typically set up in designing the information system. For product and market classification the system is likely to ensure that wherever possible these conform to external data sources, so that internal company data can be compared with product market data as well as across countries and regions. For cost and financial data, this requires input from local operating units concerning measurement standards, local accounting procedures and taxation laws and other fiscal requirements (Choi and Meek, 2005). A standardized company-wide system can then be established for cost accounting and reporting results. Local subsidiaries compile and input data according to standard company accounting procedures. In some cases, this entails keeping a double set of records, one based on local accounting procedures and the other on international reporting standards.

A key problem here is the burden placed on local operating units in inputting data conforming to a uniform format into the international information system. This is likely to be viewed as particularly onerous where data are used primarily for control purposes, little or minimal feedback is received from corporate headquarters, and relatively little use is made of the information system at the local level for tactical or strategic planning.

Similar issues are likely to arise with regard to the inputting of other types of data into the information system. Particularly in inputting information relating, for example, to new product launches or experience with specific promotional marketing programs, management in local operating units may have limited time available or incentive to input this type of data. Equally, time pressures may limit the dissemination or exchange of information via e-mail unless appropriate incentive structures are created.

Where a company is highly decentralized and organized around local profit centers, there may be limited incentives to disseminate or exchange information with other organizational units. The integration of markets worldwide and the need to develop and coordinate strategy across country markets has encouraged greater horizontal communication and the establishment of mechanisms facilitating transfer of information across geographical borders and organizational units (Ghoshal, 1997; Ghoshal and Bartlett, 1990).

## *Updating and Maintaining the System*

Closely related to the question of inputting data is that of updating and maintaining the information system. Here again, greater difficulties are likely to be encountered in relation to product market data and data from internal sources than with regard to macroeconomic data.

Macroeconomic data from existing electronic data sources merely needs to be linked up and integrated into the company's system. As noted earlier, these sources are typically updated on an ongoing basis. However, data that are not available in electronic form need to be updated regularly. While greater customization to specific company requirements will be feasible, this also requires monitoring to ensure data are appropriately updated.

Product market data are likely to pose some problems where data are not available in electronic form or on an ongoing basis. Where Nielsen or other syndicated services are available, these may provide an appropriate basis for monitoring product market trends. Integration of data from other sources, however, requires the patching together of data from different sources and diverse origins and can pose problems in establishing their comparability.

In the case of internal company data, considerable attention needs to be paid to obtaining data on an ongoing basis and updating it. This problem is likely to give rise to some conflict if local country managers perceive this as particularly burdensome or of little value to themselves. Attention therefore needs to be paid to the ease of reporting, data access and development of software to facilitate use of data and its integration into decision making at all levels, from strategy formulation to tactical decision making.

Once procedures have been developed for collecting and updating information on a systematic basis, procedures for analyzing these data need to be implemented. Here, a key issue is the use to be made of the information system and in particular how this is integrated into management decisions. Heede and his colleagues (Heede *et al.*, 1995) have developed a market information system for marketing managers that integrates data from multiple countries and facilitates access to the data to aid decision making. To illustrate its application they compiled a series of databases on the European automobile market. The different databases were:

- Monthly car sales and car production in several countries (OECD).
- Consumers' expectation of a future car price (GALLUP).
- Structure and finances of retailers and importers of cars (Købmandsstanden).
- Trade of cars between different countries (EUROSTAT COMEXT).
- Finances of the car producer business in different countries (EUROSTAT CRONOS/INDE).
- Development of macroeconomic variables in different countries (OECD).
- Economic performance of a particular car producer (AMADEUS).

In addition to the data, Heede *et al.* have incorporated a number of sophisticated analytical tools to allow the manager to analyze the data. These include SYSTAT, which is a comprehensive package of statistical methods, SYBIL/RUNNER, a time series program, as well as CFO Advisor, a budget simulation program that allows the manager to assess the financial implications of various decisions. The combination of the statistical analyses and the financial modeling allows the manager to develop a solid rationale for decisions and then evaluate the impact of different options.

# Applying the Information System

The international information system has four major uses in relation to international strategic planning and decision making: (1) scanning the global environment to monitor trends and pinpoint those with specific implications for the geographical areas and product markets in which the company is involved; (2) assessing how to reallocate resources and effort across different countries, product markets and target segments so as to achieve desired rates of growth and profitability; (3) monitoring performance in different countries and product markets throughout the world; and (4) transferring ideas and experience from different countries and areas of the world throughout the organization (Roche, 1992).

# Scanning the Global Environment

In the first place, the international marketing information system can be used to scan the environment in order to monitor changes and emerging trends in different countries and regions throughout the world. It is particularly crucial to keep abreast of such developments, especially in view of the rapid rates of change in many international markets. These can have a profound impact on the company's ability to compete effectively in world markets and maintain desired levels of profitability.

In scanning the environment, it is important not only to assess what is happening at the macro-environmental level, for example economic growth or social change, but also how events or trends in one country or region influence those in other countries and regions, and also how these trends affect the specific product markets in which the company is involved. Advances in communications technology together with the growth of business and interaction across national boundaries have resulted in increased interlinking and integration of markets. Consequently, events and trends in one market have repercussions elsewhere. This implies that a company needs to maintain a broad focus in monitoring markets worldwide, not just those in which it is currently involved but also in other related markets. News services such as Bloomberg and CNN are helpful in keeping abreast of breaking events and short-term trends. Monitoring and anticipating long-term trends is, however, considerably more problematic, given the rapid pace of change and its unpredictable nature. Here, reliance on expert opinion, such as use of Delphi techniques, may prove helpful. Assessment of the impact of emerging trends on both the product markets and countries in which the company is involved is also critical. However, the rapidity of change makes it difficult to assess both the impact and its timing on strategic decision making.

The experience of various large multinationals suggests the importance of scanning the environment to anticipate future social, political, economic and technological conditions. A key issue is how to integrate this information with that used in assessing the investment climate in different countries, and with various measures of company performance in different countries in developing a global marketing plan. Appropriate frameworks and procedures for systematic global planning are next discussed.

# Assessing Expansion, Retraction and Reallocation of Resources in International Markets

For companies already involved in international markets, the international information system can provide a key input in assessing the reallocation of resources across countries or regions, product markets and target segments. This includes determining not only which geographical areas, product markets and market segments offer the most attractive expansion opportunities, but also whether the company should divest unprofitable operations, or shift from less profitable operations to those with higher expected rates of return.

A global portfolio approach provides an appropriate conceptual framework for analyzing market expansion and divestment decisions (Douglas and Craig, 1996). This is based on the product portfolio approach, which assumes that maximum long-run return will be achieved through a balanced mix of products at different stages of maturity with different cash flow positions and capital requirements (Day, 1977). The optimal portfolio of products will consist of a mix of products, including mature products that produce large cash flows and are used to finance products with considerable growth potential.

The same approach can be used in international markets, replacing products with countries or geographical regions. A company needs to achieve a balance between high-growth and mature markets (product markets and geographical areas) to ensure that the firm is well placed for the future. Thus, involvement in mature product businesses has to be balanced with involvement in new, rapidly growing product businesses, and involvement in mature countries and regions of the world such as the US and Japan has to be balanced with involvement in rapidly growing areas such as China and Latin America. At the same time, the company needs to assess its own performance in existing markets to ensure that this matches market growth potential and to assess whether there are opportunities for improved efficiency and performance through integrating and consolidating operations across borders.

Achieving this balance between growth and mature markets implies that for any given product market, a company needs to assess growth opportunities and risks in different countries and regions of the world both at a macroeconomic and product market level (Douglas and Craig, 1996). Data from the international information system can be helpful in making this assessment. Specifically, information at the three levels discussed earlier will be needed. This includes macroeconomic data such as GNP per capita, growth of GNP, private consumption per capita, political risk to assess opportunities and risk at the macro level; product market data such as sales growth, number of competitors, market share and so on; and internal company data relating to ROI, sales and other indicators of performance in different countries, regions of the world and product markets.

First, opportunities and risks need to be assessed at the macroeconomic and product market level to determine whether the firm is appropriately positioned in the light of expected future growth. This assessment may trigger consideration of a shift of resources from mature markets to future growth markets. A firm may find that it has a lopsided emphasis on certain regions or specific markets, and that it has no or only a weak position in long-run growth markets for that specific product business.

The decision to divest resources from a market has to be tempered with the potential for economies of scope across product markets and product lines. Divestment of a product business within a given country could affect profitability in other product lines or businesses due to shared marketing expenditures, production or distribution facilities, or product complementarity.

At the same time, opportunities for improved performance within existing country or regional markets need to be considered. Comparison of growth potential with actual performance may suggest opportunities for improvement. Equally, opportunities exist for standardizing product lines, brands and marketing programs across countries or integrating R&D or production within a region or worldwide, to achieve economies of scale and efficiencies.

The primary advantage of the portfolio approach is that it provides a global perspective for developing marketing strategy and allocating resources rather than a country-by-country perspective. Guidelines for resource allocation, whether in terms of financial or management time and effort, can thus be established on a global basis rather than for each country separately. This can aid not only in decisions with regard to which country and product markets to invest in, but also decisions about which countries and product markets to divest, and how far strategies should be integrated across countries or specific geographical areas, segments and product markets.

Along these lines, Li (Li and Davis, 2001) developed a hybrid decision support system, Glostra, to assist in the development of global marketing strategy. The system comprises a database and a knowledge base along with five analytical modules that synthesize and analyze the information. The system can be used to assess the global environment and evaluate the attractiveness of various countries. Further, it can support development of the global portfolio and provide guidance on the development of global marketing strategy. It was viewed as particularly helpful by marketing experts in dealing with fuzziness and uncertainty. It was also viewed as useful in understanding the factors that affect marketing strategy and in providing guidance for the development of marketing strategy.

# Monitoring Company Performance

Another use of the international information system is to monitor performance in different product markets and countries throughout the world. Data entered into the system can be useful in assessing the effectiveness of activities in different countries and regions, and in benchmarking performance under different environmental and market conditions.

In evaluating performance in domestic markets, a number of standard measures are typically used, such as market share and ROI. This is based on the assumption, which has consistently been supported in various studies, that high market share is related to high levels of profitability. Furthermore, emphasis on product-related variables such as product quality has been consistently found to lead to high market share. Use of such criteria for evaluating performance and emphasis on similar marketing mix variables in an international context assumes that similar relationships will hold in foreign markets. A number of factors suggest, however, that this may not necessarily be the case. Differences in demand factors, for example concern with product quality or new product development as well as more fragmented markets, and differences in competition suggest that market share may not always be associated with high profitability. This raises some issues concerning appropriate measures of performance.

Focus on the use of financial criteria does not take into consideration market potential and the extent to which this is currently exploited. Some countries may be experiencing rapid rates of growth and have greater potential for market development and expansion than countries with relatively stagnant or low rates of market growth. This needs to be considered not only in the perspective of existing products and product lines, but also in that of the addition of new lines, product variants and product market expansion. The markets that are growing are likely to be better candidates for expanding and upgrading existing product lines and for adding new items. Certain economies may be achieved in relation to the sales and marketing organization within a country, either because overhead expenses are extended over a broader range of products or as a result of scale economies.

In some cases, low levels of ROI may predominantly reflect poorer product performance or inappropriate or ill-adapted market strategies. Changes in marketing tactics may improve performance and thus result in changes in ROI. Situational factors such as political instability or economic fluctuations may affect rates of return in the short run. This is particularly likely to occur in relation to products with a substantial proportion of imported components that are subject to short-run trends or currency fluctuations. Such factors may have an artificial impact on rates of return. Manipulation of transfer pricing may also imply that financial measures are biased and do not accurately reflect actual performance.

In addition to the likelihood of bias, emphasis on financial criteria implies a focus on short-run profitability. This may not always be appropriate, particularly in international markets, where company goals may center on market expansion and growth in order to build world market share and remain competitive in world markets rather than on short-run profitability. Such considerations suggest that factors other than purely financial criteria should be taken into account in evaluating performance in international markets. Criteria such as market growth and productivity levels should also be examined. Measures such as sales per sales person, advertising to sales ratios, promotional expenditure to sales ratios and employee turnover rates might be evaluated, providing a more detailed evaluation and a broader horizon for evaluating performance.

In using these criteria to evaluate and compare performance in different countries, differences in operating conditions and the market environment need to be taken into consideration. These might be evaluated based on aggregate measures at the country or industry level, for example rate of growth of GNP or rate of market growth. These can be used as benchmarks in evaluating and comparing performance from one country to another. The evaluation is made relative to differences in environmental factors as well as in absolute terms.

# Transferring Ideas and Experience from One Market to Another

The international information system can also be helpful in disseminating information more broadly throughout the organization, and particularly across geographical regions. While data relating to performance tends most commonly to be transferred vertically within the organization – that is, from country or local operating units to regional, area or central headquarters – information facilitates the development of more complex horizontal flows of information.

Local country managers can then input information relating to their operations into the system. This might include, for example, information relating to new product launches, marketing programs, price changes or promotional ideas. This information can be filtered centrally and ideas or experience that appear to have relevance or be applicable in other countries or regions can be disseminated more broadly. This can be refined into a system of 'best practices'. Local managers feed information concerning successful experience and programs in their own markets into the information system. A central committee examines these reports and determines which are designated 'best practice' and disseminates them as such throughout the organization.

An important element for the successful creation of these horizontal flows is the motivation of local managers both to submit and also to access and act on 'best practices'. As noted earlier, time pressures may make managers reluctant to submit information on successful programs, unless they are provided with incentives to do so. Equally, limited time available may restrict managers' willingness to access and absorb information and apply best practices. To the extent that such practices are endorsed by a central committee, the risks of unsuccessful implementation are to some extent mitigated.

# Summary

Information is a key element in developing and implementing effective international information strategies. Maintenance of an international information system is an important priority for companies committed to global market expansion. This can play an important role in keeping management current on events in markets worldwide and in integrating worldwide operations.

The four major components of the international marketing information system are macroeconomic data, market infrastructure data, data relating to specific product markets, and internal company sales and performance data. In each case, the specific information that is collected should be tailored to individual company requirements and objectives and will also vary depending on the product or services concerned. A number of issues arise with regard to the comparability of information obtained in different countries due to differences in reporting systems and procedures. Generally, it is desirable to standardize reporting units and reporting procedures to ensure comparability of information worldwide.

The information system can thus be helpful in a variety of decision areas. In particular, the information system can provide an important input for decisions relating to entry and expansion in markets throughout the world. It is essential to evaluate performance in different countries and product markets. It can also be used to scan the global environment and to monitor trends and changes in existing patterns. Finally, a global information system is essential in developing strategies that are integrated worldwide and that provide the optimal combination of countries, product markets and marketing strategies to maximize long-run profitability. Developments in telecommunications and in computer and communications technology have extended considerably the scope of global information systems as well as facilitating their use by managers.

# References

Choi, F.D.S. and Meek G.K. (2005) *International Accounting*, 5th edition. Prentice Hall, Upper Saddle River, NJ.

Day, G.S. (1977) Diagnosing the Product Portfolio. *Journal of Marketing*, **41**, 29–38.

Douglas, S.P. and Craig, C.S. (1996) Global Portfolio Planning and Market Interconnectedness. *Journal of International Marketing*, **4**, 93–110.

Farley, J.U. and Lehmann, D.R. (2001) The Important Role of Meta-analysis in International Marketing Research. *International Marketing Review*, **18**, 70–79.

Ghoshal, S. (1997) *The Individualized Corporation: A Fundamentally New Approach to Management*. Harper Business, New York.

Ghoshal, S. and Bartlett, C. (1990) The Multinational Corporation as an Interorganizational Network. *Academy of Management Review*, **15**, 603–625.

Gwynne, P. (2001) Information Systems Go Global. *MIT Sloan Management Review*, **44**, 14.

Heede, S., Pettersson, M. and Bab, K. (1995) Market Information Systems for Marketing Managers. *ESOMAR Seminar on Information Technology*, Brussels, Belgium, 25–27 January, pp. 117–134.

Kim, B. and Oh, H. (2000) An Exploratory Inquiry into the Perceived Effectiveness of a Global Information System. *Information Management and Computer Security*, **8**, 144–154.

Knight, G.A. and Cavusgil, S.T. (2004) Innovation, Organizational Capabilities and the Born-global Firm. *Journal of International Business Studies*, **35**, 124–141.

Konsynski, B.R. and Karimi, J. (1993) On the Design of Global Information Systems. In Bradley, S.P., Hausman, J. and Nolan, R.L. (eds) *Globalization, Technology and Competition*. Harvard Business School Press, Boston, MA, pp. 81–108.

Leonidon, L.C. and Theodosion, M. (2004) The Export Marketing Information System: A Integration of Extant Knowledge, *Journal of World Business*, **39**, 12–36.

Li, S. and Davis, B.J. (2001) Glostra – A Hybrid System for Developing Global Strategy and Associated Internet Strategy. *Industrial Management and Data Systems*, **3**, 132–140.

Pagell, R.A. and Halperin, M. (1998) *International Business Information: How To Find It, How To Use It*, 2nd edition. Oryx Press, Phoenix, AZ.

Roche, E.M. (1992) *Managing Information Technology in Multinational Corporations*. Macmillan, New York.

# Chapter 14

# CHALLENGES FACING INTERNATIONAL MARKETING RESEARCH

## Introduction

A key theme throughout this book has been the challenges that marketing researchers face when they conduct research in a multicountry environment. On one level they face the challenges of coordinating and controlling research activities spread over vast geographical expanses. On another level they face the challenges of achieving comparability and equivalence in sampling, instrument design, data collection procedures, analysis of the data and interpretation of the results. Addressing these challenges adequately ensures that marketing research conducted in a multicountry environment is of the highest possible quality and is adequate to support management decisions or test theory.

As markets change and the pace of change quickens, there are some specific challenges that are becoming increasingly salient as research is conducted in the twenty-first century. These added challenges can be viewed within the more general context of what is happening to the businesses that the research community serves worldwide. Businesses are becoming increasingly global in their activities. All firms regardless of their size are beginning to craft strategies in the expanded context of world markets to anticipate, respond and adapt to the changing configuration of these markets. As the ways in which firms conduct their business change, research suppliers need to change if they are to remain relevant and competitive.

This chapter is devoted to exploring these challenges and examining how they affect the conduct of marketing research. Emphasis is placed on how developments open up new opportunities and how international marketing researchers might respond to these. The goal is ultimately to conduct research that both enhances understanding of consumers in world markets and guides management decision making.

# The Changing Global Environment

Firms attempting to compete effectively in global markets are faced with four interrelated challenges, the challenges of *change, complexity, competition and conscience* (Craig and Douglas, 1996). The same factors that have an impact on businesses affect the marketing research firms that conduct research for global businesses. Like their clients, they must respond to the challenges if they are to grow and survive. The rapid pace of change implies that the ways in which marketing research is conducted must be monitored continually and adapted to take into account new economic, technological, political and social realities. The interplay of these forces in diverse geographical areas creates a new complexity as market configurations evolve. As firms expand the scope of their operations, their research needs change, both in terms of the types of research they require as well as its geographical extent. Finally, differing standards of ethics in different environments mean that researchers need to establish a consistent code to guide research in diverse contexts. As firms consolidate or enter into new partnerships to provide the geographical coverage required by their clients, new organizational forms emerge, changing the complexion of competition.

The most far-reaching challenge is occasioned by the rapid changes in the marketing and mass communications infrastructure, which in turn are the result of and driven by rapid changes in technology. Technological change is pervasive and has profound implications for both marketers and consumers. Change influences not only how and where business is conducted and hence the scope of research needs, but also the way in which research is conducted. Marketing researchers must be able to adapt and incorporate changes in technology into the research process. Many of these changes enhance marketing researchers' ability to conduct and coordinate diverse research projects. Mastery of the new techniques in turn creates new organizational forms.

One of the most dramatic challenges is created by the increased amount of research that will be conducted in emerging market economies. Growth in the industrialized nations is in the low single digits, while countries like China, India and Russia have the potential for rapid double-digit growth. This adds to the complexity of conducting marketing research as the range of research contexts becomes increasingly heterogeneous. As emerging market economies evolve and become more important to firms, there will be an ever-increasing need for sound marketing research to guide decisions in diverse markets.

Changes in the competitive environment present direct challenges to marketing research suppliers as they face both a changed and a more intense competitive environment. The increased intensity and accelerated speed of competitive reaction create a dynamic environment for marketing research

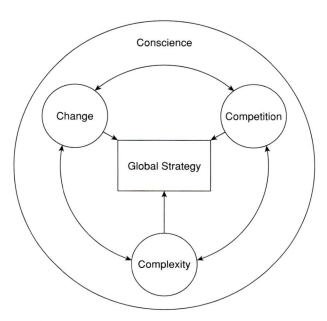

**Figure 14.1** Challenges facing the global marketer
*Source*: adapted from Craig and Douglas, 1996.

suppliers. With fewer larger firms competing for multinational clients' business, a research firm's ability to respond quickly on multiple fronts is critical. Competitors' actions also serve to accelerate change and increase the degree of complexity.

Growing awareness and concern with social responsibility and ethical issues require that research firms develop a social conscience and abide by this in conducting marketing research worldwide. The challenge is to conduct marketing research in multiple diverse settings on the highest ethical plane. It is imperative that researchers respond to this challenge, so that the results of research studies are trusted and management has confidence in them as a basis for decision making. This is an overarching challenge that encompasses the other three (Figure 14.1).

# Coping with Change: Marketing Infrastructure and Technology

Not only is the accelerating pace of change permeating all aspects of life, from daily life patterns and social relationships to changing market boundaries and value delivery systems, but also patterns of change are becoming more fluid and discontinuous. Knowledge and technological obsolescence can dramatically change market configurations and behavior from one day to the next, creating instability and uncertainty, making predictions of future trends and developments difficult if not virtually impossible. At the same time, customers are becoming more mobile and are exposed to new ideas and behavior through global media. They also have instant access to an overwhelming volume of information that is continually changing.

Against this backdrop, it becomes ever more difficult for the firm to track consumers' changing preferences and behaviors and to predict the diffusion of new ideas, products and services. Yet, tracking these changes becomes increasingly imperative for the marketer anxious to respond to rapid change in customer choices and to stay ahead of competition. High-quality marketing research becomes increasingly imperative and at the same time more difficult to design and execute. One of the more visible aspects of change has to do with the changing nature of the marketing infrastructure and the technology that is part of it.

# The Changing Market Place

Developments in mass communications technology and global and regional media such as CNN, MTV and STAR TV create an environment where certain segments of the population worldwide are developing a common set of expectations, familiarity with a common set of symbols, similar preferences for certain products and services, and an overall desire to improve their standard of living. This globalization of consumers means that it is more difficult to compartmentalize marketing research. The design of research must take into account these new complexities. There is an increased need for global sampling frames, multilanguage versions of questionnaires, well-coordinated research efforts that can be conducted simultaneously, rapid coding and analysis of results from multiple sites, and a means to disseminate research results rapidly.

The extent to which the same brands are recognizable worldwide facilitates construction of a 'universal' questionnaire. However, while certain brands may be available in most markets, the set of local competitors will vary considerably. Mass media has also helped educate consumers worldwide and given them a consumption vocabulary, as well as educating them on product class attributes and decision criteria for brand evaluations. Differences in per capita GDP will influence their ability to actually consume these products or affect the quantity eventually purchased.

The expansion of retailers worldwide is also facilitating marketing research. As chains expand, they incorporate their 'best practices' in the new stores. They incorporate POS (point-of-sale) scanner technology, modern merchandising practices and product mixes that both respond to local tastes and reflect the firm's desire for economies of scale in buying from suppliers. The development of shopping malls where they did not previously exist makes possible mall intercept interviews. Another consequence of the development of the marketing infrastructure is the greater need for marketing research. As firms invest more in the development of the marketing infrastructure, they need more marketing research to guide their decision making.

In some countries of the world, notably Africa and parts of Asia, technological developments mean development of the basic infrastructure: roads, electricity, running water, rudimentary transportation and distribution systems. The developments are essential for further development of the marketing infrastructure. Electricity not only powers television sets that carry commercials, but also refrigerators that make possible home storage of perishables. Further, a dependable electrical supply makes possible retail stores with refrigeration for staples and some convenience items, often soft drinks and ice cream. With the arrival of branded products, issues of choice, product attributes and competition become salient and require marketing research.

# Technological Change

Changes in technology continue to have a dramatic impact not only on how marketing research is conducted but also on how the results are disseminated and incorporated into management decisions. Advances in computer technology have dramatically reduced the time required to conduct marketing research and present results to the client. The impact of technology is felt in two main areas of marketing research, the collection of data and the dissemination of data. Technology such as scanners, the Internet, CATI (Computer Assisted Telephone Interviewing), and CAPI (Computer Assisted Personal Interviewing) are well established in the developed countries and are beginning to be used elsewhere in the world. They represent faster and more accurate ways of collecting data, but do not dramatically alter the practice of marketing research. Developments with the Internet are beginning to change not only the way research is conducted but also how it is disseminated.

## Computerized Data Capture

Whether it is product purchase data or responses to questions, computer technology makes possible the rapid and accurate collection of data. The widespread use of scanners at point of sale means that information on brand sales and market share can be quickly and accurately captured and tabulated. The limiting factor is both the scanner infrastructure at retail and the demand for the services by marketers in a country. An added difficulty is the consistency of product class definition across countries. A brand may be in one product category in one country and in a completely different product category in another.

CATI and CAPI greatly facilitate the collection of primary data from respondents. The development of CATI depends on household penetration of telephones. While CATI is used widely in developed countries, its use will spread only as the telecommunications infrastructure in other countries reaches the point where it is feasible. Not only does the infrastructure need to develop, but respondents in a particular country need to feel comfortable answering questions over the phone. CAPI is not infrastructure dependent, but its use is limited due to the cost of the computer equipment as well as respondents' lack of familiarity with computers. Even if a pen or touch screen is substituted for the keyboard, it will be difficult for individuals with low levels of literacy to respond in that fashion. Even if the computer interface can be made extremely 'user friendly', the novelty of the computer may serve as a distraction.

Technology will continue to evolve and create innovative ways to present stimuli and collect data. Multimedia CAPI makes possible the presentation of highly complex stimuli and facilitates getting consumer reactions to video and audio stimuli (Thomae, 1995). Developments in virtual reality CAPI will heighten the realism in stimulus portrayal and expand the range of topics on which marketing research can meaningfully be conducted (Needel, 1995). Developments in Interactive Voice Response Interviewing can eliminate human interviewers.

On another front, software to translate questionnaires automatically will facilitate conduct of multicountry research; although given some of the subtleties involved with abstract constructs, human intervention will still be necessary. Related to this are developments in textual analysis that will facilitate analysis of qualitative responses and responses to open-ended questions from large groups of respondents. This will be increasingly feasible as questionnaires are administered over the Internet. Respondents, in addition to providing pre-coded responses, can also type lengthy open-ended responses to questions. These will already be in a machine-readable form and can be analyzed using computer software.

## Using the Internet for Data Access and Collection

The Internet continues to evolve and affect business practice and the everyday lives of millions of people (Craig *et al.*, 2003). One of its major impacts has been the ready access it provides to vast amounts of secondary data. Rather than have to visit a traditional research library, the marketer can have virtually instant access to data from traditional sources as well as sources that are only available on the Internet. Web sites can provide all kinds of useful information, on topics ranging from countries to customers. The use of the Internet to access secondary data serves to change the timing of access to data and expands the range of information sources available. It enhances the timeliness of data as some of the sources are updated daily.

Another use of the Internet, which is growing rapidly, is the collection of primary data. Data can be collected in three different ways: (1) from visitors to a web site; (2) through electronic question-naires sent over the Internet; and (3) via questionnaires posted on the Internet to which individuals are directed. When information is collected from web site visitors, individuals are typically offered some inducement or incentive to provide basic demographic data and answer a few simple questions. This use does not provide a projectable sample, but it can be employed to suggest characteristics of those who visit the web site and how they feel about certain issues related to the products or service being offered. More specifically, it indicates how those who *chose* to provide the information feel. Data can also be collected without the visitor's knowledge through the use of 'cookies'. More insidiously, spyware can monitor an individual's use of their PC and use this data later for some other purpose. This use is controversial as it encroaches on an individual's right to privacy.

The Internet can be used to collect data in a more systematic fashion, which is closer in character to more traditional marketing research practice. Subject to the availability of suitable Internet sampling frames, questionnaires can be administered directly over the Internet. The individual can respond to the e-mail by filling in the blank space in response to a question. More typically, links to a questionnaire are sent via e-mail to a list drawn from the sampling frame. Respondents visit the site and are led through the questionnaire. The Internet represents a means to conduct a survey over a broad geographical scope. Further, the results are available almost instantaneously as the responses are captured automatically and can be analyzed in real time as they are received. This approach is most suited to surveys among respondent populations that are technology literate. However, as use of the Internet becomes more commonplace, e-mail surveys will begin to replace mail and telephone surveys. Progress is occuring most rapidly in the US and Europe and will take place more slowly in other parts of the world. The limiting factors will be the extent of Internet penetration and the availability of sampling frames that correspond to respondent populations that are of interest to marketers. Factors such as overall response rate and item nonresponse will also continue to be important. One key advantage of obtaining results rapidly is that it allows additional sampling to be conducted with enhanced incentives, to compensate for shortfalls in the initial phases.

## Linking Information via Intranets

Perhaps a more important benefit of the Internet for international marketers is the extent to which it facilitates the establishment of intranets. These are company-specific networks that link individuals within a firm. They help link individuals who perform the same job function in the same country and in different countries. Further, there are also links to different functions within the organization, again in the same country and in different countries. These are particularly important for firms operating on a highly decentralized basis. The intranet facilitates coordination and control of activities across many countries.

Often information exists in some part of the organization that would be helpful to someone in another part of it. This information can be obtained informally through the use of electronic bulletin boards or more formally through the establishment of 'best practices' compendia. Procedures can be established to collect information systematically on effective marketing practices throughout the world. These are put into a standard format and organized. A manager facing a difficult pricing or promotional decision can search the database to see how others have approached the problem and determine what would be the most effective solution. For the database to be effective there must be good editing and data collection procedures at the front end and it must be continually updated so that the information is current.

# Contending with Complexity: Conducting Research in Emerging Markets

Complexity in marketing research can be a function of many factors. It may relate to the research design, the respondent population, the sensitive nature of the topic or the sophistication of the analytical techniques. It may also be a function of the preceding factors as well as the range of different environments in which the research is conducted. When marketing research is conducted in multiple similar environments, the same approach can be used in each environment. However, when diverse markets such as India, China, Indonesia, Brazil, Russia and South Africa are part of the research plan, the overall process becomes exceedingly complex.

The areas of the world that offer the greatest growth potential for marketing research are the areas outside of Europe, Japan and the US. Currently, 86% of all marketing research is conducted in these three parts of the world. As firms seek to expand globally, markets beyond the industrial triad are being incorporated into their global marketing plans. As firms expand into emerging markets, they need sound marketing research to guide and shape their expansion. However, conducting research in emerging markets is not the same as conducting research in highly developed markets. Firms encounter a range of problems that may affect the validity and reliability of the results. In some instances, the environments are so different that it is extremely difficult to obtain comparable and meaningful results.

Research in emerging markets poses challenges to the marketing researcher for a variety of reasons. First, there are dramatic differences in the context in which the research is conducted. This makes the actual conduct of research not only different but often more difficult. A related issue is the increased difficulty of ensuring comparability of results. Finally, there are issues related to the cost of conducting research in emerging markets. Often, this is not so much the absolute cost, but the cost relative to likely sales in that market.

## *Contextual Differences*

When one thinks of the things that make conducting research in the US, Europe and Japan relatively straightforward, they relate to the availability of a well-developed market research infrastructure, a general acceptance and understanding of marketing research, familiarity with the conventions used to collect data, a communications and mail system that facilitate collection of data, common language within defined groups, high levels of literacy and so on. The factors that are taken for granted in developed countries often do not exist in emerging markets. Table 14.1 summarizes some of the key contextual factors that affect the ability (or desirability) of conducting marketing research.

First and foremost is the lack of a well-developed marketing research infrastructure. Many of the factors are interrelated. Often the reason that the marketing research infrastructure – specifically organizations that conduct and facilitate marketing research – is not developed is that the standard

---

**Table 14.1**    Contextual factors that have an impact on the ease of conducting marketing research

Development of the marketing research infrastructure (primarily number and size of
   research suppliers)
Proximity to countries with well developed marketing research infrastructures
Level of overall economic development
Level of communication infrastructure development
Level of development of marketing and distribution infrastructure
Degree of urbanization
Homogeneity of inhabitants and language

---

of living is so low that firms are not interested in assessing market potential or entering the market. In some instances, there may not be a large number of marketing research organizations in a specific country, but an adjacent country with a more developed research infrastructure may be relied on. For example, bilingual marketing researchers from Germany could be used to design studies, train interviewers and so on in nearby Eastern European countries that may lack the same degree of sophistication. This is going to be more difficult in parts of Asia where the countries are not only geographically dispersed, but there may also be greater cultural differences.

There are other factors such as the degree of urbanization that facilitate marketing research. Developing countries that have a large percentage of the population in urban areas are easier environments in which to conduct marketing research than countries where the population lives mainly in rural areas. A higher degree of urbanization means that even if there are not good lists for sampling, the respondents can be contacted through other means. The extent to which the population of a particular country is relatively homogeneous and speaks the same language facilitates the collection of marketing research data.

A well-developed general communications infrastructure will also facilitate the conduct of marketing research. A high level of telephone ownership and an efficient mail system make marketing research easier. Related to this is the mass communication infrastructure. If print and broadcast media are well developed, then consumers will have knowledge of a range of products and services. This general exposure to information will enhance their ability to respond in a meaningful way to questions on a questionnaire. Finally, the development of the overall marketing infrastructure influences the ability to conduct marketing research. It is difficult to conduct mall intercept interviews without the existence of shopping malls or their equivalent. Further, if scanners are not widely used it is difficult to provide the types of data and analysis that Nielsen and IRI routinely provide to their clients.

# Comparability

In addition to contextual factors, there are a series of issues that relate to the difficulty of achieving comparable results in emerging market economies. Throughout the book the issues of comparability and equivalence of results have been key themes. Many of the factors that make it difficult to achieve comparable results are tied to some of the contextual factors identified above. However, they also relate to fundamental cultural and developmental differences that exist between highly developed countries and emerging market economies.

There are major differences in the level of literacy between countries. Most, although not all, of the differences relate to the level of economic development. More highly developed economies tend to have higher levels of literacy, while developing countries tend to have much lower levels of literacy. As indicated in Chapter 1, in some of the poorest countries in the world less than 50% of the population is literate. Consequently, when conducting research in countries with low levels of literacy, it will not be possible to use a mail or self-administered questionnaire. Where the research is also being conducted in developed markets, this will necessitate development of a new instrument that relies on pictorial or other types of stimuli.

Basic familiarity with the stimuli can influence the ability of respondents to provide meaningful data. For example, Serpell (1979) administered a pattern-copying task to children in Zambia and the UK. Their ability to copy a pattern was assessed in two ways: (1) using a pencil drawing; and (2) using wire to model the pattern. The children from the UK performed better when using a pencil to copy the pattern, while the Zambian children performed better when using wire to model the pattern. Wire modeling is a popular pastime among Zambian boys and suggests why their performance was superior. The impact of stimulus familiarity is also illustrated in a study by Deregowski and Serpell (1971). They gave Scottish and Zambian children two tasks: (1) sorting miniature models of animals and motor vehicles; and (2) sorting photographs of animals and motor vehicles. There were no differences between the two groups when the task was sorting the actual models. However, the Scottish children performed better when the stimuli were photographs. The greater familiarity of the Scottish children with the two-dimensional portrayal of objects accounts for the difference in performance. These types of differences exist in different forms in many developing countries and require special attention when designing instruments for data collection.

## Cost

The cost of conducting marketing research in emerging markets can vary dramatically. The absolute cost of conducting marketing research can be very high or very low. When there is no local capability to conduct marketing research, all the design has to be done on site but with foreign nationals who are temporarily stationed in the emerging market. In addition to salary costs, all living expenses would be part of the cost of conducting the research. Further, once the research is designed, research supervisors have to be brought to the country and considerable time spent training interviewers so that they can do the fieldwork. At the other extreme there are emerging market economies, such as India, that have a well-developed marketing research industry that is capable of conducting high-quality research at a low cost. The information presented in Chapter 2 suggests that on average marketing research can be conducted in India or Bulgaria at about a third of the average cost of conducting research.

The absolute cost of conducting research is only one half of the equation. The other component is the value of research in terms of the types of decisions it will facilitate and the sales over which the cost of the research will be spread. A usage and attitude study may cost $60 000 in two different countries. In one country the brand may have sales of $300 million and in another country sales of only $30 million. In the first country, the research expenditure is spread over ten times the sales revenue as in the second country, and is only 0.02% of sales. In the second country the research amounts to 0.2% of the brand's sales. From the manager's perspective, the research cost ten times as much. Since this would not be the only research expenditure, the manager may look for ways to limit expenditures and possibly conduct less research than might be necessary.

## Confronting Competition: Marketing Research Services in a Global Environment

One of the greatest challenges facing marketing research firms is to develop an effective strategy to remain competitive in the changing global environment. The multinational firms that are their clients are dealing with the rapid changes and increased complexity of global markets. Research firms must be able to meet the changing needs of these firms as they expand globally. At the same time, there are also major changes that have been occurring in the marketing research industry.

The industry is consolidating, with the top 25 research organizations accounting for around 65% of the total market. Despite this concentration, with the exception of Research International, Millward Brown International and Taylor Nelson Sofres, the major firms do not have significant global presence (Barnard, 1997). Most are organized on a national or regional basis and have operations in the US and the major countries of Western Europe. While the research industry is somewhat concentrated, it remains highly fragmented, with over 3000 serious research companies worldwide (Barnard, 1997). The large number of firms has resulted in many of them competing on price for *ad hoc* research studies, which has eroded profit margins.

Competition is taking place on a variety of fronts. Nielsen and IRI continue to battle it out in the market for data on market share of consumer packaged goods in the US and Europe. Specialized firms such as IMS continue to expand their service for their clients in the pharmaceutical industry. Smaller specialized research firms continue to focus their efforts on the needs of companies in specific industries. There is also considerable growth of marketing research for firms other than consumer packaged goods. Marketing research is becoming increasingly important for business-to-business marketing and for the financial services industry. One of the more important aspects of competitive change, particularly from the standpoint of this book, is that increasingly competition is taking place on a regional or global scale, rather than being confined to one country.

## *Organizational Options*

Business organizations are restructuring themselves, making acquisitions and entering into strategic partnerships. One consequence of the consolidations on the client side is that before a merger there may have been a need for two marketing research organizations to service the two firms. After the merger, there may only be a need for one. On a more positive note, as firms make cross-border acquisitions, they have a requirement for a research supplier that has the capability of doing research in the new countries. Further, since many of the firms are highly decentralized, each division or product group will have its own set of preferred research suppliers.

To remain competitive, research organizations must find ways to expand the geographical scope of their operations to meet the ever-changing needs of their clients. The critical issues are: (1) market presence and access – having or appearing to have the capability to conduct marketing research in country X, as well as access to the resources necessary to conduct marketing research in that country; (2) market knowledge – sufficient knowledge of a country to be able to plan a research project that takes into account local nuances and idiosyncrasies; and (3) local capability – the ability to execute a marketing research project in that country, including all the fieldwork. While these three components are not independent of one another, all three must be present for the firm to be credible.

Each of these capabilities can be achieved in a number of ways. If the research firm does not have offices in some of the new countries, it can either form strategic partnerships with local research organizations, acquire an equity position in a local supplier or establish an office. Each of these approaches has to be looked at in terms of what it provides and how it enhances the firm's ability to supply high-quality market research. As an initial step, firms will typically enter into strategic partnerships with local suppliers. This can be done on a project basis or may entail some more formal relationship that involves sharing of resources and an understanding that the relationship will involve multiple projects. These relations can also be reciprocal, where two firms agree to provide research capability for each other in their respective home markets. Another advantage of strategic partnering is that it allows research to be conducted immediately and provides considerable knowledge of the local environment. However, it does not give as much control over local operations and may not offer as sound a basis for future growth.

Based on a favorable first experience with research in a particular country market and the growing importance of a particular market, a research firm may decide to take an equity position in its partner. Sometimes this is necessitated by increased capital requirements as the local partner attempts to expand and at other times simply by the growth ambitions of the larger firm. At the extreme, a firm may acquire a local firm. Negotiating an acquisition may take time and there is also some uncertainty as to how effective the acquired firm will be after the acquisition. Often there will be multiyear performance goals for the acquired firm, with the full price being contingent on meeting the goals.

Starting a greenfield operation in a country takes time and it is likely to be difficult to find qualified personnel. If the country is going to be very important for the future, typically a current employee who speaks the language can be charged with setting up the new office. Recruiting and training of additional employees can then occur at the local level. This process takes time and often it is easier to acquire or take an equity position in a strong local firm. The local partnership also removes a potential competitor from the local market and creates an important ally.

# Conforming to Conscience: Ethics in International Marketing Research

So far the discussion has focused on ways to ensure that the research carried out in international markets is of the highest possible quality. Having data that are comparable, equivalent reliable and valid allows conclusions to be drawn that form the basis for sound business decisions or build on existing theory. An overarching issue concerning the conduct of research, whether by academics or commercial firms, is that the research process adheres to the highest possible ethical standards. When research is conducted in multiple countries, there may be more than one set of ethical standards. Further, what is considered ethical in one country may be considered highly unethical in another country. This section will not attempt to resolve the inherent differences in different religious, moral and ethical traditions. It will look at the virtue of conducting research according to high ethical standards so as to ensure the integrity of the research results.

Much has been written on the subject of ethics in marketing (Schlegelmilch, 1998; Smith and Quelch, 1993), as unethical or illegal behavior is often manifested in the market place. Most typically, the unethical behavior involves some aspect of the marketing mix, deceptive advertising, price fixing and so on. Unethical behavior can result in negative publicity in the media, loss of consumer confidence, and in some cases legal action. Ethics are also extremely important when it comes to conducting marketing research (see Kimmel, 2001; Kimmel and Smith, 2001). Just as unethical market-place behavior can undermine trust and confidence in the firm and its products, unethical marketing research practices can undermine trust and confidence in the research and the research process. If research is not conducted on the highest ethical plane, then those who are asked to participate will decline to do so, those who supply research will find that their results are called into question or ignored, and those who need sound research on which to base decisions will not trust the results, or increasingly not commission research in the first place.

Ethics in marketing research can be viewed in terms of those who are involved in the research process. The specific issues relate to the four main parties to the research process: (1) the respondent; (2) the interviewer; (3) the research supplier; and (4) the client. Each party has a specific role in the research process and a different stake in the outcome. Respondents play a relatively passive role in the process and have limited interest or knowledge in the outcome of the research. Ultimately, they may benefit in the aggregate through, for example, products that better meet their needs or enhanced services. However, their participation is voluntary and critical to effective research. The

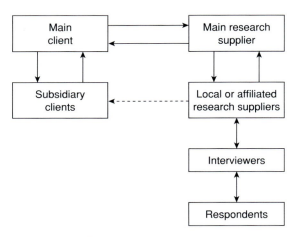

**Figure 14.2** Multicountry research. Solid lines represent direct transfer of information. Dotted lines represent influence on the process. Arrows represent the direction of the flow while two lines indicate exchange of information at different points in time. The flows of information are influenced by expectations, knowledge, standards and cultural backgrounds

interviewer and research supplier gain economically from the conduct of research and are concerned about repeat business from the clients that hire them. This depends on producing research that can be relied on and is valued by the client. In assessing value most clients consider the quality of the research, but there are some that may also be swayed by the outcome; that is, whether it supports a planned course of action. The client needs to know that the research that is conducted will be valid, reliable and provide a sound basis for important business decisions. The client is also concerned that the research is worth the expenditure that has been made.

While these issues are far from straightforward when conducting research in one country, they take on an added complexity when the research is conducted in multiple countries (Figure 14.2). In multicountry research, there may be multiple clients, multiple research suppliers, certainly multiple types of interviewers, and respondents who differ on a variety of dimensions. Each of these parties will have different expectations, cultural background, standards and so on. Further, each of these components will interact with other components. For example, a research supplier from one country may have more difficulty in understanding the research requirements of a client from another country.

The types of research being conducted can range from large, multicountry studies to those involving a few contiguous countries. Typically, one entity within the firm will commission the research to help solve a particular problem facing it. If the issue is developing a global brand, corporate head-quarters will be the client and very actively coordinate the research. However, there may be heavy involvement from the country managers where the research is actually being conducted. This particip-ation will help ensure 'buy-in' at the local level. Other marketing research projects may be organized regionally and conducted on a more decentralized basis. When the research project is more decentral-ized, it is more difficult to ensure that the same ethical standards are applied throughout.

ESOMAR has established a set of guidelines for the conduct of research to help ensure that it is conducted on the highest ethical plane. The first code was published in 1948 and has been revised periodically. The most recent version was prepared in 1994 and is available on the Internet at www.esomar.org. In 2001 an amendment to the code was added to cover the data protection principles established by the EU Data Protection Directive. In addition to the code of conduct, ESOMAR has established guidelines for different types of research. These are available at its web site and cover areas such as the distinction between marketing research and direct marketing, pharmaceutical marketing research, and conducting marketing research on the Internet.

To enforce the code of conduct, in 2000 ESOMAR established disciplinary procedures. These consist of a Professional Standards Committee (PSC) and a Disciplinary Committee (DC). Both committees are charged with examining alleged infringements of the ESOMAR Code of Marketing and Social Research Practice at the international level. The PSC can issue a warning, a reprimand, or refer the matter to the DC, which can impose more stringent penalties, including suspension, expulsion or notification of appropriate authorities. Details of the procedures can be found at the ESOMAR web site.

The ESOMAR code covers the rights of respondents, and by implication the role of the interviewer, the professional responsibilities of researchers, and the mutual rights of researchers and clients. It also specifies that research studies must comply with national and international legislation applicable in the various countries. The next three sections are based on the ESOMAR code.

# Respondents and Interviewers

The rights of the respondent are the most fundamental to the marketing research process. Without respondents, there would be no research. Further, the primary means of obtaining information from respondents is through interviewers; although this is changing somewhat as data can be collected through the mail or directly over the Internet without the intervention of an interviewer. However, the general ethical concerns are relevant, whether or not an interviewer interacts directly with the respondent.

To begin with, respondents' participation in the research project must be entirely voluntary and it is unethical to mislead them in an attempt to gain their cooperation. Respondents must also be assured that their responses will be held in strict confidence and that their right to privacy is ensured. A related aspect is respondent anonymity. If data are to be passed on, subject to respondent approval, then steps must be taken to ensure that the identity of the respondent is not revealed. Respondents must not be harmed in any way by the research process and they must be informed if observation techniques or recordings are to be made of their responses. Mechanisms must be put in place to allow respondents to verify the identity of the researcher and that the researcher is connected with a legitimate research organization. Special care must be exercised when children or young people are interviewed. In most cases this will involve obtaining parental consent. There is a separate set of guidelines for interviewing children and young people, available at the ESOMAR web site.

## *Researchers*

The researcher has certain obligations to the client and more broadly to the research profession. Researchers have to conduct themselves so as not to discredit the marketing research profession or do something that would lead to the loss of public confidence in the research profession. Researchers have to be truthful in making claims about their skills and experiences so as not to mislead clients. This can be problematic in multicountry research as it may be more difficult to interpret or verify claims made by research organizations. Researchers must always endeavor to design and conduct research in the most cost-effective manner. Given the different cost structures in different countries discussed in Chapter 2, this may be more difficult than it appears. Fieldwork may be conducted in a certain country because of the need to understand that particular market. However, the tabulation and analysis can be conducted in another location, which may be more costly. The issue is whether this is being done for the convenience of the researcher or because it provides the best approach for the client.

Security of the data is a key issue. If the right of respondents to privacy is to be preserved, then the researchers must take steps to ensure the security of all data that they have collected. Also, researchers have an obligation to see that any research findings that are disseminated are adequately supported by the data. The interesting dilemma is where results obtained in one country, for example country A, may be disseminated in country B, as being indicative of responses in country B. However, this may be less of an issue for the researcher and more one of how the client uses the research.

There are a number of issues that relate to the conduct of the researcher, independent of any direct interaction with the client. For example, the ESOMAR code specifies that 'Researchers must not unjustifiably criticize or disparage other researchers'. In addition, research firms need to establish a clear delineation between their research activities and any nonresearch activities undertaken. This can be a problem if a research firm has a large database and also engages in direct marketing and promotional activities. As long as the research information about individuals is not used in the nonresearch activities, there is no ethical breach.

## Clients and Researchers

The client enters into a specific contractual agreement for a particular research project. The contract spells out all the terms and conditions covering the specific research engagement. All provisions of the contract should be consistent with ethical guidelines established by ESOMAR, the American Marketing Association or another professional body. The researcher must inform the client if the collection of the data is to be done in combination with the data collection for another client. The researcher must inform the client if any part of the research process is to be subcontracted to others. Both of these provisions fulfill the need for full disclosure so that the client is fully aware of how the research is being conducted.

In addition, documents that the client provides to the researcher remain the property of the client and should not be disclosed to others. Typically information provided to the client, such as research proposals and cost information, remains the property of the researcher and should not be disclosed to others. The research organization should maintain records of the research for a period of time after the research is conducted. This is likely to present more of a problem when the research project is highly decentralized and spans a number of countries. Further, the researcher should not disclose the identity of the client for whom the research is being conducted.

The above guidelines and obligations of the various parties establish the minimum standards for the conduct of ethical research. Specific countries may have more stringent laws that prohibit certain practices, for example pertaining to the privacy of individuals. Problems of misunderstanding, particularly between the client and the researcher, are most likely to arise outside the Western European countries, Japan and the US. The research infrastructures are less sophisticated and the amount of research being conducted is far less in less-developed countries. Consequently, things that are taken for granted in the major markets may require special arrangements.

# Summary

Change is occurring in virtually all aspects of business and personal life. Businesses are both being buffeted by change and acting as change agents to bring about change in markets throughout the world. Consumers face a much more complex consumption environment and have more choices than ever before. These changes are being played out at different rates in different parts of the world. Against this backdrop, marketing research firms are being challenged to conduct research that is of the highest possible quality, as quickly as possible, in multiple diverse settings. The issues that marketing researchers face are multifaceted and relate to where and how research will be conducted, who the respondents will be, and the tools and techniques that will be used.

To prosper and grow, marketing researchers must find creative ways to harness the new technologies to facilitate the conduct of research and enhance its value to clients. At the same time, research organizations must begin to develop the capability to conduct marketing research simultaneously in the developed and the developing world. Increasingly, multinational marketers are designing and selling international brands and need research to guide their decision making across a diverse and disparate world. To accomplish this, marketing research organizations need to acquire the capability to meet their clients' needs through strategic partnerships and acquisitions. Finally, marketing researchers must strive to ensure that the research they conduct adheres to the highest ethical standards, so that it is trusted and relied on by their clients.

# References

Barnard, P. (1997) Global Developments and Future Directions in Marketing Research. *Globalization and the Millennium: Opportunities and Imperatives.* Marketing Science Institute, 16–17 June, Brussels.

Craig, C.S. and Douglas, S.P. (1996) Responding to the Challenges of Global Markets: Change, Complexity, Competition and Conscience. *Columbia Journal of World Business*, **31**, 6–18.

Craig, C.S., Douglas, S.P. and Flaherty, T. (2003) The Internet and International Marketing. *Journal of Internet Commerce*, **2**, 107–123.

Deregowski, J.B. and Serpell, R. (1971) Performance on a Sorting Task: A Cross-cultural Experiment. *International Journal of Psychology*, **6**, 273–281.

Kimmel, A.J. (2001) Deception in Marketing Research and Practice: An Introduction. *Psychology and Marketing*, **18**, 657–661.

Kimmel, A.J. and Smith, N.C. (2001) Deception in Marketing Research: Ethical, Methodological, and Disciplinary Implications. *Psychology and Marketing*, **18**, 663–689.

Needel, S.P. (1995) Marrying Marketing Research and Virtual Reality: Implications for Consumer Research. *Information Technology: How Can Research Keep Up With the Pace of Change?* ESOMAR Conference, 25–27 January, Brussels, Belgium, pp. 65–75.

Schlegelmilch, B. (1998) *Marketing Ethics: An International Perspective*. International Thompson Business Press, London.

Serpell, R. (1979) How Specific Are Perceptual Skills? *British Journal of Psychology*, **70**, 365–380.

Smith, N.C. and Quelch, J.A. (1993) *Ethics in Marketing*. RD Irwin, Homewood, IL.

Thomae, M. (1995) Multimedia CATI/CAPI. *Information Technology: How Can Research Keep Up With the Pace of Change?* ESOMAR Conference, 25–27 January, Brussels, pp. 89–101.

www.esomar.org

# Chapter 15

# FUTURE DIRECTIONS IN INTERNATIONAL MARKETING RESEARCH

## Introduction

With the accelerating pace of market globalization, communication and movement of firms, people and goods across national boundaries, the need for information on international markets continues to grow. This has to be timely, reliable and accurate as well as to furnish an adequate basis for making complex decisions in today's fast-paced markets. Yet, it is not enough simply to keep pace with the latest technological developments in collecting and delivering information: rather more fundamental issues relating to the design and comparability of information collected in multiple and diverse environments have to be addressed. In particular, issues relating to the comparability and equivalence of theoretical constructs or research questions, developing the research design and measurement instruments, and selecting appropriate analytical methodologies become more pressing and pertinent.

As an increasing volume of research is conducted in cross-cultural psychology, comparative sociology, political science and other social sciences, as well as in consumer behavior and marketing, more knowledge is accumulated about variations in behavior in a broader range of environmental and cultural contexts. Frequently these are, however, directed toward examining the universality of theories and constructs developed in a single sociocultural context or anchored in a specific research philosophy or paradigm. More attention is needed to identify issues or constructs specific to a given context or situation, and to assess the cultural embeddedness and dependency of constructs.

Such concerns imply a need for greater rigor in the design of international marketing research. This entails explicitly building in procedures to examine and evaluate the comparability and equivalence of constructs and phenomena in different contexts, as well as to 'decenter' the impact of a dominant culture or research philosophy on research outcomes. In addition, theories and constructs need to be studied in a broader range of environmental contexts to examine variation under different conditions (Triandis *et al.*, 1972). At the same time, attention needs to be paid to clearly defining the relevant unit of analysis so as to isolate the impact of contextual and other influences on the phenomena studied. Finally, more emphasis needs to be placed on developing more rigorous and better calibrated measurement instruments and methods of analysis. This entails greater attention to pre-testing and calibrating measurement instruments. In addition, multiple methods of analysis should be adopted in examining the patterning of the phenomena studied in order to assess and eliminate potential method bias.

Each of these issues is next further probed in more depth and some directions for future research suggested. While the discussion is not intended to provide an exhaustive list, it is nonetheless intended to establish important priorities for future research. These need to be addressed if further progress is to be made in the development of more rigorous, reliable and useful research on international markets.

# Comparability and Equivalence Revisited

Comparability and equivalence issues have been a central theme throughout this book. These have traditionally been and remain a fundamental concern of cross-cultural and comparative researchers throughout the social sciences. It should be noted that considerable ambiguity exists with regard to the terminology used in relation to equivalence, comparability and bias. In this book, we have relied primarily on terminology used in cross-cultural psychology and notably that used by Van de Vijver and Leung (1997). They distinguish between equivalence and bias. Equivalence relates to comparability in the level at which different cross-cultural groups are compared. Three levels are identified: construct equivalence, measurement unit equivalence and scalar equivalence. Bias, on the other hand, is a more general term that relates to any factors that may jeopardize the validity of a cross-cultural comparison and is a function of the measurement model and procedures, rather than the nature of the comparison. Bias and equivalence are related, in that the presence of bias will lower equivalence. Absence of bias does not, however, imply equivalence. Consequently, establishment of equivalence and the absence of bias are essential to any meaningful comparison.

Considerable progress has been made toward developing procedures to identify and deal with problems arising from measurement and instrument equivalence and use of scales in different cultural environments and settings. Yet, it is clear that much remains to be done in the earlier stages of research in identifying and examining issues related to conceptual and construct equivalence, in 'decentering' theories and constructs, and in examining the reliability and validity of constructs and operational measures of these in different contextual settings.

# Decentering Theories and Constructs

A key issue closely related to that of assessing conceptual equivalence is the 'decentering' of theories and constructs, or removing the influence of a dominant culture or philosophy. While this has been extensively discussed in relation to measurement and particularly with regard to translation (Werner and Campbell, 1970), it is also pertinent in relation to many of the theories and constructs used in international marketing research. Often these have been developed and their reliability and validity tested in relation to a single environmental context, frequently the US. Such constructs typically reflect the specific characteristics, values, philosophy and organizational structure of a given economic and sociocultural setting. For example, the two-step flow of influence model, hypothesizing that the impact of mass media is filtered by opinion leaders, was initially developed by Katz and Lazarsfeld (1955) based on research conducted in the US. In examining this theory in Sweden, Cerha (1985) found the flow of influence to be horizontal, across interest groups, rather than vertical, reflecting the flatter societal structure in Sweden.

Similarly, research approaches tend to reflect the dominant research paradigm or philosophy of a given culture. Again, this is closely related to the self-referent criterion or bias whereby researchers tend to perceive and interpret stimuli and other phenomena in terms of their own cultural background (Lee, 1966). In some cases, this may result in a lop-sided emphasis on issues and concerns that are of primary interest in the dominant culture but not in others. For example, a study might examine issues relating to consumerism in a culture where a consumer culture has not yet emerged. At worst, it may result in a framing or forced fitting of research questions in terms of those that are relevant in the researcher's own culture.

Decentering of theories and research design typically requires the participation of researchers from different cultural backgrounds and research paradigms. For example, in conducting research in another country or environment, it may be helpful to enlist the collaboration of colleagues in the country studied as well as from other countries or backgrounds. Here, two different approaches can be adopted to design a culturally balanced study, which is not dominated by a single culture (Van de Vijver and Leung, 1997). A *decentered* approach can be adopted in which researchers from different cultures participate in the design of the study, develop the research instruments, and add culture-specific measures and/or concepts to a common core. Alternatively, a *convergence* approach can be followed, in which a researcher from each culture designs his or her own instrument. These are then combined and administered in each culture. Similarity of findings across instruments provides strong evidence of validity, while discrepancies may highlight sources of bias. The latter approach is likely to prove time consuming and cumbersome, as well as being difficult to organize and coordinate.

# *Examining Construct Equivalence*

A widely recognized and yet persistent issue in international marketing research and in cross-national comparative research in the social sciences is that of 'construct' equivalence. As discussed in Chapter 6, this is concerned with whether the underlying construct or concepts studied have the same meaning or salience in another environmental context or setting, and whether, if so, they are best expressed in the same way, for example attitudes, behavior and so on. The issue is not whether the same measurement instrument can be used effectively in another and different context, but rather whether the underlying construct that the instrument is designed to tap has the same function or meaning in a different societal or cultural context.

While this issue has been widely discussed in surveys of international marketing research methodology (Cavusgil and Das, 1997; Sekaran, 1983), in practice it is rarely considered in empirical studies. Typically, the researcher focuses on examining the reliability and validity of a specific measurement instrument in another social setting or context, without questioning the appropriateness or relevance of the underlying theoretical construct (Douglas and Craig, 2004). For example, the reliability and validity of a specific innovativeness scale are examined in different countries or sociocultural settings, without investigating whether the concept of 'innovativeness' *per se* is expressed in the same way in each sociocultural context.

More attention is needed to conducting emic or culture-specific studies relating to the particular construct or phenomena of interest. This will help to identify relevant construct dimensions and to determine how best to construe the concept in a given context. Conduct of studies specifically assessing the conceptual equivalence of constructs in different settings is, however, extremely rare.

# *Greater Reliance on Unstructured Approaches*

Use of an unstructured approach to research design can prove helpful in further probing the contextual embedding of attitudes and behavior and identifying culture-specific concepts or contextual influences. Using this approach, culture and other environmental factors are viewed as providing the context within which other attitudinal and behavioral processes occur or develop. This is in contrast to a structured design, which views culture as an independent variable with a direct influence on the object or behavior studied (Lonner and Adampoulos, 1997).

In international marketing research a primary advantage of qualitative methods is that they do not require the imposition of a pre-specified conceptual model or structure to the research. This reduces the likelihood of cultural bias and at the same time increases the probability of identifying new constructs and concepts of relevance to the study. Observational techniques may shed further light on the situational context and its role in shaping processes and behavior. Projective techniques or depth interviews may bring to light new attitudinal dimensions or aspects of behavior, as well as providing deeper understanding and fresh explanations of motivational factors and relationships between variables. These can then be further probed and may provide input to develop and further refine research hypotheses in subsequent phases of research. Technological developments also allow the use of richer stimuli and the collection of data online or through computerized techniques, facilitating data analysis (Pawle and Cooper, 2002). Qualitative data collection techniques can be combined with quantitative techniques to develop a 'qualiquant' approach.

# Developing the Research Design

Developing a rigorous research design that enables the researcher to focus on examining the phenomena and constructs of interest, while isolating the impact of other confounding influences and eliminating plausible rival hypotheses, is critical (Harkness, Van der Vijver and Mohler, 2003). This is invariably an important issue in research design throughout the social sciences. However, cross-cultural research poses particular problems in this regard due to the multiplicity of levels in the research design and their hierarchical character. In addition, the increased intermingling and flow of people, ideas and information across markets imply that it is increasingly difficult to isolate the impact of diverse influences on the attitudes and behavior of any particular group or set of respondents. This is further compounded by the rapid pace of economic and social change, implying a growing need for attention to tracking changes in the environmental context and monitoring the underlying dynamics of behavioral change.

# Extending the Range of Contexts

Conduct of studies in a broad and diverse range of sociocultural contexts constitutes another important priority. This is particularly critical where the purpose of the study is to examine how concepts and theories are manifested in different societal contexts; or to identify the impact of societal or contextual factors on specific attitudinal and behavioral phenomena.

Systematic examination of both constructs and the relationships among constructs in a broader range of sociocultural settings may help to provide further insights into the nature of these relationships and to broaden understanding of these constructs. Where studies 'replicate' a theoretical framework developed or used in a study conducted in a 'base' country or context, they may also provide further evidence relating to the universality of this framework. In this case it is important to allow for the addition of emic or culture-specific measures of theoretical constructs, in order to glean further insights into how these are expressed and vary in different cultural contexts.

Where the purpose of the study is to examine the impact of the cultural context on attitudinal and behavioral phenomena, the specific types of cultural contexts or elements making up a cultural context need to be clearly identified and categorized. This may include specification of relevant elements of the sociocultural setting at the macro-, meso- and microenvironmental levels, as well as in terms of the specific behavioral, consumption and purchase situations. Insofar as the latter vary from one society or macro context to another, it is often preferable to build up the range of cultural contexts to be studied based on different scenarios or sociocultural situations in structuring the research design.

# Establishing Geospatial Boundaries

Despite widespread recognition of its limitations, the country remains the dominant geospatial unit used in international marketing research. This stems in large measure from its historical role as the dominant organizational and political unit. The market research information structure is typically organized around country units, and most secondary data, particularly at the macroeconomic level, are collected or available on a country-by-country basis.

With the growing integration of markets and flows of communications across national boundaries, the country is no longer the focal unit for the organization of marketing activity. Firms are increasingly targeting global or regional market segments, such as teenagers or affluent consumers, which span national boundaries and are present in markets worldwide. Even where the target market is broader in scope and not segmented, firms are developing and organizing marketing plans relative to geographical regions or world markets as these become more integrated. Equally, sampling frames are becoming available on a world or regional basis, for example lists of world or regional trade organizations, consumer organizations and Internet groups.

The changing spatial configuration of markets suggests that research units should be defined on a market-specific basis rather than with reference to geopolitical entities. For example, research should be conducted relative to natural market units or segments with common consumption or behavioral patterns, for example heavy users of cooking oil or small and medium-sized exporters of high-tech goods.

# Isolating Confounding Influences

A second problem closely related to that of defining the geospatial boundaries of the research design is how to isolate confounding influences on behavior within the unit or units studied. Since international marketing research typically focuses on comparing or understanding differences and similarities between different cultural or social entities in different spatial locations, communication and interaction between units will plague the researcher and contaminate the research results. These problems become particularly acute insofar as respondents are not only exposed to direct and indirect influences from other units, but also move from one unit to another.

As Galton noted in his remarks following Tylor's 1889 presentation of his classic cross-cultural paper, it is typically impossible to obtain cross-cultural sampling units that are independent of each other (Tylor, 1889; Naroll, 1965). Supposedly culturally distinctive traits have often spread between neighboring or historically related regions through historical fusion, diffusion or migration of people. This problem, apparent over 100 years ago, has been further accentuated by increased consumer mobility and the spreading influence of mass media and the Internet.

In recent years massive waves of migration (Hispanic and Asian peoples to North America, North African Arabs to France, Russians to Israel and Germany, Turks to Switzerland and Germany) have added further complexity to changing customer patterns. Where once migrants from other cultural backgrounds would gradually become absorbed into the host culture, today a more complex pattern of cultural interpenetration and cultural pluralism is taking place. Migrants are intermarrying and adopting certain facets of the host culture, but also retaining distinct features or traits of their own ethnic or cultural identity.

As a result, new cultural entities are emerging and the boundaries of cultural groupings are becoming more intertwined and more fluid. Consumers may belong to multiple groupings, crossing boundaries. In any given situation, the relevant identity of an individual or the dominant social influences may vary depending on the situational context, or the people with whom he or she is interacting. Consequently, isolating the impact of these diverse influences and particularly the nature of their interaction and influence in the formation of preferences and response patterns has become even more problematic.

## *Extending the Time Dimension*

The rapid pace of change in consumption patterns in emerging markets, as well as the emergence of new market segments and behavioral and purchasing modes, implies an increasing need to track change in world markets. At the same time, the nature of the market infrastructure, how consumers obtain information as well as systems for the delivery of goods and services are all changing, altering the forces underlying purchase, consumption and disposal behavior.

Such trends mean that increased attention is needed to the time dimension of research. In the first place, studies tracking attitudinal and behavioral patterns among specific consumer groups are required. Second, longitudinal studies of how consumption patterns and behavior are changing over time in different situations and contexts will help to shed light on the forces underlying change. Of particular interest here is how behavior and consumption changes as a result of movement to a new geographical location or interaction with a new societal grouping, as also is how newcomers in turn influence the behavior of others. Further complexity is thus added in attempting to distinguish the impact of these structural changes from those of natural evolution or those associated with a specific cohort.

# Improving Analysis of Cross-cultural Data

A final issue is the selection of analytical procedures that provide unambiguous means of testing the research hypotheses developed earlier. Here, of primary concern is the development of more rigorous and better calibrated measurement tools. Closely related is the selection of analytical procedures that fit the nature of the design and are capable of capturing and testing the hypothesized patterns of relationships, as well as being free of method bias. Use of multiple methods or procedures, while time consuming, provides greater confidence in the robustness of the research results and enables analysis of the data from different angles and perspectives.

## *Developing More Rigorous and Better Calibrated Measures*

Greater emphasis on developing more rigorous and better calibrated measures of constructs is a key concern. This includes not only examining the reliability and validity of existing measures in different societal contexts, and in a range of different environments, but also developing improved versions of instruments and better adapting these to specific research contexts.

All too frequently, largely due to the use of 'borrowed' constructs and theories, measure reliability and validity are at best only cursorily examined in other research contexts. Often tests, where conducted, are limited to examining internal reliability (for example, Cronbach's alpha). This in itself is not a particularly stringent test of internal reliability (Rossiter, 2002). Frequently attention is centered on assessing whether or not the measure works; that is, whether there is limited measurement error and adequate respondent comprehension. Rarely is effort devoted to examining whether the instrument in fact measures what it purports to measure and whether measuring the construct in a given culture is at all meaningful.

More extensive pre-testing of measures and concepts prior to their inclusion in a study is an essential first step to developing more rigorous measures. Specifically, this might begin with testing alternative formulations of measures on a broader and more diverse subject pool. Often measures, where pre-tested, are administered to small student samples. However, students are unlikely to be representative of a broader spectrum of the population in terms of age, education and other key factors underlying differences in response. In particular, problems relating to comprehension of wording or familiarity with stimuli in the broader population are likely to go undetected.

In addition, testing and measure validation typically focus on examining existing measures and constructs. As noted earlier, much research focuses on applying measures and constructs borrowed from prior studies. Relatively little attention has been paid to developing and testing new or different formulations of existing constructs and measures that are better adapted to another cultural context. This is essential if progress is to be made in developing better measures and measurement procedures, and in further understanding cross-cultural concepts.

# Triangulation

A procedure widely recommended in cross-cultural research in the social sciences to assess method bias is triangulation, or the use of monotrait multiple methods (Marsh and Byrne, 1993). This approach uses multiple diverse methods to examine the same phenomenon or construct. Where responses are consistent across methods, greater confidence can be placed in the results. Low consistency in response, however, suggests the existence of method bias. Wherever feasible, the methods used should be as diverse as possible. For example, results obtained through use of the experimental method could be compared with telephone interviewing. Equally, results obtained using different procedures for recruiting or questioning respondents can be compared. Convergence of results using different methodologies and research approaches provides greater confidence in the validity and reliability of results and in the absence of bias due to use of a particular approach.

Triangulation is particularly helpful in situations where other procedures for assessing the reliability of results cannot be applied. For example, examination of results from qualitative approaches can be contrasted with statistical approaches. This approach is also useful where attention is focused on single-item measures or contextually dependent measures, or where replication is not feasible.

# Fitting Analytical Models

Another related issue concerns the fit of analytical models with the structure of the research design. As noted earlier, the design of cross-cultural research is frequently complex and hierarchical in nature. Attention is centered on examining and comparing relationships between a number of variables in different sociocultural settings and contexts. This implies not only examining differences in the configuration or patterns of relationships among these variables, but also in comparing the impact of the sociocultural context or scenario on these patterns. Consequently, analysis occurs at two levels, at the level of the country or sociocultural setting or scenario, and at the within-country level. An added element of complexity is that some variables are measured at the country level and some at the individual level. To incorporate both types of variables adequately into the same analytical framework requires the use of sophisticated analytical techniques.

Application of covariance structure models and confirmatory factor analysis (LISREL and EQS) means that multicountry individual-level data can be analyzed at different levels. Data can be analyzed at the country level to examine the measures and relationships within that country; at the multigroup level to determine whether patterns of measurement and constructs are invariant across countries; or pooled to examine the entire sample. Recent developments in hierarchical analytical techniques provide an appropriate set of techniques to examine the impact of country-level and individual-level variables. Hierarchical linear models can be used to examine variables, such as Hofstede's measures of national culture, in the same model with individual-level variables. While as yet limited in application, use of hierarchical linear models offers considerable promise in examining the impact of different types of variables as well as the interaction between variables at both levels. As more researchers become familiar with these techniques and apply them to multicountry data, knowledge and understanding will advance dramatically.

# The Growth of Internet Research

The increase in Internet penetration in countries around the world has had a substantial impact on international marketing research. Individuals with Internet access can now be reached at relatively low cost no matter where they are located. In numerous cases, in order to ensure adequate response, companies have established large Internet panels such as the Harris panel or American Consumer Opinion, which has over 3.5 million members in the US, Canada, Latin America and Asia. While these panels are not necessarily fully representative of a national population, they are likely to tap innovators, the segment of greatest interest to marketers who are launching new products. In addition, they typically cover a broad spectrum of different interests, activities and product ownership.

Internet surveys offer the advantage of enabling the researcher to conduct research rapidly and at relatively low cost. Surveys can be sent out worldwide, responses received and a report delivered within a week, enabling research to be done at a speed that was previously impossible. The cost of conducting an Internet survey is also less than that of a comparable telephone or face-to-face survey.

According to one estimate, an Internet survey can be completed, analyzed and presented to the client for approximately 60% of the cost of a traditional survey.

Use of an Internet survey also enables the targeting of specialized market segments who could only be reached at much higher costs, if at all, by conventional methods. Richer visual stimuli can also be used on the Internet, for example advertising stimuli or product concepts, in order to provide a more realistic effect. Where respondents have broadband access, the survey can be transmitted in streaming video, closely paralleling the live impact. Respondents can also be sent products and instructed on how to use them, and their reactions can be probed interactively.

A subtle problem is that conduct of research on the Internet also tends to reduce the researcher's exposure to the local research environment. Traditionally, members of the research team would visit a site where research was to be conducted to organize and oversee the research. With the Internet, research is organized centrally, eliminating the need for travel to the site. As a result the researcher may lack understanding and familiarity with the local context and may have a limited basis on which to interpret and understand research results.

In brief, the spread of the Internet in many industrialized countries and among certain segments in other countries provides a relatively inexpensive approach to tapping such international populations, as well as a means of obtaining rapid responses. While undoubtedly this medium will grow rapidly in the future with the expansion of Internet access, its use needs to be tempered with a certain caution. There is an inherent danger that researchers will become too enamored of its speedy, low-cost features and fail to look closely at the inherent biases and limitations, as well as at its suitability for collecting specific types of data.

# Conclusion

International marketing research offers tremendous promise as a means to expand knowledge about consumption and purchase behavior and the impact of the market environment and marketing activities on that behavior in other contexts and cultures. It is, however, also evident that for progress to be made, greater attention is needed to rigor in the conceptualization of research programs, research design and application of research tools. While considerable progress has been made with regard to measurement issues, this needs to be matched by equal attention to 'decentering' the research approach and broadening theories and constructs to remove the dominance of a single culture or research paradigm.

Greater attention therefore needs to be paid to the earlier stages of research design to examine the issues of conceptual and construct equivalence and the relevance of theories in different sociocultural contexts. Ideally, researchers from diverse sociocultural backgrounds and research paradigms should participate in the initial phase of the research design. This provides perspective and input relating to the local research context and sociocultural setting, as well as the manifestation of behavioral phenomena within that setting.

While posing complex organizational challenges, international marketing research offers considerable promise for deepening understanding of unique emic or cultural-specific phenomena, and also for explaining how universal or etic constructs and theories are manifested in diverse sociocultural settings. At the same time, it helps to provide insights into how cross-border and cultural influences are changing these patterns and their underlying dynamic. This is imperative in an increasingly global and interrelated world. Such research will provide a more comprehensive and less parochial picture of the phenomena studied. It will help managers and academics to reach beyond a nationally embedded perspective and lead to a better understanding of the complex collage of a constantly changing global environment.

# References

Berry, J.W., Poortinga, Y.H. and Pandey, J. (eds) (1997) *Handbook of Cross-cultural Psychology*, 2nd edition. Allyn and Bacon, Boston.

Cavusgil, S.T. and Das, A. (1997) Methodological Issues in Empirical Cross-cultural Research: A Survey of the Management Literature and a Framework. *Management International Review*, 37, 71–96.

Cerha, J. (1985) The Limits of Influence. *European Research*, 2, 141–151.

Douglas, S.P. and Craig, C.S. (2004) *International Marketing Research: Constructs, Countries and Confounds*. Stern School of Business, New York University.

Harkness, J.A., Van de Vijver, F.J.R. and Mohler, P.Ph. (2003) *Cross-cultural Survey Methods*. John Wiley & Sons, Hoboken, NJ.

Katz, E. and Lazarsfeld, P.F. (1955) *Personal Influence*. Free Press, New York.

Lee, J.A. (1966) Cultural Analysis in Overseas Operations. *Harvard Business Review*, March/April, 106–111.

Lonner, W.J. and Adamopoulos, J. (1997) Culture as Antecedent to Behavior. In Berry, J.W., Pawle, J.S. and Cooper, P. (2002) Using Web Research Technology to Accelerate Innovation. *Excellence in Research 2002*. ESOMAR, Amsterdam.

Marsh, H.W. and Byrne, B.M. (1993) Confirmatory Factor Analysis in Multigroup Multimethod Self-concept Data: Between and Within-group Invariance Constraints. *Multivariate Behavioral Research*, **28**, 313–349.

Naroll, R. (1965) Galton's Problem: The Logic of Cross-cultural Analysis. *Social Research*, **32**, 428–451.

Pawle, J.S. and Cooper, P. (2002) Using Web Research Technology to Accelerate Innovation. *Excellence in Research 2002*, ESOMAR, Amsterdam.

Rossiter, J.R. (2002) The C-OAR-SE Procedure for Scale Development in Marketing. *International Journal of Research in Marketing*, **19**, 305–335.

Sekaran, U. (1983) Methodological and Theoretical Issues and Advancements in Cross-cultural Research. *Journal of International Business Studies*, Fall, 61–73.

Triandis, H.C., Malpass, R. and Davidson, A. (1972) Psychology and Culture. *Annual Review of Psychology*, **24**, 355–378.

Tylor, E.B. (1889) On a Method of Investigating the Development of Institutions Applied to the Laws of Marriage and Descent. *Journal of the Royal Anthropological Institute*, **18**, 243–269.

Van de Vijver, F. and Leung, K. (1997) *Methods of Data Analysis in Cross-cultural Research*. Sage, Thousand Oaks, CA.

Werner, O. and Campbell, D.T. (1970) Translating, Working through Interpreters and the Problem of Decentering. In Narroll, R. and Cohen, R. (eds) *A Handbook of Cultural Anthropology*, American Museum of Natural History, New York, pp. 398–419.

# SUBJECT INDEX

# AUTHOR INDEX

# ACKNOWLEDGEMENTS

The Publisher would like to thank the following who have kindly given permission for the use of copyright material.

**American Marketing Association**
Table 2.3. Reprinted with permission from *Marketing News*, published by the American Marketing Association, J. Honomichl, 'Honomichl Global Top 25,' **38**(August 15 2004).

Figure 4.2. Reprinted with permission from *Journal of Marketing*, published by the American Marketing Association, H. Takada and D. Jain, 'Cross-national Analysis of Diffusion of Consumer Durable Goods in Pacific Rim Countries,' **55**(1991), 48–54.

Table 4.2. Reprinted with permission from *Journal of Marketing*, published by the American Marketing Association, K. Helsen, K. Jedidi and W.S. DeSarbo, 'A New Approach to Country Segmentation Utilizing Multinational Diffusion Patterns,' **57**(1993), 60–71.

Table 4.8. Reprinted with permission from *Journal of Marketing Research*, published by the American Marketing Association, J.O. Rentz, F.D. Reynolds and R.G. Stout, 'Analyzing Changing Consumption Patterns with Cohort Analysis,' **20**(1983), 12–20.

Table 4.9. Reprinted with permission from *Journal of International Marketing*, published by the American Marketing Association, S.P. Douglas and C.S. Craig, 'Global Portfolio Planning and Market Interconnectedness,' **4**(1996), 95–110.

Figure 10.3. Reprinted with permission from *Journal of Marketing*, published by the American Marketing Association, J.G. Klein, R. Ettenson and M.D. Morris, 'The Animosity Model of Foreign Product Purchase: An Empirical Test in the People's Republic of China,' **62**(1998), 89–100.

Table 10.1. Reprinted with permission from *Journal of International Marketing*, published by the American Marketing Association, S.T. Thelen and E.D. Honeycutt Jr., 'Assessing National Identity in Russia Between Generations Using the National Identity Scale,' **12**(2004), 58–81.

Table 10.2. Reprinted with permission from *Journal of Marketing Research*, published by the American Marketing Association, T.A. Shimp and S. Sharma, 'Consumer Ethnocentrism: Construct Validation and the CETSCALE,' **24**(1987), 280–289.

Figure 11.3. Reprinted with permission from *Journal of Marketing*, published by the American Marketing Association, M. Colvin, R. Heeler and J. Thorpe, 'Developing International Advertising Strategy,' **44**(1980), 73–79.

Table 11.1. Reprinted with permission from *Journal of Marketing*, published by the American Marketing Association, M.C. Gilly, 'Sex Roles in Advertising: A Comparison of Television Advertisement in Australia, Mexico, and the United States,' **52**(1988), 75–85.

Table 11.6. Reprinted with permission from *Journal of Marketing*, published by the American Marketing Association, J-B.E.M. Steenkamp, F. ter Hofstede and M. Wedel, 'A Cross-national Investigation into the Individual and National-Cultural Antecedents of Consumer Innovativeness,' **63**(1999), 55–69.

Table 12.1. Reprinted with permission from *Journal of Marketing*, published by the American Marketing Association, K. Helsen, K. Jedidi and W.S. DeSarbo, 'A New Approach to Country Segmentation Utilizing Multinational Diffusion Patterns,' **57**(1993), 60–71.

**Amanda Broderick, Aston University**
Figure 12.8. Reprinted from 'Utilising Consumer Involvement for International Decision-making in the Food Retail Market,' (1998) in *Proceedings of the 27th EMAC Conference*, 481–500.

**Karen Blakeman, RBA Information Services**
Table 3.3. Reproduced with permission from http://www.rba.co.uk/sources/index.htm. © Karen Blakeman.

**Cambridge University Press**
Figure 8.3. Reprinted from J.D. Morris, 'SAM: The Self-Assessment Manikin: An Effective Cross-cultural Measurement of Emotional Response,' *Journal of Advertising Research* (1995), 63–68, by permission of Cambridge University Press.

**Elsevier**
Figures 12.1 and 12.2. Reprinted from *Journal of Business Research*, Vol. 42, G. Bostchen and A. Hemetsberger, 'Diagnosing Means-end structures to Determine the Degree of Potential Marketing Program Standardization,' pp. 151–159, Copyright (1998), with permission from Elsevier.

Figures 5.2, 5.3 and 5.4. Reprinted from *International Journal of Research in Marketing*, Vol. 14, S.P. Douglas and C.S. Craig, 'The Changing Dynamic of Consumer Behavior: Implications for Cross-cultural Research,' pp. 379–395, Copyright (1997), with permission from Elsevier.

**Euromonitor International**
Table 3.5. Reproduced from *Consumer Asia*, representative data 1997–2002 (www.euromonitor.com) by permission of Euromonitor plc.

Table 3.6. Reproduced from *Consumer Europe*, representative data 1998–2003 (www.euromonitor.com) by permission of Euromonitor plc.

**Harvard Business School**
Table 4.7. Reproduced from D. Narayandas and J.A. Quelch, Orbital Sciences Corporation ORBCOMM. Copyright © 1997 by the President and Fellows of Harvard College. Harvard Business School Case 9-598-027.

**The Haworth Press**

Figure 12.3. Reproduced from P. Valette-Florence and B. Rapacchi, A Cross-cultural Means–End Chain Analysis of Perfume Purchases. *Proceedings of the Third Symposium on Cross-cultural Consumer and Business Studies* (1991), pp. 161–173 by permission of The Haworth Press, Binghamton, NY.

**INFORMS**

Table 11.3. Reprinted by permission from M. Lubatkin, R. Calori, P. Very and J.F. Veiga, 'Managing Mergers across Borders: A Two-nation Exploration of a Nationally Bound Administrative Heritage,' *Organization Science*, volume 9 (1998). Copyright 1998, the Institute for Operations Research and the Management Sciences (INFORMS), 901 Elkridge Landing Road, Suite 400, Linthicum, Maryland 21090-2909 USA.

**International Monetary Fund**

Table 2.5. INTERNATIONAL FINANCIAL STATISTICS YEARBOOK 2002 (PAPER) by IMF, INTERNATIONAL FINANCIAL STATISTICS. Copyright 2002 by INTL MONETARY FUND. Reproduced with permission of INTL MONETARY FUND in the format Textbook via Copyright Clearance Center.

**Michigan State University**

Figure 3.1, Table 4.4. Taken from globalEDGE website – http://ciber.msu edu or http://globalEDGE.msu.edu. Reproduced by permission of Michigan State University CIBER.

**The PRS Group, Inc.**

Table 3.7 is from their publication, *International Country Risk Guide*, and it is an extract of Table 2B.

**Psychology Press**

Figure 6.1. Reprinted from Berry, J.W., 'Imposed Etics-Emics-Derived-Etics: The Operationalization of a Compelling Idea,' *International Journal of Psychology*, **24**(1989), 721–735, by permission of Psychology Press (http://www.psypress.co.uk/journals.asp).

Table 12.2. Reprinted from Watkins, D., 'The Role of Confirmatory Factor Analysis in Cross-cultural Research,' *International Journal of Psychology*, **24**(1989), 685–702, by permission of Psychology Press (http://www.psypress.co.uk/journals.asp).

**University of Chicago Press**

Figure 12.6. Reprinted from Durvasula, S., Andrews, J.C., Lysonski, S. and Netemeyer, R., 'Assessing the Cross-national Applicability of Consumer Behavior Models: A Model of Attitude Toward Advertising in General,' *Journal of Consumer Research*, **19**(1993), 626–636, by permission of University of Chicago Press.

The Publisher has attempted to contact all those from whom permissions are required. They would welcome hearing from any copyright holders whom it has not been possible to contact.